Sexuality, Sexual Behaviour and Reproductive Health

About the Editors

Prof. R.K. Mutatkar pioneered teaching of Medical Anthropology in India in 1974. He has been the first Head of the Department of Anthropology, and first Director of the Interdisciplinary School of Health Sciences at the Savitribai Phule Pune University.

Prof. R.K. Mutatkar chaired the Curriculum Development Committee at the University Grants Commission, to prepare model curriculum for Anthropology (2001). He has been Chairman of the first working group on 'AYUSH in Public Health' at the Planning Commission. He has been the Principal Investigator of the Ford Foundation capacity development programme to generate research on Sexuality issues at the School of Health Sciences.

He has authored the books, "Caste Dimensions in a Village", "Society and Leprosy", "AYUSH in Public Health" (2 volumes), and "Tribal Health and Malnutrition". He has been Chairman, Indian National Confederation and Academy of Anthropologists (INCAA), President, Indian Association for the Study of Traditional Asian Medicine (IASTAM), and President, Maharashtra Association of Anthropological Sciences (MAAS). He is Chairman, Indian Association of Human Behaviour (IAHB), and Patron, Society for Indian Medical Anthropology (SIMA).

Prof. Mutatkar has been the recipient of 'International Gandhi Award for Leprosy', 'Adiwasi Puraskar' of the Government of Maharashtra and 'Tagore Research Fellowship' at the Anthropological Survey of India.

Dr. Aarti Nagarkar is an anthropologist and currently the Director in-charge of the Interdisciplinary School of Health Sciences, Savitribai Phule Pune University. With twenty years of teaching and research experience, she has been working on reproductive health issues, especially translation research, in the field of women's health from the perspective of public health. She also works in the area of geriatrics and longevity and has developed curriculum on Gerontology. She has been closely associated with the capacity building programme on Sexuality, Sexual Behaviour and Reproductive Health at the School of Health Sciences. She organized the National Dissemination Meeting of the Ford Foundation Programme which has culminated in the production of this book.

Sexuality, Sexual Behaviour and Reproductive Health

Social Science Perspectives

Edited by
R.K. Mutatkar
Aarti Nagarkar

Jointly Published
for
Interdisciplinary School of Health Sciences
Savitribai Phule Pune University
by

CONCEPT PUBLISHING COMPANY PVT. LTD.
NEW DELHI-110059

ISBN-13: 978-93-86682-91-8

First Published 2019

Published and Printed by

Concept Since 1974

Concept Publishing Company Pvt. Ltd.
A/15-16, Commercial Block, Mohan Garden,
New Delhi-110059 (INDIA)
T: +91 11 25351460, +91 11 25351794
E : publishing@conceptpub.com; *W* : www.conceptpub.com

Cataloging in Publication Data--Courtesy: D.K. Agencies (P) Ltd. <docinfo@dkagencies.com>

Sexuality, sexual behaviour and reproductive health : social science perspectives / edited by, R.K. Mutatkar, Aarti Nagarkar.
pages cm
Includes bibliographical references and index.
ISBN 9789386682918

1. Sex—Social aspects—India. 2. Sex (Psychology)—India. 3. Reproductive health—India. I. Mutatkar, R. K. (Ramchandra Keshav), 1936- editor. II. Nagarkar, Aarti, editor. III. Savitribai Phule University of Pune. Interdisciplinary School of Health Sciences.

LCC HQ18.I4S49 2019 | DDC 306.70954 23

Foreword

This book bringing out the social science perspective of Sexuality, Sexual Behaviour and Reproductive Health reflects the nature of the Interdisciplinary School of Health Sciences, established at the then University of Pune (now Savitribai Phule Pune University) in 1991. The School was established by Prof. P.V. Sukhatme with inputs and support from Dr. N.S. Deodhar, the eminent public health scientist, with Prof. R.K. Mutatkar, the medical anthropologist from the Social Science Faculty as its first Director.

Erstwhile Prime Minister of India, Dr. Manmohan Singh, who had a brief stint as the Chairman, University Grants Commission, expeditiously granted the three faculty positions and a matching grant for the building, duly recognizing the need to provide interdisciplinary education related to health, outside typical medical environment.

The Masters (M.Sc. and M.Phil.) and Doctoral programme at the School provide training in disciplines such as Biochemistry, Molecular Biology, Biometry, Public Health, Nutrition, Plural Systems of Medicine and Social Sciences. A proper balance is maintained between laboratory work and community based field research training. Recently, Center of Excellence has been bestowed by AYUSH Ministry providing opportunities for mainstreaming AYUSH potential in public health system. The School remains a pioneering effort where both the social sciences and biomedical sciences are part of the mainstream curriculum.

It is but natural that the threat of AIDS pandemic demanded the need for social science research on sexuality, sexual behaviour and reproductive health. It was felt necessary to build the capacity of the researchers and institutions to undertake research in the new research areas of sexuality. Ford Foundation, New Delhi, offered a capacity building programme to the School under the guidance of Prof. R.K. Mutatkar, who as Honourary Professor of Medical Anthropology after superannuation, readily accepted the responsibility and completed the task by December 2003. The majority of the fifteen small grant awards were given to young research fellows, besides three Ph.D. fellowships. Their research reports in an abridged form provide the bulk of this book. The Ford Foundation capacity building programme permeated in the Masters' curriculum where reproductive health and gender issues are being discussed in depth. The workshops, seminars and symposia organized under the capacity building programme enhanced the research capabilities of young researchers and have developed wide networks.

I feel happy to have shared the process of Ford Foundation Programme in its entirety, while I was Director of the Interdisciplinary School of Health Sciences at the University.

The book, I am sure, will further enhance the research process in developing the adolescent and reproductive health policies, and intervention strategies to control the HIV infections. More focused campaigns could be designed based on research material presented in this book.

Prof. Bhushan Patwardhan
Vice-Chairman
University Grants Commission
New Delhi

Preface

Sexuality and sexual behaviour have been discussed in Indian mythology. There are treatises like *Kamsutra* and many others which could be classified as manuals on sexual behaviour. Aphrodisiacs have been promoted in these books, which are available in markets. Foods are classified as per their aphrodisiac characteristics. The erotic art sculptures at Khajuraho and Konark are world heritage sites. However, sexuality has never been on the academic agenda for objective and scientific discussion in India.

HIV-AIDS has brought sexuality and sexual behaviour as a researchable issue eliciting empirical evidence in order to priorities the risk behaviour and identify groups which are at great risk of getting infection.

In India social science research on sexuality and sexual behaviour started in the late eighties. Research studies about sexual behaviour have mainly focused on commercial sex workers (CSW) and their clients, youths and adolescents, urban educated, truck drivers and other groups, engaged in risky behaviour. Studies have not been carried out among other groups of society like urban and rural poor, exploited women, migrant, occupational groups etc. Almost all the studies are of KABP type quantitative surveys. Qualitative research on sexuality and sexual behaviour and reproductive health is lacking (Nadkarni, 1999).

With no solution of effective and cheap treatment in sight, behavioural change is the only answer for preventing HIV-AIDS. It is in these contexts that social science research on sexuality and sexual behaviour has gained prime importance.

Ford Foundation took initiative in starting a project for building social science research capacity for studies regarding woman's reproductive health. Several NGOs and institutions received grants to develop their capacities particularly in qualitative research training. I had the opportunity to be a resource person at the first workshop held at Delhi in early 1990, which took me to a village in Haryana with Dr. Pertti Pelto for fieldwork. I also had an opportunity to interact with Margaret Bentley from the John Hopkins University. Subsequently, I attended the "Indo-US Workshop on Behavioural Research Priorities: Developing Effective Strategies for Prevention of HIV in India" at the Tata Institute of Social Sciences in 1995.

Dr. Moni Nag and Dr. Pelto visited us at Pune to discuss the priority issues for organizing workshops, ranging from research techniques, analysis of data to report writing. The series of workshops and meetings starting with reproductive health issues later turned to discuss sexual aspects of AIDS prevention.

A working group was formed to further design the programme on Sexuality and Sexual Behaviour, the first meeting of which was held at Banglore (Bangaluru) in December 1995, the second being hosted by us at the University of Pune in August 1996. The Pune meeting was funded by Dr. Margaret Bentley from the John Hopkins University for local expenses and was chaired by Dr. Isabelle de Zoysa. I had an opportunity to supervise a rural research study on Adolescent Sexuality at the KEM Hospital Research Centre, Pune, with Dr. Hemant Apte, which was funded by Rockefeller Foundation through International Centre for Research on Women (ICRW). On an earlier occasion, I had an opportunity to participate at a meeting on STD at Chennai in 1986 convened by UNICEF, which was inaugurated by the Director General of Health Services, Government of India, who had the other agenda at Chennai in connection with female sex workers who tested HIV positive, probably the first confirmed HIV infected cases in India.

Dr. Michael Koenig, who was Reproductive Health Programme Officer at the Ford Foundation, Delhi, offered a capacity building programme comprising two Ph.D. fellowships, small grant projects, national level meetings and training workshops. The programme aimed at developing skills and generating research in the social and behavioural aspects related to sexuality, sexual behaviour and reproductive health. The programme began by eliciting the concept notes from prospective young researchers. The capacity building programme supported 18 research projects including three Ph.D. research fellowships. The projects were broadly classified under three broad themes:

- Sexuality and Sexual Behaviour,
- Gender and Sexuality, and
- Reproductive Health.

Initially five studentships were offered at Master's level for field based dissertation work on sexuality which a batch of students undertook in one village. Another studentship was reserved for M.Phil. work which remained vacant due to procedural issues about instituting M.Phil. at the School. Dr. Stephen Schensul was present with Dr. Pelto while the five students were selected for M.Sc. dissertation. For logistic reasons, the M.Sc. and M. Phil. studentships were abolished to create one more Ph.D. fellowship.

Small grant award scheme was widely circulated across the universities, research institutes and NGOs doing academic work. Concept papers were invited for primary selection; those selected being invited for a proposal development workshop at a later date. Simultaneously, a national meeting was convened to discuss research priorities on sexuality and sexual behaviour in March 1999 at the School of Health Sciences. We pleaded at this meeting to go beyond the topics immediately concerning HIV-AIDS and to study the socio-cultural contexts and related issues like gender and reproductive health also, if good proposals were presented. Most of the small grant awards did not exceed Rs. One lakh (One Hundred Thousand) each. The awardees and Ph.D. fellows participated in several workshops on research methodology, data analysis and report writing, specially organized for them. Dr. Pelto, Dr. Hemant Apte and Dr. Neeta Mawar were the resource persons for all the workshops. Dr. Asha Bhende was invited for some workshops. Moreover, she was also available at her Mumbai residence for individual consultations to the awardees, like other resource persons. The draft research results were presented at a National Dissemination Meeting at Pune in October 2003. The programme funded by Ford Foundation was to close in December 2003.

The programme not only developed the capacities of young researches but also created good data base on various issues of reproductive health, sexuality and sexual behaviour. The thrust of the research projects has been on the use of qualitative research techniques. One of the last workshops held at Leslie Sawhney Centre, Devlali, District Nashik, under the guidance of Dr. Asha Bhende was devoted to Intervention Research. The young researches designed drafts of intervention research proposals which were submitted for discussion at the National Dissemination Meeting in October 2003. A workshop was also held to orient the young social science researchers from National AIDS Research Institute and other academic NGOs, along with Ford programme awardees in qualitative research techniques. Two seminars with broad themes about Bio-ethics and about National Health Policy and National Policy on Indian Systems of Medicine were organized at the University of Pune for larger participation and exposure to policy issues.

Dr. Pertti Pelto has contributed a paper on research methods about data collection concerning sexuality and sexual behaviour. Dr. Hemant Apte and Rohini Sahani's paper pertains to linguistic anthropology and discusses the semantics of terms used mainly to denote a woman in sexual relationship. Many terms are still in use in literature or in colloquial expressions. The paper throws light on the historical aspects of sexual behaviour. Broadly, the colloquial terms label all exposure of women in public as actual or potential prostitution, while in actual life, there has been a great difference between dancing girls and CSW. There are studies on male and female adolescent sexual behaviour in the tribal, rural and urban settings. There are studies on migrant youth from rural area around Pune and also from distant places, engaged as hotel workers at Pune. The slum dwelling adolescent girls are influenced by Bollywood presentations of love and marriage. The permissiveness among tribal youth has been well documented and in the era of AIDS, presents situations of risk behaviour. The studies on commercial sex workers in Rajasthan who are traditionally associated with the profession while living in the families, and those in Pune red light area, present ethnographic evidence of sexual relationships. Reproductive morbidity of CSWs has been presented which brings out their plight as mothers and women. The emotional and stable relationships of CSW with their clients and with the managers of their occupational dwellings in the earmarked locality provide clues to the logistics of 'flesh market' and human factors involved therein. Concerns of the rural parents about their wards working at Pune for livelihood, has developed awareness about AIDS, and has developed community diagnosis about mortality and morbidity among the young migrants. The category of hotel workers is a special category particularly those working in restaurants around the red light area since they have to interact constantly with CSWs and their clients. The couple of studies on reproductive health and morbidity among the slum dwelling adolescent girls and women in rural area, enlighten us about the degree of ignorance of women about menstruation and white discharge. A study of the males indicate awareness about condom, with the belief that it was to be used only with CSWs. Some of these studies bring out the need of effective communication to translate awareness into acceptance resulting in behavioural change. Persons living with HIV-AIDS have problems concerning concealment of their positive status, due to associated social stigma. Issues like job security, dependence on family for care and unsympathetic attitudes of health professionals, raise concerns about self-stigma and fear of social isolation, as happened in case of leprosy afflicted persons.

There are methodological issues in social science research on sexuality and sexual behaviour. These are issues of confidentiality. Since information has to be sought about intimate private episodes of sexual behaviour, winning the confidence of the community and participants is of crucial significance. That is the reason, qualitative methods developed by anthropologists are significant in sex research.

Dr. Bhattacharya had to adopt the technique of non-participant observation and in-depth informal interview in the study of CSW. Dr. Agashe had to live in a tribal village and go 'native' to get the details of sexual behaviour of the young tribal males, Lokesh Gujrappa and Sandeep Rasalpurkar did the same for studying hotel workers as also Dr. Abhay Kudle for the study of migrant youth. Ms. Maushmi Joshi could win the confidence of adolescent girls from an urban slum, winning the role of an elder sister to whom they revealed everything.

Dr. Bhattacharya's paper on 'Brothels and Brothel Clients' was published, with our permission, in a book 'Sexuality in the Time of AIDS' edited by Ravi Verma, Pertti Pelto and others (2004), since she was an awardee with our programme to undertake this research.

This book puts together all studies done under the Ford funded capacity building programme of socio-cultural issues on Sexuality and Sexual Behaviour. In addition, there is a paper by Pertti Pelto on Methods of Data Collection specially written for the book and a paper by Aarti Nagarkar based on her Ph.D. work on Reproductive Health. The book also includes the inaugural address by Dr. Saroj Pachauri at the National Dissemination Meeting advocating the need to bring together applied research from the academic institutions and the grassroots level experiential evidence from the lives of people, by the NGOs. The introductory essay deals with anthropological issues pertaining to sexuality and sexual behaviour.

The contributors to this book represent the disciplines of Anthropology (8), Health Sciences (6) and Medical Sciences (4). Dr. Aarti Nagarkar and Dr. Susmita Bhattacharya have contributed three papers each, based on field research. The project and the book, justify the interdisciplinary spirit of the School of Health Sciences. About one hundred scholars, senior faculty as also research fellows, drawn from different disciplines, representing universities, research institutes and NGOs, across India, attended the national meetings. This interdisciplinary interaction continues to contribute significant socio-behavioural research and training inputs, in several research institutions, dealing with HIV-AIDS and reproductive health.

Acknowledgements

The Ford Foundation funded capacity building programme comprising Ph.D. fellowships, small grant projects, national level meetings and training workshops spread over a span of five years, 1999-2003, could not have been fruitfully organized and completed without the efforts and support of several persons and institutions.

Dr. Michael Koenig of the Ford Foundation, New Delhi, and Dr. Margaret Bentley of the John Hopkins University, School of Hygiene and Public Health (Later at the University of North Carolina), supported by Dr. Isabella de Zoysa, Dr. Pertti Pelto and Dr. Moni Nag reposed confidence in the Interdisciplinary School of Health Sciences, Savitribai Phule Pune University (S.P.P.U.), and personally in me, by offering the programme. Dr. Pelto, earlier Professor of Medical Anthropology at University of Connecticut, U.S.A. with his residence at Pune, during the period of the Ford programme, was always available formally and informally, at his residence or at the School, for all the guidance in all workshops, consultations and individual attention. Dr. Asha Bhende, formerly Professor of Sociology at the International Institute of Population Studies (IIPS), Mumbai, readily arrived at Pune, on all occasions that she was invited, to provide guidance.

The Scholars across the country readily accepted our invitation to participate at the national meetings towards the beginning of the programme and at the end. (The list of participants is given in the annexure). Dr. Saroj Pachauri, Regional Director, South and East Asia, Population Council, New Delhi needs special mention, who was the prime mover at the Ford Foundation to initiate reproductive health programme and research on sexuality. She inaugurated the National Dissemination Conference in October 2003 and provided guidance.

The National AIDS Research Institute (NARI) and the scientists and officers, notably Dr. R.S. Paranjape, Director, Dr. Sanjay Mehendale, Deputy Director, Dr. Neeta Mawar and Dr. Gangakhedkar, always provided support to all the programmes. Dr. Neeta Mawar as Member of the Coordination Committee took great interest in the programme and attended all events of the programme to provide guidance. Dr. Kalpana Mutatkar as an Obstetrician and Gynaecologist provided guidance at all stages of training, research and report writing.

The Coordination Committee and the Technical Review Committee who took all the executive and technical decisions have been very positive and supportive of all the activities. The University administration, particularly, the Finance Department made it possible for us to act as funding agency in awarding and executing the small grant awards outside the geographical jurisdiction of the University of Pune and even outside Maharashtra to scholars in Gujarat and Rajasthan. Prof. B.K. Patwardhan, Director of the Interdisciplinary School of Health Sciences, who has recently shifted to Delhi as Vice-Chairman of University Grants Commission, gave us a free hand in administering the programme. The School administration shared the responsibilities, particularly in organizing workshops and meetings. The Ph.D. fellows completed their Ph.D. dissertations on time. There have been no dropouts among the small grant awardees and the reports were submitted on time.

Dr. P.S. Agashe and Dr. Ms. Apoorva Pandit, as research coordinators helped the academic administration of the programme. Ms. Swati Salunke as Secretary took all the administrative responsibilities with great efficiency and understanding. I am personally grateful to her since she unburdened my personal load of responsibilities. Ms. Sharvari Nisal has prepared the copy of the book for publication.

Dr. Hemant Apte who has done commendable work in sexuality research has been a great help to the programme, particularly, during training workshops. He has also been a mentor to several grant awardees and gave all the time to help them. He has been a great support to me personally. Another person, on whom I relied greatly and put the responsibilities, has been Dr. Aarti Nagarkar, senior social science faculty member at the School. She organized the National Dissemination Conference and helped in editing this book.

We are grateful to the people who participated in the research process of the grant awardees and Ph.D. fellows, that has led to the large database being presented in the book which would prove useful for planning the course of action to mitigate and prevent the morbidities on account of HIV.

We are thankful to Concept Publishing Company Pvt. Ltd., New Delhi, for offering to publish the book with the sole aim of disseminating and promoting discussion on the significant issue of Sexuality, Sexual Behaviour and Reproductive Health.

October 2018
Interdisciplinary School of Health Sciences
Savitribai Phule Pune University,
Pune.

R.K. Mutatkar
Principal Investigator
Ford Foundation Research
Capacity Building Programme on
Sexuality, Sexual Behaviour and
Reproductive Health

Savitribai Phule Pune University
Interdisciplinary School of Health Sciences

The Interdisciplinary School of Health Sciences, an autonomous post graduate school of Savitribai Phule Pune University (formerly University of Pune), offers post graduate courses in Health Sciences and Public Health. Masters course in Biometry extended as a course in Biometry, Health and Nutrition was upgraded as an Interdisciplinary School of Health Sciences. Established through funding from the University Grants Commission (UGC) in 1989, the School was conceived by Prof. P.V. Sukhatme, former Director of Statistics at FAO, Rome, through a series of interdisciplinary summer workshops.

The School was the first institution in the country to offer a Masters programme in Health Sciences and a distinct Public Health programme supported during the brief tenure of Dr. Manmohan Singh, as the Chairman of U.G.C. Recently, a 'Centre for Complementary and Integrative Health' has been instituted through funding by the Ministry of AYUSH, Government of India. Besides, Ph.D. programme in Public Health and Health Sciences, Certificate programme in 'Traditional Medicine and Integrative Health' and Certificate course in 'Integrative Dietetics' are offered at the School.

Contents

Foreword by ***Prof. Bhushan Patwardhan*** v
Preface vii
Acknowledgements xiii

1. Social Science Research: Sexuality, Sexual Behaviour and Reproductive Health 1
Saroj Pachauri
2. Anthropology and Sexuality 7
R.K. Mutatkar
3. Research Methods: Sexuality and Sexual Behaviours 20
Pertti J. Pelto

SECTION I

Sexuality and Sexual Behaviour

4. Linguistic Terminology for Female Sex Partners 51
Hemant Apte and *Rohini Sahani*
5. Brothels and Brothel Clients 75
Susmita Bhattacharya
6. Female Sex Workers among Nat Community 92
R.C. Swarnkar
7. Sexual Behaviour of Persons Attending HIV-AIDS Counselling OPD 110
S.V. Gandham
8. Condom Use among Married and Unmarried Males 126
Alka Barua
9. Sexuality and AIDS Awareness among Diamond Workers 137
Binod C. Agrawal
10. Sexuality and Sexual Behaviour of Tribal Males 153
P.S. Agashe

11. Sexual Behaviour of Migrant and Non-migrant Youth 166
Abhay M. Kudale
12. Perspectives of Sexuality among Adolescent Girls 186
Maushami Joshi
13. Sexual Behaviour among Migrant Hotel Workers 209
Lokesh Gujjarappa and *Sandeep Rasalpurkar*
14. Coping with Stigma among PLHA 224
Jyotsna Bapat

SECTION II

Gender and Sexuality

15. Construction of Sexuality among Male College Students 241
Ram D. Gambhir, Saju Joseph and *Shantanu Ozarkar*
16. Gender Construction and Rural Health 269
Aarti Nagarkar
17. Male Involvement in Family Planning Decision Making 283
Anjali Ganpule
18. Menopause as Multivariate Issue 303
Aarti Nagarkar

SECTION III

Reproductive Health

19. RTI and Genital Hygiene 315
Bhupali Mhaskar and *Kalpana Mutatkar*
20. Reproductive Health Issues of School Going Adolescent Girls 334
Susmita Bhattacharya
21. Reproductive Health Practices among Urban High Caste Women 352
Aarti Nagarkar
22. Reproductive Health Issues of Sex Workers 363
Sushmita Bhattacharya and *Geeta Pardeshi*

Epilogue 384
Annexure 1—List of Small Grant Awardees 389
Annexure 2—List of Participants who Attended National Meetings 390
References 391
Index 399

1

Social Science Research

Sexuality, Sexual Behaviour and Reproductive Health

SAROJ PACHAURI

I feel truly honoured to be invited to inaugurate this national meeting on Social Science Research on Sexuality and Sexual Behaviour organized by the Interdisciplinary School of Health Sciences of the University of Pune. It is a great privilege to be with you today as you share the results of research undertaken by scholars at this institution. I am, indeed, impressed with the wide-ranging issues that have been explored by the researchers and look forward to the learning's that the studies that you have undertaken will, no doubt, provide. Needless to say, the importance of this research is immense. This is, indeed, pioneering work in an area where there is immense need but huge research gaps.

I am confident that the results of the research will have great bearing on several of the issues that we are all grappling within our country. Unless we have some answers to key research questions that relate to sexuality, sexual and reproductive health behaviours, and decision-making processes that determine these behaviours, as well as the use or non-use of services, sexual and reproductive health programming would be extremely difficult to operationalize in a meaningful way. Developing social science research capacity within academic institutions as the longer-term goal of this project is, therefore, clearly a priority for our country.

We are specially pleased to learn about your work because the programme that you are undertaking builds on the work that we had initiated during the late 1980s in my earlier incarnation with the Ford Foundation. While developing a sexual and reproductive health programme at the Foundation, it had become quite clear that policy-and programme-relevant social science research was urgently needed if we were to move forward in implementing the national programme in India.

The impeding HIV-AIDS epidemic had further re-enforced this belief. In fact, the problem of HIV-AIDS had begun to generate an even greater sense of urgency a hidden and forbidden area was truly challenging at that time. In fact, even opening up a discussion on sexuality was daunting! However, we took the plunge and initiated the programme. This was the genesis of the programme to develop social science research capacity on sexuality and sexual behaviour that is now underway at this prestigious university.

The rationale for the programme was very clear. Research was urgently needed. Research capacity in the country was generally weak. To address complex issues related to sexuality and sexual behaviour, it was necessary to combine the skills and methodologies of different disciplines. It was, therefore, important to undertake multidisciplinary research. However, universities in the country had built strong walls between disciplines and departments which presented a major barrier for bringing sociologists and anthropologists together with epidemiologists and demographers in such a research endeavour. Most research conducted in the 'ivory towers' of universities tended to be very theoretical. What we needed was applied research. We needed intervention research and operations research to address community-based and household-level problems.

University faculty did not have the tradition of grappling with on-the-ground problems. But this land is blessed with large numbers of creative and innovative NGOs and several NGOs are involved with addressing the needs of the poor in rural, tribal, and urban slum communities. Some NGOs had begun to reach reproductive health services to the unreached. Others were on the forefront of undertaking advocacy to promote the sexual and reproductive health agenda. But few NGOs are researchers. So herein lay our dilemma! How could we 'marry' these two different sets of institutions with widely differing world views, skills, and styles of functioning to undertake high quality research that had meaning in people's lives.

Our earlier experience with developing institutional networks had taught us that although developing and sustaining such networks was very time-intensive, if it worked well it had important long-term benefits. Consequently, we took the decision to support what was then called the Women's Reproductive Health Research Network. The aim was to strengthen social science research capacity by generating a synergy between academic institutions with training and research skills and action agencies that were close to the people and were grappling with real on the ground problems. The strategy was to set in place a process of learning and sharing.

A major emplasis was on promoting interdisciplinary research by integrating qualitative social science methods with quantitative survey and epidemiological methodologies. Thus, studies were designed to obtain epidemiological data on the prevalence and determinants of reproductive morbidity and social science research methods were used to understand women's perceptions of reproductive illnesses, their beliefs, attitudes, and health-seeking behaviours. The programme focused on creating a body of knowledge and experience by combining epidemiological and social sciences and by drawing on the experiential learning of grassroots NGOs implementing community-based programmes.

These research efforts were integrated with documentation, networking, technical support, and advocacy activities. We organized a series of workshops that emphasized hand-on experience in conducting research, managing actual field data, and preparing written documents. The workshops enabled participating institutions to share experiences, design research programmes, and develop research skills in data collection, management, and analysis. This interactive workshop process, coupled with on-site visits, was mutually rewarding as it enabled experience sharing among an unlikely peer group academically-focused institutions and activist-oriented, community-based NGOs. The workshops stimulated much interest and were in great demand.

Participating institutions identified reproductive health research priorities for addressing national policy and programme needs. Thus, the network members undertook research to study maternal mortality and morbidity, gynaecological problems, reproductive tract infections (RTIs), sexually transmitted infections (STIs), HIV-AIDS, and adolescent sexual and reproductive health problems.

While HIV-AIDS appeared to pose a serious threat at that time, the national programme had yet to be implemented. STIs had become an important concern because of their link with HIV transmission. Research was urgently needed to assess the levels of RTI/STI morbidity and to understand sexual behaviours that contribute to the spread of STIs including HIV. With the growing realization that the only viable and feasible intervention strategy for HIV-AIDS prevention at least in the foreseeable future was behaviour modification to ensure safer sexual practices, information on sexuality and sexual behaviour had become an urgent need. Therefore, the Network members undertook epidemiological research to assess the load of STI morbidity and behavioural research to examine perception of risk, sexual behaviours, and health-seeking behaviours of men, women, adolescents, sex workers, truck drivers, and others.

Information dissemination was a key element of the programme. Several mechanisms were used for sharing information. We undertook a dynamic programme of publication, documentation, and dissemination concurrently with our ongoing networking and research activities.

Some examples of the Network's contributions include:

- Bringing the invisible problem of RTIs in women on the national agenda by building a body of knowledge on the epidemiological and behavioural dimensions of this problem. This initial work stimulated further research in this neglected field.
- Initiating work on the sensitive areas of sexuality, sexual behaviour, STIs and HIV-AIDS. This work was recognized nationally and use by the National AIDS Control Programme when it was subsequently established.
- Most importantly, this programme made a significant contribution to the Government of India's effort to translate the ICPD agenda within the national programme.

The work that has been undertaken at this institution builds on the early work that we have just described. We congratulate you not only for sustaining the initial programme of work, but for significantly advancing the agenda. The research undertaken through this small awards programme has provided deeper theoretical and empirical insights into the areas of sexuality and sexual behaviour. Research that you have undertaken on the construction of sexuality and its relationship with perceptions of risk and vulnerability is critically needed for bringing about sexual behaviour change in our gender-stratified society. Your work on sexual behaviours of urban, rural, and tribal communities would have an important bearing on the design of interventions for migrants, youth, clients of sex workers, and others at risk. We need a variety of context-specific interventions for different sub-populations because one lesson that we have learned through long years of experience is that interventions must be tailored to the needs of particular communities. A universally applicable 'one-size-fits all' model is not a reality for any country and is clearly not a reality for a country as large and diverse as India.

We are specially pleased to see that research supported through this initiative has a strong gender focus because we firmly believe that gender issues lie at the heart of the problems that we are trying so hard to address. Gender-power relations in sexual decision-making and the powerlessness of women to negotiate safe sexual behaviours stand out vividly as major barriers to effect change in India's male-dominated patriarchal society.

But research on sexuality deals with the most intimate and private aspect of human lives and while this research is needed to further our programming efforts we need a deeper understanding of sexual dynamics, sexual networks, and sexual behaviours of men, women and especially of young people including adolescents breaking the silence in an area which has for centuries been carefully hidden from the public domain is clearly a challenge! It also poses a threat because such research will, no doubt, unveil the carefully disguised reality of many socially unacceptable forms of behaviours that exist in our society but have, so far, been kept carefully concealed-hidden from the public domain. Sexual coercion, sexual abuse and incest are but a few among many others.

Bringing into the public domain, behaviours that are often interpreted as 'normative' in the private sphere within the household and within the family is certainly a threat! These issues are politically and culturally sensitive in most societies. In our traditional, patriarchal society perhaps they have even heavier political and cultural connotations. We also know that in traditional societies such as ours there is a strong denial of these issues. And that there are clear boundaries between the private and public domains. We as researchers must, therefore, remain aware of these sensitivities as we open a discourse on these potentially explosive issues. Such a discourse is likely to generate a debate on what is 'normative' and what is 'deviant'. It is extremely important to ensure that such a discourse is steered positively. It is also important to recognize the political and cultural realities within which this discourse is conducted. It is critical that discussions on such potentially volatile issues are carefully managed so that when policies are framed and programmes implemented they are, indeed, responsive to the findings of the research that we have conducted.

It takes considerable courage for scholars to undertake such research so I applaud your efforts. It is also a challenge to identify and implement appropriate methodologies so that valid and reliable information can be obtained on this privately guarded and very silent aspect of people's lives. The need for combining a variety of research methods is, therefore, obvious. Multi-disciplinary research is needed to obtain valid data that can enhance our understanding of complex issues in very diverse contexts.

We must not only ensure that we obtain valid and reliable information as we undertake this research, but we must also adhere to ethical standards and ensure that these are rigorously maintained. Ethical issues related to obtaining informed consent and maintaining confidentiality of research subjects are paramount, particularly since such research explores private and intimate thoughts, attitudes, and sexual practices of men, women, and young people. Maintaining ethical principles though challenging cannot be compromised. In fact, we must think of creative ways in which communities can be informed of the risks and benefits of such research. It would be important to draw lessons from your experience as the larger research constituency expands the frontiers of research on sexuality and sexual behaviours in India.

We would like to say a few words about the dissemination of research findings. We are strong believers in the dissemination and utilizing of research. We believe that we should strive to undertake high quality research that can be published in peer-reviewed journals and books. We recognize that it is important for young scholars to have publications on their CVs. However, we also firmly believe that this form of dissemination can only reach our own peers. We need to reach much larger audiences of policy planners, service providers, activists, and others. For these diverse audiences to be reached effectively, we must specifically tailor our research outputs.

We believe in research that can make a difference in people's lives. We, therefore, feel strongly that key stakeholders must be partners throughout the process of research so that they can have a feeling of ownership of the research that is undertaken. Our objective is to provide research-based evidence and also ensure that research findings are, in fact, used. Only then can research impact policies and programmes on sexual and reproductive health and rights.

I heartily congratulate Prof. Mutatkar and all of you who have participated in this important and pioneering research initiative. We would urge you to carry forward the momentum that you have generated through this project so that future research can benefit from the holistic, multidisciplinary approaches that you have so arduously developed and implemented. Today, the need for such research is greater than ever before. The work that you have begun must be certainly carried forward. You must, therefore, set in place mechanisms for achieving the goal of strengthening social science research capacity to advance the agenda.

The initiatives that this Institution has taken will take us further in policy formulations and implementation about addressing the issues regarding reproductive health in general, focusing on the epidemiological and social issues concerning HIV and AIDS.

2

Anthropology and Sexuality

R.K. MUTATKAR

I

Human society has always strived to institutionalize the biological urges so as to ensure order between and within groups and communities. In the process, food and sex have emerged as commercial, marketable commodities. They get therefore linked with poverty issues. The indicators of affluence also lead to variable consumption of food and sex gratification. In patriarchal societies, the powerful always have been trying to grab land, cattle and other means of production, as also women. One peasant total me in a Gwalior village way back in 1958 that *Kaliyug* meant commercialization of land and women as marketable commodities. Sexual activities could not be looked in isolation. They are linked with social, cultural and economic context, not only biological. Now there is neither biological determinism nor cultural determinism. The social, economic and political dynamics has brought in life styles which are not culturally controlled, thereby resulting in increased risk behaviour. However, since the Basic Personality is shaped by culture, and the social structure of caste, tribe, class, kinship, family and endogamous marriage is still intact, as also the religious rituals and ceremonies, the interventions could be planned systematically. The behaviours are not universally irrational, they could be understood as aspects or patterns in a bio-cultural system.

Sexuality research undoubtedly has become priority research agenda due to risk of contracting HIV infection, which is understood by lay people as AIDS, which is perceived as fatal. Interventions or policies cannot be properly planned without valid, reliable data. Qualitative research which takes into account historical perspective and different contexts would help in such research. Although hard core of belief systems appear to continue, life style variations have influenced soft core of culture, including sex behaviour, which offer potential risk of HIV-AIDS.

II

Anthropology as a discipline studying Man in holistic perspective discusses the biological and socio-cultural dimensions of sexuality and sexual behaviour. The anthropological classics detailing ethnographies of isolated communities commonly referred to as tribes or primitive people, have given accounts of sexual life of these people. The generalizations drawn from empirical evidence about plurality of ways of life have developed the theory of culture, which in detail, talks of integration of culture suggesting the stability or equilibrium in culture. Anthropology is trapped in the discussions revolving around the concepts of cultural determinism or super-organic nature of culture, and cultural relativism. Cultural relativism signifies and justifies the functional variability of behavioural patterns which might be traced to social evolution, adaptability to environment, and history.

Homo Sapiens share sex instinct with other animals, more particularly with the primates. Desmond Morris has discussed this aspect in great details in his two books, 'The Human Zoo' and 'The Naked Ape'. He has brought out the similarities and differences among the other primates and human animal. In his latest presentations on the Discovery Channel of television about 'The Human Sexes', he has brought out the male and female behaviour patterns about attracting each other, dominantly for procreative purpose.

Human animal as compared to other primates has a mind, and intellect, not only physiological brain. The soul which could transmigrate into other living forms after death of body, according to Hindu theology, rationalizes rebirth. The *Ashram* system guiding the life of an individual among the Hindu or among the Indians (since Hindu customs are largely shared by other religious groups in India) enjoins upon the householder to indulge in sex for procreation and for pleasure. Basham in his classic book, 'The Wonder that was India' has discussed sex briefly as under:

"The literature of Hindu India, both religious and secular is full of sexual allusions, sexual symbolism and passages of frank eroticism... the process of cosmic creation was figured as the union of god and goddess and figures of closely embracing couples *maithun* were carved on the walls of temples. Sexual activity was indeed a positive religious duty—the husband must have intercourse with his wife within a period of eight days at the close of every menstruation...*Kamsutra* attributed to the saga *Vatsayana*...written in early centuries of Christian era or perhaps in the Gupta period....gives detailed instructions on erotic techniques, aphrodisiac recipes and charms.... The ideal of feminine beauty in ancient India...thick thighed, broad hipped but very slender-waisted, and with heavy breasts, seems evidently chosen for physical satisfaction" (1967: Third Revised Edition). The artistic, erotic sculptures of *Maithun* at Khajuraho and Konark exhibit Basham's narrative about beauty and sex.

Gita Govinda the 'Song of Love' by 12th century poet, Jayadeva and translated in English by George Keyt about the sensual passionate emotions of Radha and Krishna is well known 'for its delights in erotic experiences and for sheer excellence of romantic poetry'.

> *There on the bed of tender leaves, O lotus-eyed embrace his hips, his naked hips from whence the girdle drops.*
>
> *Those hips from whence the garment falls, those loins which are a treasure heap, the fountain and the source of all delight!*
>
> *He dwells, the garland wearer, in the forest by the Jamna, in the gentle breezes there,*
>
> *The swelling breasts of gopi girls who crushes ever with his restless hands.*
>
> *Pressing upon me your breasts so hard, entwining me with your vine-like arms, biting me with your merciless teeth, inflict upon me foolish one, the suitable penalty!*

The sexual urges among the male and female would follow the biological instincts and would be age specific, and may be manifested in variations in sex related activities and behaviour. All human societies have tried to institutionalize the sex instinct in marriage forms. There are rules of endogamy, exogamy, hypergamy and hypogamy and culturally acceptable norms regarding monogamy, polygyny and polyandry which guide man-woman relationships. Sexual relations outside marriage also tend to follow the limits set by these norms of behaviour. Premarital and marital sex may be guided by class, caste, *gotra* regulations as also extramarital relations, guided by rules of hypergamy. Sex relations violating these rules would be labelled as deviant behaviour and may be punishable by society. Murders and violence on account of deviant liaisons are not rare in Indian rural and urban life. There are permissible liaisons guided by rules of levirate and sorrorate whereby the joking relations between a woman and young brother of her husband, and between a man and younger sister of his wife could lead to marriage and/or sex relationship. Levirate marriages have been commonly approved to rehabilitate young war widows in the family. Several case studies are available in literature, whereby *Bhabhi* educates *Devar* about negotiating sex-play on the first night after marriage. Untouchability in the traditional caste system or different religion, did not prohibit or defer sex relations between a man of high caste and a woman from outcaste group. Hypogamous sex liaisons are, however, frowned upon, punishable even with honour killing. The latest, very popular Marathi movie, *Sairat*, followed by a Hindi remake movie *Dhadak* documents such honour-killing. Such killings are widely reported in media. The harems of kings could have women from various castes and religious communities. There are ample references to sex liaison in '*Arabian Nights*'.

Indian mythology including the epics of *Ramayana* and *Mahabharata* have stories about sex liaisons. Sita charged Laxman, her husband Ram's younger brother with *mala fide* motives about her, since he did not rush to help Ram in distress, who shouted for help, which was actually a mimicry call made by a devil. Draupadi in *Mahabharata*, as also her mother-in-law, Kunti, have been polyandrous. Krishna in the parlour of diplomacy tried to allure Karna, the son of Kunti, born out of premarital relationship with Sun-God, to join the Pandavas as the eldest brother and claim Draupadi as his legitimate wife, besides getting anointed as King. Karna earlier had abused Draupadi in *Durbar* as a prostitute, since she had married five brothers. Attempts were made to disrobe Draupadi in King's court labelling her as a slave, being the wife of five Pandav brothers who became slaves, having lost in the game of dice.

Indra, the king of heavenly kingdom, *Devlok*, had several sex workers in his celestial kingdom, known as *Apsara*, heavenly beauties. Even then, he molested Ahilya, the wife of sage Gautam, feigning himself as the sage for which, both were cursed by Gautam. He also directed an Apsara, Menaka, to seduce sage Vishwamitra who had attained spiritual and intellectual powers by sublimating sexual energy to arouse *Kundlini*, situated in the cerebral region. Menaka was successful in begetting a daughter, Shakuntala, from the sage, thereby lowering his spiritual powers, as a result of consumption of seminal fluid. India is called *Bharat* after the name of the son of Shakuntala married to king Dushyant.

Another *Apsara*, Urvashi expressed sexual favours from Arjun, the great Pandav archer in *Mahabharata*, whose biological father was Indra. While Arjun declined the offer saying she was like mother to him, being the mistress of his father, he was cursed by Urvashi to become impotent. Indra limited the life long period of curse of impotence to one year. During the period of one year, Arjun played the role of Brihannalla a eunuch dance teacher, in the kingdom of Virat during Pandavas' incognito period of one year, prior to beginning of *Mahabharata* war. Another name of *Apsara,* Rambha is commonly known and the term is used to taunt a woman who overtly exhibits her beauty, dress and hairstyle in public.

Another legend in Hindu mythology refers to the great God Vishnu destructing a demon *Bhasmasur* by presenting himself as a beautiful female dancer Mohini. The term *Bhasmasur* is now commonly used to refer to a powerful and authoritative person having achieved that position in a very short period, who is cruel and behaves like an unbridled devil.

Vishwamitra as a *kshatriya* king could become a *Brahmin* through penance. It is believed that through *yoga*, one could transform seminal power into spiritual-intellectual-divine power by awakening *kundalini.* These are the issues of body metabolism, of formation of seminal fluid, of its judicious use for procreation and pleasure, which are described in Ayurveda and Yoga and which influence the psyche of Indian people about masturbation, about over indulgence in sex, about losing body immunity, thereby becoming vulnerable to TB or AIDS.

It is not for any economic or political reason that a political leader of the stature of Indira Gandhi lost power and position personally. It is believed to be the result of crusade for vasectomy to have been campaigned by her son, Sanjay Gandhi. Vasectomy continues to be compared with castration resulting in loss of physical power and energy bringing in overall weakness. The illiterate rural women in her constituency could be persuaded to vote against Indira Gandhi with the argument that they would become *de facto* widows after their husbands underwent vasectomy operation for family planning. Widowhood is considered the worst curse for traditional Indian woman.

The most frequently asked questions by adolescent males in the course of research on adolescent sexuality bring out their concerns about loss of semen and the resultant weakness or possible impotence in case of masturbation. The IEC material of the government dismissing such concerns as psychic issue and masturbation or involuntary discharge of seminal fluid in sleep or dream, as natural body function, does not convince the adolescent boys. Ayurveda recognizes the dominant sex drive but advises to channelize it in legitimate sex relations with the spouse, and to restrain or control it according to age and other conditions as pregnancy, menstruation and early days after child birth.

Mahatma Gandhi has also discussed *Brahmacharya* (Celibacy) in great details, citing his own experiences and experiments. *Gita* respected as the guidebook of Hindu philosophy also cautions restraint in matters of sexual pleasures and sex. Sex drive is believed to be so powerful that the great God Shiva had to use all his powers by opening his powerful third eye to demolish the sex deity Kamdeo, presiding over the creation and sustenance of sex and sexual pleasures, when he tried to entice Shiva to become romantic with his wife Parvati for procreation. The legitimate sex is recognized in Hindu philosophy whereby the deities, gods and goddesses have spouses save for one monkey god Hanuman (But he also involuntarily procreated a child Makardhwaj from his sweat gulped by a fish). The sages respected for their wisdom as teachers and preachers had the wives who helped their husbands in the management of hermitage schools. Although celibacy has been advocated as a great virtue, it has never been practised widely, only monogamy has been preached. *Sanyas* whereby a person had to give up all worldly possessions and sexual pleasures including his property, family, personal and family name and caste affiliation, could be adopted at a ripe old age, only after the duties of householder were performed as enjoined by social norms. Only in rare cases, could a younger *Brahmachari* (Student stage in *Ashram* System) become a *sanyasi* (Monk) jumping over the two *ashrams*—*Grihasta* and *Vanaprastha*, thus avoiding the responsibilities of young and elderly householder, as husband, father and grandfather. Swami Vivekanand was one such *Sanyasi* who became internationally famous.

Of the four *ashramas*, i.e. stages of life, *Grihastashram* (Householder) has the longest period of life. Sex and procreation are the duties of a householder, to be treated as debts to be settled with the parents and society. Ayurveda enjoins not to hold back the biological bodily urges of hunger, sex, thirst and excretion beyond a reasonable period, failing which health would be affected.

It is thus being argued that human animal shares the biological instincts and urges with all living beings, more so as a mammal and as a primate. However having developed brain, mind and intellect, making him the only culture building animal, there is wide socio-cultural variability in sex behaviour. Cultures provide the permissible range of variability in order to ensure that the social structure does not collapse; the children as future members of society are properly reared and enculturated. Episodes of plural sex have by and large been among the permissible social relations in traditional societies guided by rules of endogamy, exogamy and hypergamy. It is mainly in the urban areas, that commercial sex workers and their clients have transgressed caste and religion. But there too, the recruitment to CSWs have been largely from particular caste groups and regions. The economically, politically and ritually powerful always exploited the women for sexual exploits from weaker sections and poor, and continue to do so in the present. It is a contradiction that untouchability did not proscribe sex between high and low caste members, the high caste men usually exploiting the low caste women as per the principles of hypergamy in a patriarchal system. While I causally asked the powerful *Brahmin* landlords in a village in Sagar district of Madhya Pradesh as to how there were several beautiful and fair skinned girls among the untouchable castes, they said, they were their 'daughters'. However, hypogamous sex crimes evoke large protests from the community of a high caste female victim, as happened in 2016, in a village Kopardi in Ahmednagar district of Maharashtra. A girl from a dominant caste Maratha was raped and murdered by three persons of low caste, probably ex-untouchables. There were very big protest marches from Maratha Community all over the state demanding capital punishment to the culprits.

There has been a clear distinction between CSW and dancing girls. During the feudal rule of princes and *jagirdars-zamindars*, even during British rule in India, the dancing girls or *nautch* girls were not commercial sex workers. They were invited on some occasions as birth or marriage ceremonies to perform with their team of instrumental musicians, to entertain the audience. In Maharashtra, *Lavni* dance and *Nautanki* in Hindi belt, are performed by such dancers who are quite famous for their art. In my village study in Gwalior in 1958, people would say, if the engagement cash money was Rs. 1000, there would surely be a dancing girl performing at the marriage ceremony.

A dancing girl could develop a lasting relationship with one of the clients and could beget a child but not as commercial sex. Having a mistress or a live-in relationship was considered a status symbol of power and money. As a result, female actors were not available to play female roles in drama or film. A Marathi actor Balgandharv became famous due to his playing excellent female roles in Marathi theatre.

There are several famous Hindi and Marathi movies, that we know of, portraying the life of dancing girls, during Moghal and British rule. It used to be a common sight or experience during feudal rule to hear the sound of dance and music if one passed through the area in a city where the dancing girls were located, usually on the first floor, ground floor having shops. Dance and music were considered as art professions, hereditary in nature, and had no linkage with commercial sex.

During my Master's level fieldwork in a village in Gwalior region, on a *Kojagiri Poornima* day in 1958, I was invited at a tehsil capital to participate at the milk party, which is widely practiced across India to enjoy the brightness of first time full moon after the rainy season is over. The party was held at the Police outpost located in a small fortress like building termed as *Garhi*. The participants were the block, tehsil level officials and some prominent professionals like lawyers and doctors. There was a dance performance by a *nautch*-girl during the milk party.

Homosexuality till recently considered as abnormal behaviour has been legitimized in several countries as same sex marriage, also termed as gay and lesbian. There are issues about third sex, transgender or eunuchs. Sex change is being formally recognized by way of change of name and not losing employment status, facilitated by surgery. One of my anthropology student from India, settled in New York, told me that he was earning his living by pursuing counselling as an occupation, to counsel the same sex partners to resolve their discord.

Recently, there has been a movement, more particularly in the West, termed as 'Me Too' about the alleged exploitation of female actors by film producers to award them plush roles in the films.

III

Anthropologists developed culture theory from the empirical studies of isolated people, the islanders or the tribal people in forests and hills. The communities who lived in 'time freeze' had developed coping mechanisms to deal with human behaviour, including sex behaviour. Being close to nature, they constructed their sexuality observing animal behaviour which suited their needs. Cow's milk is meant for the calf as mother's milk for the babies, could be rational, if they had to the raise the bulls at home, not purchasing from the market. Cow could be drafted for ploughing along with the bull. If a woman could work in the field, why not the cow? A woman's breasts, therefore, have no erotic appeal for tribal youth since their primary and important function is to feed the babies unlike the caste peasant communities where cow's surplus milk could be given to the baby and sold in the market. A paper in this book on "Construction of sexuality among Male College Students" bringing out the comparison between caste and tribe responses needs careful attention. Verrier Elwin has also discussed the issue of tribal response to women's breasts as mammary glands in his autobiography. The discussion about 'seed' and 'field' in *Mahabharata* in the context of who should be invited for *Niyoga* for procreation if the husband was not capable for insemination or was deceased, has its context in the society which was transforming from pastoral stage to settled agricultural stage. Irawati Karve has discussed this issue in her book '*Yugant*' which is anthropological analysis of *Mahabharata*. Anthropologists, therefore, have discussed sexuality in the context of culture, along with the discussion about marriage and kinship. It is the functional explanation provided in British Social Anthropology influenced by Durkheim from France. "Within the anthropological corpus, there is limited information of a direct kind of sexual behaviour, but a great many issues, such as marriage, divorce, family formation, fertility beliefs and practices, initiation rites and gender relations, all bear upon the social construction of sexuality" (Hilary Standing: *Social Science and Medicine*, Vol. 34, No. 5, p. 475, 1992). There is an opinion that anthropologists have not looked at sexuality and sex behaviour outside the domain of culture which was "conceptualized as autonomous and super-organic", and "did not assimilate sexuality—sex in itself—to its theoretical programme". "Thus, from the 1920s onward sex came to be treated either anecdotally or as an appendage to normative, propositional system such as kinship and marriage, or, more recently, gender ideology. Behaviour, as such, was abandoned to the psychologists, while sexual behaviour, in particular, became a research specialty largely associated with reproductive physiology, sex therapy and the Sunday supplement" (Donald Tuzin, *Social Science and Medicine*, Vol. 33, No. 8, p. 869, 1991).

It is also believed that Victorian moral standards guided legislation relating to adultery as a criminal act, as in India, which is being advocated for repealment. Tribal Communities also frown upon extra-marital relations since divorce by consent was an easy social process, even regulating the partial return of bride price paid during marriage.

The relationship of sexuality and gender received a new framework for analysis and interpretation under feminist thought. Contraceptive technology has questioned the concept of biological determinism, about the natural functions of procreation by women. Gender as a social construct has since then been discussed and accepted widely. The bride price paid in tribal society against dowry paid in caste Indian society (caste is a pan-Indian phenomena, not a Hindu phenomena) markedly differentiates position of woman in these communities. It needs a thorough probe as to why a tribal woman is never threatened of molestation or rape by a tribal man. While divorce and remarriage are not social issues in tribal society, social reform movements had to be launched in caste society to propagate widow remarriage. In case of adultery, man is punished or reprimanded in tribal society while a woman is punished in caste society. The social construction and cultural explanations thus become relevant to discuss sexuality and gender.

Carole S. Vance in the paper "Anthropology Rediscovers Sexuality: A Theoretical Comment" in *Social Science and Medicine* (Vol. 33, No. 8, 1991) has discussed Social Construction Models (1975-1990) and Cultural Influence Models of Sexuality (1920-1990) as distinct thought. "Social constructionists differ in their views of what might be constructed, variously, including sexual acts, sexual identities, sexual communities, the direction of erotic choice (object choice) and sexual desire itself."

The cross-cultural ethnographic accounts of single societies bring out variations which are functional for respective societies. "In this respect, it rejects obvious forms of essentialism and universalizing." "Culture is viewed as encouraging or discouraging the expression of generic sexual acts, attitudes and relationships. Oral-genital contact, for example, might be a part of normal heterosexual expression in one group but taboo in another; male homosexuality might be severely punished in one tribe yet tolerated in another."

As mentioned earlier the concept of beauty expressed in Indian sculpture is different from that in Greece or modern Europe and America. Cross-cousin marriage may be preferred in some parts of India and reflected as such in kinship terms while in other regions, it may be labelled as incest. Similar is the case with levirate. In Haryana in India, war widows could be married to husband's younger brothers in a public ceremony while this may be proscribed in south India.

"A social construction approach to sexuality would examine the range of behaviour, ideology and subjective meaning among and within human groups and would view the body, its functions and sensations as potentials (and limits) which are incorporated and mediated by culture." On the other hand "the cultural influence model recognizes variations in the occurrence of sexual behaviour and in cultural attitudes which encourage or restrict behaviour but not in the meaning of the behaviour itself...Anthropology's commitment to cross-cultural comparison made it the most relativistic of social science discipline in regard to the study of sexuality...The variability it reported suggested that human sexuality was malleable and capable of assuming different forms." It suggested that sexuality was not "largely a function of physiological functioning or instinctual drives". "It began to develop social and intellectual space in which it was possible to regard sexuality as something other than a simple function of biology" (Carole Vance: *Social Science and Medicine*, Vol. 33, No. 8, 1991). The anthropological account of sexuality and sex behaviour as in the writings of Malinowski or Verrier Elwin about single society, has been good demonstration providing the cultural context and function of sexual practices. The effects of these practices could be managed by the respective communities to contain them within the communities and groups. Sex was linked with social, cultural and economic life, not with the disease, at least not to our knowledge. There have been no documented epidemics of STD in tribal communities.

Now, with the potential risk of Tsunamic dimension of AIDS epidemic, sex is directly linked with disease, with chronic morbidity and mortality. The variations in sexual behaviour are all within the risk behaviour of AIDS. Sex has thus become a bio-medical concern. Sexuality is getting medicalised with research on therapy and vaccines. In the absence of effective treatment, and preventive vaccine, the emphasis is on behavioural change which calls for documentation of behavioural variability. "The AIDS crisis surprised anthropologists into the realization that there is apparently much we do not know about sexual behaviour; missing facts that are essential to our understanding of the epidemiology of this and other sexuality transmitted diseases" (Tuzin, *Social Science of Medicine*; Vol. 33, No. 8, 1991).

Anthropologists are no more dealing with isolated tribal communities only. They have been the first to bring out ethnography of peasant society following the conceptual and methodological model of primitive society as if they were isolated communities. The developing nations through their programmes for directed change have set in motion urbanization and industrialization which lead to rural to urban migration and mobility on an ever increasing scale. The political awareness in a democratic set up in countries like India have made the tribal and peasant communities dynamic and are moving them towards the global economic forces. The traditional occupations of caste societies have been modified while the tribal communities are migrating to other areas as workforce, being drawn in the cash economy, and for want of food security.

This scenario has developed various life styles, which may vary from the life style, that was co-terminus with culture patterns. There is drastic change in life styles between the pre-industrial urban centres and post-industrial cities. Like food, sex is also a marketable commodity. Woman as a sex object is being paraded in all advertisements to sell every product. The concept of affluent behaviour as always revolves around variation in food and sex. The main visual media like TV has become very popular and affordable making its impact on the adolescents. As a result, there have been surveys to find out the groups at risk of getting HIV infection like the truckers or CSWs. The need has also been felt to identify the risk behaviour in which some people indulge. The migrant youth including the hotel workers who are not subjected to family controls but are exposed to opportunities of sex in a metropolitan area could indulge in risk behaviour. It has been found necessary to understand the perceptions and knowledge of young about sexual activities and the behaviour which could be labelled as risk behaviour.

The concern of the parents about sex security of girls get reflected in their marriage immediately after attaining puberty. The concern of the parents about young males is rooted in the exposure of youth to blue films and poronographic literature as also urban influences particularly the urban peer groups. The social construction approach and cultural influence model may need to be reinterpreted to analyze the situations in the context of AIDS. At the same time, there are people who are living with AIDS and they have to live life with dignity. Flow of information and knowledge becomes important in the awareness campaigns. The biomedical approach being linked with disease, its causation and lack of treatment, is likely to give messages which develop a fear and stigma. Social stigma and self-stigma are two sides of a coin. There are instances on the increase that this is leading to suicides and murders within the family as coping mechanisms to salvage the honour of the family. These are all challenges to social science research.

There are issues about transmission of HIV to baby during pregnancy. It is, therefore, necessary to know more about reproductive biology and morbidity and to communicate it to women. Women in the rural area do suffer from reproductive tract morbidities as a result of their visiting husbands who work in cities and indulge in risk behaviour. If the wives have undergone tubectomy, it is difficult for these men to use condoms which would manifest breach of trust in marriage. Anyway, the perceptions about condom use is, they have to be used only in contact with CSWs. Even the CSWs who have developed emotional or long duration relationships with a particular client do not persuade use of condoms since the condoms are not meant for husband-wife relationships. These are the cultural influences which are to be documented and modified.

Sex research in the context of AIDS thus is crucial since the research results could help plan the interventions. General awareness about AIDS has permeated even to the rural areas, but it is accompanied by scare about the disease. Scare does not necessarily modify the behaviour. It tends to make it secret and underground. It also contributes to accentuation of stigma. Community's experience of leprosy stigma has a tendency to be transferred to AIDS, probably much more, since AIDS has moral connotation being linked with sex.

While initiating a research study about Reproductive and Child Health in Velha taluka of Pune district, we organized a meeting of elected representatives from villages, to inform them about the project and seek their participation. At the largely attended meeting, concerns were expressed about the risk of contracting AIDS by the youth in the villages who stayed in Pune city for work, or visited markets for sale of farm produce. Sympathy and concerns were also expressed about the young women getting infected from their husbands who had city connections and probably visited red light areas in Pune. Meetings were also conducted in respective study villages, mostly held in temples at night, after dinner after 8.0 P.M., due to availability of spacious and clean place for men and women audience. While we focused our discussion on reproductive and child health, there were demands to know about AIDS, despite pointing out the sacred space of temple with the idols of deities in place. Normally discussion about sexuality and risk behaviour would be a taboo in temple premises. This indicates the severity of people's concerns about risk behaviour in urban areas with a scare about AIDS. In case of any death of a young person, the community diagnosis would be death due to AIDS.

In Summary, we have to admit that sex research by way of documentation by anthropologists of sexuality and sex behaviour in their ethnographic monographs to complete the holistic picture of respective cultures has been different than what is required now in view of its implication for AIDS. The quantitative epidemiological surveys are no doubt required by policy planners to plan and implement the policies based on numerical and geographical events of the issues. However, in order to understand the contextual reasons for behaviour in the dynamic and changing societies in the days of globalized economic, political and health systems, it is necessary to follow the qualitative methods which has been appropriately modified to study issue specific focused ethnography.

3

Research Methods

Sexuality and Sexual Behaviours

PERTTI J. PELTO

Introduction

The studies in this collection presented in this book were carried out with a number of different data-gathering techniques. Some researchers, particularly Mr. Agashe and Dr. Swarnakar, used general ethnographic methods, based on their anthropological training. Mr. Agashe immersed himself in the field situation among the tribal people, living for some months in the villages, while engaging in extensive participant observation as well as in-depth interviewing of his informants. Others, such as Dr. Bhattacharya, Ms. Maushami Joshi, and Dr. Alka Barua, carried out structured, quantitative surveys in their research sites, in addition to qualitative, open-ended interviewing. Dr. Hemant Apte conducted a thorough-going review of written sources in order to carry out his study of the language of sex work and sexuality as reflected in the historical Marathi literature. Several of the studies made excellent use of a combination of qualitative and quantitative research methods.

Recent studies in the field of sexuality and sexual behaviours in India have relied heavily on qualitative methods. Excellent progress has been made in refining these data-gathering techniques in order to get more thorough understanding of the complexities of socially sensitive areas of sexual behaviours and sexuality in a variety of different sub-groups and settings.

In this review I will examine some of the features of the qualitative data-gathering methods that have been developed in the course of studies of sexuality, sexual behaviours, and related topics in India. The examples are taken from the various small-scale research projects funded by the

Ford Foundation in a number of different locations over the past six to eight years. Examples are also included from recent work in Nepal in connection with the HIV-AIDS campaign in that country.

Reasons for Emphasizing Qualitative Methods

Both quantitative and qualitative data are important in social sciences research, but qualitative methods are especially important for situation assessments before programmes are launched, and in certain other situations where detailed descriptive information is needed about specific communities or populations. Qualitative descriptive data are also essential as preparatory information for developing and refining quantitative surveys. I am focusing particularly on qualitative data-gathering techniques in this review because these methods are much less well understood than quantitative surveys, and a great many misconceptions are still circulated about qualitative research.

Qualitative methods are particularly useful in the following circumstances:

1. When the topics to be studied are sensitive because they are linked to socially disapproved behaviours, so that general survey interviews result in widespread evasion, denial, and under-reporting.
2. When very little is known about the details of a complex social and cultural domain, so that researchers do not have clear ideas of what kinds of questions should be explored.
3. When programme people have very little time for generating useful background information before intervention activities are to begin. In such situations qualitative data can be analyzed quickly, and the research can continue while intervention operations are getting underway.
4. When behaviours related to HIV-AIDS programmes and other sexual matters are strongly influenced by cultural idea systems that require in-depth analysis, including information about local vocabulary, concepts of illness and treatment seeking, and other cultural information.
5. When the results of quantitative surveys produce puzzling, unexpected results that need to be explained through detailed questioning of people within the study population.
6. When a comprehensive quantitative survey is planned, but

researchers lack information about the composition of the target population(s), from which to develop strategies of sampling, as well as estimating appropriate sample sizes.

Defining Qualitative Research

In simplest terms, qualitative data consist of verbal, textual, descriptive materials and other forms of information that are presented primarily or wholly without reference to numbers. (*Note*: Data is a plural word, though it is often misused as singular.) Although we usually think of narrative descriptions (text) as the prototype of qualitative data, maps, pictures and diagrams are also basically qualitative in nature. Contrary to some writers, particularly some who have anti-science philosophies, we believe that qualitative, textually and graphic data can be intermingled with quantitative data, and the two sorts of information are generally more convincing when an integrated qualitative-quantitative approach is presented.

A large part of the strategy of qualitative research is the collection of 'emic data'. The concept, 'emic', refers to information that reflects the point of view of local people in the study population, including their vocabulary and their categories for understanding sexual behaviours and other information. The concept 'emic' is used as a contrast to 'etic data' (and categories), which present the language and categories of the researchers, or the 'outside' biomedical ways of conceptualizing knowledge. The ethnographic, qualitative focus on emic data is also paramount in the uses of free-listing, pile-sorting etc., methods described below. One clear example of the differences between 'emic' and 'etic' information is in the terminology used for sexually transmitted infections. Local people in much of north and western India use words such as *garmi* and descriptive words for 'pus discharge,' 'sores on penis,' and 'burning urination'. These 'emic terms' are in contrast to the 'etic' biomedical language of 'gonorrhoea,' 'syphilis', and other technical vocabulary.

Qualitative Research and Science

It has become fashionable for people to equate science with quantified research, often dismissing qualitative data as 'humanistic' and 'unscientific'. However, historically and still today a very important component of science is qualitative in nature. One of the most significant scientific works of all time, Darwin's 'The Origin of Species', in which he set forth the theory of natural selection and biological evolution, is entirely qualitative. Large parts of the biological and geological sciences are qualitative in their basic theoretical propositions and data-gathering techniques. For example, a major activity in palaeontology, the study of the history of living things through analysis of fossil remains, consists of the discovery and collection of fossil materials, and the detailed description (and depiction) and categorization or classification of the fossils. Of course, all such areas of science now-a-days also include plenty of computerized work and complex mathematical analysis as well.

Mapping: Geographical Mapping and Social Mapping

Mapping is a very important component of much applied research on sexuality and sexual behaviours, because all programmes, whether in HIV-AIDS or other topical areas, need to have a sense of: "Where are the target populations?" "Where are the problem areas?" And "where are our resources and personnel carrying out their activities?" Mapping is also essential for developing a clear sampling strategy for data-gathering, particularly when a quantitative survey is planned.

Geographical Mapping

'Ordinary' geographical mapping refers to putting key features communities, health facilities, locations of target populations, supporting resources, and other information onto more or less accurate maps prepared by the researchers from their own observations plus inputs from key informants and other sources. Ethnographic researchers generally carry out mapping activities, with the help of local informants, in order to identify special subgroups and features within their study communities. Such mapping operations are often essential for on-going planning and research logistics.

Social Mapping

Social mapping is a process of data-gathering in which researchers ask members of a target population, or informants familiar with a specific target area, to draw maps on which they indicate important locations and information on the maps. For example, researchers who were studying men's sexual health problems in a district in Tamil Nadu approached groups of men in the study villages and in various neighbourhoods of the city, asking them to indicate on schematic maps the locations of sex workers, medical practitioners who treat sexual health problems, and other salient features. The researchers collected 14 of these 'social mappings' in the rural area, and 8 maps in the urban area of Vellore. On the basis of these maps they compiled a comprehensive mapping of 'pockets of risk behaviours', as well as locations of the most usually contacted providers in one large rural block, and in the city of Vellore (Peedicayil, 2003). Similar social mapping strategies have been employed in a number of rural and urban projects, including a low income area in Mumbai, a rural region in Gujarat, and a study of treat children in Bangalore (Verma *et al.*, 1998; Lakhani *et al.*, 1997; and Murthy and Karott, 2000). Social mapping is seen as a technique for getting the perceptions of places and locations from local people, so it is a method for collecting 'emic data'. In addition to data about sexual behaviours, social mapping has proved very useful in wide range of other topics, such as health care seeking, understanding the distribution of health services, and mapping the patterns of crops and other activities in rural areas.

In addition to data-gathering, the technique of social mapping has also been widely used as a device for developing rapport in local communities, and also as a way to identify who are the most useful key informants, particularly among those individuals who play prominent roles during the social mapping process.

In-Depth Interviews

In-depth, open-ended interviews are the real backbone, the most important data-gathering technique in qualitative research concerning sexuality and sexual behaviours related to HIV-AIDS, and other community health topics. Most of the studies in the University of Pune (School of Health Sciences) small grants programme relied on in-depth interviewing as the primary investigative tool.

People who have experience in survey research (with carefully worded, structured questions) often have difficulty in understanding the technique and 'philosophy' of in-depth interviews. Many experienced interviewers with survey research experience wish to construct very clear, structured questions, perhaps because they feel uncomfortable with a relatively unstructured format, in which the dialogue often takes unexpected directions. The concept of the in-depth interview is much different from structured interviews, as the objective is to get the informant, the interviewee, to 'take control', and to narrate in her or his own style and timing. It is worthwhile to explore the differences between the two styles of interviewing, particularly for those persons who will have the responsibility of training the field researchers.

In-depth Interviews are Very Different from Survey Interviews

In-depth interviews are a central element of qualitative situation assessments, and many other types of data-gathering. At the outset it is important to be clear about the differences between in-depth interviews and survey interviews.

In survey interviews, the aim is practically always to get numerical data, or frequencies, of specific pieces of concrete information. How many sex workers report having such and such symptoms of STIs? How many men report using condoms in the most recent sexual encounter? How many this? How many that?

In-depth interviews, in contrast, seek to get extensive descriptive information, in the form of narratives, actions, events, that can give verbal pictures of systematic behaviours, such as "where are all the places that people go for sex?" "What are the steps and processes for a bunch of young men to embark on a group sexual activity?" "What are the different kinds of men who come to this area for entertainment, including sex?" "What are the various factors and attitudes that affect peoples' likelihood of using condoms?" And so on. In each case, the aim of the interviewing is to get as much narrative detail as possible from individuals, often in the descriptions of specific events, actions, or episodes.

Other Points of Difference between the Two Types of Interviews

1. In-depth interviews should be like conversations. Very informal, with very few, or no, prepared questions. The interviewer seeks to establish a friendly social interaction with the informant. The sequence of topics can be very different from one interview to the next, depending on the kinds of information the informant happens to bring up; and depending on the specific situations and experiences of the informants.
2. Interviewers should avoid the question answer sort of interaction, and try to get the informant to narrate, to talk, to describe events and actions in detail.
3. In-depth interviews are designed to get a lot of concrete detail; while survey interviews eliminate almost all details.

4. In-depth interviews do not follow a set sequence of questions. The goal is to get the informant to talk in detail; and then to follow up with 'probes' to get further details about important features.

One main goal of in-depth interviews is to get 'the full story' with plenty of details, about specific 'events of interest' such as a man going to treatment for his STI problem; a trucker's narrative of his meeting and behaviours with a sex worker; or a person getting tested for HIV and then the first weeks and months of coping with the knowledge that he is HIV positive.

Using a Checklist of Topics

Instead of having a prepared set of questions, such as used in quantitative research, the interviewer seeking qualitative, descriptive information often carries a checklist of topics to be explored. It is recommended that the interviewers memorize all or parts of the checklist, so they do not have to consult the list during the interview. Sometimes, near the end of an interview, the checklist can be consulted to see what items have been left out.

Probing for More Details and Examples

One of the most important tools in in-depth interviewing is the technique of asking for more details about some of the information that informants narrate. Usually informants give only sketchy, partial information when they are answering our questions. Interviewers must listen carefully, and respond to the informant's narratives by asking for more specific information on certain key points.

For example, in an interview a sex worker said that "Some men argue with us that they don't want to use a condom; so we have to try to convince them."

Interviewer: "Can you give me a recent example when you had that kind of argument with a man?" Please give me a 'play by play' description: what he said; what you said, and so on.

Key Informants and In-depth Interviewing

Key informant interviews are discussions with persons who have knowledge about conditions and events in the community, and particularly about the specific topic of study. For example, in the studies in Pune brothels by Dr. Bhattacharya and her colleagues, the key informants were experienced persons in NGOs working in the area, as well as some of the *gharwalis* (brothel-keepers). Studies of school students, on the other hand, generally rely on some interviews with teachers, parents, local community leaders, as well as some particularly expressive and communicative girls who are able to generalize about their peers.

Such interviews should be very open-ended, as the researcher tries to learn as much new information as possible from the informant. The interview is not about that person and her or his own personal behaviours, beliefs, or knowledge about HIV-AIDS, so the interviewer does not need to ask the key informants about their age, education, and other background data.

Since our interest in the key informant is basically concerning information about events or situations in the immediate area, or in some special aspect of the community, it is generally not useful to ask the key informant about his or her own knowledge and attitudes about HIV-AIDS, or whether he himself practices safe sex, or other details about that person. The main personal knowledge about the key informant that we care about is the background features that make her or him (relatively) 'an expert' about some topic of information. So, the individual's occupational role, how long he or she has been in this location, and amounts of contact with the different kinds of key persons in the area, are potentially useful to ask about.

Who/What are Key Informants?

Key informants are people whom we expect will have considerable knowledge about some specific topic or area that we wish to find out about. For example, when a research team in Nepal was mapping and counting injection drug users (in the Kathmandu valley area) they relied heavily on NGO outreach workers who were familiar with IDUs, and also former drug users who were familiar with some areas that IDUs frequented. Those informants were, in a sense, 'local experts' concerning the information the researchers wanted to know about.

In many situations NGO outreach workers are likely to be very good key informants. There are many other types of 'local experts' who can be good key informants. If you want to know about commercial sexual activities in certain areas, the taxi drivers, *paan* shop and tea-stall operators, and other 'street people' are likely to be excellent sources of information.

Sometimes, people think that key informants should be persons in authority, such as government officials, health authorities, school teachers, and other 'leaders'. Such persons may have a wide range of information, but often they are not your main key informants. They are too busy; and often they prefer to give you 'official' information, rather than giving realistic descriptions.

Very often key informants are persons whom we consult on a number of different occasions; not just a one-shot interview. In community assessment fieldwork you should try to find two or three persons that you can continually go back to, to ask questions as you learn more about your research topic.

Sampling and Numbers of In-depth Interviews

Sampling is the process of selecting 'cases,' or informants (or other units of observation) in a manner that will be representative geographically, socially, and in other ways, of the population(s) or situations about which we are seeking information. We select our 'samples' basically for the purpose of making the resulting information as credible and useful as possible.

Sampling is always important, even though in most cases (in qualitative research) we do not do random sampling. If the study area and population is spread out (over an entire valley, or a long stretch of highway) then sampling should be from the different geographical locations. Along a stretch of highway, the researchers should look for key informants in each of the main population clusters and/or truck and bus halt places. At the same time it is important to insure that data are collected from both female and male informants, and it is usually good to get information from people in different occupations and/or different kinds of establishments.

Case Interviews

Unlike key informant interviews, 'case interviews' are primarily focused on the individual herself or himself. Depending on the focus of the research, the interviewer inquires about the personal history of the person, and probes in detail concerning events and actions that person has been involved in. Most of the studies in this collection included 'cases'. Studies in the brothel included the cases of individual sex workers and also case interviews of individual clients of sex workers. Studies of the young men working as hotel workers involved semi-structured interviews with one hundred 'cases,' concerning their sexual behaviours and experiences.

The clearest example of case interviews is in studies about treatment-seeking. A number of studies in various parts of India have been based on in-depth interviews (sometimes multiple sessions) with persons who have had (for example) STI symptoms. The research of Joshi and her colleagues (2004) was based on a total of 124 in-depth interviews among men in rural Gujarat. They collected detailed narratives of the men's experiences with symptoms that appeared to be sexual health problems. They obtained step-by-step accounts of the treatment-seeking behaviours, and also descriptions of the types of girls and women with whom the men had sexual encounters. Thus, each interview contained detailed information about the men's behaviours, as well as their interpretations of the sexual health problems, expectations about treatment from health providers, and other contextual information. The interviews also included details of the vocabulary of men's sexual health problems in the rural region.

A 'case interview' about treatment seeking often begins with a request for a narrative about going for treatment. Based on the narrative, the interviewer then probes for more details, based on a checklist (which has been memorised). Usually the researcher would like to have certain standard background data from the informants, including age, education, and other features. (These individual background data are much less important in our interviews of key informants, since the information they give us is not about themselves.) In some situations it is a good idea to wait until the end of the interview to collect background data concerning age, education, marital status, and other information in 'case interviews'.

A Useful Style for Case Interviews (e.g., for Cases of Treatment Seeking) (Sequence of questions)

1. Start with general social chatting (to break the ice and create social rapport).
2. Ask the informant to give the play-by-play narrative of going for treatment seeking (very open-ended, unstructured).
3. Then probe with the informant to fill in details from your checklist.

a. First noticed symptoms—what, when?
b. What did you do first? (Anything at home; home remedies?)
c. How long did you wait?
d. Who did you talk with? Who gave you advice?
e. How did you decide to go to that particular provider?(etc. etc.).
f. Did you go to any other provider? (Get the whole sequence). *Note:* In some cases it is very useful to use a time-line, drawn on paper, onto which you put the sequence of steps in the treatment seeking.

4. Go on to your other topics in your checklist, perhaps past history of problems; or other information.
5. Near the end of the interview: Collect the background information about the person: age, education, marital status, occupation, etc. etc.

Statistical Analysis of Case Materials: The Qualitative/Quantitative Mix

Whenever a project includes at least 30 or 40 cases, it is useful to give some numerical statements about the data, such as:

a. "Nineteen (about half) of the women spoke about—as a big problem."
b. Treatment seeking usually includes home remedies, going to chemists/medicine shops, private practitioners, government hospital, traditional healers, and others. It is useful to give the breakdown of numbers going to each of those different categories. Perhaps the health problems mentioned can be grouped into several categories, then you might have a table (Table 3.1) something like this:

Table 3.1: Matrix of Treatment-Seeking for Different Types of Health Problems

	Home Remedy	*Med. Shop*	*Priv. Pract.*	*Govt. Hosp*	*Traditional Healer*
Menstrual problem	5	7	1	0	0
Burning Urination	9	2	2	0	0
Itching in genitals	6	7	0	0	1
Sores, ulcers in genitals	1	6	7	3	1
Totals	**21**	**22**	**10**	**3**	**2**

Source: Hypothetical Example.

The table supports the generalization that the people in the study population seem to rely more on home remedies and getting medicines from the chemists and medicine shops, instead of going to private doctors or government services. Results very similar to this table were found in a study of treatment-seeking among sex workers in Kathmandu, Nepal.

Note: In studies with fewer than 100 cases it is generally not good to use percentages. Simply the numbers of cases should be given, as in the following examples:

1. "About half of the younger age group (16 of 30) experienced this problem; while only three people in the older category (of 32 persons) mentioned it."
2. "Very few persons (three cases) went to traditional healers for this type of problem."

Structured Qualitative Interviews: Free-listing, Pile-sorting and Ratings (*cf.* Weller and Romney, 1988)

Free-Listing

Free-listing is one of the easiest, and most useful, techniques for getting lists of the contents or 'inventory' for any topic or subtopic. The beginning inventory from a free-listing can be used for a variety of subsequent data-gathering activities. Some of the most productive and interesting free-lists in recent research in reproductive/sexual health include lists of:

A. Male sexual health problems.
B. Types of drugs used in the local IDU population.
C. Types of problems experienced by sex workers.
D. Women's health problems.
E. Health providers in the area.
F. Types of clients of sex workers.
G. Many other topics are amenable to free-listing.

These are only a few examples of the many different topics for which free-listing has been useful. Table 3.2 is an example of free-listing of drugs, collected from injection drug users in the south-eastern region of Nepal. Such lists can be collected very rapidly, as it requires only 5 to 10 minutes (usually) for an informant to give his or her answer to the question. The free-listing question is often introduced early in an interview, after the informant has relaxed and good rapport has been established. The interviewer can simply ask:

> "Now I would like to know about all the different types of *maal* or drugs, or things that you know about, or that you have heard of people using among the guys in this area. Please take your time. Think of all the different types of drugs, and I will write them down."

Table 3.2: Top 15 Drugs Mentioned by IDUs, and Corresponding Local Terms Listed in Biratnagar

Sl. No.	*Name of drugs*	*Local terms*	*N=15*	*%*
1.	Tidigesic	Maal, T, Tata, Ampoule, TD, Snooker, Pool, Bullet, Dose, Masi, Bhala, Bhitti, Dot	15	100.0
2.	Nitrosun	Bhatmas, N, Sun, Gedagudi, Makai, Taak, Button, Naatibabu, Ten, BP, Nitro	15	100.0
3.	Phensydyle	P, Dyle, Pyachche, Jhol, Beer, Liquid, Kalo, Horlics, Bottle, Chadole, Sano Bhai, Maal, Black tea, Dose	15	100.0
4.	Calmpose	—	14	93.3
5.	Ganja	G, Butti, Shankarji ko buti, Makada, Join, Jharpat, Osi, Chir, Grass, Prasad Gansh	14	93.3
6.	Spasmoproxi bon/S.P.	Kala daiza	14	93.3
7.	Rakshi	Buch, Tharra, Kho.Bi., Bam, Daru, Sarab, Ghachchu, Wangepani, Chiso chiya	14	93.3
8.	Avil	—	13	86.7
9.	Corex	Jhol, Beer, C, Jholjhal, Dyle	13	86.7
10.	Phenargon	—	11	73.3
11.	Cyclofam	—	8	53.3
12.	Chares	Black, Koila, Kaalo	7	46.7
13.	Fortwin	—	7	46.7
14.	Brown sugar	BS	5	33.3
15.	Valium-10	—	5	33.3

**Data from Research by CREHPA, 2002.

After collecting the list, the interviewer can go ahead to ask about each item, to get more information, and perhaps to ask about "other words people use for the same *maal.* The example above shows that the more popularly used drugs are known by a number of different slang labels. One of the important features of free-lists is that you can quickly find out which items are 'uppermost in peoples' minds,' or 'most common' in the area. In the example, it is clear that tidigesic, nitrosun and phensydyle are well-known in the area, as every informant mentioned them. The pharmaceutical preparation, Tidigesic, is the most commonly injected drug in almost all parts of Nepal, and is known by many nicknames. In contrast to the top three well-known drugs, the much lower frequencies of mention of 'brown sugar' and valium-10 show that those are less common, or less well known in this population.

The researchers only needed to collect lists from 15 respondents in order to get a nearly complete inventory of the drugs used by the injection drug users (IDUs) in the Biratnagar area of south-eastern Nepal. Free-listing and other structured qualitative methods generally require only small samples for most purposes. The sample sizes depend on the nature of the topic and the purpose of the listing. If researchers wished to compare the above list of drugs with the free-list of another area, it would be good to have perhaps 25 informants instead of only 15. For a topic such as 'sexual health problems,' the sample size for free listing should be at least 20-25 respondents, because of the complexity of the topic.

Sometimes the free listing of "what are the kinds of problems that you encounter in your work?" is a good way to start an interview with sex workers and others who may be wary of being interviewed. It is also a very good beginning with community outreach workers. Most people like to talk about their problems, so when you ask them about their problems near the beginning of an interview, it helps to build rapport.

Very often the contents from a free list give a good framework for the next steps in an open-ended interview. Suppose that in an interview with a sex worker, the first comment is that 'some of the *goondas* refuse to pay.' When her listing is finished, the researcher can start with a probe:

> *You said that some of the goondas don't pay you. Could you give me an example—a recent case when this happened? I would like to know more about this kind of happening, and what kind of people these are...*

Pile Sorting

Pile sorting is used to find out how people group or categorise the items that are collected in free listing. The process is very useful to discover peoples' 'cultural categories,' and the underlying assumptions or reasons for their groupings. For example, in some communities in India and Nepal, if people are asked to group or categorise a series of illnesses, some of the informants may group together some illnesses because they are 'heaty' (*garmi* in Hindi), versus 'cold' (*thandi*). In Nepal, some people categorise or group certain illnesses as *thulo* (big) *versus saano* (little) (Beine, 2003).

Ravi Verma and his colleagues used pile sorting to find out about categories of 'men's sexual health problems' in Mumbai (Bombay). The resulting pile sorting showed that the men in the low income community made a clear distinction between sexual health problems that were thought to be due to sexual contact (STIs) *versus* 'non-contact' problems such as excessive masturbation, night discharge, and impotence (Verma *et al.*, 1998).

Pile sorting is usually carried out using index cards. Each item is written on a separate index card. If we were using the different drug items in the listing above, we would have 15 cards, which individual informants would be asked to sort into groups. The informant is told to use as many different groups or piles as he/she wishes, and that there are no right or wrong answers. After the informant has sorted the items into groups, the interviewer should ask about the reasons or 'criteria' for the groupings.

Rating and Ranking

The same set of index cards (items from free lists) can also be used for rating or ranking. In research on male sexual health problems in a low income community in Mumbai (Verma *et al.*, 1998), male informants were asked to rate the degree of 'seriousness' of the various sexual problems that emerged in the free listing. The ratings showed that men considered AIDS to be the most serious disease, and in general the symptoms that appeared to be due to sexually transmitted infections (STIs) were rated as more serious than the 'non-contact' sexual problems. However, the fifth item in the ratings, *dhat patla hona* (thinning of the semen) is often a non-contact sexual problem, according to local understandings, believed to result from excessive masturbation and other non-contact causes (*see* Table 3.3).

The 'etic terms,' gonorrhoea and syphilis are known to some people in the low income population of Mumbai, but the meanings are likely to be different from the biomedical understanding of these words.

The rating task, using index cards, is performed in much the same way as the pile sorting, except that the informants are directed to "put the most serious, or most severe conditions on the far left hand side," and "put the least serious conditions over here, on the far right hand side." For informants who cannot read the cards, the interviewer can read out the words on each card, and then ask the informant to indicate which

Table 3.3: Ratings of Severity of Sexual Health Problems in Mumbai Low Income Neighbourhood (N=56)

Sexual Health Problems	*Mean Rating (4-point scale)*
AIDS	3.94
Gonorrhoea**	3.20
Syphilis**	3.00
Pus nikalna (pus discharge)	2.78
Dhat patla hona (thinning of semen)	2.43
Ling se khoon (bleeding from penis)	2.39
Jakham hona/fori/foda (sores on penis)	2.37
Garmi ('heat') 'probable STI'	2.33
Ling main dard (pain in penis)	2.31
Peshab main jalan (burning urination)	2.29
Dhat girna (white discharge)	2.27
Khada na hona (lack of erection)	2.27
Dane nikalna (boils, sores)	2.24
Khujli (itching)	2.14
Kamjori (weakness)	2.10
Jaldi girna (early ejaculation)	2.02
Hasthamaithun (Masturbation)	1.55

Source: Verma *et al.*, 1998.

severity rating he wishes to assign to the item.

Rank ordering is carried out in the same fashion, with index cards, except that the informants are asked to put all the items in rank order, so they have to make more small-scale distinctions, from high to low. Thus, rank ordering is much more time consuming than simple ratings.

Rating and ranking has been effectively used, for example, for the following:

1. Which problems are most serious? (sex workers)
2. Which sexual acts are most *maja* (pleasure)? (Street boys in Bangalore)
3. Which drugs are most easily available? (drug users in Nepal)
4. Which health providers are most preferred? (villagers in Pakistan)
5. Many other kinds of information can be rated (and pile-sorted) in the same manner.

Free listing, pile sorting and rating/ranking are a curious mixture of qualitative and quantitative data. The technique of data collection is qualitative, yet the process results in information that is managed numerically. The statistical software programme, ANTHROPAC is used for processing the data into readily usable formats. The results of pile-sorting data are often presented in the form of two dimensional plots, or 'cognitive maps'. Thus, the numerical results are 're-translated' back into a qualitative, pictorial representation. Weller and Romney (1988) have presented a handy review of this package of qualitative-*cum*-quantitative data collection and analysis.

These data-gathering techniques are extremely versatile, and relatively easy to use, even by less qualified and experienced interviewers. The techniques generally require relatively small samples, as they focus on cultural information which is relatively common in the usual study communities. The data-gathering using index cards has been found to be more interesting and congenial for informants, as compared with the usual interviewing formats. Many innovative approaches can be used, including picture cards, photographs, or other kinds of materials. The frameworks provided by free-listing and pile-sorting also offer abundant opportunities for probing into details, or even branching off into in-depth narratives about individual experiences related to the categories in the index cards.

Quantitative Surveys

Among the papers presented in this collection, several studies relied heavily on quantitative surveys. For example, the study of condom use among married and unmarried men in Ahmedabad, reported by Dr. Alka Barua used a structured format for interviewing of the sample of 300 male respondents. Similarly, the study of reproductive health issues among adolescent girls (Bhattacharya and Pardeshi) used a structured quantitative instrument administered to 370 girls in a low income area of Pune. Joshi's study of 'sexuality of adolescent girls' in a Pune low income area included structured questionnaires with 300 school girls.

The main purpose of these surveys was to provide numerical estimates of how many or what proportion of the study population displayed or reported specific characteristics that the researcher specifically focused on as target questions. The quantitative questions that were answered in the surveys gave concrete estimates of targets for intervention. For example, the data in Barua's study of condom use indicated that only about 50 per cent of men going to sex workers used condoms. That gives an estimate of the magnitude of a problem that further interventions must address. The quantitative data also permit the identification of sub-groups that are particularly at risk, e.g. of failure to use condoms. In most data of this type the more educated respondents show somewhat greater use of condoms. The researchers who use quantitative data must often employ sophisticated, complicated statistical procedures in order to develop clearer designations of the most 'at risk' sub-populations. In many cases the researchers using quantitative techniques can develop more refined statistical measures for identifying the sub-groups in their populations that are particularly engaging in risky sexual behaviours; and at the same time, the careful use of qualitative methods can give further definition and understanding about the specific situations and types of people that can be the focus of intervention programmes.

Other Qualitative Data-gathering for Sexuality and Sexual Behaviour Research

Many other techniques of data-gathering are found in the wide range of recent research concerning sexual and reproductive health and issues related to HIV-AIDS. Direct observation is often an important component of qualitative research, especially ethnographic research, but is seldom feasible in research focused on sexual behaviours. However, Agashe's research in a tribal community included considerable opportunities for direct observation of events in the study communities; and Bhattacharya's research in the brothels of Pune also included some opportunities for direct observations of the organisation of activities in the brothel settings.

Some research projects have used group discussions (so-called focus group discussions) for part of the data collection. The group sessions are most useful for collecting information on the publicly or socially approved versions of behaviours, along with local stereotypes about the people who practice the socially disapproved behaviours. The group discussions are also very important in studies of adolescents, as such meetings with groups of parents help to develop a positive feeling towards the research directed to the sexual and reproductive health issues in the younger generation.

Use of Computers in the Data Management and Analysis

Until the decade of the 1990s most of the qualitative, ethnographic, research in India was carried out without the use of computers. Larger survey projects made use of computers, but that meant that local NGOs and other small-scale programmes could afford, or were unable to carry out such data-gathering, as they had little or no access to computers. All that changed during the past decade, as relatively inexpensive desktop computers became more widely available, and the skills in computer use (and availability of appropriate software programmes) spread to mid-size and even small NGOs, particularly those who were receiving research and programmatic funding from international sources.

Throughout India it has now become standard practice that in-depth interviews are entered into computerised form, using WORD or other word-processing software. More and more research and intervention groups are using 'text management' programmes such as ATLAS/ti (Muhr, 1997) and ETHNOGRAPH to code and process the complex text data for easier analysis and writing. Those programmes do not actually 'analyse' the data, but they are very useful for coding, sorting, and retrieving pieces of text materials as needed by the researchers.

The data from free-lists, pile-sorting and ratings are generally analysed using the ANTHROPAC software programme (Borgatti, 1993), which is now widely known in many parts of India. Processing of free-lists, for example, quickly produces the summarized list in descending order of frequency, and also a measure of the 'salience' of each item, in terms of frequency of mention, weighted by how near the 'top of individual lists' an item appeared. For pile-sorting data, ANTHROPAC provides both a cluster analysis programme and a 'multidimensional scaling' (MDS). The MDS gives a 'cognitive mapping,' or spatial display of the items that were grouped by the informants. That display shows which items were grouped together, and which groupings and items are relatively distant from other groups. In the example about sexual health problems cited above, for example, the MDS shows that items suggesting STIs are relatively closely grouped, and are distant from the group that includes masturbation, premature ejaculation, and other 'non-contact' problems.

Researchers with quantified data sets, on the other hand, commonly use SPSS as the computer tool for processing data and carrying out statistical analysis. In earlier times, fifteen years ago, such statistical analysis required computer specialists, who carried out the analytic procedures on mainframe computers in the universities or large research institutions. Now-a-days those statistical skills are much more widespread in even small research organisations.

Training and Technical Assistance for the Researchers

The development of research programmes such as the group of projects at the School of Health Sciences (SPPU) has required extensive training activities, in the form of workshops as well as one-on-one consultations.

Most of these small grant programmes began with proposal development workshops as well as intensive training in data-gathering techniques. After those initial workshops there were further training sessions, including workshops on data analysis and writing. In addition, individual researchers met with their mentors for individual problem solving.

Although a primary objective of these research programmes focused on developing useful information about sexuality and sexual behaviours in relation to the campaigns against HIV-AIDS, the research activities have also had the objective of expanding the research skills of individuals, NGOs and other action groups. The methods of data-gathering and analysis that have been disseminated in these efforts are intended to have wide applicability in the different sectors of community health and related action research.

Summary and Conclusions

Almost all of the recent research in India on sexuality, sexual behaviours, and related topics has made use of several different data-gathering procedures, in order to put together detailed qualitative and quantitative portrayals of the research populations and topics. In most cases the 'all purpose' in-depth interview has had a central place in the research strategy, but supported by a variety of other data-gathering techniques.

In the course of the various projects the researchers have found that the information about sex and sexuality is not as hidden or 'taboo' as had previously been thought. Some of the hesitations about discussion of sexual behaviours and sexuality have stemmed from shyness among the researchers, rather than attitudes in the general population. In any case, in-depth interviewing has resulted in a great deal of detailed information about sexual behaviours, sexual health problems, and many other related topics. In a few cases researchers found that female interviewers can get fairly detailed information about sexual topics from male informants, although the most usual practice has been that the interviewers and informants are of the same sex.

The results of these rounds of research have helped to 'de-mystify' some areas of sexuality and sexual behaviours in Indian society. At the same time, the processes that brought about these research results have also de-mystified the approach and techniques of qualitative and quantitative research in this sector of the social sciences, allowing the younger researchers to develop their skills in data gathering as well as in the use of computers for data analysis.

Annexure

Research studies on Sexuality, Sexual Behaviour and Reproductive Health at Interdisciplinary School of Health Sciences, SPPU 1999-2003.

Section I **Sexuality and Sexual Behaviour**			
Sr. No	*Title*	*Issues*	*Methods of data collection*
1.	Linguistic Terminology for Female Sex Partners	Historical review of terms cultural meanings and association with cultural and social aspects	Library research
2.	Brothels and Brothel Clients	Typology of brothels and profile of clients	Key informant interview Observation Semi structured interview schedule Case study
3.	Female Sex Workers among Nat Community	Description of traditional commercial female sex workers' life style	Key informant interview Indepth interview FGD Observations
4.	Sexual Behaviour of Persons Attending HIV-AIDS Counselling OPD	Profile of participants visiting counselling centre about condom use and sexual behaviour in relation to HIV	Semi-structured interview schedule FGD Documentation of counselling sessions
5.	Condom Use among Married and Unmarried Men	Utility of condom as a barrier to conception and infection	Structured interview schedule Informal indepth interview
6.	Sexuality and AIDS Awareness among Diamond Workers	To design communication strategy to meet information needs and behavioural change of migrant diamond workers.	Social mapping Participant observation Indepth interview Case study Group discussion

7.	Sexual Behaviour of Tribal Males	Description of sexual behaviour and perception of sexuality.	Indepth informal interview Group discussions Non participant observation House hold survey Secondary data from Health Centre
8.	Sexual Behaviour of Migrant and Non-Migrant Youth	Comparison of migrant and non-migrant youth about perception and behaviour about risk in sex relationships	Indepth informal interview Semi structured interview schedule
9.	Perspectives of Sexuality among Adolescent Girls	Understanding context of sexual behaviour and risk behaviour	Informal indepth interview Key informant interview Group discussion Questionnaire
10.	Sexual Behaviour among Migrant Hotel Workers	Perceptions and practices about sexual and risk behaviour	Key informant interview Observation Indepth interviews Group discussion
11.	Coping with Stigma among PLHA	Techniques of information management in regard to coping mechanisms by PLHA	Informal interview with the help of interview guide
	Section II **Gender and Sexuality**		
12.	Construction of Sexuality among Male College Students	Tribal-Rural comparison about conceptualizing gender and sexuality	Structured questionnaire Few indepth interviews
13.	Gender Construction and Rural Health	Women's perception of gender differences in village	Semi-structured interview schedule indepth interviews
14.	Male Involvement in Family Planning Decision Making	Inter-spouse communication, male involvement and decision making	Key informant interview Informal indepth interview
15.	Menopause as Multivariate Issue	The symptoms and the perceptions about post menopausal life	Questionnaire indepth interview

Section III Reproductive Health			
16.	RTI and Genital Hygiene:	Perception and practices about causation and treatment of RTI	Semi structured schedule FGD Observation
17.	Reproductive Health Issues of School-Going Adolescent Girls	Correlation of education and knowledge about reproductive health	Quantitative survey In-depth interview FGD Key informant interview
18.	Reproductive Health Practices among Urban High Caste Women	Inter generational perceptions about menstruation, pregnancy and post partum period	Semi structured interview schedule indepth interview for life history
19.	Reproductive Health Issues of Sex Workers	Reproductive morbidity including pregnancy episodes and its management	Key informant interview indepth interview Group discussions

SECTION I

Sexuality and Sexual Behaviour

The global concern over about of HIV-AIDS prompted research and documentations patterns of sexual behaviour in different regions and suggest interventions to curtail the epidemic of HIV. The perceived threat of HIV-AIDS highlighted that people displayed different patterns of sexual behaviour, sexual preferences and sexuality. These researchers brought out the biological and behavioural challenges which existed in different sections of populations and in different parts of the world. For the first time, sexuality and sexual behaviour was discussed openly and became focal topics in the scientific as well as popular media.

Confronted with such a scenario, behavioural intervention efforts to alter high-risk behaviours remain the only practically available means to prevent the spread of the HIV infection. As sexual behaviour is the largest single factor (70% to 80%) of HIV transmission, behaviour interventions can direct at behavioural change.

Numerous interventions have been designed to promote safer sexual behaviour amongst young people. However, relatively few have proved effective since majority lack basic understanding of the sexual behaviour, its important determinants and theoretical insights which could have been beneficial in the development the programme. Although individual behaviour change is central to improving sexual health, efforts are also needed to address the broader determinants and social context in which sexual behaviour takes place. The evidence from behavioural interventions suggested that due to the huge regional variation in the patterns of sexual behaviour, no general approach to sexual-health promotion would work everywhere. Comprehensive behavioural interventions are needed that take account of the social context, cultural preferences, economic structure and political willingness.

The issues about HIV-AIDS are predominantly relevant in the context of biological vulnerability among women and bio-social behaviour of youth. Women's health issues focusing on female sex workers and challenges to youth due to migration and mobility coupled with issues of adolescent girls particularly in poor urban localities demand more research documentation to develop intervention strategies.

Women Vulnerability and AIDS

The risk of acquiring HIV from an infected partner during sexual intercourse is considerably greater for women than men. The lack of female controlled preventive devices exposes even to more vulnerability and women are prone to infection. Vulnerability of women is more than men due to several biological, sociological and economic factors. This may be broadly classified into two categories—biological and social vulnerability. Since biological vulnerability is the root cause of the consequent social vulnerability, it is worthwhile to explore the nature and causes of biological vulnerability in women.

The risk of infection with HIV during unprotected vaginal intercourse is as much as 2-4 times higher for women than men. The semen infected with HIV typically contains a higher concentration of virus than sexual secretions of an infected woman. In addition to biological vulnerability related to sexual intercourse, Indian women suffer from another kind of vulnerability, which stems from the general social prejudice as they are subjected to denial of access to nutritious food and basic health care since childhood. A majority of women in India suffer from anaemia. An early marriage, coupled with repeated pregnancies, worsens the situation.

The birth of a daughter was distinctly unwelcome in the patriarchal social order. The last centuries of the first millennium and the entire medieval age witnessed a rapid decline in the status of women. She was little more than an object in the hands of men. Female infanticide has been rampant, allegedly more among the higher castes in Hindi-belt, which has been shifted to foeticide with the misuse of sonography. Only tribal communities are free from these maladies, possibly due to custom of bride price as consideration for labour. Indian Law bans female foeticide and infanticide. However, pre-natal testing for sex determination is widespread.

Indeed, for girls and women in many cultures, sex is the 'currency' in which they are expected to pay for life's opportunities, from a passing grade in school to a trading licence or permission to cross a border. Millions of young girls have very little understanding of the physical and psychological changes involved in the transition of a girl into a woman. Thus, girls approach adolescence with a great amount of trepidation, only having a vague notion of retaining virginity. The boys may have already indulged in sexual experiences with Female Sex Workers or may have engaged in some form of homosexual activity. Perhaps, having no idea of safe sex or birth control, girl is seldom in a position to refuse sex or insist on condoms, even on suspicion of infidelity/extra-marital activity.

It is thus evident that a significantly large proportion of women in the reproductive active age group of 15-44 years are becoming more vulnerable to diverse socio-economic factors. These are often the cause of prostitution.

Women in Prostitution (Female Sex Workers)

Women in prostitution constitute another setting in which women have little power to protect them from HIV. Female Sex Workers (FSWs) are the most vulnerable section of the community. Girls are forced into sex as a profession before puberty and they are generally unaware of the risk from AIDS and are unable to escape from vicious circle.

Many women turn to occasional or steady sex work as an alternative to dire poverty, exchanging sex for the necessities of life for themselves and their children. She is the chief source of earning for the families with male parasites who seldom treat her as a human being. The predicament of FSWs suffering from STDs/HIV and securing access to appropriate health care services is even more acute than that of the general populace of women. They are quantitatively a small part of society but qualitatively separated from it, and denied basic rights.

Approaches to Understand Women in Sexuality

The attitude towards prostitute and women *vis-à-vis* sexuality can better be explained by three approaches. First, Institutional or Functionalist approach: It assumes that prostitution is as old as human civilization. It is a universal and inevitable social evil. Prostitution is often considered society's safety valve against the rape of innocent women and the disintegration of the institution of family (Cunha, 1972). Baba Amte told us during conversation that the CSWs from Mumbai's brothel locality, 'Kamathipura' on a visit to Anandwan, exclaimed that "your women are safe because of us". They also appealed that at least, their motherhood should be respected since they also had children. Secondly, Feminist approach: Prostitution is one of the types of gender inequality. The social sanction and moral condemnation will not wipe out prostitution. Feminist struggle against patriarchal society is also launched due to dubious partiality of social values and morality. It gives freedom to men for deriving sexual pleasure outside family while poses various social restrictions and moralistic taboos on women (Truong, 1988). Lastly, the Marxist approach: The Marxist scholars condemn the institution of marriage as such and see very marginal difference between a prostitute and a woman. A woman through the institution of marriage becomes not only the private property but also the sexual property as well of her husband.

Women's Issues

Women's health has been an issue and subject of research for more than a couple of decades. With specific reference to HIV-AIDS, both the interventions and research have focused more on female sex workers to study reasons for sex work, number of partners, knowledge about HIV-AIDS, safe sex practices, use of condoms and constraints in using them. The Ford Foundation and the International Centre for Research on Women sponsored studies in India on sexual behaviour amongst women from low-income populations. One of the first studies on female sex workers (FSWs) was taken up by Gita Bhave at the K.E.M. Hospital, Mumbai, in collaboration with the Centre for AIDS Prevention Studies, University of San Francisco. Two graphic documents on sexual behaviour research are prepared by Moni Nag and NACO, and on adolescents by Shireen Jeejeebhoy on behalf of the International Centre for Research on Women. (Nadkarni, Vimla V., 1999).

In India too, because of the social subordination, women are particularly vulnerable and the lack of availability of female controlled protective devices leave them vulnerable along with other biological factors. Not only are sex-workers at risk but also other women (Nichter, M., 1981). The link between powerlessness and the risk of exposure to HIV provides the key to understanding the special vulnerability of women to STDs and AIDS. Since women have little control over sexual decision-making, they are unable to use the information (even when they have it) to protect themselves. The sex-workers also have almost no negotiating powers with their clients to practise safe sex.

Almost one in every five male patients and one in two sex workers presenting to STD clinic were found to be HIV infected (Mehendale, Sanjay, 1999). Although prevalence of HIV infection in North India has been reported to be low (Ray, K., Sachdeva, K.G. & Others, 1995), a rising trend has been reported from South India (Jacob, M., John, T.J. &

Others, 1995). In various studies, the HIV prevalence has been reported to rise rapidly amongst high risk group. Between 1986 and 1994, prevalence of HIV infection has risen from 1.6 per cent to 40 per cent in sex workers, 1.4 to 40 per cent in STD clinics and 0 to 70 per cent in intravenous drug users in various studies (Pais, P., 1996, Salunke, S., Jagtap, M.R. & Others, 1997, Bhave, G., 1996).

Sexual Behaviour of Youth

Indian youth are facing a dilemma because of the disparities between traditional norms and western patterns of expression. As lifestyles are changing, there are greater opportunities for youth to experiment and participate in unsafe sex practices. The mean age of first sexual experience documented in various studies varies from 16.5 to 19.5 years, earlier in males than in females (Watsas, Mahendra, 1996). Boys have access to more information than girls, though some leads to more risky behaviour than preventing it: like easy access to pornographic literature in rural and urban colleges, encouraging them to experiment that involves risks (Nadkarni, Vimla V., 1999).

The girls are at a greater risk, as they are less familiar with the correct information. Unmet needs of students creates misconceptions in their minds; their curiosity and dependence on unreliable literature leads them to engage in risky behaviour which needs to be prevented through positive thoughts that enable responsible decision making for themselves and their partners (Mawar, 1998).

The relationship between science, politics, and health care policy has changed dramatically over the years since AIDS was first diagnosed in the United States. Initially politics was viewed as inimical to prevention; now it is viewed as central. The challenge is to ensure that policies facilitate prevention of the spread of HIV and do so in a way that protects those most vulnerable. The policies of the first decade of the epidemic were indifferent to research in areas such as needle exchange, condom promotion in youth and sexuality issues that were considered relevant for protection of women vulnerabilities etc. More recently, the political climate has been more sympathetic, but whether this will result in a more effective health care policy is not yet clear (Mawar, 1998). Focused ethnographic study (FES) is a strategy of research; developed during the 1990s, to provide quite specific types of data for intervention progammes.

Several studies were supported through this research programme to enhance our understanding, social science knowledge and perspective on the study of sexuality and sexual behaviour. Through these studies, we promoted the use of social science methodology with preference for qualitative methods, to investigate sexual behaviour in a variety of contexts. The researchers explored premarital relationships, sexual behaviour, and issues related to sexual preferences, condom use negotiation, safe sexual practices etc. The first chapter of this section tries to understand linguistic and colloquial way in which sexuality is expressed. Subsequent chapters identify vulnerability of different sections of the society which includes, brothel clients, diamond workers, migrant youths, hotel workers, and tribal males. A chapter on female sex workers in Nat community highlight the cultural ways in which sex work is promoted. Studies on adolescent girls, people attending HIV counselling session, married and unmarried men, and PLHA also bring out important issues. These studies have found a widespread lack of knowledge about sexual issues and protection as many were engaged in unprotected sexual behaviour and relied on traditional pregnancy preventive practices. The findings also revealed numerous categories of factors influencing sexual attitudes and behaviours: ethnic group, peer pressure and norms, and place of residence. With regard to condom use, factors such as embarrassment about condom acquisition, low perceived susceptibility to sexually transmitted infections (STIs), and perceived efficacy of traditional and folk methods of contraception, were uncovered from the discussions.

Enough information is available about the non-use of condoms among emotionally or socially accepted hetero-sexual partnerships. Even relationships between CSWs and their frequent clients preclude the use of condoms in the relationships. In the patriarchal societies there are double standards of permitted and tolerated sex behaviour for men and women. If a woman uses any method for preventing fertility or morbidity without the knowledge of the male partner, a needle of suspicion is directed to woman about infidelity. The use of condoms continues to be associated with deviant sexual relationship. In tribal communities where pre-marital sexual relations are not uncommon and are permitted, the pregnancy consequences are not denied and could culminate in socially approved marriage. The idea about sex in tribal societies differs from that of the caste peasant society. In tribal society, adultery is frowned upon since the divorce and re-marriage are relatively easy and approved with social and economic procedures.

The insistence by CSWs of the use of condom by clients is fairly successful since the clients are now aware about the potential risks. For the same reason, the use of condoms is not favoured between married couples. The migrant youth from rural areas around Pune who work at Pune as rickshaw drivers, hotel workers and as labour have started using condoms in relation to CSWs, but would not use them in their relationship with village girls.

On the basis of the key findings of these studies, culturally tailored interventions to delay sexual initiation and promote safe sex practices in young people of India is required. These studies have identified factors associated with young men and women's sexual behaviour and contraceptive use and identified areas that health authorities could assess and target for interventions. These studies have both theoretical and empirical implications for future research. Finally, through this publication we are sharing experiences that could be used to assist other similar studies.

4

Linguistic Terminology for Female Sex Partners

HEMANT APTE AND ROHINI SAHANI

Introduction

Cultural traits are expressed in language. Words as terms are coined to reflect nuances of an attribute. Vocabulary develops through coinage, borrowing, preservation etc. Marathi language has accumulated over 200 words for an occupational or behavioural trait termed as prostitute, culturally defined in a patriarchal society. They do not necessarily mean a sex worker but include mistresses, servants, performers etc. Now some terms have changed their meaning; some are out of usage while a few continue to be used without change in the original meaning.

The terms meant to denote female sex workers throw light on society's attitude towards women, gender discrimination through language, and linguistic bias against women. By analyzing overt linguistic semantics we get an insight into the covert social psychology of a particular linguistic group—the Marathi speaking population. The terms are clearly symptomatic of the underlying social psycho-pathology of a woman's sexuality. Terms for a prostitute have been accumulating in the language for several centuries. Though many of the words were used in literature, there is not much evidence to be found to conclusively say that these words were not used in colloquial expressions. With the decline of Mughal rule in India and Peshwa regime in Maharashtra, spread of education, decreasing influence of Sanskrit on Marathi language, many words have gone out of use because of change in social context.

Monogamy as the ideal pattern of sex relationship institutionalized in marriage does not proscribe polygyny or polyandry in some cultural groups. Patriarchy and tendal social structure imposes strict sex behavioural parterns on women. Anything outside marriage, exposure to more than one man outside family or kin-group by way of dance and music was also termed as pnostitution as documented in this study. Do the tribal ethnic communities have such terms, where there is no concept of prostitution and pre-marital sex liaisons are not frowned upon where divorce is easy and remarriage not uncommon?

The objectives of the study have been to understand why so many synonyms for a common term prostitute had emerged over time in Marathi language. These terms denote the variety in heterosexual relations. An attempt has been made to study the etymology of some of the terms and find influences of other languages and find the changing connotations that these words acquired over time. The study was carried out in order to identify the avenues that led women to prostitution in different time periods, how prostitution was perceived in oriental and occidental cultures. The extensive literature search was carried out in public and personal libraries, websites etc. to trace the history of prostitution. Efforts were made to study the origins of the terms and their use in literature to trace the time period in which these terms were in use. The terms were then categorized into different groups that reflected a particular attribute of sexual relationship or of commercial sex work. Words borrowed from other languages were identified. An analysis was undertaken to recognize terms that had become obsolete, words that had changed their meaning and terms that had retained their use and original meaning.

In every language, words are subject to a variety of cultural meanings. A living, growing language contains words that have specific meanings—either embedded in the root of a word or that have developed in the course of history and usage. The terms that have been studied here demonstrate the various attributes of prostitution and other deviations from the social norms of sexuality. They also bring into light a gender bias; reflect moral values and covert patriarchal influences.

- The historical review of prostitution revealed that pathways that led women into prostitution had been changing according to the changing social structure. The status of a prostitute gradually deteriorated as the profession got more commercialized. Some words that defined historical avenues and attributes remained in use though the actual context changed.

- A review of connotations of 'prostitute' traces the changing perception of the concept and the changing function/role of a prostitute in a given society.
- The existing schemes of classification categorize prostitutes *per se* into groups based on their function, status/role, number of clients etc. The present classification, however, tries to classify terms into categories that indicate pathways to prostitution, attributes of the profession, physical attributes, morality and marital status. The categories are as follows—
- Words as terms have been coined in particular contexts for example, deviation from ideals of feminity. Words have an ascribed meaning and an achieved meaning. Ascribed meaning is the original meaning while achieved meaning, in this case, is when another connotation is added on. For example, actual availability for sex, an add-on, denotes a deviation from sexual morality. Many words are borrowed from over a dozen other languages indicating the phenomenon of linguistic acculturation. There are several words that are to be found only in literature, while some others are used largely colloquially. Within the domain of colloquial use, some are mainly used by the elite and some by others. Some have an abusive tinge while some others have an element of respectability.
- A large number of terms have gone out of usage over time. Presently about 53 words are in use. Out of these 29 terms have retained their original meaning while 24 are used without the connotation of prostitution. Out of the 29 that have retained their meaning, eight of them are understood to denote as women of easy virtue, 5 mean a mistress while 16 terms continue to mean a prostitute, commercial sex worker.

Since culture and language are two sides of a coin in classical anthropology, language reflects the cultural traits of people. Words are coined to reflect nuances of an attribute. Vocabulary of a language develops through coinage, borrowing and preservation. Marathi, a standardized language over 700 years old, has accumulated about 200 words and terms that are synonymous to the English word prostitute, now expressed as Commercial Sex Workers (CSW). All these terms do not necessarily mean a sex worker, but convey terms for mistresses, servants, performers etc., deemed to be involved in multi-partner sex. The research question is why are these so many words for prostitute or a

Vyabhichaarinee (a fallen woman)? It was found that Kodava—a language spoken in southern India (Rajyashree, 2001)—does not have a single word for prostitute. People speaking that language do not have such an institution. Marathi, on the other hand, has accumulated a wealth of such terms. Although the terms were accumulated over a long period of time, it was still indicative of the fact that there were many overt and covert ways to express sexual relations outside the institution of marriage and all such relations were equated to prostitution. It may be borne in mind that in a traditional patriarchal society, the moral code of conduct was very strict, particularly in the case of women and a slightest deviation or even suspicion of deviation was considered immoral for the woman to be labelled as a *Vyabhichaarinee* (a fallen woman), the meaning of which is given as a *Veshyaa* (a prostitute).

It was felt that the dictionary was a part of a heritage that documented the wealth of words. The question then was to understand the need for so many words that reflected the finer shades of heterosexual relations that may have existed in history. The contexts in which many of the terms had emerged were gradually changed but the terms continued to exist at least in a dictionary. Many words are understood differently today than in the earlier period.

Methodology

As a part of an earlier research project on Pune's sex workers (Apte, 2002), the authors came across some 20 words in Marathi that basically meant either a prostitute or a 'loose' (of easy virtue) woman. Looking at those words it was realized that each word expressed a slightly different shade of meaning. It was also found that the words were used interchangeably and were under a broad category indicating a prostitute or *Veshyaa*. This led the authors to a more comprehensive exploration with the help of an eight-volume lexicography written in the first half of the 20th century. This exploration resulted in an even larger number of synonymous words (more than 200). In order to understand the meanings of these words it was felt necessary to look into the history of prostitution in India and also at some of the ways in which scholars defined a prostitute/ a loose woman. This study does not really follow the classical research design, because it entails searching through secondary data and a descriptive documentation of evidence found in the literature. Based on the documentary evidence, the analysis presented here is based on deductive logic.

The objectives of the study were to identify terms, accumulated over time, those denote nuances of heterosexual relations and societal attitudes towards women; categorize the terms synonymous to the term prostitute on the basis of certain attribute; study the etymology of some of the terms and study the linguistic acculturation; find the changing connotations that the terms acquired over time.

Prostitution in India

Evidence from ancient period in Indian history indicated that prostitution was an accepted occupation to which were attached certain definite rights and duties. The early Indian societal attitude towards prostitution was that, it was a necessary element in the organization of society. The presence of *Apsaras* among the godly personages of *Rigveda* is a clear evidence of the existence of courtesans and perhaps common prostitutes in the society during the *Vedic* period. In the *Ramayana*, *Mahabharata* and other mythologies of the Hindu, we find frequent references to prostitution and prostitutes.

Prostitution during the Buddhist Period

There are references to prostitution in spite of adverse opinion and punishments, during the *Buddha* period. The courtesans formed a significant section of the then society. At that time, it was thought that a woman became a prostitute on account of the working out of her *Karma*. Though prostitution was looked down upon by *Jainism*, no special stigma was attached to it. Prostitution was rampant at that time and the Jain nuns were cautioned against it.

The Maurya Period (324–300 B.C.)

During this period, it was mentioned, that any food to be eaten, garments, flowers, ornaments, scents to be used by the king had to be tested by the courtesans before it was to be given to him. These women acted as the security force for the personal safety of the king. *Arthashastra* (written by Kautilya), a treatise on governance, written approximately 300 years B.C., discusses the duties of the superintendent of prostitutes (*Ganikaadhyaksha*). It has also been mentioned that in the cantonment areas *Rupajivas* were to be given accommodation along the main highways. A *Dasi* or a low-grade prostitute was employed for regular spying, while whores (*Pumschali*) spied on thieves. It may, therefore, be said that prostitution as an institution was a well-developed and socially recognized institution at this time in history.

The Ashoka Period (273 B.C.–232 B.C.)

King Ashoka felt the need to appoint Mahamattas to look after the welfare of women. Their work included supervision of prostitutes also. It was the duty of the State to make necessary arrangements for the prostitutes who were unable to earn their livelihood. A beautiful girl (would be courtesan) used to receive training in music and dance at the expense of the State. The *Ganikas* were controlled by the State under special laws promulgated from time to time.

Gupta Period (622 A.D.)

As in the Mauryan period, courtesans played an important role in the social life during the Gupta Period. They were engaged to sing and dance during the celebrations made in honour of the birth of a child in the homes of wealthy persons as well as worshipping in the temples like that of *Mahakal* in Ujjain, where they danced.

During Chalukya Period (6th-8th Century A.D.)

In Karnataka there are references to courtesans. In the *Chola* period the institution of *Devadaasee* was very well organized and one finds a mention of temple women in the famous Tanjor inscription dated 1004 A.D.

In the Vijayanagar Kingdom (1336 A.D.–1565 A.D.)

Prostitutes used to give sexual pleasures to the army personnel. There is a clear and vivid description of the residential area inhabited by the prostitutes.

Prostitution in Mughal Period and Thereafter

In the Mughal Period (1526 A.D.–1767 A.D.) prostitution was a recognized institution. For their proficiency and skill in dancing and singing, prostitutes were considered as one of the best sources of enjoyment and pastime for the rich and the aristocrats. Emperor Akbar

(1556–1605 A.D.) made some regulation to impose certain restrictions on the profession of prostitutes so that their services might not be freely available to the public. He forced the prostitutes to live together in a place outside the capital city. This place was known as *Shaitanpura* or the devil's quarters. However, Akbar maintained a seraglio (Harem) in which there were five thousand women (Mukherji, 1936) and Emperor Shahjahan (1627–1657 A.D.) gave sufficient encouragement to the dancing and singing girls. Following the Mughal tradition of keeping large harems in the palaces, the Palace of King Shahu, the Maratha king of Satara, also had a large harem. Shahu, son of Sambhaji and grandson of Shivaji was captired as a child by Mughals and imprisoned for a long time. It is alleged that he got sorialised in adopting Mughal princely life style. During the Peshwa regime, in Pune, we get enough references to prostitution and to the singing and dancing girls. Despite social legitimacy to the custom of having more than one wife, the practice of keeping mistresses also seemed prevalent and accepted. The great warrior, Bajirao Peshwa had a Muslim mistress (Mastani) who hailed from Bundelkhand. His son, Nanashaheb Peshwa (1744) alleged to be a sensualist and had his harem. The harem of Raghunathrao Peshwa and Sawai Madhavrao had over 700 women. *Bavankhani*—the mansion with 52 rooms was the first established brothel in Pune city.

Prostitution thrived on a large commercial scale during the British period. Social disabilities and economic hardships made the dancing girls easy victims to the gangsters in the profession. The patronage, which had ended after the downfall of the Mughal kings, was once again extended to them by the Jagirdars, Zamindars, and Nawabs. After abolition of Zamindari system and the merger of princely states after Independence, protection of the aristocracy once again disappeared and the girls and women in the profession felt orphaned.

Several scholars, at various times, have tried to define a prostitute or prostitution. Some definitions (Abraham, 2001, Barua, 1933, Mathur and Gupta,1965) highlight the genital function without considering instances where sexual relations go beyond a mere genital function. Legally, prostitution is the sale of sexual services. The services may consist of any sexual acts, including those, which do not involve copulation. While payment may be any non-sexual consideration, most commonly it is in the form of money. This definition takes cognizance of the fact that 'sexual act' necessarily does not mean penetrative peno-vaginal intercourse. The legal framework also recognizes the fact that the mode of payment for the service availed could be monetary or a kind of barter. According to the sacred books of Hindu religion a prostitute is a fallen woman, who has deviated from the normal life and made her looks as the means of commerce. The definition in the sacred books is based on moral grounds as indicated by the words 'fallen woman' and 'deviated from'. Some definitions by Western scholars in the earlier times are also quite moralistic. Wardlaw (1842) defines them, as women who temporarily loan the use of their bodies to a miscellany of men in return for money. According to Scott these definitions are too narrow and restricted. He feels that to include mistresses in the category of prostitutes is to give to prostitution too wide a scope. However, according to Kapur (1995), mistresses who she calls private prostitutes occupy the highest position in the hierarchy of prostitutes.

According to Delora and Warren (1977), A prostitute is a person who engages in sexual relations for money. Such relations are promiscuous, fairly indiscriminate, largely without affection, often anonymous, and not made legitimate by marriage. Even with the addition of a few more components to the basic issue of sex and money, there continue to remain a few more ambiguous cases, since acceptance of money or gifts in exchange for sexual favours may be found among mistresses, girlfriends and wives (Gebhard, 1969).

It is felt that different understanding of the various types of sexual relations outside marriage and the profession of prostitutes by different sections of society is probably the basis of coinage of various words in a language.

Till date many attempts have been made to classify prostitutes into several categories. The earliest attempt of classifying prostitutes is found in *Kamasutra* by Vatsyayana. According to him, there are three types of prostitutes—Courtesans (*Ganikaa*), girls who live on their charms (*Rupajeevaa*), and slave water carriers (*Kumbhadaasee*). These three categories correspond to the three upper, middle and lower levels.

Mukherji (1936) mentions that in the ancient sexual works, prostitutes have been classified as follows: Married women prostituting with other men, Clandestine Prostitutes, Actresses, Widows who became prostitutes, Professional prostitutes, Dancing Girls, High Class Courtesans and Prostitutes of the street.

Rajwade in his treatise on sex titled *Nasadiyasooktabhashya* has referred to a classification of women as presented in the *Mahabharata*. This classification is based on the number of partners. A *Kulata,* has two partners while, *Gharshani,* has three partners. *Pumschali,* has four partners and the one who has five or six paramours is called *Veshya.* A woman who has six or seven partners is called *Pungi* and the one who has gone beyond all this is called a *Mahaveshya.*

The classification presented by Joardhar looks like an extension of the classification done by Vatsyayana.

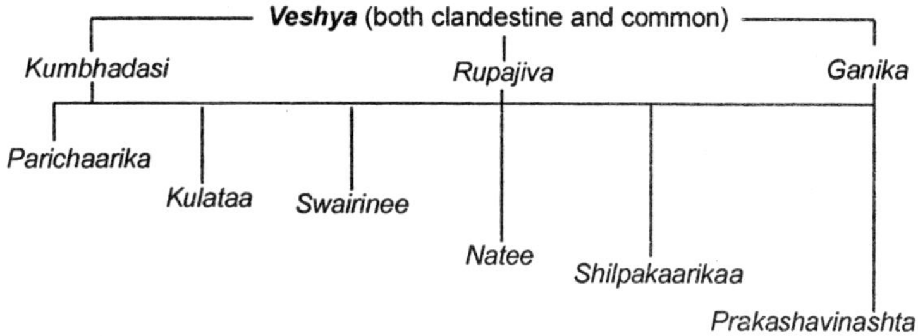

A *Kumbhadaasee* was the low-class woman who used to act as a maid servant and often ministered up to the lust of the menials of the household. A *Rupajeevaa*, the clandestine prostitute was mainly dependent on her youth and beauty. *Parichaarikaa* was almost like a lady-in-waiting or maid-of-honour in a respectable house. The *Kulataa* was a married woman who occasionally but very secretly slipped out of her house to enjoy one or more lovers. The *Swairinee* is not afraid of her husband and entertains her lovers either in her husband's house or that of another. The *Natee* generally lives on dancing, music and acting on the stage and entertains people of her choice for an extra earnings. The *Shilpakaarikaa* is the wife or even sometimes the daughter of a man engaged in petty handicrafts. The *Prakashavinashshtaa* may belong to any caste or class. She forms indiscriminate liaison with any man according to her choice. To her, both money and sexual satisfaction are equally important. Thus she is little better than any common prostitute.

Kapur (1995) categorizes the modern prostitutes hierarchically with regard to their status in a society as follows: the kept women or mistresses who may be called private prostitutes are at the top, then come the clandestine and independently operating prostitutes who are generally known as call girls, while at the lowest of all are the common prostitutes, the typical brothel inmates.

Classification given in the sacred *Tantras* or mystic books (*Nirvanatantra*, (trans.) Dutt, M.N., Bombay, 1900, p. XXVIIf.) is *Rajveshyaa* or Royal whores. *Naagaree* who drew her patrons from the well-to-do citizens. *Guptveshyaa,* a clandestine prostitute. *Devaveshyaa,* the strumpet of the Gods and *Brahmaveshyaa* the prostitute of the bathing places who catered for pilgrims.

The present study deals with the different categories of terms that indicate various dimensions of multi-partner man-woman relationships. The categories are as follows:

1. Kept Women/Mistresses
2. Performing Artists
3. Servants
4. Temple Prostitutes
5. Those that refer to Body Parts
6. With Reference to the Concept of *Saubhaagya*
7. Women Enjoyed by Many
8. Market Related Words for Prostitutes
9. Words Meaning Deviation from Norms
10. Miscellaneous

The words refer to women who engage in multi-partner heterosexual contacts. They reflect nuances in each type of relationship and social status of women and their honour in a patriarchal social structure.

Marriage is an institutionalized 'control of sexuality' hence, for women who are out of marriage, sexuality is not controlled. Women who are singers and dancers, those offered to a deity, being a widow, being in a powerless position like a servant, being a low caste person with pronounced sexuality and so on, have been understood and labelled as fallen.

After looking at the diversity in the meaning of words that directly or indirectly mean a prostitute, it appears that the society (at a time when the dictionary was compiled—1930s to 40s) perceived any heterosexual relationship other than the one within marriage as 'prostitution'. Similarly, those who did not follow the prescribed code of conduct and the prevalent ideals of femininity were all addressed by words that suggest that these women were like a prostitute. The society seemed to have a very clear idea about what an ideal wife was and what was ideal femininity. Unmarried girls and married women from respectable families were supposed to adhere to the code of conduct that was culturally prescribed or else they were likely to be misunderstood as females deviated from norms, essentially sexual norms.

Three words commonly seem to refer to what was understood as a prostitute. They are *Veshyaa*, *Swairinee* and *Vyabhichaarinee*. The word *Swairinee* in the Marathi dictionary is given to mean a woman without restraint *(Unaad stree),* deviated from common rule, an adulteress *(Vyabhichaari stree)*, Prostitute *(Veshyaa)* or a self-willed person, bent upon the gratification of the devices and desires of his/her own heart *(Swachhandee stree).* In the common usage the words *Unaad* or *Swachhandee* when used in the case of a man do not necessarily have any sexual connotation but when used in the case of a women, there is an understanding of sexual freedom/liberty. It also highlights the fact that any mention of the term *Vyabhichaar* denotes adultery. Apte's Sanskrit-English dictionary defines *Vyabhichaar* as 'to go astray, deviate from, to transgress against, be faithless to etc. *Vyabhichaar* is thus exclusively equated to sexual activity. Any woman, therefore, who transgressed the sexual norms, was equated to a prostitute even if she was really not into sex work as we understand today.

The word *Veshyaa*—a word that is commonly used for a prostitute even today has following meanings (Molesworth,1994):

1. A woman who sells her body to anyone for earning money;
2. *Raand* which means—A widow (always used with contemptuous implication), a female slave, a courtesan, any woman of easy virtue.
3. *Kasbeen*—a dancing girl, a harlot.
4. *Kalaavanteen*—a dancing girl.
5. *Naayakeen*—the mistress of any establishment, a dancing girl.
6. *Nartakee*—a dancing girl.

Thus one finds that there is a range of different categories that emerges, namely, slave/servant, a widow, a courtesan/dancing girl, a woman of easy virtue etc. which implicitly implies that these categories of women were thought to be potentially being available for sex.

Here it is important to note that two seemingly synonymous concepts emerge from the meanings. One is the deviation from norm and the other is prostitution. It may also be noted that for a woman to be without any restraint or being self-willed was also considered to be something beyond prescription. It also shows that if a woman is bent upon gratification of her own heart, it was considered inappropriate. Women who did not follow the code of conduct prevalent in the society were called *Swairinee* which according to Molesworth means women that walk according to their own will; loose or unchaste women or an adulteress.

Words for Women who have Deviated from Norms

A *Vyaabhichari* is a person who is understood to be wanton (having sex with other man or woman). If a woman engaged herself in sexual relations with a person other than the husband, she was labelled as a prostitute at the time when the dictionary was compiled.

Words like *Pardwaargaamee, Pararata, Paradwaaree, Parapoorvastree* mean a woman who has sex with a person 'other' than the husband while the word *Pativanchakaa* means the one who has cheated on the husband. *Apativrataa* and *Asatee* mean a woman who is not faithful to her husband. The words *Chhinaal, Shindal, Sinal, Sinalee* etc. mean a fallen woman. The words *Badakhyaalee* and *Badafailee* are taken from Persian language, which mean the one who indulges in unchaste behaviour or thought. The word *battaa* means blemish, stigma or stain. Thus the meaning of the word *Battebaaz* means the one who is fallen. In a society where women did not have much freedom of thought, expression or behaviour, someone who transgressed these codes of conduct was called a *Swairinee*. Another word equivalent to a *Swairinee* is *Pumschalee* which means a prostitute. One may include the word *Khelavanee* in the category of deviation from norm, because she is a woman who ensnares/entices a man with her charms.

The word *Veshyaa* which is the word equivalent to a prostitute has many corrupt forms like *Vesanaa, Vesavaa, Vesvaa*. The words *Jaarinee, Jaareen or Jaarkarmi* denote a woman who has deviated from norm and is understood in English as an adulteress. *jaar* means a lover who is not a husband.

A few other words for deviated women are *Kulataa Sutaaroo, Zodge, Bisane, Chumbhalee, Shobhanee, Phetaal, Baahiree, Vaavtal Laagore and Chyavan*. The word *Vakal* an Arabic word, means a prostitute. Words such as *Lalanaa, Lalitaa* or *Lankaa*, which only mean a woman in today's context, also meant a fallen woman. The word *Chyavan* comes from the verb *Chyuta* that means to have fallen.

This category has the largest number of words. The words include those for the one who has cheated the husband to a prostitute and a go-between. It includes women who are of easy virtue and those who do not follow the societal norms. They necessarily are not the ones who indulge in commercial sex work as we understand today.

Kept Women or Mistresses

The keeps/mistresses are not prostitutes, as we understand today but the

Dictionary has given the meaning as Prostitute. They are women who are committed to their man and are like his wife but without the sanction of marriage. Historically, having a mistress was a common practice, as a status symbol.

A *Naatakshaalaa* was a woman who was kept by a man attracted to her by her beauty and artistic achievements. An *Avaruddhaa* was a mistress who resided in the house of the master while a *Bhujishyaa,* was a mistress who did not stay in the house of her master.

A *Khaandaaraanee* was a woman kept by a warrior. There was an old custom among the Rajputs where kings married themselves with their swords and such women were called a *Khaandaaraanee.*

Mistresses primarily provided erotic pleasures and satisfied the sexual urge of the master and hence dear to the master. This gets reflected in terms like *Priyaa* (a beloved female), *Pyaar* (loved, beloved and dear), *Priyatamaa* (most beloved or dearest), *Velhaalee* (beloved woman), *Vallabhaa* (any beloved female) etc.

Other terms for a mistress are *Baail, Angaakhaalchee baayko, Upastree, Upapatnee* etc. The words *Stree, Patni, Baayko* mean a wife while the prefix *Upa* literally means vicinity, nearness, inferiority, likeness or resemblance. Terms like *Rakshaa, Raakh, Rakhel, Rakhelee, Rakhaau* etc. which are used even today, arise out of the Sanskrit verb *Raksha* which means to protect. Hence, a woman who is to be kept or protected is described by the words mentioned here. The word *Paatra* means an assumed character. Hence the words *Paatraa, Paatra, Prem-paatra* covertly mean the one who has assumed the role of a wife.

The words *Haram and Maashuk* are borrowed from Arabic and mean a beloved woman or a mistress while *Dhagadee* is borrowed from Gujarathi language and *Aawaa and Awaa* are borrowed from Kannada. The word *Zangdoo* borrowed from Marathi language spoken in the region of Kolhapur in western Maharashtra seems to have originated from the word *Zangat* which means clandestine love affair.

The terms like *angavastra, upastree, upapatnee* etc. were used for mistress of people belonging to the higher social and economic strata whereas the words *rakhel, thevlelee baai, angaakhaalchi baayko* etc. are not used respectfully. The term *dhagadee* is used abusively.

The English equivalent words for this type of women as found in Molesworth's dictionary are a keep, a mistress, a concubine, a lady, inferior wife and an inamorata. The masculine counterpart of the word *Upapatnee* is *Upapatee* meaning a paramour but other than this, there are no equivalents for the masculine gender.

Words Related to Body Parts

There is a small set of words which have a mention of body part or genitals of a man or a woman, to denote a prostitute.

The word *Angaheena* is a compound word *Anga* + *Heena*. The word *Anga* means a woman's genitals and *Heena* means of a low quality, inferior. Thus the word *Angaheena* means a prostitute or a woman exposed for sale, or that may be bought; a courtesan or harlot, a strumpet. The word *Gaandaal* means a woman who has large buttocks or posteriors, an adulteress (*Jaarinee*), a loose/libertine/dissolute woman (*Vyabhichaaree stree*). A woman with large buttocks seems to be equated to an adulteress or a loose woman. The word *Ziparee* is commonly used for a woman whose hairs are not properly combed. According to societal norms a respectable woman must have her hair done up when she presents herself to anyone and hence a woman whose hairs are unkempt, is equated to a prostitute. The meaning of the word *Ziparee* as given in the dictionary is the one who is worthless or one who has licentious tricks (*Ajaagal*), disorderly (*gabaalee*) or of an ugly, ill-formed face and deviated from norm (*Gobaree parantoo vyabhichaaree stree*). The word *Shepaaloo* means either a woman who commits whoredom (*Chhinaal*) or the one who is a sensualist, voluptuary, epicurean (*Vishayee*) or a lewd/amorous woman, a wanton (*Kamuki*), is derived from the Sanskrit word *Shep* which means a penis.

Religious Prostitutes

The custom of offering girls/women to a deity/temple is known to exist almost all over the ancient world. Scholars have dated this custom to have originated between the Third century (Kathare, 2000) and Sixth century (Jogan Shankar, 1994). The female dancers and singers attached to temples were generally referred to by the term *Devadaasee,* which literally means 'female servant of the deity'. They were not allowed to marry any mortal man and their dedication to temple service was considered as constituting a marriage with the deity. These 'temple marriages' were considered lucky for a girl since she would never be considered a widow. Molesworth's (1994) gives the meaning of the word *Devadaasee* as a female dancer or a courtesan. It may be said that prostitution was forced upon the *Devadaasees* at a time when the society was going through structural changes and upheavals caused by external aggression (Chawla, 2002). Today the word *Devadaasee* has got equated with prostitution.

The devotees of *Yogeshwari* (*Yallammaa*)/*Renukaa,* essentially performing functions similar to that of the *Devadaasees,* are called *Jogteen.* Some other words for temple women are *Bhaaveen, Devlee, Naaikeen, Bhakteen, Jogteen, Muralee, Aaraadheen, Sulee, Basavee* and *Jaanee*, borrowed from other languages like Kannada, Hindi and Goanese.

A *bhaaveen* was not allowed to dance or sing in public, while the *devlees* blew horns/trumpets in the temple (Ethnographic Survey of Bombay: 1909: No. 60). There were also the *upadaasees* who were trained in various arts like conversation to the subtleties of titillation. *Muralees* and *Bhakteen* are girls devoted to *Khandoba* and *Bhairoba*, the incarnation of Shiva. The word *Aaradheen* means the priestess of *Khandoba,* while *Jaanee* is a girl offered to Lord *Khandoba.*

The word *Sulee* in the Marathi language spoken in Tanjore (erstwhile Maratha Kingdom in South India) means a *Devadaasee, Kalavanteen* or *Naikeen* according to *Maharashtra Shabdakosh.* The word *Basavee* in Marathi means a woman who sits in the bazaar. It also means a reputable woman who indulges in immodest behaviour. The word also means a dancer or a singer belonging to the Jangam sect. The word is borrowed from Kannada.

It could be seen that except for the meaning of the word *Devadaasee,* which means a courtesan, no other words have any connotation of prostitution. However, it is commonly understood and believed that women who are offered (married) to any deity practice prostitution for survival.

Prostitutes from Heaven

There is one word in Marathi that refers to all the women offered to different deities. This generic term is *Devaanganaa,* a compound word meaning women of the deities (Dev = god or deity + angana = woman). The other words synonymous with *Devaanganaa* are *Suraanganaa, Devastree, Suryuvatee* and *Apsaraa.* The *Maharashstra Shabdakosh* (dictionary) does not equate these words as directly being synonymous to a *Devadaasee.* However, evidence from mythology suggests that *Devadaasee*s are the incarnation of *Urvashee,* the celestial nymph (*apsaraa*). The word *apsara* means courtesans of heaven. The word *Rambhaa* according to the Dictionary means a prostitute, though she too like *Urvashee* is another celestial nymph. *Devadaasees* trace their origin to *Urvashee.*

The word *Apsaraa,* today, means a beautiful woman. However, the word Rambha is sometimes used as a mild abuse for an untidy girl.

Market Related Terms

Scholars have talked about certain socio-political and economic conditions that have led to the commercialization of sex at some point in time (Kapur, 1995). It is now established that sex is a commercial activity and is flourishing despite serious health hazards like contracting HIV infection. When one looks at the words that are used for a prostitute in Marathi language, one feels that the commercial nature of a prostitute's activity and her consequent nexus with the market was understood for a long time.

The concept of a market essentially has some attributes like, buying and selling items/goods and a price. These attributes get reflected in the terms that fall under this category. The commoditization of women for sexual relation is reflected in these words. The word *Panyaanganaa,* means a woman exposed for sale or that may be bought, a cortesan or harlot; a strumpet. *Hatavilaasinee* is another word which also indicates a market place (*hata*). The word '*haat*' is a colloquial version of the word '*hatta*' in Sanskrit. The word *Vilas* means pleasure seeking, voluptuary, and coquetry, prudery or flirting. *Vilaasinee* is a woman who seeks pleasure, indulges in flirting and coquetry. The meaning of the word *hatavilaasinee* is 'A woman exhibiting herself and sporting in public places, a harlot or strumpet'. The word *Vaanasee* is also a compound word *Vanik* + *Stree* (tradable + woman). All the three words have Sanskrit origin.

During the period of Muslim rule in India, Urdu and Farsi (Persian) languages were in use. The word *Maaljaadee* (*Maal* means an item on sale and the word *Jaadi* means a girl) has its roots in these languages. The word *Basava* in Kannada means a bull that freely roams all over the town and *Basavee* is the feminine form, which means a foot-loose woman (Jogan Shankar).

The word *Baajaareen* means a woman of the market or the one on sale. The word *Bajar* is a corrupt version of the word *Bazzar.* It may be said that words, which are compounds along with the word *bajar*, may have originated during the Mughal period where the language of the royal court was Persian. There are more words like *Baajaarbunagee* and *Baajaarbundgee.* Yet another phrase, which is far more explicit, is *Baajaarchee Khaat.* A *Khaat* means a bed, so the phrase literally means the bed of the market. Traditionally, women in Indian brothels exhibited themselves in windows to solicit customers. The word *Baajaarbasanee,* means the one who sits in the *Baajaar*. The word *Baajaarbasavee* is commonly used even today. These words connote the saleability of a woman in an open market.

Terms for a Public Woman (A Woman of Collectivity)

The terms in this particular category refer to women who were available in the 'market' for men. As mentioned earlier, despite a strict moral code propounded by the '*Smritikaras*', we have cited references that go to show that 'public women' existed even during the *Ramayana* period. These women were then called *'Nagarvadhoo'* which literally means the wife of the town. A marriage gave a man exclusive conjugal rights and in a patriarchal society, a wife was considered the private property of her husband. Women who had sex with many men obviously were the ones on whom nobody could/did claim exclusive rights. From this concept of non-exclusiveness of conjugal rights arose this category of words that indicate a public woman (a prostitute).

The word '*vaar*' means a group or a collectivity. So all the words that begin with '*vaar*' followed by words meaning a woman, mean a woman available to more than one man. The following words were found to be in usage in Marathi language—*Varaanganaa, Varayoshitaa, Varavilaasinee, Varavanitaa, Vaaryuvatee, Vaarnaaree, Vaarvadhoo* and *Vaarastree.* The word *'Vaarayoshita'* literally means the one who serves (offers sexual services) many people.

Another sub-group of words mean the 'woman of the town/village'. The terms are *Gaav-Bhavaanee, Gaav-gaai, Gaav-mavshee, Gaav-mehunee* and *Nagar-Bhavaanee.* The word *Mehuni* means wife's sister. In most of the cultures, one could have a joking relationship with his wife's younger sister. Hence, the word *Gaav-Mehuniee* means one with whom the entire town could have a joking relationship (which presumes sexual liberty). A similar term, '*Sarvaanchee Mehunee*'—a 'common' sister-in-law is also found in Marathi.

Another way to address a woman who was considered sexually available to many was by calling her '*Ushtee Stree*' or '*Ushtee Patraaval*'. The words *Ushta* means leftover or rejected food. A *Patraaval* means a leaf plate which is used for food only once and thrown away. These two words clearly show the derogatory sense in addressing prostitutes.

The word *'Bahuvas'* means a one who stays with many while the word '*Sarva-Vallabhaa*' means someone who is dear to all. The word '*Sabhaanganaa*' means a woman of the assembly.

The term *Vaara* and *Sabha* in Sanskrit means 'a multitude', 'large number' and the word *Saamaanya* means 'common or general'. *Saadhaarana* means 'common (to two or more), joint' and *Sarva* means 'all or every'. The word *Bahu* means 'numerous'. Hence, all the words beginning with *Vaara* mean a woman enjoyed by/available to a large number of men or a public woman. All the words in this category are either Marathi words or have been borrowed from Sanskrit.

Servants

As mentioned earlier, many terms eventually came to mean prostitute/ loose woman, though their original meaning may have been different. They generally indicate a particular avenue or pathway which when taken as an occupation by a woman was likely to lead her into prostitution.

This category includes words that have 'acquired' the meaning of a prostitute in the course of time. The word *daasi, batik or Kunbeen* essentially means a maidservant. Like in other countries in the world in the 17th and the 18th century, Maharashtra also had a custom of keeping female slaves. Not only the kings, noblemen, rich and the elite kept women slaves, but even those families who could afford to feed a slave twice a day also kept *daasees* and *Kunbeenees*. The women referred to by these words are maidservants. But when the duties of maidservants/slave girls/ women also implied sexual availability, either through coercion or as a part of the duty, many of the words meaning servants/slaves also came to be understood as 'prostitutes'.

Batakee and *Kunbeenee* were servants who in many instances were not paid any salary (Shirgaokar, 2001). The word *Kunbeen* and *Naatakshaalaa* have been used synonymously, but in reality a *Naatakshaalaa* was a mistress who did not have a status equivalent to that of a man's wife, while a *Kunbeen* was a housemaid who in some cases became a *Naatakshaalaa*.

The meaning of the word *Bateek* is given as *Daasee/Molkareen* (a maid servant) in the dictionary but the word *Bateekpuraa* means a red light area. The fact that a word such as *Bateekpuraa* was coined is indicative of the fact that there was a place (a red light area) where the *Batakees* would end up as common prostitutes if they lost their employment/patronage. The dictionary further states that a *Bateek* was a woman who originally came from a good family but became

Vyabhichaarinee (one deviating from sexual norms) at some point. The words *Bandhakee, Baandee* also means a *Daasee* or *Vyabhichaarinee.* Occasionally, the meaning of the word *Randee* is given as a *Daasee.* The word *Bateek,* has also been used synonymously with *Raandbhaand* and *Raandwadaa,* which are abusive in nature.

The terms *Lavandee/Laundee/Laundhee* (from Persian language—Lavand) also means a *Bateek/Daasee/Veshyaa/Rakhelee.* A word is found in the literature for *Daasee* who accompanies her master in bed—*Sejwaala* (*sej* means bed). The dictionary has another word *Sahalee* which means a *Daasee/Sakhee.* The word *Saamaanyaa,* meaning 'a common woman' also means *Bateek.* The word *Daashiru/Daasri/Daasru/Daasee* seem to be different versions of the same word and all of them mean a female slave or a keep. A woman, who is a maidservant since birth, is called *Garbhadaasee.*

The words *Jagjhodee, Adhaswee* and *Khaangee* are equivalent to a *Daasee*/keep. The word *Urdaabeganee,* means a *Daasee/Bateek* (During the regime of Aurangzeb, the chief of the women's army was called '*Urdubegi*'. The term *Urdaabeganee* seems to have originated from this word). Another phrase that one finds being used for the *Daasees* during the Peshwa regime is '*Khaasechakareeteel Striyaa*' which means women in the service of the noblemen. The words *Yoshaa* or *Yoshitaa* mean the one who serves. The different words that are used for a maidservant also seem to interchange with words that mean a keep and a prostitute. This suggests that a *Daasee* (maidservant) might be changing her roles from a servant to a keep to even end up as a common prostitute.

Words Related to Saubhagya

In a patriarchal society, marital status determines a woman's honour within her family and the society. It stipulates specific norms limiting a woman's sexual behaviour to monogamy. The marital status also determines a woman's lifestyle. Any deviation from the accepted norms means dishonour and punitive measures taken against the woman, whether a married one or a widow (Chakravarty, 1996). The words in this category use the institution of marriage as a point of reference while describing a prostitute or a loose woman.

A woman who is married is termed as *Saubhaagyavatee* (A woman blessed with the joy of wedlock). Looking at the words synonymous to a prostitute, one finds that the words either mean the one who is exempted from widowhood/the one who is blessed with unbroken joy of wedlock.

Since in the Indian society sex is institutionalised through marriage alone, these words also mean indirectly, that such a woman has the fortune of always being sexually gratified. A prostitute is referred to as '*akshay savaasheen*', '*akhanda-saubhaagyavati*', and '*janma savaasheen*' the words '*akshay*' , '*Akhanda*' *and* '*Janma*' mean lifelong. These terms denote that these women could never become widows.

The term *raand* which is commonly used in an insulting sense for a 'loose' woman primarily means a widow. The word, however, is also sometimes used to mean a woman or a wife. There are many words that have stemmed from this particular word, like *randakee, raandkhaand, raandbhaand, raandavadaa, phatraand.* All of these terms originally meant a widow, but have acquired a derogatory connotation to indicate a woman with a 'loose' character. There was a fear that a young widow could go astray and hence regarded 'potentially' immoral. It was also possible that a young widow could lose the support of her husband's family as well as her parents, and could turn to prostitution for want of a livelihood. Thus, their sexual availability, real or imagined, could have given the word such an acquired meaning. The laws of Manu (*Manusmriti* V 156-160) state that "The sex desire in a widow is so great that she will cohabit with any man she meets, irrespective of his age or appearance."

Artists

The association of prostitution with the theatrical profession is not peculiar to India. In the West, dancers and famous actresses were 'kept' women or else practised serial marriage. Courtesans played an important role in the ancient urban society. Familiar with arts, it is through them that the refined techniques of music and dance were transmitted, a role they continued to play for centuries (Danielou, 1994). The Nauch girls were traditional dancers in Hindu temples but by 1830 had become a well-established entertainment at royal courts (Mughal and the British).

Since singing and dancing as an occupation was not considered modest or desirable for honourable women to pursue, women who performed and entertained, such as *Kalaavatee* (artist), *Nartakee* (dancer), *Natee* (an actress) rarely married. They were sometimes available for sexual pleasures and hence the words acquired an additional meaning to their occupation, that of prostitution. Words like *Naachan, Naachanghugaree* and *Naachantiparee* also indicate dancing girls though probably of lower class.

The words *Chhataaki* or *Chhatel* mean a coquetteous woman who may sing or dance for men. Both these words have a colloquial character. The word *Gaayikaa* (singer) and *Saajindee* (woman who plays a musical instrument) also acquired the meaning similar to a prostitute though the words merely state a woman's profession.

The *Ganikaa*, who was a high class courtesan in the ancient times was expected to be proficient in sixty four art forms. Words for singers and dancer, synonymous to a prostitute, are: the *Kalaavanteen, Kanchanee, Kasbeen* who could sing and dance.

Maharashtra Shabdakosh (dictionary) points out the difference between the words *Kalavanteen* and *Kasbeen*. A *Kalaavanteen* is a one who sings while dancing whereas the *Kasbeen* is the one who sits while singing. The *Kalaavanteen* earns her livelihood through her art, but the *Kasbeen* sells her body for her livelihood. There are many terms that are colloquial versions/corrupt forms of the word *Kalaavanteen*. The words are as follows, *Kalvant, Kalaavati, Kalvantin, Kalaateen, Kalaapaatra, Kalaavatee, Kalaavantee* etc.

It could, therefore, be seen that those women who were engaged in singing and danc ng were perceived to be those of a 'loose' moral character and hence sexua.ly available.

Findings and Conclusion

The position and status of women in Patriarchy has always been secondary to a man. The basic assumptions of liberty and freedom are different for men and women. Even a woman's attire and adornments are defined by the social norms of 'ideal' femininity leaving women with almost no space or freedom to deviate from the rigid framework for fear of being labelled immoral and hence degrading the family honour. Patriarchal family norms operate differentially for men and women. While men are expected to remain ideally within the confines of monogamous marriage, there is a social indifference to their indulgence to extra marital sex. Any woman who does not confine to the norms of monogamy (or is believed to deviate from norms) is labelled as 'a fallen woman' and consequently equated to a prostitute.

Over 200 terms were found in the *Maharastra Shabdakosh* (dictionary) perhaps the largest lexicon of Marathi language published between 1930s and 1940s, spreading over eight volumes. The terms include words for keeps, religious prostitutes, common strumpets, artists/ performers, women who have deviated from the sexual norms and the ones indicating various attributes of the occupation of prostitutes. The time during which the dictionary was compiled was a period of social awakening and social reforms, particularly those concerning the upliftment of women. The common understanding of some of the concepts was also changing, but the changing norms were still not as well defined as they are today. For example, a *gayikaa* (a singer) was not considered as low as a prostitute, but also did not command the same respect as married women from respectable households and a '*natee*' (a film actress) probably was understood to have a status lower than the one who sang classical music. And all these women were thought to be moral deviants. Words like *lalanaa, lalitaa, apsaraa* which were earlier understood as 'fallen' women now meant only beautiful women. These words have been used in Marathi fiction and poetry. The rich and aristocrats still had maidservants and keeps. But in the society at large, the maidservant was not expected to provide sexual services. The dictionary has documented the meaning of the words prevalent in the older times, as also prevalent in the times when it was written. As a result, the meanings of many words are interchangeable and are given as synonyms in the dictionary. For example, the various meanings of the word *naikeen* are given as a dancer, an artist, an unmarried singer, prostitute, a fallen woman and a keep. This shows that the status, roles/functions, moral hierarchy of women in various occupations was not clearly defined and hence in a state of flux.

The earlier attempts of classifying prostitutes were based on their functions, personal charms, accomplishments, place of residence and their patrons/customers etc. Kalyan Malla has classified women in various aspects of love, while Rajwade has referred to the classification of prostitutes, given in *Mahabharata*, on the basis of moral hierarchy. The *Devadaasee*s were also categorized according to their mode of entry into temple prostitution. Kapur has classified the modern prostitutes on the basis of their status in the society. Classification in the old texts of the *Tantrik* sect (*Niruttar Tanra*) is based on the class of people served by prostitutes and also their place of work.

This study does not classify prostitutes *per se*. The classification is essentially of terms synonymous to a general term prostitute in Marathi language. The classification is based on the avenues of entry into the occupation or based on the different attributes of prostitution. This classification shows that there were potentially certain occupations, which if a woman pursued, could lead her into prostitution. Other categories include the one where marriage is used as a point of reference to indicate a prostitute and the other category is of words that have a derogatory reference to body parts. Many of the words are not in use today, either in literature or in colloquial language. Because of the redefinition of the meanings of certain words in today's times, even if they are in use, they do not denote a prostitute or even a fallen woman. A large number of terms out of these words have gone out of usage over time. Presently, about 53 words are in use. Out of these 53 words only 29 have retained their original meaning, while 24 are used without the connotation of prostitution (e.g. *Sajindee, Ntrityaanganaa, Nartakee, Kalavatee*). Out of the 29 words that have retained their meaning, eight of them indicate women with loose morals (e.g. *Nadafailee, Chhainaal, kultaa, Jaarinee* etc.); Five means a mistress (*Thevalalee, Rakhelee, Rakhel* etc.); and the remaining 16 still mean a prostitute or a sex worker (*Veshyaa, Randee, Raand, Naikeen, Baajaarbasavee* etc.).

Language grows through borrowing from other languages. India was repeatedly attacked by Muslim invaders and their empire was extended to the South well beyond Maharastra. Hence, in the process of acculturation it is not surprising to find that words were borrowed from the languages of the rulers. One finds words being borrowed from Arabic (*Vakal, Mashuk*), Persian (*Lavandee, Khangee, Maljaadee*), Urdu (*Badakhyaalee, Badafailee, Urdaabeganee*). Because of the geographical proximity to the states like Goa and Karnatak, there are words borrowed from Goanese (*bhaveen, naikeen*) and Kannada language (*Basavee, Sule, Avvaa*). Some of the Sanskrit scholars who had migrated from Maharastra to Tanjore Maratha kingdom, spoke a dialect that had a combination of Kannada and Marathi. The word '*suli*' is from Tanjore Marathi, whereas the word *Zodge* is from Rajapuri Marathi, a part of the coastal region of Konkan (The colloquial language changes to some extent within the State). Since Marathi has originated from Sanskrit, a great deal of influence of Sanskrit is to be found in the coinage of the words as also a direct borrowing (*Swairinee, Vaaraanganaa, Vaaryoshitaa, Paradwaargaamee, Pararat*).

The other and probably more significant force was the changing economic, political, social and cultural scenario throughout history. The opulence of the ancient kingdoms during the Maurya and Gupta period as also during the Vijayanagar empire had '*Ganikaas*' (courtesans), who were well educated, beautiful and rich women who were trained and skilled in the art of providing erotic pleasures to the elites and the aristocrats. The wealth of these kingdoms prompted construction of huge temples and women were brought in to serve the deities in the temples. Then came a period during which the Mughals repeatedly attacked India and destroyed several temples. This forced the women serving in the temples to leave the temples and make a living through performing arts like singing and dancing. Additionally, the Mughals captured many women and recruited them in their harems as maidservants or mistresses and keeps. The Peshwa regime followed the same pattern of grandeur and amorous blandishments. There were many maidservants, camp-followers and keeps in the harem of the Peshwas.

The British who came to India also indulged in the entertainment provided by the '*nauch* girls' (dancers). After Independence, when the small principalities merged to form a unified, Independent India, the feudal patronage provided to the prostitutes, singers, dancers, artisans by the chieftains came to an end and many women had to relocate themselves in brothels. The terms that came into the language came to stay and presently, even if they have gone out of common usage, still find a place in the expanse of words in Marathi language. (When Naipaul was shown the Red Light Area of Mumbai, the person showing him around used the word *Ganikaa* for the sex workers, though we know that they are quite different from the *Ganikaa* as of the past).

A powerful evidence of gender discrimination in a given society comes from the language of the society. Each language abounds in expressions which are indicative of society's differential treatment of women. Linguistic data can be interpreted as manifestations of hidden attitudes towards women. Our linguistic behaviour is a diagnostic tool of our hidden feelings and thoughts. Linguistically gender discrimination finds expression in the language descriptive of women. For example, the word *Raand* (a widow), which means a prostitute and is commonly used in an insulting manner does not have a parallel word for a widower with any derogatory sense. Also, there is no word for a male prostitute either, who seem to be on way to become an urban occupation to serve the affluent women.

There are quite a few offensive phrases that mean a prostitute. For example, the term *Taangal* means a cow that is in the habit of kicking and this word is synonymous with a prostitute. The word *Kadbaa naayakin* means an old prostitute as cheap as hay/dry grass or the expression *Vaavaachi Maashi* meaning a useless fly is also used to refer to a prostitute.

It can be concluded that by analyzing overt linguistic expressions in Marathi, one can have an insight into the covert social psychology of the Marathi speaking people. The examples cited in this chapter are illustrative and by no means exhaustive. Nonetheless, they are clearly symptomatic of the underlying social psycho-pathology of discrimination and cruelty against women in our society.

5

Brothels and Brothel Clients

SUSMITA BHATTACHARYA

Introduction

Presence of sexual networks has facilitated the rapid and wide dissemination of the infection of HIV. The clients of Commercial Sex workers are part of the sexual network and vulnerable to acquire the infection and are the major source of spreading the disease to other partners/members in the community.

The present study focuses on exploring the profile of the clients, their sexual behaviour and safe sex practices. The present study was carried out in the historically known (since Peshwa times) red light area in Pune city. About 100 clients visiting low and middle level brothels were interviewed supported by the data collected using observation technique. Interviews of the clients were taken at different locations, near eight middle and six low class brothels. The researchers used various channels to reach the area and spent more time, resources and efforts, to gain confidence of the CSWs and their house managers.

The age of the clients ranged from 16 to 59 years while, 75 per cent of them were in 20-39 years of age. 64 per cent of them had studied beyond 10th standard and 71 per cent had no fixed income. About 45 per cent were married and 25 per cent were migrants. Average one to two hundred rupees were spent on habits including tobacco chewing and smoking. Alcohol consumption was reported by 45 per cent of them. About twenty clients had disturbed family relations during childhood.

About 30 clients reported that they had a fixed sex worker as a sexual partner, while remaining had multiple sex partners including wife, girl friend or a sex worker. Mean age at first contact with sex worker was 20 years and majority of them 68 per cent were unmarried at that time.

Condom use was reported common but 38 per cent reported to have used condom 'always' while 44 per cent mentioned 'sometimes'. History of STDs, fear of getting AIDs, and protection of wife from infection were the main motivating factors for use of condom. About 106 contacts were reported by 69 clients in one month, of which they had not used condom 26 times. Practice of condom use was dependent on CSWs attitude, perceived threat of infection and romantic perceptions. Repeated history of sexually transmitted diseases was given by 24 clients. About One-fourth clients did not have any knowledge about mode of spread of HIV. Rest of them got information through television. A large proportion knew that HIV could be diagnosed by testing blood, and condom use could protect them from infection.

There is thus a need to promote information about safe sex practices, and awareness about STDs and HIV among the clients. Since present condom use policy is CSW centred it is felt necessary to promote condom use amongst CSWs through informal education. At the same time focus of the policy should be on socially deprived and economically marginalized young men to prevent risk of infection.

Locale

Pune city has a very active sex trade, including large number of women who work in brothels that are clustered in the area of Budhwar Peth and Somwar Peth in the heart of the city. The brothels of Pune have a long history, since it existed during Peshwa Rule. The location is in a very busy commercial zone, in which hundreds of shops, markets and other business enterprises are jostling with residential buildings. The area attracts large number of peasants, as they bring their vegetables and farm produce to the bulk markets located in this zone. In the vicinity, there are bulk markets of cloth, dry fruits, plastics and household utensils.

In recent decades, the rapid industrial growth in and around Pune city has brought migrant workers from rural areas of Maharashtra, as well as large number of newcomers from neighbouring states. The city is a major transit route for the trucks that carry goods between south India and Mumbai. A large number of truckers pass through the metropolitan region everyday contributing a steady stream of clients to the commercial sex work sector of the city. Although the bulk vegetable market has been shifted to an area on the fringe of the city, the area continues to be the hub of Pune retail markets.

There is a seasonal influx of clients to the brothels from the

was very apprehensive and uncertain about the response of the brothel owner and the client(s). The brothel was located on the second floor of a multi-story building. The staircase leading up to the brothel was littered with empty cigarette packages, tobacco spit, scraps of paper and dirt. Our team made way past the curious eyes of sex workers standing at each landing of the staircase, along with young men involved in negotiations with the sex workers.

As we entered the brothel, we were met by the informant, who had been contacted earlier by our peer worker. This man was a regular partner of the brothel owner, and was very open and informative. He said he had been informed by his partner that a team of doctors was coming from the 'big hospital' interested in researching about brothel clients. A sex worker was sent to get cold drinks for us, and the man invited us to sit down. Gradually our team relaxed as the interview proceeded. Subsequently, we carried out four interviews at the same location. On each occasion, the peer worker came with us and introduced us to the brothel owner and explained about the purpose of our study. After we had interviewed several clients (during several visits) at that site, the brothel owners became uneasy, and suggested that we should go to other locations for our interviews.

We then shifted our activities to a 'lower level' brothel area. (The 'lower level' designation is used by various key informants, with reference to brothels that have lower rates per sex act, and are, therefore, visited by men with less money to spend.). We found the 'lower level' brothels to be poorly furnished and maintained. During our first visit, our team had to sit on wooden boxes used for storing the belongings of the sex workers. In addition to the visits to brothels, we had frequent meetings with the peer workers connected to the NGO. We also met with local leaders, including a local youth group known as Mitra Mandal. Gradually several local groups and individuals showed interest and helpful attitude towards our study. All of our data-gathering activities were greatly facilitated by the head of the local NGO with whom we were working very closely. She became our chief advisor and facilitator throughout the study.

Structure and Functioning of the Brothels

The brothels are located in a highly congested area, in which ordinary family dwellings and numerous shops, are jostling with the brothels. The buildings are identified by house numbers allotted by the Municipal Corporation, in addition to which many of the buildings have names—

often quite poetic. Most of the brothels are located in multi-story buildings; five or six story buildings are the usual pattern in the area. Rents are high because the area is a busy commercial sector of the city; thus, much of the income of the brothel operations goes towards rent.

The middle level brothels (as designated by key informants) are generally more spacious than lower level brothels, with sufficient room for clients to sit on sofas or benches, while the sex workers are seated on the opposite side in the 'reception room'. These brothels pay greater attention to overall cleanliness of the premises, compared with the lower level establishments. The sex workers are usually young, and dressed in clean, flashy modern clothing and make-up. Their dress is often *salwar kamiz*, but some also wear western style tops and skirts, showing their legs. The individual 'cabins' in these brothels are generally clean, and the cots are covered with good quality mattresses and sheets and some of the brothels have air-conditioning. Their inside toilets include washing facilities for the use of the clients as well as sex workers. Clients who visit the middle level brothels are usually skilled workers, office workers, small businessmen, contractors, shop owners, and some students. Rates charged per sex act are substantially higher in the middle level brothels, but they vary considerably, depending on the attractiveness of individual sex workers, and the negotiating styles of both clients and sex workers. On an average, the rates in the middle level brothels were reported to be in the range of Rs. 70 to 100, per episode.

Compared to the middle level brothels, the lower level places have significantly less space and furniture, as well as a lower level of cleanliness. Some informants, referred to these brothels as 'third class'. They usually do not have proper toilet or washing facilities and the cots in the individual cubicles are usually covered with a worn and dirty looking 'rug'. Our researchers noted that the sex workers often appeared weak, pale, and sickly. Rates in these 'bottom of the line' brothels are generally in the neighbourhood of Rs. 40 to 50, per episode.

A major difference between the two levels of brothels is the degree of interaction on the streets. Whereas the middle level sex workers generally avoid soliciting on the streets, the lower level sex workers go out and loiter on the streets to find clients. In addition, street based, 'floating' sex workers (*rastya-varchi* in Marathi) often bring their clients to the low-level brothels, paying the brothel owner Rs. 5 for 'rent' for the temporary use of a cubicle. Thus, day-time sexual activity in these brothels is largely based on the floating sex workers, many of whom are from nearby villages and peri-urban areas, and return to their respective homes after a day's work. They do not reside on brothel premises.

Informants in the brothels and among the peer workers told us that the sex workers who stayed in the brothels were generally considered 'clean' and safer from infections, whereas street-based sex workers, and sex workers from the brothels who solicited in the streets were considered to be 'unclean' (*gandi*).

Organization of the Brothels

Each brothel is headed by a female owner, generally referred to as *gharwali* (literally: house owner). Another term is *malkin* which is derived from the word for 'owner'. Many of the brothel owners are women who worked as sex workers in the area during their youth, and then accumulated sufficient money and experience to set up their own business. Frequently, the owner is married, with children, and lives somewhere outside the area.

The majority of the brothels are under the day-to-day supervision of a 'manager', who works under the direction of the owner. The managers are also generally 'graduated sex workers', who have earned the trust of the owners. The managers bear the brunt of police raids, as they are often taken into custody by the police, and must then be bailed out by the owners. Daily control of cash intakes and other administrative tasks are the work of the managers, who must also maintain order, intervening to prevent quarrels among the sex workers, as well as disputes with clients.

The brothels are open from 7:00 AM to midnight, although rather little traffic occurs before noon. During the daytime, some of the sex workers could be seen sleeping on the floor or in their cubicles, while (especially in lower-level brothels) floating sex workers and their clients circulate in from the streets, pay the manager, and go out again. The brothel manager keeps account of the number of clients by using multi-coloured tokens.

The numbers of sex workers vary from brothel to brothel, but generally range from 5 to 15 per day. Lower level brothels usually have more sex workers, even though they often have less space and poor accommodations. The other regular members of the brothel community are the sex workers' children—often 3 or 4 small children in each brothel. The children are sometimes seen in the waiting room, watching TV, but usually they are out of sight, somewhere in a back room.

Sex workers collect the money from each client and immediately put the money into their own storage boxes. However, each sex worker pays from 20 to 50 per cent of her earnings to the owner. From her earnings each sex worker pays for her own necessities such as make-up, clothing, and food. They also contribute Rs. 10 to 20 each month for cable television, as each brothel has at least one television set. Among the sex workers there is very little cooperation or sharing. They quarrel over clients, try to control their tiny bit of space, and they often must borrow money from the *gharwali* if they need health care, or wish to give financial assistance to a family member back in their home village. When they borrow money from the *gharwali* they must pay high rates of interest on the borrowing. Some are heavily indebted, so they have no option but to continue in the brothel. Others, more fortunate, with more clients, can save some money, or perhaps find a partner who will take them out of the brothel life.

Some of the sex workers reported that they undertook 'fast'. The fast does not refer to food restriction or abstinence, but instead to refraining from sex. Those who observed a 'fast day' bathed, and then visited a temple to pray. Those who go to the Durga temple observe a Friday fast, while the special day for *Yellamma*, goddess of *devdasis,* is Tuesday. The more fortunate sex workers, with greater freedom, also spend afternoons in shopping and perhaps going to a cinema. However, very few of the sex workers (perhaps 10 or 15%) appeared to have those special privileges.

The managers of the brothels try to bar entry of intoxicated individuals, and other unwelcome 'guests'. Those include local *goonda*s or rowdies, who often try to obtain sex without paying. According to informants, the local rowdies sometimes take away sex workers, to keep them as sex partners. Local boys from the immediate neighbourhood are not allowed in the brothels, since they also try to have sex without paying, and are seen as causing serious quarrels. It was observed that these local boys were addressed as 'brother' by the sex workers in the area.

The brothel owners discourage sex workers from accepting food or drink from clients, although sometimes clients bring things to the brothel, particularly alcohol and *paan* (mixture of betel leaves, areca nut and lime, for chewing). The *gharwalis* are suspicious of men who bring food or drink, although the practice is generally permitted for the 'regular' clients who are known to the brothel people. Well-off clients who come frequently to the brothel bring food, drink and sometimes small gifts, and the sex workers who receive these things are happy for the treat and the special attention, given to them.

Normally, each client stays with the sex worker for only 10 to 15 minutes, but some clients pay extra amount for staying overnight (Rs. 100

to 200). Brothel owners discourage the sex workers going out with clients, as they fear the sex worker would abscond (especially if she owes money to the owner) or may be harmed by the client.

The largest numbers of clients come in the evening, from 7:00 or 8:00 p.m. until closing time at midnight. Sundays and Thursdays appear to be particularly busy days, as more men have free time. During the first 10 days of the month brothels see more clients, as those who are paid monthly have more spending money.

Characteristics of the Clients

There are many misgivings about the clients of the brothels, for example, they are drunk, disorderly, come from the lowest socio-economic status, with various anti-social features and are truckers and other out of town visitors. Also, it is often expected that many clients of brothels are truckers and other out-of-town visitors. Our data, however, indicates a somewhat different picture of the brothel clients.

We interviewed a total of one hundred men who visited the brothels. They ranged in age from 16 to 59 giving a mean age of 29.4 years (SD = 8.3). The largest age category in our sample consisted of men between 20 to 39 years 75 per cent. Twenty men were 40 years or above and five were less than 20 years of age. There were not many illiterates, but eleven of our total sample reported that they had received no formal education, while 18 clients had education above 10th standard and three men were university students, or had studied at the university level. Perhaps the most surprising feature of our client sample is that they are preponderantly residents of the city itself, with only 17 individuals from outside the city. Most of those 'outsiders' were from nearby towns and villages and only 3 men said they were from other states.

The men in our sample were almost evenly divided between married and unmarried (46 ever married; 54 unmarried). Only one was a widower and two reported that they were divorced. As would be expected, the unmarried were mainly from the younger age group. Many of these young men expressed the desire to "marry a good girl and settle down in life".

We used the clients' reported occupations as a proxy for socio-economic status (SES). In the 'high SES' group (N = 12) we included men who are professionals, landowners, contractors, estate agents, and men from middle level government or public sector jobs. In the 'low SES' category (N = 41) we included day labourers, street vendors, and men who make their living by doing occasional odd jobs. The 'middle level (N = 47) included a wide variety of occupations falling between the high and low groups. In the wide range of reported occupations we had three engineers, three post-graduate students, a few large-scale farmers, and four men who worked in government offices.

Nearly half of our samples (45 men) reported regular alcohol use. Men from lower income jobs generally consumed *desi daru* (country liquor), while those from higher income occupations reported that they drink *videshi daru* (foreign liquor), though the whiskey, gin and other alcohol they refer to are actually manufactured in India. In our discussions with informants from the area, and with some of the clients, there emerged a prevalent feeling that "a man cannot go to a sex worker without consuming alcohol". It was reported that, at least during the initial contacts with sex workers, there was a strong need to allay inhibitions and fears. None of our interviewees were drunk at the time of the interview, though many of them reported that they had consumed alcohol before coming to the brothel. We observed three cases of clients bringing alcohol with them and they coaxed the sex worker to drink with them.

About half of our client interviewees also reported use of tobacco, in the form of cigarettes, *bidis* (country cigarettes), and *gutka* which is a general label for various mixtures of tobacco plus other substances for chewing. It is interesting that our informants referred to all of the substance use (alcohol, smoking, tobacco chewing, drugs) as well as relations with sex workers as *vyasan* (addiction). When we asked them to calculate the amounts they spent for *vyasan* per month, they replied by adding up the costs of 'substances' plus costs for sex worker contacts. These estimates of monthly expenses for 'addictions' ranged between 100 and 1000 rupees.

Rakhel (Keep) Fixed Relations between Sex Workers and Clients

It is generally believed that brothels are places where sex is exchanged in return for money and the interaction or encounter is devoid of any kind of bonding or support. We found that there are significant exceptions to that pattern. Although 70 per cent of our informants said, they generally visited different sex workers, often in different brothels, each time they came for sex, 30 per cent of our interviewees said that they had regular, on-going relationships with a particular brothel woman.

Those men referred to their partner as *rakhel* which means 'woman kept by a man'. They were also referred to as *samaan*, meaning a 'commodity'. The men in this type of relationship are referred to as *yaar*, which means 'dear friend with sexual commutation'. The word *yaar* is commonly used to refer to a male friend, but the word *rakhel* is considered a derogatory term in most situations. In *rakhel* relationships, the men visited their fixed partner usually on weekly holidays (Sunday). The frequency of visits to an individual *rakhel* varied from once a week to once fortnightly. Some of them visited their *rakhel* in the evening and stayed till late night, while some visited in the morning and stayed the entire day, returning home only at late hours in the night. The *rakhel* relationships were usually an outcome of a typical pattern of risk behaviour of men who started visiting sex workers in brothels, while they were still teenagers. They visited multiple partners in the first phase and after some years, anytime between 2 to 10 years, they settled down with one sex worker. However, these relationships often break up after two or three years, due to quarrels, abuse or suspicion of illness of the *rakhel*. A few men said that they continued the relationship for a longer period, up to 8 or 10 years, and in three cases, the relationship with their *rakhel* had continued for 15 years or longer.

We probed for the reasons which prompted a man to enter into *rakhel* relationships, and also for the motivations of sex workers who consented to such an arrangement. While it was clear that sex workers wanted some support and security, financial, social and emotional, the men kept a *rakhel* because they were 'bored' with going to a new and different sex worker each time. We observed that there were a few destitute young men (some of them sons of sex workers) who were keen to keep a *rakhel* at quite a young age. This was done in order to get shelter in the brothel, or to extract money from the *rakhel*. Although some clients reported that they gave support to their *rakhel*, we learned from key informants that in many cases the relationships were unsupportive and exploitative. The following case shows the exploitative side of these relationships:

> Mr. R ran away from his native place near the city of Bangalore at the age of 17. He has no education in spite of the fact that his father owned 40 acres of land. He first came to Mumbai and searched for a job but was unsuccessful. After three months he came to Pune. He got a job in a restaurant near the red light area. He got food and shelter along with his wages from the hotel owner. A sex worker named Kamal used to come there to eat *biryani* quite frequently. He liked her, got friendly with her, and became sexually involved. At first, the sex worker used to demand money from this man, but for the past three years she gives him money. This 25 year old man said that he is enjoying the situation, as his *rakhel* is providing for food, drinks and other needs. He said that his *rakhel* is good looking and her business is good and she gets

> many clients. Mr. R commented that *I treat her like my wife and do not keep relation with other sex workers*. He has two children aged two years and seven months from her, and both stay with his *rakhel*. He reported that he has been using condoms for the past three years, after one of his friends died of AIDS.

Many of the older men with fixed partners reported that they regularly gave money to the *rakhel*. The usual amounts mentioned were Rs. 1000 to Rs. 1500 per month. In addition, during festivals they gave clothes and gifts. Several of the men said that the relationship is 'like husband and wife'. In our study, out of 30 clients with *rakhel* relationship, 18 reportedly did not go to any other sex worker. Many of these men denied that their relationship involved any risks of infection, so condom use was less among the men with these fixed relationships. The following case recorded by us presents some of the above points:

> Mr. M is 32 years old and hails from Nasik, where his family has a large farm and property. He is the youngest of five children. His elder brothers and sisters are all married, so his unmarried state is the cause for concern in the family. Mr. M went to school in an area near the brothels, and he passed through the red light area scene everyday on way to school. He dropped out of school in 8th standard. He joined a group of young boys who sold flowers to sex workers. His flower selling prospered and he also began to have sexual contacts in the brothel at the age of 17. In his early years he went to different girls in the brothel, but after two or three years he decided to keep a *rakhel*. He stayed with her for 4 years but left her and began living with another sex worker, Sonam. His flower business expanded and he is financially well off. He reported to us that he does not smoke or drink and has developed a strong dislike for sex. Nonetheless he has sexual contact with Sonam once or twice in a week.
>
> He has strong opinions about AIDS and condom use and believes the solution to AIDS control lies in education of brothel owners, to maintain strict condom use rules. Presently they are indifferent, as they are afraid that this might drive away the clients.
>
> Mr. M believes that he is not at risk of AIDS as his *rakhel* is 'like his wife' and he would marry her but she advised him to marry someone of his parents' choice. Several months after our interview we learned that Mr. M had married a girl of his parents' choice. First he went for an HIV test, as "he did not want to ruin a girl's life".

Some of the clients who had *rakhel* relationships provided extended support, not only financial but also during illness. They also supported children of the *rakhel*.

Mr. K. is a 36 year old auto-rickshaw driver, who had his first contact with sex workers at the age of 16. After having multiple sex partners, he developed a relationship with one woman in the brothel, whom he supported financially for 4 to 5 years. Subsequently his *rakhel* developed AIDS and died. According to his account he had been supporting her two children, a boy and a girl, for the past five years. He now has another *rakhel*, whom he lives with in the brothel and is paying rent to the brothel owner.

It was observed that older men were generally supportive towards their *rakhel,* while younger men who started their relationship recently tended to be more exploitative.

All the clients who had a *rakhel* were residents of the city, whereas there were 17 'outsiders' among the other, *non-rakhel* clients. Some of them were visiting Pune for business, employment opportunities or to buy or sell their agricultural produce in the local market; three men were from outside the state. 70 per cent of the interviewed clients in the *rakhel* relationship category were unmarried, while only about half 47 per cent of the *non-rakhel* clients were unmarried.

Clients Who Did Not Have a *Rakhel* Relationship

These men were the majority in our sample. Most of these men began visiting the brothels when they were adolescents. These brothel clients preferred to visit multiple partners, and expressed liking variety in their sexual partners. Key informants commented that most men do not visit the same sex worker more than four or five times. The brothel managers also prefer that men do not form regular relationships with specific sex workers. Many of these clients were also aware of the risks involved in their sexual activities. Some of them commented that "many men come to these sex workers, so one can get AIDS from them if you visit them frequently."

The clients expressed their desire to have sex with good-looking young girls and they were of the opinion that when they were buying sex they should receive good service. In one such case a client said, "I do not like my wife. She is not good looking. Here all the girls are smooth, so I come here. I am paying so I want a new *maal* each time". The term *maal* is used for 'commodity' in both Hindi and Marathi.

> Mr. S is 32 year old man who works in a large industrial plant near the city. His formal education is up to the 10th standard, and

his present job earns him about Rs. 10,000 per month. He was interviewed by our team in a middle level brothel which is well-known in the area as a place where the girls command high prices. He lives with his father, mother, wife and two children. He said he got married at the age of 18 to a 16 year old girl. He said that his wife is beautiful. However, two years after marriage, influenced by his friends, he visited a sex worker. Since then this behaviour has become habitual. He visits the brothels at least twice per month. Initially he did not use condoms, but for the past three or four years he regularly uses condoms with sex workers. He is well aware about HIV-AIDS and he said that is why he regularly uses condoms and also cleans himself with soda water after each sexual encounter. He claims that he has never suffered from STD.

During the interviews, we tried to get some information about the impact of extramarital sex activities on family relationships. Many of the men were hesitant to talk about their relationships with their wives. But some clients who had *rakhel* relationships said they faced opposition from parents as well as their wives. Many of the interviewees expressed their desire to stop the risky behaviour, but seemed to consider it an addiction, and difficult to overcome.

The following tables show that there are important differences between the two types of brothel clients:

Table 5.1: Age and Educational Status of *Rakhel* and *Non-Rakhel* Clients

Characteristic	*Rakhel Clients N=30 (%)*	*Non-Rakhel Clients N=70 (%)*
Age		
Median	30	27
Range	18-59	16-49
Age <20 years	2(6.7)	3(4.3)
20-29 years	13(43.3)	38(54.2)
30-39 years	5(16.7)	19(27.1)
40 and above	10(33.3)	10(14.3)
Education		
No Education	6(20)	5(7.1)
Up to 7th std.	15(50)	10(14.2)
8 to10th std.	9(30)	37(52.8)
Above 10th std.	–	18(25.7)

χ^2 (education) = 23 $P<0.001$; χ^2 (age) = 5.04 $P<0.05$

Source: Field Investigation.

Table 5.1 indicates that there is a main difference in age between the men with *rakhel* relations and *non-rakhel* relations. The percentage of men with regular ties is much higher for those 40 years and over. The difference in education is much more striking than the differences in age. The *non-rakhel* clients are much better educated than their counterparts.

Table 5.2: Condom Use in *Rakhel* and *Non-Rakhel* Clients

	Rakhel Clients		*Non-rakhel Clients*	
	N = 30	*(%)*	*N = 70*	*(%)*
Condom Use:				
Always used	4	(13.3)	34	(48.6)
Sometimes used	14	(46.7)	30	(42.8)
Never used	12	(40.2)	6	(8.6)

$\chi^2 = 18.7$ $P<0.001$

Source: Field Investigation.

We can see in Table 5.2 that clients who had *rakhel* relationships report much less regularity of condom use. As many as 40 per cent reported that they never use condoms. This is partly due to their belief that there is less risk when they only visit one sex worker. They said 'my *rakhel* is like my wife' and it is not common to use a condom between husband and wife for reasons other than contraception. However, in some of the interviews, clients did agree that the relationship is not like husband-wife, as the *rakhel* continues with her sex work with other men. One of the clients who has maintained a *rakhel* relationship for the past 16 years commented "these women are like public tap, anyone comes and washes his hand." The lower educational level among the *rakhel* clients is probably a factor contributing to their lack of regular condom use, although the nature of the relationship ('like marriage') also contributes to condom non-use.

Table 5.3: Relation between Condom Use and Education in Clients

Characteristic	*Always used N = 38(%)*	*Sometimes used N = 44(%)*	*Never used N =18(%)*
Education			
No education	1 (2.6)	6 (13.6)	4 (22.2)
Up to 7th std.	5 (13.1)	13 (29.5)	7 (38.9)
8 to 10th std.	23 (60.5)	16 (36.4)	7 (38.8)
Above 10th std.	9 (23.7)	9 (20.4)	–

$\chi^2 = 12.7$ $P < 0.001$

Source: Field Investigation.

Our data are similar to many other studies which show that education is a major factor influencing condom use. Table 5.3 shows the relationships very clearly. In the category of 'always use condoms' 84 per cent had at least eight years of education, while none of the clients with education above 10th standard were in the 'never used' category. Education influences the employment levels, income, peer group relations, as well as access to information. Therefore, it is not surprising to find that men with more education are more regular condom users. As would be expected, there was also a relationship between socio-economic status (rated in terms of occupations) and condom use [higher SES is related to higher condom use (chi-squared = 6.19; $p<.05$)]. However, this relationship is not as strong as the correlation with education, so we feel that education is the most significant predictor.

Recent Developments in Condom Use

Though the brothels and sex work in the area have had a long history, the use of condoms is quite a recent phenomenon. A peer informant who was formerly a sex worker in the area told us *ten years back the condom was not used by sex workers. We never used to take condom in hand if a customer brought one with him. We felt dirty to touch it.*

In the past five years, there have been strong campaigns of AIDS awareness and condom promotion from the government health department and non-government organizations (NGOs). Condoms were initially available from government sources, and are now found in many nearby shops, so the availability has greatly increased in recent years. Workers from the NGOs told us that they met with fierce opposition from *gharwalis* when they first began condom promotion in the early 1990s. The brothel owners feared that insistence on using condoms would reduce their clientele. However, that resistance gradually dissipated in the mid-90s, particularly as the spread of AIDS cases became more apparent. Now the *gharwalis* say that condom use is mandatory in their establishments, though violations of that 'rule' are widespread. Fear of AIDS is almost universal among the sex workers, and the protective role of condoms is widely known. However, many men, particularly the less educated clients, still resist condom use, and the women in the brothels are unwilling or unable to enforce strict condom use rules. Non-use is still common in both the *rakhel* and non-*rakhel* situations. On the other hand, some of the clients said that their *rakhels* insist on condom use so they have to use it. One *rakhel* commented that *these men are like dogs. We cannot trust them, they go to all places, to so many girls, rakhel must use condom to protect her.*

Summary and Conclusions

In our study we found that there are wide variations in the types of brothels in the red light area, with corresponding differences in clientele. The 'lower level' brothels tend to be crowded, poorly furnished and badly maintained, and cater to lower income, poor and less educated clients. 'Middle level' brothels have more amenities, are cleaner, with slightly more privacy, and usually have smaller numbers of sex workers.

A major finding in our study was that a substantial minority of the clients have fixed relationships with specific women, who are referred to as *rakhel.* The *rakhel* relationships tend to be found in cases where the men are less educated, and a number of them are men over 40 years of age. Men involved in *rakhel* relationships are less likely to use condoms, as many of them regard the relationship to be similar to a marital relationship.

While condom use in the brothels has become common since the mid-1990s, there are still many situations in which condoms are not used. The various NGOs and government health workers in the red light area have continued to promote safer sexual practices, trying to overcome the long-term resistance and negative connotations of condoms. Fear of AIDS is common among the brothel sex workers and their clients, though many people are still willing to take risks, believing that protective measures, such as, washing after sex can prevent the sexually transmitted infections, including AIDS.

The continued resistance to condom use among some of the brothel clientele demonstrates that there is a need for continued intervention programmes and condom promotion. However, our data show that the less educated men, particularly, those involved in *rakhel* relationships, are the hardest to reach, and the hardest to persuade concerning condoms. Therefore, outreach workers in intervention programmes need to use varied approaches in relation to different types of clients, in the various types of brothel environments.

6

Female Sex Workers among Nat Community

R.C. SWARNKAR

Introduction

According to Colonel Todd, '*Rajwada*' or Rajputana were the terms used for the state of Rajasthan. In the 19th century, British ruled Rajputana whose earlier local feudal lords were classified into '*Riyasat*' and '*Thikana*' or '*Thikanedar*'. They were invited on festive ceremonies like marriage, birth etc. in which singing and dancing was performed by the Nat women. Nats were gifted with cash and kind for their traditional skills demonstrated in the form of dance and song. They were part of the '*Jajmani*' system and had relationship of '*Jajman-Jachak*' (pattern and performer) in the traditional social structure.

Women belonging to Nat, Rajnat, Bedia, Kanjar communities of Rajasthan have been practicing commercial sex for a long time as a profession. Women particularly belonging to caste 'Nat' used to perform '*Notanki*', street plays, dance and music. They were involved in prostitution too. 'Rajnats', a clan of Nat, were associated with the princely houses (Swarankar, R.C., 1999). In fact, prostitutes from the '*Kothas*' were invited to each '*mahfil*' on the occasions of joy by the leisured class for singing, sensuous and sexual pleasure. A large '*harem*' of keeps and concubines (including slaves) were maintained by both Hindu and Muslim rulers which occupied much of their time (Modi, I.P., 1985). Nat communities leading nomadic life were involved in the occupation of entertainment, *Khel-Tamasha* (street plays) to people. Their women were engaged in dancing and singing with bodily charms. Prostitution locally known as *dhandha* practiced by these women (FSWs) has social permissiveness by the Nat community. Their perception and value system about sex and attitude towards sexuality, sexual relations are different from the normative pattern of high caste Hindus.

Commercial sex work has proved to be the most challenging problem of contemporary times. In the state of Rajasthan 20,000 CSWs are reported by International Institute of Population Sciences (IIPS), Mumbai. Majority of whom may be Nat women.

In Rajasthan, total 2708 HIV positive cases and 95 AIDS cases were reported in June 1999. It was maximum 14 cases in Ajmer district and 6 in Jaipur district. Out of 95 reported AIDS cases, 81.1 per cent got infected through heterosexual route followed by 5.3 per cent through blood transfusion, while 13.7 per cent could not be traced. Of the total 95 AIDS cases, 80 were male and 15 females. A majority of them belong to age group 21-30 years (39 cases), 31-40 years (34 cases) according to Rajasthan State AIDS Control Society, Jaipur, 1999.

The first case of AIDS detected in the year 1987 from the pilgrimage centre Pushkar, was a drug addict tourist from Switzerland. Four foreign students were again found to be AIDS carrier who came for seeking admission to pursue higher education at Udaipur University. Few persons of Rajasthan origin found to be AIDS carrier were sent back from Quwait, Quatar and other Gulf countries during 1992-93. HIV positive is not only found among tourists and people exposed to outside world but also indicated by a woman from the remote tribal district of Dungarpur. Here, prostitution by tribal women with truck drivers and others is rampant. In fact, the culture of 'Bhil', 'Garasia' and other tribal permitting pre-marital sexual relations among themselves is being exploited as well by the non-tribal in the process of 'culture contact'. It is as well true for the Nat caste women who are left with no option but to go for multi partners heterosexual sex for traditional and economic reasons.

A study carried out in selected rural and urban sites of Ajmer and Udaipur districts reveals that 16 per cent men admitted that they had sexual relationship with other women. Of them, more than 80 per cent men did not have fear of contracting STD during sex with other women. And only 14 per cent of men used condom every time, while having sex with other women. They carried condom with them. The major reasons reported for not using condom, were inconvenient to use and lack of satisfaction (IIHMR, Jaipur, 1998).

A high rate of multiple sexual activities along the highway by the truckers was attributed to their prolonged stay away from home, alcohol intake, sexual urge and sex being the only form of entertainment along the highway. Majority of FSWs denied ever being affected by STDs because of the fear of losing clientele. On the whole, they were cautious of their general health as it affected their income directly. While poverty had pushed majority of them into the profession, they did not want their daughters to enter into this profession (ORG, 1995).

However, like other states in India, measures are taken by the Government of Rajasthan to prevent and control AIDS. The widespread availability of contraceptives to prevent pregnancy and antibiotics for the treatment of STDs, led to behavioural changes in the population.

The study about sexual behaviour of female sex workers (FSWs) among Nat nomadic community in Jaipur region in the eastern region of Rajasthan was carried out with focus on their perception and practices related to sexual behaviour, knowledge of AIDS and practice of safe sex. The study was carried out in 4 hamlets, 2 near national highway-8 (Jaipur-Ajmer) and 2 in the interior located in Jaipur district. Data were collected from Nat males (elders and youth), females (elderly retired FSWs, working FSWs and married) a few truck drivers and other clients, using interview guide and observational techniques. In-depth interviews with key informants were also taken.

The economic compulsions and social approval permit the Nat women to act as commercial sex workers with truck drivers and other clients. This high-risk group practicing unprotected sex is resulting into the transmission of HIV among increasing number of population in the society. Nat caste population also interacts with other castes and ethnic groups in their surroundings.

Nat led nomadic life in the traditional social structure of Rajasthan. Decision to encourage girl child to become FSW depended on several variables such as, number of females or retired FSWs in the family, economic compulsion, and sometimes, glamour, easy money, freedom, modern life style etc. After attaining puberty, the girl was brought into proximity with the '*Patelan*' (retired FSW) and inducted in the profession with rituals and festivities. The sex worker remains active in the profession from15 to 35 years of age. The first client was considered as husband and given priority over other clients. No Nat male can become the client. Truck drivers, transporters, youth, labourers, immigrants and students were the main clients. Sexual gratification and enjoyment may take place with regular client or *Ghar janwai*. Nat women also worked in the hotels and bars in Mumbai where other Nat relatives play important role. Exploitation of FSWs by pimps, agents, *Patelan*, police and relatives could be observed.

Television 55 per cent was a major source of information about

HIV-AIDS followed by the peer group of FSWs 18 per cent, staff members of NGOs 15 per cent and healthy highway project 10 per cent. In the case of 2 per cent of FSWs, information of AIDS were first time provided by the *Ghar Janwai*. Condom was used to avoid undesired pregnancy and the infection of AIDS and STD. It was observed that FSWs initially insisted on the use of condom, but if a client was willing to pay more, it was not insisted.

About half of Nat women practised this profession for economic reasons. Immediate action on mass awareness about HIV-AIDS, promoting condom use as necessary and long term plans to improve the socio-economic conditions, improving literacy rate and female status are advocacy and implementation issues.

Objectives

The present study on sexual behaviour of female sex workers from the Nat nomadic community in Jaipur is carried out with the following objectives:

1. To undertake an ethnographic documentation of 'Nat' families in their socio-cultural context;
2. To study the socio-economic, psychological and situational factors resulting into commercial sex by their women;
3. To understand their perception and practices related to sexual behaviour;
4. To assess about their sexual pattern *vis-à-vis* the knowledge of AIDS and practice of safe sex, such as the use of condom;
5. To investigate about the inter-relationships and interdependence at the levels of
    (a) Nat female commercial sex worker (FSW) with other members of family and kinship groups,
    (b) FSW with those in sexual trade i.e.; hoteliers, transporters, middlemen, clients etc., and
    (c) Nat community with castes and other social groups in the village(s) and surroundings.

The study attempts to look at the following issues:

1. The historical, socio-cultural and economic background of Nat community.

2. The type, extent and network of interaction and inter-relationship among FSWs, Nat community, Clients, Sex traders and Caste groups.
3. The factors responsible for making the Nat women commercial sex workers. What is their status and role *vis-à-vis* other members of the family?
4. What are the concepts among FSWs related to body, beauty and sexuality? How sex is perceived, and sexual behaviour is evaluated by the Nat and other caste people in the surroundings?
5. Whether or not FSWs know about the STD and AIDS? What is the extent of infection and perception of getting infection from sexual activity including HIV-AIDS?
6. What traditional and modern (condom) measures are taken by them to prevent transmission of AIDS or HIV? Where from the condoms are accessible, quality of condom, duration of use, and its disposal practices?
7. What are the socio-economic and other changes experienced by the Nat community in general and FSWs in particular over the decades?

Research Methodology

Both secondary and primary data using qualitative as well as quantitative methods were used in the study.

The literature, directly and distantly related to the objectives of study mentioned above was reviewed. The books, journals, magazines, newspapers, report etc., available in the libraries and documentation centres have been scrutinized. The experiences of social scientists, medical experts, government officials, voluntary organizations, NGOs working on the similar problems were also obtained.

Primary data of qualitative and to some extent quantitative types were collected from the respondents by the trained investigators. Research tools mentioned below were used to gather the informations from the field.

- Observations: related to commercial sex activities,
- Key Informants Interviews,
- In-depth Interviews,
- Focus Group Discussions, and
- Semi-structured and structured interview schedule for a survey.

Nat Community

Nats are distributed in almost all the districts of Rajasthan. Four hamlets were selected for the study, two hamlets on national highway-8 (Jaipur-Ajmer), one on state highway of Jaipur and one in the rural interior, in Jaipur district.

Nat women as CSW were interviewed from the hamlets in the eastern district of Jaipur and adjoining areas. The truck drivers and other clients were asked to share information and experiences with female sex workers.

Dhabas (Highway eating places) parking and resting places of truckers, grocery shops, liquor shops located close to such road site hamlets of FSWs were used as the contact points, to interview persons.

Nat as entertainers were traditionally patronized by the Rajput rulers. Zagirdars used to invite Nat women as dancing girls at the time of birth, marriage and other ceremonies to entertain the guests with dance and music. After zamindari abolition, commercial sex *(Dhandha)* has become the primary occupation of Nat women for the survival of family.

Nat caste *panchayat* plays a dominant role in the socio-economic life of Nat Community. A Nat girl who has accepted *Dhandha* cannot make nuptial alliance within the community, but she is allowed to marry a non-Nat caste person. Clients from other castes, known as *kajja* in Nat language, is free for sex with a FSW, but a Nat boy is not allowed to have sex with Nat FSW. Even the boy could be socially boycotted from the Nat community, if he violets the social norm.

Nat woman who is a sex worker does not marry. FSW is supposed to abandon *dhandha* after having *Ghar janwai*, who lives at FSW's residence.

The family structure consists of a FSW, her children and *Ghar Janwai* in the nuclear type family. The joint family structure of Nat caste comprises one or more than one FSW, unmarried sisters with or without *Ghar Janwai*, brothers, unmarried and married with their wives and children and parents. The woman particularly FSW is the axis of the economy of the whole family, although Nats are patriarchal.

Women occupy lower status in the patrilineal male dominated social structure of the Nat community. Despite FSW being an earning member for the family, she is ranked lower to married women. Brother's marriage is considered essential to sustain the lineage amongst the Nats. A FSW earns to meet the expenditure of marriage of brothers.

Child marriage is prevalent among the Nats. A Nat woman working as a FSW or retired, does not enjoy social standing even within her own caste.

Nat traditionally have linkages with the Rajputs. Inter-community marriage is not allowed. Nat women practicing commercial sex (*Dhandha*) are looked down upon by the people living in the neighbourhood villages. Villagers have experienced difficulties in marrying off their sons and daughters in villages where Nat women are pursuing *Dhandha* in the hamlets at the periphery of the village. Nat live socially isolated life in the caste villages and women do not go frequently in the main village. People are reticent to have marriage alliances in villages inhabited by Nats. Nat led nomadic life in the traditional social structure, while now they have started living sedentary life on the periphery of caste villages.

Commercial Sex as an Occupation

The *Patelan* (retired FSW) initiates the socialization of a girl for becoming a FSW. Such a girl comes in closer contact of retired FSWs and eventually with the clients. Elderly married women monitor the younger FSW in the family. Active FSW peer educates about the occupation to the girl undergoing the process of socialization.

The norms of *Dhandha* amongst others include sex as an occupation, nominal time to be spent with clients, sentimental attachment forbidden with clients, no Nat male can be a client etc. These norms are inculcated by the retired FSW to new FSW. First time, sex initiated with a client is known as *Nath Utarai* (*Nath* means nose ring).

After *Nath Utarai* the *Patelan* (retired FSW), acquaints the newly inducted FSW about sex behaviour and nuances about the profession, e.g. minimum time for penetrative sex to be given to clients.

FSW from Teelawala hamlet had visited hotels at Jodhpur earlier. The earnings from dance in hotel are more than the commercial sex practised by a FSW at native hamlet. In the hamlet, FSW charged Rs. 60 from a client and Rs. 200-500 for staying overnight. Maximum of Rs. 3000–5000 could be income a FSW per night as stated by a FSW.

The retired FSWs involved in sex trade are termed as 'aunty' or 'madam' in Mumbai. Aunty provides the accommodation and place to FSW to perform heterogeneous sex with clients. In case the police trap any FSW, then the financial burden is equally shared between the *Mukhi* and the FSW concerned.

The *patelan* is responsible for introducing a FSW to the clients. Rs. 10 was charged from each FSW towards the use of place for commercial sex activity.

Nat FSWs are classified into two categories; local Nat women working as FSWs and outsiders who are hired for *dhandha* from other villages. FSWs are kept as tenants in the houses owned by the retired Nat FSW.

FSWs go to another place when the number of FSWs become more at one location as compared to the demand of clients. FSW may shift to a new place to attract more clients who are interested in new faces.

FSWs are taken to other villages under a contract, which materializes between the FSW, '*Patelan*' and sex traders. Nat women in Teelawala hamlet practise *Dhandha*. Besides the girls of the hamlet, FSWs are brought from other villages to practise commercial sex in the hamlet.

Nat perceive a girl to be sexually matured soon after the onset of menstruation. In consequence, before the age of 16 years, some girls are made to accept commercial sex work. The economic, traditional and family conditions are the factors responsible for it. The preference for sex with the girl child for sexual pleasure, perceived cure of STD etc. are the other reasons. The considerable amount received at first time sex (*Nath utrai*) by a client with a girl child is an attractive carrot for parents or guardians.

The age of a girl, i.e. 13 to 16 years is considered the ideal age for initiating commercial sex work (*dhandhe par Baithne ki umra hai*). The period for which a sex worker usually works range between 15-16 to 35-40 years. If the offsprings of a FSW earns, she may withdraw herself from *Dhandha* at an early age. But she may extend it further if the prevailing economic condition is not favouring her retirement from *Dhandha* and if she is considered fit for sex.

It is seen that 35.7 per cent of sex workers were found to have been working for 4-6 years and little more. It was followed by 28.6 per cent who had an experience of about 1-3 years as sex worker.

As the FSW approaches her retirement age and realizes that after 3-4 years, she would not be able to continue her sex profession, she seeks to develop some sort of matrimonial bond, to make the old age secure and comfortable.

In Dantri hamlet, *Kutcha* houses constructed of mud with small rooms are used for commercial sex. *Dhandha* is practised exclusively in these rooms, built for this purpose only. Hired FSWs are also brought here from outside. Such rooms are without proper ventilation and electricity. One *charpoy* (a knitted cot), mirror, small waste container for used condoms and earthen pitcher of drinking water are kept inside the room. Light connections were not available in all the houses. A tunnel type structure is dug to rescue FSWs in the event of police raid.

In *Chamand-Ka-mand* and *Dantri* hamlets, beddings were usually not found on the cots, while in *Teelawala* and *Bandar Sindri*, mattress or bed cover with pillow, were seen on the cots (*charpai*).

Presently, the role of police is seen by the actions taken against the FSWs, pimps and clients. Intermediaries approach and ensure police officials about discontinuing commercial sex work by FSWs. The constables posted at police *chowki* outside the Nat hamlet may charge 'money' from the clients. Some police official may help in diluting the cases against FSWs and clients, in the court of law. A networking among FSWs, clients, intermediaries and police officials exist which bales out everybody from legal action. Sometimes, police register false cases, against FSWs as well as clients in order to make money. As a result, some girls practicing *dhandha* migrated either to Mumbai or to some other hamlets.

Clients

With the highways and their connectivity, local as well as outside clients of FSWs have increased over the decades. Truckers, transporters, youth, labourers, immigrants and students are seen in and around the Nat hamlets. Most of them belong to young age groups (20-40 years). It is pertinent to mention about the study undertaken in two villages of rural block of Shirur in Maharashtra which found that about 10 per cent unmarried and 30 per cent married males indulged in sex with multiple partners before marriage, including the visit to sex workers. Data shows that pre-marital sexual activity does exist among rural adolescents and that protection through condom use is extremely low on account of several difficulties (Mutatkar, R.K. and Apte, Hemant, 1999).

Majority of clients of FSWs are truckers and labourers, army men, local political activists, police personnel and college students. Clients approach in the hamlets close to the highways. Nat boys act as pimps in assisting FSWs to solicit new clients. Majority of the clients are 20-30 years old, age varying from 20 to 45, years irrespective of marital status and occupation. Climatic season does not have any significant impact on *Dhandha*. Usually the regulars visit during 9.0 p.m. to 12.0 midnight, who commute on the road. According to a FSW at Bandar Sindri, clients usually came after midnight. "We are not selective about clients. It is the money that matters."

Majority of FSWs showed their preferences to the healthy, handsome and non-alcoholic clients, who left silently after sex. Two FSWs of 25-30 years. categorically mentioned that they liked college students, not the truck drivers as their clients. Two-fifth of FSWs were not in favour of having sex with alcoholic clients if a choice was given. As high as 50 per cent of FSWs accepted it to be a part of occupation and life, where money mattered.

Sexual Behaviour

Sexual behaviour of FSWs with clients in Mumbai was different from the one that was practised in the native hamlets of Rajasthan. At Mumbai, a FSW has to remain at the disposal of a client for a longer period who paids her manifold more, as compared to the rates received by her at the native place. She often takes active part with her sexual partner at Mumbai, which includes kissing, hugging and fondling of body parts and sexual organs, culminating in penetrating sex. The use of condom depends on the choice of a client. Average 2-3 clients per day could be engaged by a FSW in Mumbai, unlike intercourse with many clients by a FSW in native hamlet. In Mumbai, FSWs went around with the clients for sight seeing, watching movies etc. Enjoyment could become revelry including tobacco smoking.

Sexual behaviour of FSW varies in different situations. With a common client, sex was only penetrative sex. FSW avoided indulging into any other sexual activity except penile penetrative sex. Usually the clients after sex wanted to leave the place as soon as possible, due to the fear of police, and to protect identity from recognition by the known persons.

Common clients did not develop any attachment with the FSW and *vice versa*. Clients who were drunkard and untidy were ignored by the FSWs but for money.

FSW developed sentimental attachment usually with the regular clients, referred as *yaar* (friend/lover) of the FSW. This relationship goes beyond commercial sex episodes only.

As mentioned earlier, *Ghar Janwai* is treated like a husband by the FSW in the given situation. He owns economic responsibility and is entitled to enjoy sex with FSW turned wife, as desired by him. He usually does not use condom. There are cases of *Ghar Janwai* who stayed permanently with FSW in 'live-in' relationship in Nat hamlets.

It was inferred from a few FSW respondents that the meaning of sex perceived by them was merely copulation. Kissing, fondling, hugging etc. are taken as meaningless sexual activities, which are neither encouraged nor practised with the clients. Oral sex and anal sex too, were neither practised nor liked by the FSWs. If a client demanded or approached for oral or anal sex, the FSWs did not agree to such demands. A majority 80 per cent of FSWs reported opposition to oral and anal sex, remaining 20 per cent were neutral, while no FSW favoured such sexual practices.

Commercial sex work is taken as an occupation for earning livelihood. Sexual gratification and enjoyment may take place with a regular client or *Ghar janwai.* Sex is enjoyed in different postures with a person with whom emotional sentiments are developed. Children born to FSWs are from such persons. Sexual satisfaction is, thus, confined to specific persons and not with all types of clients. FSWs insist the use of condom for sex, without which they do not entertain the clients. Regular clients are permitted to have sex without condom. Unlike common clients, they may also spend more time with FSWs. Occasional clients are given only 10-15 minutes to be with the FSW.

Knowledge about AIDS

Almost all the respondents have heard about AIDS as a disease. Highways and infrastructure development have promoted the risk of contracting HIV infection commonly referred as AIDS, due to unsafe sex practised by male clients with female commercial sex workers of Nat community. As high as 160 cases of AIDS and more than 50,000 cases of HIV infected patients have been reported in Rajasthan. About 95 per cent of them got infected through heterosexual route, followed by 3 per cent through blood transfusion and 1 per cent through pregnant mothers to their children. Available data about the age distribution shows maximum 41 per cent cases in 21-30 years followed by 36 per cent in 30-40 years and 14 per cent above 41 years of age category. Remaining 6 per cent and 3 per cent belong to 11-20 years and below 10 year age groups respectively. Sero-positive rate of 26 cases per thousand estimated for the state is alarming (Dainik Bhaskar, Jaipur, 22 October, 2000).

The unprotected commercial sex practiced by Nat FSWs compounded the existing situation of AIDS. The perception of FSWs of not getting infected because of commercial sex practised for generations by the Nat women, and indifferent attitude towards safe sex, and ignorance about the transmission of HIV, are the causes for the pathetic state of affairs. They neither go for blood and other investigations nor are motivated for it by the officials and NGOs. But these days, condoms which are accessible are stated to be invariably used while having sex with the clients. It was also revealed by some FSWs that to attain sexual pleasure or to conceive child, condom was not used with persons like permanent clients, clients of choice, *Ghar janwai* etc.

With the connectivity and convenient reach, government and NGOs have been carrying out AIDS awareness campaign and other activities to prevent the transmission of HIV-AIDS. The distribution and use of condoms, counselling and preventive measures are stated to be taken up with FSWs, clients and the community. Information, education and communication (IEC) activities are operationalised through various methods. Availability of electric connections and television sets in some of the houses of Nats has facilitated the communication process. Now, more FSWs are exposed to the information about AIDS, and accordingly they stated to have been taking preventive measures to avoid infections. However, the unsafe sex of the FSWs with some of the clients could not be ruled out. The FSW's personal hygiene and sanitation seem to have improved over the years.

Commercial sex work by Nat women appears to add to prevalence of HIV infection and other sexually transmitted diseases (STDs). Condom is used as a precautionary measure. Without the use of condom, there is always a possibility of minor infection like irritation, burning while urination and boils on the genital organ, say FSWs. It was known that a married man from the village Bandar Sindari, died due to HIV-AIDS in the December 1999.

Source of Information about AIDS

Table 6.1 shows that television is a major source of dissemination of information of AIDS and allied aspects to as many as 55 per cent respondents. It is followed by the peer group of FSWs 18 per cent, staff members of Jeevan Asha Project 15 per cent and healthy highway project 10 per cent. In the case of 2 per cent FSWs, information of AIDS were first time provided with by the *Ghar Janwai.*

Use of Condom

Clients are not entertained by FSWs for sex without using condom. Condom is being used to avoid undesired pregnancy and the infection of AIDS and sexual diseases. However, the FSWs initially insist for the use of condom, but if a client is willing to pay more than her usual rate, the

Table 6.1: Source of Information about AIDS

Sr. No.	*Source*	*%*
1.	T.V.	55
2.	Jeevan Asha Project	15
3.	Healthy Highway Project	10
4.	*Ghar janwai*/Client	2
5.	Retired FSWs	Nil
6.	Peer group of FSWs	18

Source: Field investigation.

proposal may be accepted for having sex without condom. It is likely that insisting for the use of condom may as well be a strategy in some situations to spin more money from the clients. FSWs also provide condom to the clients, who arrive without it for sex. Condom is neither placed nor removed by the FSWs, but if the client insists, then she charges extra amount for it.

The following Table 6.2 indicates that all the FSWs practice sex with *Ghar Janwai* without the condom. About 30 per cent of them had sex without condom with the common clients who paid more than their usual rate for the same.

Table 6.2: Condom Use and Type of Clients

Category	*Yes*	*No*	*Can't say*
Ghar janwai	Nil	100	–
General client	30	70	–

Source: Field investigation.

At Teelawala hamlet after the use, condom is dumped into a container (paper box) placed in the room meant for *Dhandha* by FSWs. The box is thrown away next day morning. FSW uses clean cloth or cotton to clean her genitals or wash with water after intercourse with client. At Dantari hamlet used condoms are disposed of carelessly in open or sometimes in polythene covers. Sometimes, they may be thrown in the backyard of the houses.

Health and Health Care

Nat use both traditional and modern methods of health care. Young generation including FSWs prefer allopathy for an early cure of diseases.

They have favourable attitude towards family planning measure. Nat women have now become vigilant about the diseases like polio, measles, cholera etc. The newly born are now immunized at the appropriate time.

Nats of Dantari hamlet either go to Kishangarh or Dudu for the treatment of disease. For the treatment of worm disease in infants and children, *Heeng ghutti* (a medicinal preparation of asoeftida) is given and also a piece of asoeftida in cloth is tied up on the wrist of infected child. Smell of asoeftida is believed to cure the effect of worms. For diarrhoea, fever etc. a private practitioner from neighbourhood is consulted, but in case of acute disease, private doctor at Jaipur is approached.

To save the child from any evil effect (*Nazar se bachana*), pieces of sandalwood are tied around the neck of the child. To cure the effect of evil eye (one chilly, one pebble and one salt crystal) is waived around the body of child seven times preferably on Saturday evening. After passing under the left leg it is thrown into the hearth. It is done seven times with separate chilly, salt and pebble. It is believed that by doing so the 'evil eye' (*Nazar*) of jealous kin and others would wither away, with the burning of this material into the fire of hearth.

Gutkha (tobacco product) is a very common addiction among Nats irrespective of age, gender and occupation. All the FSWs had addictions. As high as 71.4 per cent were taking *gutkha* and tobacco even before the induction into *dhandha* and 28.6 per cent were also taking liquor in addition to tobacco with advancement in age. These habits are picked up from peer group, elders and clients.

Non-Government Organizations and HIV-AIDS

Involvement of non-government organizations (NGOs) in HIV-AIDS control in India is imperative focusing on key concepts as 'safe sex', 'behaviour change', 'empowerment' and 'community'.

World Vision, India, an international, non-profit, Christian organization dedicated to serve the poor has been working for the development of Nat community in the hamlets located on national highway-8. Under the Jeevan Asha Project (JAP) a number of activities have been undertaken for the upliftment of Nats in general and for the emancipation of FSW in particular. AIDS awareness campaign for at risk along the population highway is the major task under it. Water reservoir and pipeline to meet the basic needs of drinking water to inhabitants is considered to be the major contribution under Jeevan Asha Project. It is sustainable with participation and ownership by the community.

Three-fourth marriages of Nat girls solemnized in the year 1999-2000 were considered to be the achievement of workers of NGO. The girls sent off to live married life with their husbands were prevented from becoming FSWs.

Discussion and Summary

Ethnic Identity Crisis

Nat community claiming themselves to be the descendents of Rajputs are likely to face the severe crisis related to ethnic identity. About half of their women are commercial sex workers who cannot marry within Nat community and are socially permitted to have children without marriage from non-Nat clients, lovers, *ghar janwai* live-in, with whom so called symbolic marriage is solemnized. The maternal uncle of children looks after the children born to his sister, from non-Nat male belonging to any caste and religion, playing the role of sociological father. Due to the Nat females pursuing *dhandha* not permitted to marry within the caste, and their dwindling number, has forced Nat males to search for their brides from analogous community known as the Kanjar. With the matrimonial alliances of Nat with Kanjar caste, the increasing number of Kanjar women, mostly other than those married to Nats, are becoming FSWs and migrating to pursue *dhandha* on the highway hamlets of Nats. Kanjar girls are accepted as daughters-in-law, but Nats do not marry off their daughters to boys of Kanjar caste, considered lower in the social hierarchy. The caste endogamy of Nat is disappearing very fast. Clan remains an exogamous group. Heavy bride price is practised amongst the Nat and Kanjar caste too. In addition to children born from FSWs, the marriage of Nat males with Kanjar girls and births given by them may create the crisis of ethnic identity of Nat in due course of time.

The process of socialization by parents, and prevailing culture equip girl children mentally to accept *dhanda,* institutionalized in the Nat community. *Dhandha* is stated to be inherited, nurtured, transmitted and practised by their women over the generations. A girl by the age of 12 to 13 years is persuaded by the members of family and kinship that becoming a FSW is good for economic, social and emotional reasons, while marrying off and going to live with husband and in-laws elsewhere would not be beneficial. The charms of a comfortable life with all facilities and freedom coupled with the 'demonstration effect' of elderly FSWs life style in the surroundings ultimately act as predominant factors which influences girls' mind to accept the *dhandha*. The family conditions, economic, traditional and social factors, are considered to be responsible for the practice of *dhandha* by the women. However, female sex workers perceive married life to be better, as married women not in *dhandha,* attain relatively better status in the Nat community. An elderly woman retired from the occupation of commercial sex, plays vital role in making a girl female sex worker. The custom of *nath utrai* symbolically removal of nose ring, refers to an act of intercourse initiated first time with the girl by a client who pays maximum amount amongst the contenders for the purpose. Many rituals are performed and community feast is organized on the occasion.

Nat girls from Rajasthan opted for commercial sex referred as *dhandha* as per the norms of caste panchayat. They were invariably inducted into it by the age of 16 years, although few started commercial sex before 16 years. A girl child is perceived fit physically and mentally to pursue commercial sex after the onset of puberty by the Nats. A FSW practise indiscriminate heterogeneous commercial sex with clients for about two decades in her career. The Nat FSWs belonging to the hamlet may deal with the clients directly, while those in migrants from elsewhere, operate under the supervision and management of *patelan*/retired sex worker. The *patelan* keeps the migrant FSW at her home on lump sum monthly commission basis, as per the contract between them. A few of them are able to catch hold of regular client turned lover, who may stay with live-in relationship (*ghar janwai*) for some period with her. They also intend to become the mistress of some willing person for security reasons, in the old age, but rarely accepted as regular wife by the males. It is the responsibility of brother's family and other dependents to look after her in old age, who have been fed by her through her income as sex worker.

FSWs are conscious and sensitive about the body and beauty to attract the clients. Unlike married women of Nats, they are differentiated in terms of cosmetics, dress pattern and life style. There is no specific diet intake by the FSWs except the traditional items like *ladoo* with herbs and dry fruit ingredients which are consumed after delivery by other Nat and Hindu caste women. Delivery is preferred in private nursing home and private medical practitioners are contacted for the allopathic treatment of general diseases. Sexually transmitted diseases and reproductive tract infections are not reported for the adverse effect on *dhandha*. Local home remedies and other ritualistic methods too are practised by the women including for their children's ailments. Most of the Nat, irrespective of age and gender, are addicted to tobacco available in the form of *gutkha* everywhere.

FSWs have heard and know about AIDS, causes of its transmission and preventive measure for safe sex. Condoms supplied by government and NGOs are kept by them. They are able to use the condom with casual clients for penetrative sex, but not with the lovers, *ghar janwai* and other clients who pay more to have sex without condom for the pleasure. In fact, penetrative sex is merely an act of earning to FSWs, with majority of clients. A FSW besides the sex worker is also a woman with biological desire for sex who intends to become the mother for her security and to lead family life with her own children. She conceives from the clients of her choice to give birth to children which is socially permitted in the Nat community.

Migration of Nat women in search of *dhandha* and for more income, to Mumbai has emerged as a trend over the years. The sex traders, intermediaries and net work of operators provide patronage to such women. They are assisted in finding out employment of dancing and subsequently commercial sex with clients in hotels and elsewhere in Mumbai. The major impact of highways, infrastructure development and connectivity has been in terms of the increase in number of clients. FSWs mainly go to Mumbai where they pursue the sex profession in hotel, brothels and private flats hired on rent. Such migrated women worked as cabaret, hotel dancer and sex workers. An investment in terms of providing facilities like T.V. sets and music systems, fridge to provide cold drinks, chilled bear and wine to clients in the hamlets by some local FSWs is also being made. In the changing scenario, the easy mobility of Nat FSWs and clients, has facilitated promiscuous and unprotected sex by them. The role of police is said to be protective as well as problematic to the female sex workers in Mumbai as well as in native hamlets. It has been informally reported that police personnel enjoyed sex with FSW without paying for it, by way of a bribe.

Mass awareness campaign against AIDS and the practice of safe sex launched by Government of India at different levels has to be increased. The Nat FSW being illiterate and ignorant need to be made aware of the fact that even one time unsafe sex with infected clients may cause STD/RTI/AIDS. They need to be convinced about safe sex each time, irrespective of the type of clients. Congenial atmosphere in the community and proper rapport building with FSWs are indispensable. Although modern IEC media have significant role in bringing about mass awareness against AIDS, but its translation into the practice should be ensured.

It is imperative to provide economic activities to Nat males who are dependent on the earnings of their female sex workers. They remain idle and make the FSW economically responsible to fulfil family and social liabilities.

Adolescent girls could be encouraged for marriage after attaining their legal age of marriage. To delay their marriage, adolescent girls be given opportunities to participate in educational, recreational, cultural and skill development activities. In fact, retired FSWs, *Patelan* perform socialization of a female child to become FSW and train her for the sexual behaviour in *dhandha*. The adolescent girls should be made to learn and realize the adverse affect of sex profession in changing conditions for the happy and healthy life of youngsters in future.

This would require alternate employment and security to old women under pension and such other schemes of the Government of Rajasthan. Sex traders and *Patelan*, pimp, intermediaries associated with hotel, transport, tourism industry etc. in the urban areas, are the challenge. Nats assisting female sex workers for *dhandha* need to be provided alternate employment to abandon the sex trade.

Police and administration ought to be clear in their task and role, towards the commercial sex activities. Clients too need to be educated to understand the effects of commercial sex to change their sexual behaviour and practices accordingly. The coordinated and concentrated efforts of police officials, NGOs and representatives of Nat caste may help attain the desired goals.

The traditional caste panchayat is the strong and effective local political institution, which governs the socio-sexual behaviour of Nats. It perhaps requires rethinking in the changing scenario by the caste panchayat members and '*Panchs*', the social elite. It is equally important to emphasize that Nat women are sex workers not due to the social sanction of the caste panchayat alone. It is more so due to the patriarchy and freedom to males to have sex outside their homes and families. The existing situation calls for the integration of Nat caste with the mainstream society to become the beneficiary of development schemes, getting preferential treatment as backward community. It is a matter of disability and rehabilitation.

7

Sexual Behaviour of Persons Attending HIV-AIDS Counselling OPD

S.V. GANDHAM

Introduction

Counselling plays very crucial role in the prevention of HIV infection and the role of such centre is to bring about an attitudinal change and enhance the decision making skill of individuals in order to prevent the spread of HIV-AIDS through high risk sexual behaviour. The study on sexual behaviour of persons attending the HIV-AIDS education and counselling centre in Pune was conducted during which a total of 218 individuals visited the centre.

Of the 218 subjects majority 72 per cent of the visitors were males, the number of females was significantly high 28 per cent as compared to the earlier figures. The mean age of males and females were 30.6 and 25.6 years respectively and the range of age group was from 17 to 57 years. Only 9, 6.3 per cent individuals were illiterate, of whom 5 were females. Almost 75 per cent of the respondents were from Pune. The predominant occupations were service and labour. Almost three-fourth of the study population had a monthly income below Rs. 5000.

There were 29, 20 per cent individuals who reported only once, and their HIV status could not be ascertained. Nearly 60 per cent of the total 144 individuals were married of whom 46 were HIV positive. Of the 43 unmarried male individuals, 10 were infected. There were 10 widows, 5 of whom were infected. Of the total 40 women, 22 were infected. One female, a CSW and one male counterpart of an infected female respondent died of AIDS during the study period. 73 per cent of the total 68 infected individuals were symptomatic. Weakness, weight loss and fever were the most commonly reported symptoms. Family and social support was available to most of those who were infected.

There was a wide range of high risk sexual behaviour including visit to CSW, female friend, multiple unprotected sex with known and unknown females, bisexuality, homosexuality, oral as well as anal sex (receptive as well as insertive). Visit to CSW was the commonest as reported by 59, 60.2 per cent males. 17-22 years was the frequent age range of first experimentation with sex. Majority of those who reported extramarital sex had premarital sex with CSWs. Several respondents felt that visiting non-CSW was safe and condom was unnecessary. Among those 8 respondents who reported bisexuality, childhood sexual experience was a major determinant.

Condom use rate in study population was only 22 per cent and most of the users did not use it consistently. However, among those who were HIV negative, most of them used condoms consistently. Unmarried and young males were most likely to use condoms than married men. The main reasons for non-use of condoms were dislike and fear of suspicion by wife. Education was a major determinant influencing condom use.

Awareness of AIDS in the study population was quite good in most of the areas except STDs and their relation to HIV-AIDS. However, many respondents reported lack of adequate and timely counselling and improper or unnecessary referral. Thus, study recommends that 'Premarital counselling' is a vital element in the preventive components of HIV-AIDS and its scope should be explored. Health care infrastructure existing in the form of primary health centres and sub-centres should be strengthened and basic diagnostic facilities, trained manpower to deal with 'counselling' and referral services should be provided on priority.

The most rapid spread of HIV has been documented in the state of Maharashtra. Pune city, once known for its historical, cultural and educational background is today gripped with the HIV-AIDS pandemic. A recent study by Brookmyer *et al.* (YEAR) demonstrated that the sero-incidence rate in Pune, the eighth largest city in India, was as high as 18 per cent per year among patients attending two sexually transmitted disease (STD) clinics in the city. Recent data from Pune (YEAR) has shown a relatively high prevalence rate among 'low risk', married, monogamous women whose only risk factor was sexual contact with a husband who had experienced an STD. Past prevention strategies focused solely on women in sex work and have ignored women at risk for HIV due to their subordinate social status. Research on sexual attitudes and practices amongst the diverse ethnic, cultural, religious and socio-economic groups in India is limited. There is an urgent need to understand the sexual behaviour of individuals who have had history of STDs, multiple sexual partners or both and hence the present study attempted to investigate the sexual behaviour of persons attending the HIV-AIDS education and counselling centre in Sassoon General Hospital, Pune with the objectives to study the range of sexual behaviours of the attendees, their perceptions regarding vulnerability to HIV-AIDS and the pattern of condom use with special reference to HIV-AIDS.

The research questions to which answers were sought were: What are the factors contributing to the type of sexual behaviour of the respondents? What are the various sexual preferences and ways of achieving sexual pleasure? What is the frequency, duration and reason for condom use? Does HIV status affect the sexual behaviour of these individuals?

Methodology

The present study was conducted using a combination of qualitative and quantitative methods to collect data. The principle method adopted for data collection was through in-depth interviews during the counselling sessions at the HIV-AIDS education and counselling centre.

Of the total 218 visitors (169 males and 49 females) who attended the counselling centre during the period of 6 months between March and August 2000, 74 visitors (65 males and 9 females, who primarily reported to Sassoon for other reasons not related to HIV-AIDS) were not included in the analysis. Thus the final study group consisted of 144 subjects of whom 104 were males and 40 were females. Information on household composition, residence infrastructure, economic status, marital history and reason for visit to the centre was collected from all 144 subjects.

Considering the past experience of the centre where over 50 per cent individuals report only once and never turn up for a second visit, maximum information was collected from the attendees at the first visit.

A pre-tested semi-structured interview schedule was used to collect basic demographic data and data on knowledge about AIDS and sexually transmitted diseases (STD) and symptomology. Attendees were encouraged to come for monthly follow-up or as and when required. Repeated visits by participants allowed for multiple interview sessions which were possible in the case of 68, 47 per cent of the 144 attendees. Information on sexual behaviours, sexual preferences, HIV status, family support and treatment seeking behaviours (in cases of HIV positive individuals) was obtained through in-depth interviews for which an interview guide mentioning the key areas to be probed was used. Some case studies were also made.

Details of sexual behaviour including the range of sexual activity, sexual desires and means to satisfy them, situations leading to high risk behaviour, vulnerability to HIV-AIDS, worries, fears and/or guilt about sex were obtained wherever possible and relevant. In addition, a focus group discussion with a group of 7 youth, all bachelor males was also conducted to enrich the data on issues related to sexual behaviour, magnitude of problem of HIV-AIDS in community, commonly used sex related terminologies and ideas about treatment and prevention of HIV-AIDS.

Detailed field notes were made immediately after the interviews and counselling sessions. Every effort was made to record narratives, exact words and views expressed by the persons. Data were carefully transcribed later.

Manual and computer assisted analysis were done for quantitative and qualitative data with a focus was on objectives and research questions framed earlier. Qualitative data were coded and analyzed thematically. Knowledge and type of counselling received (wherever applicable) were graded.

The organizational framework consisted of 2 specialists in Preventive medicine, 2 medical social workers and a trainer. The study was approved by the Institutional Ethics Committee and informed/written consent of the attendees was obtained.

Study Setting

Established in October 1992, the OPD No. 58 (popularly known as the HIV-AIDS counselling centre) is located in Sassoon General Hospital, Pune and is managed by the department of Preventive and Social Medicine of B.J. Medical College between 9.00 a.m. and 12.00 noon everyday. It is located between the medicine OPD and the pathology laboratory. One doctor and a medical social worker provide counselling services to all persons attending the centre. Voluntary HIV testing facility is also provided at a nominal fee of Rs. 10 through Microbiology Department. The average OPD attendance varies between 25-50 persons per month. The visitors include known HIV positive cases (symptomatic as well as asymptomatic), AIDS cases, relatives and friends of patients, individuals with high risk behaviour and occasionally some indoor patients.

Over 90 per cent of the attendees are males. People come from Pune and also from neighbouring districts of Ahmednager, Solapur, Satara, Beed, Latur, Dhule and Nasik. Sometimes, migrants from Karnataka, Rajasthan and Andhra Pradesh also report at the centre.

Results and Discussion

Profile of the Participants

A total of 218 persons visited the counselling centre during the period of 6 months from March-August 2000. Out of these, 74 persons (65 males and 9 females), mostly from Pune, visited the centre to get information on AIDS. Their visit to the centre reflects the awareness and concern about the disease in the general population.

The remaining 144 individuals were the ones who had specially come to the centre for some problem directly related to HIV-AIDS. There were 104, 72 per cent males and 40, 28 per cent females. The mean age of males was 30.6 years while that of the females was 25.6 years. The youngest attendee was 17 years old while the oldest was 57 years old (both males). Majority of them 45.2 per cent were between the age group 25-35 years.

Only 9 attendees 6.3 per cent were illiterate of whom 5 were females. There were 22, 15.3 per cent individuals who had higher education (diploma/degree) of whom only 3 were females.

Majority of the respondents were from Pune district of which 85 were from Pune city. Out of the 35 individuals from neighbouring districts (Beed, Latur, Nagar, Solapur, Nasik), 24 were from rural areas.

Among the males, service was the predominant occupation, which was followed by labour class. The labour class consisted of migrant construction workers. Of the 40 females, 70 per cent were housewives. The sample also included other categories like a professional thief, a CSW, a maid servant and 3 institutional destitutes.

Family income was revealed by 140 individuals, of whom 86 had a monthly income of less than Rs. 1000. Seventeen had income between Rs. 3000 and Rs. 5000 and 37 had a monthly income of over Rs. 5000. Nearly half of the attendees 48.6 per cent belonged to a nuclear family setup while 41 per cent were from joint family setup and about 10 per cent lived singly.

A little over half, 54.8 per cent were married and 30 per cent were unmarried of whom 4 unwed mothers. Eleven individuals had separated because of their HIV positive status. Among the female respondents, there were 10 widows (husband died of HIV-AIDS).

The sex-wise distribution of the participants as per their HIV status is given below:

Table 7.1: Sex-wise Distribution According to HIV Status

HIV Status	*Males*		*Females*		*Total*	
	No.	*%*	*No.*	*%*	*No.*	*%*
HIV positive	46	31.8	22	15.4	68	47.2
HIV negative	32	22.1	9	6.3	41	28.4
Unknown status	20	13.8	9	6.3	29	20.1
HIV test not indicated	6	4.3	–	–	6	4.3
Total	**104**	**72.0**	**40**	**28.0**	**144**	**100.0**

Source: Field Investigation.

Views on Reporting at the Counselling Centre

A Majority of them said that it was difficult to come again to the centre and unless something serious happened, they would prefer to get tested at their place of residence only. Though, they expressed their satisfaction over the counselling and advice received, they were not willing to stay in Pune or come again merely for the HIV report. There were another 11 individuals from Pune city who did not report again. They expressed their view that rather than waiting in queues to receive a report after 3-5 days, they would get themselves tested at a private facility.

Table 7.2: Number of Visits by the Attendees

Number of Visits	*%*
One	52.8
Two	22.9
> Two	24.3

Source: Field Investigation.

Consistent presence of the same counsellors over a long time helped in building rapport which could be one of the major reasons for more number of follow up visits by the people. Majority of those who reported frequently (4 or more times) expressed that attending the supportive counselling sessions made them feel better. Of the 18 individuals who reported four or more times, 12 were HIV negative. They came for testing either to rule out window period or to discuss about sex related issues.

One of them said that it was difficult to control himself despite attending two counselling sessions and reported having sex with a CSW but had used two condoms. Though it is difficult to give up certain behaviour suddenly, a change from 'high risk' to 'low risk' could be considered a positive indicator of behaviour change as reflected in this case.

Condom Use, HIV Status and Related Determinants

Findings of the 98 males and 40 females in relation to condom use in the context of HIV-AIDS are given separately as follows:

> Condom use among the male population was only 22 per cent. Of the 22 individuals who reported condom use in high risk sexual behaviour, 16 used it consistently. In the non-user group (n = 76) 55.3 per cent were infected with HIV. The influence of 'age and education' on the pattern of condom use revealed the following:
>
> Of those who reported consistent condom use, most were below 25 years of age and unmarried. Married individuals were hesitant to use condom with spouses.

In the 'never used' category, a similar trend was observed 78.0 per cent were above 25 years of age. The younger generation, most of them being unmarried and aware of the consequences of HIV-AIDS could be 'playing safe' as compared to the married and elderly population where usually there is an inhibition to use condom with spouse except as contraception. Educational status of those who always reported condom use was significantly higher than those who did not.

One respondent even said, "if I am going to die of AIDS, my wife should also die with me, then why should I think of protecting her". Another one said that their religion (Muslim) does not permit to use condom in marital sex.

Occasional users said that influence of alcohol and sometimes non-availability of condoms with CSWs were the reasons for not using condoms.

Influence of HIV Status on Subsequent Condom Use

HIV status, either positive or negative did have an impact of subsequent condom use though long term impact could not be assessed. Most of the individuals who were reported negative on subsequent follow up said that they had stopped visiting CSWs. A few said that they reduced their frequency of visiting CSWs and used two condoms or good quality condoms purchased from outside. This pattern was peculiar of unmarried youth but amongst the married males, several found it difficult to use condoms with wives, either because they had not revealed their positive status or because they feared that their wife could suspect something if they suddenly started using condoms. A few reported started using condoms with wife and some even said that they had stopped having sex with wife and practised masturbation. 38 out of the 40 female participants reported that their partners never used a condom. Many of these females were not aware of the infected status of their spouses and even when they knew his status, they could not say 'No'. They reported that the frequency of sex had declined after knowing their positive status. Out of the 40 females, 4 were unwed mothers and they had engaged in unprotected sex.

Of the two, who reported condom use, one revealed that her husband started using condom after both were infected as she frequently had fowl smelling vaginal discharge and was under treatment. The other who reported condom use by partner said that she had separated from her husband due to his infective status and was having sexual relationship with a married person, who was her current partner. One of the females, a CSW, reported non-use of condoms by majority of her clients.

These findings bring out the need for a females barrier method as a preventive measure.

Sexual Behaviour in the Context of HIV-AIDS

A. Visit to a Commercial Sex Worker

Out of 98 males, 60.2 per cent had a history of visiting a CSW for sex. Most of the sexual encounters with CSWs were 'unprotected'. Details of sexual behaviour with CSWs revealed the following: The age at first visit to CSW was between 17-22 years. One respondent had visited a CSW as early as 13-14 years. Other two went there out of curiosity but were driven out by the CSW because they were too young. Very few respondents said that they had been to a CSW only once. Minor sexual problems did not have an effect on the frequency of visits to CSWs. Recent knowledge of HIV status, counselling and ill health were the reasons for reduced or no visits to CSWs.

One respondent, an elderly male in his fifties went to CSWs frequently but said that he never had sex with any. He restricted himself only to fondling their breasts, kissing, hugging and sharing their company.

The number of CSWs with whom the male respondents had sex varied greatly. Few people reported having sex only once or twice with only one CSW. Most of them (n = 32) reported having sex with 3-5 CSWs and some reported having sex with up to 20 or more. Peno-vaginal unprotected sex was the most common type of sexual practice reported by majority of the respondents. Second common practice was anal sex. Some respondents reported oral sex. Fellatio was practiced by a very few selected CSWs and it was referred to as 'free-in-shot' in the red light area. CSWs demanded more money from clients for this act. Kissing, fondling and sucking breasts of CSWs were commonly practiced by most of the male respondents. The amount of money charged by CSWs for sex was usually between Rs. 50-100, which was affordable. Some said that their friends occasionally paid for them and others said that they did not have to pay the CSW because of acquaintance. CSWs charged more for spending the whole night with the client. Majority of the individuals were married and had visited CSWs before marriage and continued to visit them even after marriage. There were only two male respondents who had no history of premarital sex and had visited a CSW only after marriage.

It appears from the findings that having sex with a CSW was common among unmarried married men and hence targeted interventions should be specifically directed to adolescents and youth.

B. Visit to Non-CSWs (Known/Unknown Females)

Nineteen respondents reported having sex with someone other than a sex worker. Most of them visited known females who were either friends or a neighbour's wife or women who entertained people through some contact person. Three respondents, drivers by occupation, said that such women were available at road side eateries along the highways.

The respondents believed that since these women were not like the CSWs from red light area, there was no risk in having unprotected sex with them but contrary to their belief, most of them were infected with HIV. Most of them referred to such women as their private property or *saamaan*.

One respondent felt that having too much sex with wife would affect her figure and beauty hence he went to CSWs. Nobody said that marital disharmony was responsible for their extra marital relations. In general, the reasons for ever having sex with CSWs or other women were: peer pressure, fun and enjoying sex, difficult to give up the habit, lack of privacy at home, wife away for delivery, nature of job that forced them to stay away from family, and to test sexual ability before marriage etc. Only one respondent said that his father encouraged him to have sex with CSWs. Some felt that it was due to the influence of movies.

C. Bisexuality

Of the total 98 males who reported some or the other risky sexual behaviour, 8 reported of having experienced bisexuality. Of these eight, 3 were HIV positive, 4 were negative and HIV status of one could not be ascertained. All the 3 infected individuals were married and had children. They had experienced sex with males during their childhood and continued this behaviour after marriage. Two of them preferred to remain active partners while the third male preferred to remain a passive partner and enjoyed oral and anal sex. Wife of one of the 3 respondents was positive while the status of the wives of the other 2 respondents could not be ascertained. The remaining were all unmarried males in their twenties. They preferred sex with CSWs, three of whom used condom occasionally and five had never used a condom in MSM activity. Of these, 2 were hotel boys who preferred to be active partners. One was both, an active as well as passive partner and the other 2 who were engaged in sex with male friends occasionally.

D. Homosexuality

There was only one student aged 21 years who said that he was very intimately attached to a childhood friend. Since the age of 9 years they used to fondle each other's genitals. This habit became more enjoyable during puberty. They enjoyed mutual masturbation had not had sex with any other person. Recently, after having heard of HIV-AIDS, the fear of getting the disease made him report to the centre for testing. Both had unprotected, oral as well as anal sex, with each other, as active or passive partners.

E. Unprotected Sex with Known HIV Infected Partner

There were 8 married monogamous women, who reported sex with infected spouses. Six of them were detected HIV-AIDS positive and in the remaining 2, the HIV status could not be ascertained due to non-reporting. The reasons given for unprotected sex were: Inability to refuse sex, forceful sex and consequences not known. One female said that despite having knowledge of husband's AIDS status, she volunteered to have repeated unprotected sex as a suicidal attempt and even consumed poison to end life.

Table 7.3: HIV Status of Participants and Sexual Behaviour

Type of predominant sexual behaviour	*HIV Status*		
	Unknown	*Positive*	*Negative*
Sex with CSW	11	25	23
Sex with known parters (non-CSW)	3	23	6
Sex with multiple unknown persons	3	13	3
Bisexuality	1	3	4
Homosexuality	0	0	1
Sex with known infected partner	2	6	0

Source: Field Investigation.

Majority of the respondents 85 per cent with history of high risk sexual behaviour reported only one type of risk behaviour while 21 individuals reported 2 or more types of high risk sexual behaviour. Four gave history of injections or blood transfusion out of whom 2 were HIV positive. Only one individual gave 'sharing razors' as the reason for his positive status.

Majority of those who had no history of high risk sexual behaviour were the monogamous spouses of infected individuals of whom 14 were positive and 9 were with unknown status. One infected male denied engaging in any risk behaviour.

The respondents felt that having sex with sex worker, with unknown females, with known female with loose character, oral and anal sex, kissing female genitals and other body parts, sucking breast of CSWs, handling or nursing HIV infected relative/spouse, taking injections from local doctors could make one vulnerable to HIV. One infected male who denied any high risk behaviour said that his wife had undergone multiple hospital procedures during her pregnancy including family planning operation which could be the reason for his infection and another one felt that since his house was inhabited by an AIDS patient previously, he could be vulnerable to HIV.

Sexual Satisfaction—Alternative Means, Fears and Myths about Sex

Information on obtaining sexual gratification apart from visiting CSWs revealed that masturbation was commonly practised by unmarried males.

Most married males did not enjoy masturbation. One respondent felt that his penis would 'shrink' if he frequently practiced masturbation. Two youth thought that it was an abnormal behaviour. Masturbation was also thought to cause weakness. Homosexual behaviour, usually anal was considered as an alternative to satisfy the sexual urge by some respondents. One respondent who was a waiter habitually visited CSWs but when he had night duty or double shifts and no time to come all the way to the town, he preferred to have sex with men. Watching pornographic pictures/ movies, or reading pornographic books or simply talking about sex with friends were some of the means which some male respondents resorted to for satisfy their sexual desire. A few respondents said that they tried to suppress the sex desire by engaging themselves in work.

Presenting Symptoms/Complaints as Reported by Respondents

It was noted that some HIV negative individuals reported symptoms similar to those reported by a positive person. 67 per cent reported some symptom. Some of the common symptoms irrespective of the HIV status were as follows:

Table 7.4: Distribution of Respondents According to Presenting Symptoms

Common symptoms (complaints)	*Number of individuals*
Weakness and/or weight loss	58(40.3%)
Fever (with/without chills)	38 (26.4%)
Genital (discharge, ulcers, lesions)	33 (22.9%)
Respiratory (cough, breathlessness etc.)	26 (18.1%)
Abdominal (loose motions, pain)	19 (13.2%)
Anorexia (loss of appetite)	8 (5.6%)
Skin (herpes, molluscum etc.)	8 (5.6%)
Other (vague) sweating, insomnia etc.	8 (5.6%)

Source: Field Investigation.

Sixty four individuals reported two or more complaints of whom 37 were infected. There were 80 individuals with only one complaint, of whom 31 were infected. 18, 26.4 per cent out of the total 68 infected individuals reported no symptoms.

Some Issues about HIV Positive Individuals

Majority of the respondents reported for counselling within 6 months of getting detected HIV positive. A few (11 out of 68) reported between 6 months to one year and 7 reported after one year mainly with symptoms serious enough to require hospitalization.

Experience with Prior Counselling and Referral Services, if Any

An important observation as revealed by most of the respondents was that they were not told in detail about the HIV test, the implications of positive and negative tests result and the preventive aspects.

There were 19 individuals who had been subjected to HIV test without pretest counselling. Few of these were subjected to repeated tests without being told as to what was being done and why. The reports were not understood by majority of them and there was no post-test counselling. Five individuals were directed to Pune without being told anything. 20 individuals from rural areas were counselled but they were not convinced or dissatisfied with the quality of counselling. They were told that there was 'something wrong' in their blood or were labelled as AIDS cases. One respondent said that the doctor just drove him away from his clinic saying that nothing can be done and he should go to Pune at the earliest. There were 4 pregnant women who were refused admission either for an abortion or delivery and were referred to Pune. One of the infected widows from a village was refused basic supportive treatment in the form of multivitamins and haematinics at the PHC and was told to obtain the same from the Government hospital in Pune.

Almost all 98.6 per cent respondents had heard about AIDS. Only a couple from a rural area said that they had never heard about the disease. They never watched television. The wife was illiterate and husband, though educated till secondary school level never read newspapers or had not even heard it from friends etc. This was a discordant couple (positive husband). Majority of the respondents 88.4 per cent had knowledge about the non-curability of the disease. Similarly, 81.9 per cent said that AIDS was preventable and attributed it to use of condom.

There were many gaps in the knowledge regarding STDs and the relationship of HIV-AIDS with STDs and more than two-thirds 65.3 per cent had no knowledge regarding the same.

A significant proportion of the respondents had good knowledge about transmission of HIV and knew how it did not. When asked if the respondents knew anybody suffering from HIV-AIDS, 85 (59%) said they knew someone. Of these 31 (21.5%) had an infected spouse, 30 (20.8%) had an infected friend, 12 (8.3%) had an infected neighbour, 7(4.9%) knew of some person in the locality, 3 (2.1%) had an infected family member other than the spouse and 2 (1.4%) had an infected relative. Most of them were recently infected.

Condom use was higher in the HIV negative individuals as compared to the infected ones or those with unknown status. Most of the infected individuals who reported for follow up were married. Those who were newly detected or were symptomatic or were residing nearby were most likely to attend the follow-up sessions. HIV negative individuals who reported for follow up were usually young, unmarried and considered it important to rule out widow period through repeated testing.

Table 7.5: Expenditure on Investigations/Treatment and Treatment Seeking Behaviour

Expenditure on Treatment (Rs.)	*No. of Respondents*
Up to 500	20
501 to 1000	9
1001 to 5000	8
> 5000	11

Source: Field Investigation.

The general tendency was to seek 'Private treatment' which was costlier. The highest expenditure was incurred by a male from a neighbouring district who had spent over Rs. 40,000 in Kerala. He was in heavy debt and had borrowed an additional amount of Rs. 10,000 from a friend. Most patients found it difficult to bear the cost of transport, food and stay in Pune. 13 respondents reported being treated for HIV. Three of them had obtained the newspaper cuttings of advertisements claiming cure for AIDS. One couple was taking treatment from a god man. A few were taking some Ayurvedic treatment costing about Rs. 2000-3000/month. Four respondents were on Antiretroviral therapy of which two pregnant women.

Coping up with HIV-AIDS and Family/Social Support

Most of the infected individuals were married males. They had promiscuous behaviour and were coping well with their HIV status. Though the tendency of not revealing infectivity to spouse was seen in some, some had revealed their status to the spouse through counsellors. Monogamous spouses after knowing their infected status expressed shock and broke down. They were more worried about their children and husband than about themselves.

In the case of 9 couples both partners were infected. Inter-spouse support was good and husbands expressed their guilt and said that they were really lucky to have such good and caring wives who looked after them and accepted their HIV positive status. There were very few couples who were rejected by relatives and neighbours. Two widows were driven out by the in-laws and were staying with their parents. Many were escorted by relatives and friends especially those who came from places outside Pune, indicating 'Social Support'. Professional counselling helped patients a great deal. Family members of few infected members cared for them but kept their belongings (utensils, bed, soap etc.) separately.

Findings of FGD

All the participants agreed that HIV-AIDS was a burning problem and all had seen people die of AIDS in their locality. They expressed that friends/ peers influenced risk taking behaviour. Most participants were jobless and had ample free time. They felt that such 'frustrating period in life' led many to engage in high risk behaviour. Almost all had seen/visited a red light area. Of these, the one who was eldest had experienced sex. According to them people with AIDS had weakness, fever, cough or loose motions for many days and become thin day by day. Their perception of CSWs was that they were bad women who wore a lot of makeup, shiny clothes, had loose hair and solicited clients by certain gestures. Some respondents said that if they were forced by friends to have sex with CSWs they would go ahead and experience it at least once but would use a condom. All of them believed that there were some Ayurvedic preparations available in the market. They knew of a treatment centre in Cochin. Some talked of god-men curing AIDS. None of them had ever received any formal Sex Education. They all felt that sex education should be given in schools.

Summary/Conclusions

The study has highlighted the increasing burden and complexities of the AIDS epidemic. The range of individuals attending the centre even without any apparent reason, speaks of the general awareness and concern about HIV-AIDS in the community. Majority of the individuals were below 30 years and most of them had experienced sex between 17 to 22 years of age. The commonest source of receiving information about sex and HIV was through friends or television. Condom use was only 22 per cent and most of the users did not use it consistently. Condom use within marriage was virtually absent. Although visiting CSWs was the commonest sexual behaviour, sex with known and unknown females, bisexuality, homosexuality, oral sex, insertive and receptive anal sex were reported in the study. Majority of the infected individuals were symptomatic. Weakness, weight loss and fever were the commonest reported symptoms. Lack of adequate and timely counselling and improper/unnecessary referral were reported by many respondents. There was some awareness about AIDS attendees but information on STDs was lacking. Most of the infected individuals reported adequate family and social support. Inter-spouse support was commonly reported as a major factor in coping up with the disease.

Recommendations

'Premarital counselling' is important in prevention of HIV and its scope needs be explore l. Family Life Education to adolescents should be given on a large scale, especially in the rural areas. Condom promotion should focus on married individuals, especially those attending STD clinics. The health-care infrastructure existing in the form of primary health centres and sub-centres should be strengthened and basic diagnostic facilities, trained manpower to deal with 'counselling' and referral services should be provided. 'Support groups' should be considered as valuable resources to increase awareness and bring about behavioural change in the needy population.

8

Condom Use among Married and Unmarried Males

ALKA BARUA

"For most men the 'real thing' is penetrative vaginal sex without essentially associating love, caring and tenderness, which is associated with sexual relations within marriage. While most women wished to regulate their fertility through planned and limited pregnancies, men were not supportive of such interference with 'natural processes'. However, women's expectations and experiences highlighted pleasure associated with non-penetrative sexual behaviours of intimacy. Safer sex messages are limited to promotion of condoms for risk reduction and prevention of infection. But married partner's risk perception in terms of STIs and HIV is low if not totally absent. Messages about condom use thus seemed irrelevant to respondents" (Mane & Maitra, 1992).

Introduction

Over a period of time, focus has shifted from the use of condom for contraception to prevention of STDs and AIDS, and most efforts are directed towards creating awareness among high risk groups. However, evidence from different studies indicates that the focus has to include all sexual partnerships including marriage. The present study has focused on understanding awareness about condoms, their use/non-use within and outside marriage and reasons for the same among married and unmarried males.

The study was conducted in the Bardolpura area of Ahmedabad, Gujarat with the help of multiple data collection methods. Qualitative data was collected through semi-structured interviews with both married 30 and unmarried men 30 and also through focus group discussions. A quantitative survey of 150 married and 150 unmarried men was carried out using a pre-designed format.

The study found that more than 95 per cent of respondents had reported having heard of condom. The study further indicated that there were number of beliefs and misconceptions regarding the use of condom where they felt it necessary to use only with commercial sex workers in case of heterosexual relations. As a result only 7 per cent of married and 32 per cent of unmarried men who had sexual relations with girl friends reported using condoms. Nearly 50 per cent of married and unmarried men who visited CSW reported to have used condoms for protection from AIDS, fear of STIs etc. Nearly 40 per cent of the married men had used condom with their wives for variety of reasons which include spacing 82 per cent if being with another women 8 per cent and suffering from STIs 3 per cent themselves, while only 15 per cent of unmarried men used condom during sexual contact with other men and eunuchs. The medical shop 57-90 per cent, government hospitals 39-61 per cent FPAI workers 23-37 per cent were the main sources while *pan* shops, guest houses, provisional stores were the others sources of getting condom. Easy availability, reliability, protection and prevention were mentioned for the use of condom while reduced pleasure, non availability, spontaneous decision etc. were some of the reasons for non-use of the condom. When enquired about the advantages of condom, they mentioned it to prevent pregnancy 80 per cent, spacing 72 per cent prevent AIDS 60 per cent and prevent STDs 38 per cent. When enquired about their awareness regarding STD and AIDS, nearly 76 per cent to 87 per cent of unmarried and married respondents reported awareness about the signs and symptoms respectively. Both married and unmarried respondents mentioned that sex with CSW 38 per cent, body heat 23-38 per cent were the reasons for getting STD while sex with CSW 86-92 per cent, blood transfusion 25 per cent were some of the main sources of getting AIDS.

It could be concluded from the study that although it appeared that more than 95 per cent were aware about the condom and AIDS there was an apparent belief that condom was necessary only with CSWs. There has been lack of information on steps involved in condom use and information on the desirable use of condom in all sexual relations. Alternative methods of service delivery and lack of attention to unmarried sexually active group of males appear to be some of the limitations of the current programme. Dissatisfaction during use and disposal problems need to be considered seriously for acceptance and continuation of use of condom. The study recommends awareness programme focusing on unmarried youth about use of condoms in all sexual relationships.

Historically condom has been promoted and therefore seen as a 'male contraceptive' method. The rise and fall of popularity of 'condom' was parallel to that of 'male contraceptives' in the Indian government's population control programme. Immediately after Independence, the programme (later named as 'Family Planning' and 'Family Welfare programme') stressed on male methods of contraception and promoted condom use and vasectomy. With development and appearance of temporary contraceptives for women, the emphasis shifted to female methods such as Intra-uterine contraceptive devices and the use of condoms gradually reduced. The continued rise in population alarmed the programme planners and therefore came a phase of promotion of permanent contraception, mainly through male and female sterilization. The period of 'national emergency' in 1975-76 is blacklisted in this regard with thousands of forced vasectomies. This negative image once again shifted the focus of the programme to permanent female methods. This scenario persisted for the next two decades. The promotion and use of permanent female methods eclipsed the use of male methods, particularly male spacing methods like 'condoms'. To be fair, the non-acceptance of 'condoms' was equally a result of its perceived shortcomings, i.e. reduction of sexual pleasure (Dr. M.E. Khan & Bella C. Patel).

However, with the appearance of HIV-AIDS on the health scene, the role of 'condoms' in halting the galloping progress of the infection became a critical component of the 'control' programme. Thus came the next shift in the promotion and use of condom.

Until this time, the utility of condom was as a 'barrier' to conception and not to 'infection' (Apte, 1998). With the increase in information inflow about spread of sexually transmitted infections, HIV-AIDS and acceptance of the concept of 'safer sex' that extended beyond contraception, Government of India re-formulated its strategy of 'condom' promotion. It strengthened the existing network for distribution of condoms and launched awareness programme for its new *avatar* (role). Nevertheless, inadvertently the government programme continued to concentrate on the married men. The condom thus re-emerged, albeit with reduced popularity.

This chapter paper attempts to understand how far this strategy has been able to achieve acceptance in the Indian society and why? The chapter is based on a study carried out in the slums of Indian city of Ahmedabad, and suggests some changes in the present policy and the strategies for promotion of condoms in India, given the scenario (FRHS report).

Research Setting, Study Population and Methodology

The study was carried out by Ahmedabad based research organization, Foundation for Research in Health Systems (FRHS) in Bardolpura slum area of Ahmedabad city (Gujarat State, India) in 1999-2000. Ahmedabad is the second largest city in western India with a population of about 3.8 million; out of this about 40 per cent population is located in the slums. The population of Bardolpura slum is about 75,000 and is composed of Hindus, Muslims and Christians. A tertiary care municipal corporation hospital close by, and a range of private practitioners meet the health needs of the slum. Family Planning Association of India (FPAI), a non-government organization has been active in the area since 1997 and has a strong presence there.

The objectives of the study were to find out the awareness about and attitudes towards condoms, their use/non-use in different relationships, the reasons for the same and to examine any signs of recent changes in the attitude and knowledge about condoms.

The data was collected during the first quarter of the year 2000. In all 300 men (150 married and 150 unmarried) selected by systematic random sampling method were covered in the quantitative survey. In addition, 60 men (30 married and 30 unmarried men above 18 years of age) were interviewed in detail to get qualitative information.

There were separate structured schedules for married and unmarried men for quantitative survey as well as separate interview guide for both types of men. The structured schedule and the interview guide covered all the aspects of information relevant to the objectives of the study. A team of six investigators collected the data over a period of six months. The investigators were young men, with Masters Degree in either Social work or Psychology. They were given intensive training in research methodology and data collection before the actual fieldwork.

FRHS approached FPAI for help in doing the fieldwork. The existing rapport of the FPAI health staff with the community and a sensitive approach with complete explanation about the purpose of the study to the target group with an assurance of complete confidentiality helped in gaining easier access to the married men. The unmarried men were approached primarily through the male workers of FPAI who had already worked with youth groups in the community. Youth mandals (clubs) also assisted in getting access to the men.

The data were analysed separately for married and unmarried males. Data from the quantitative survey were analysed using the software EPI

Info. In the article, the findings of the quantitative survey are presented in percentages while the qualitative data are presented as quotes or in numbers.

The Men

The married men were in the age group of 19 to 45 while the unmarried were in the range of 18 to 39 years. The sample was predominantly Hindu; Muslim constituted about a quarter while the Christians formed 1 per cent of the sample. About 19 per cent married men and 11 per cent unmarried men had never been to school. All the married men were employed while about 92 per cent unmarried men were employed. Less than half of both types, 43 per cent had a family income of Rs. 3,000 or less, per month.

Their Sexual Relationships and Use of Condoms

The quantitative survey and interviews recorded mainly four types of sexual relationships:

(a) With girl friends or 'other women' (not commercial sex workers),
(b) With Commercial sex workers (CSW),
(c) With men and eunuchs, and
(d) With wives (in case of married men).

A. Relationship with Girl Friends or 'Other Women'

About 35 per cent of unmarried and 30 per cent of married men reported having girl friends (current as well as in the past). The existence of girl friends did not automatically signify a sexual relationship. The qualitative data revealed that out of nineteen married men who had girl friends, nine had sexual relationship with the girl friend, before and after their marriage.

The frequency of these sexual relations was between once a week to once a month, by both types of respondents, depending on convenience and logistic constraints. The frequency of visits to girl friends in both cases was largely dependant on the frequency of watching blue films or sexually stimulating movies.

Only 7 per cent of the married and 32 per cent of the unmarried men who had sexual relations with girl friends reported using condoms. While majority users used condom to prevent pregnancy, a few used these if the girl friend was menstruating. Overall, the use of condom was very restricted in this relationship, because it was guided by the events that preceded and culminated into sexual intercourse. Some of the respondents mentioned that watching blue films with friends was the first stage in the course of events. Since, the decision to watch blue film was not always pre-planned, these men were not prepared for the encounter, i.e. they did not have condoms with them. One unmarried man recounted his experience:

> "Once I went to meet my girl friend after watching a blue film, but could not meet her. So while coming back I consumed alcohol and met a CSW on the highway. She took me to a Dhaba where I had sex with her. I had no condom with me so I did not use one."

B. Relationship with CSW

About one-third of the unmarried 33 per cent and little more than a quarter 27 per cent of the married respondents reported that they visited commercial sex worker (CSW) regularly, i.e. at least once a month. Almost half of both the types of men claimed using condoms, mainly due to fear of AIDS. A few of them informed that they used condom because CSW asked them to do so. In such cases, the CSW provided the condom and advised them to use it in order to prevent health problems.

Among the few this awareness of STDs/AIDS and need for using condoms came in a little late, and only as result of experience. Suresh, was one such unmarried man,

> "Once I met a CSW on the highway. I was under the influence of alcohol. She took me to a dhaba where we had sex. A few days later I developed a wound on the penis. I consulted my friend regarding this who told me about the need to wear condom while having sex with the sex workers. I was scared when I heard this and after that I never had sex with a CSW."

On the other hand, an alarming 42 per cent of the men said that they would have had intercourse with the CSW even if they did not have a condom as the purpose of the visit is to have sex. One married man, a truck driver argued,

"When we go on highway at night, girls come with a torch so that we know that they are prostitutes. It is their signal to throw torchlight on the moving truck. We then have sex with them under the truck or on the roadside without any inhibitions... We know that Condom use can prevent AIDS but still we do not use it... we carry death with us all the time. Who knows when we will meet with an accident and die, so why not enjoy?"

C. Relationship with Men and Eunuchs

In all 13 per cent unmarried, 7 per cent married men had had sexual relations with another male or a eunuch. In addition, these men had multiple sexual relationships with different sexes. About two-three respondents during in-depth interview informed that the eunuchs paid them for sex. And despite their reservations about sex with eunuchs, they continued to have it for the monetary gains. One such man said,

"I have been with boys and eunuchs many times. I feel that sex with boys is not as enjoyable as with girls. Sometimes, I go on alternate days to eunuchs. I receive about Rs. 200 when I have sex with them. I use this money to pay the CSWs I visit..."

Three-quarters reported having discontinued or no longer having the relationship. Two-thirds 67 per cent because they did not like the experience any more. About a-fifth also mentioned that the relationship was a chance, one time encounter. Either they did not have an opportunity again or they had been afraid to repeat the experience.

All the married men and 85 per cent of the unmarried men who had sexual relations with other men/eunuchs did not use condoms. About a-third of the non-users did not feel it was necessary and another third said that eunuchs do not like these being used. Anil, the respondent who had regular sexual relations with a eunuch said,

"I never use condom with the eunuch because he does not like it. Also, I am not sure whether a sexual relationship with eunuchs can cause AIDS."

Ashok, another unmarried man said,

"All that one gets on having sex with CSWs and men is AIDS. But then eunuchs are those who are neither male nor female.

So, I don't know if one can get AIDS on having sex with them."

D. Relationship with Wife

This information refers to the sample of 150 married men. Most of these men 86 per cent had arranged marriages and 57 per cent of them viewed marriage as necessary to settle down in life. The majority 87 per cent were married between 15 and 21 years of age (before legal age at marriage) and there was no waiting period between marriage and consummation of marriage.

Most of the respondents 97 per cent reported satisfactory sexual relations within marriage. Though 75 per cent were aware of 'condom' as a method of contraception and 52 per cent as a means to prevent infection, 26 per cent reported ever using it. This use was also not regular as the reason for use in more than 80 per cent was to space children and in 12 per cent because the wife had menstrual period.

In the non-users, more than three-fourths were men who looked at condom only as a contraceptive, and they believed that contraception was women's responsibility. Nonetheless, almost all non-users 95 per cent reported that they did not use condoms because the wife did not like it. As many as 47 per cent also mentioned that there was no fear of AIDS with wife. According to Dilip,

> "Males should use condom with CSWs so that they are protected against AIDS. They need not use it with their wives because it is not needed and reduces pleasure."

Other Factors that Affected Condom Use

Almost all 98 per cent men had heard of condoms. While about 60 per cent of unmarried men were aware of role of condoms in preventing conception and AIDS, only a-third of the married men were aware of this rolc. Their information sources were household visits of government health workers, FPAI workers, friends, the media, advertisements on TV, roadsides and buses and of these they considered health workers as the most reliable source. Only about a quarter of these men 23-26 per cent felt they had adequate information and felt that they needed more information. Suresh, an unmarried man said,

> "I had not heard of condoms till my friend advised me to use it

> with CSWs after I had a sore on my penis. I have still not used or seen these but know that they are available in hospitals and in *pan* shops. I know that condom use can prevent AIDS. But I do not know much about AIDS and would like to know more about it. The information given by my friends does not seem to be complete. I would like to know more from a medical doctor."

While, the government sector remained the single largest supplier of free condoms, the focus of workers was mainly promotion of it as a contraceptive for married men. So was the case with FPAI. Men mentioned that they felt shy in buying condoms from shops and procuring them from depot holders. One time purchase also had its own problems as storage in crowded slum houses was practically impossible. Disposal was the next major concerns, especially in these crowded urban slums. The men said that purchase from shops, storage at home and disposal in public places was difficult as they did not want to make public this '*direct evidence of sexual activity*'.

The next important aspect affecting use was the perceived discomfort in use, in some cases leading to revulsion. One man shared his revulsion,

> "I used it just once and felt dirty as the semen remains deposited in the condom."

The anxiety associated with use was not just because of the discomfort but also the fear of the condom bursting. This anxiety was more in response to the quality of condoms supplied at the government centres. Another finding which emerged that should be a matter of concern for programme managers was that a vast majority of the respondents did not seem to be aware of the exact method of using a condom.

Discussion

The use/non-use of condom in each relationship varied as the attitudes, level of knowledge, reasons and situations varied with each respondent.

Many married men started using condom only to prevent conception. In those who did not use, the reasons were lack of pleasure in sexual act and identifying condom as a contraceptive that made them shift the responsibility to the female partner.

Thus in the context of a heterosexual, married couple, the use of condom, the government policy of 'safer sex' referred to 'no conception'.

This connotation of 'safer sex' to a certain extent was also responsible for non-use in unmarried men. Some of them justified non-use of condom saying that they would rather take the chance of conception, which they could get aborted, than compromise on pleasure in the act. And if at all unwanted conception was a concern, it would be of the female partner!

Not surprisingly a significantly higher per cent of married men reported non-use because of lack of awareness about the need to use this for 'safe sex' in the context of STDs. And though, 'safe sex' in the context of STDs figured higher as a reason for acceptance of condoms in unmarried men, the awareness appeared after a while, when they had already been exposed to 'unsafe' relationships.

In the scenario of increasing threat of HIV-AIDS, the notion of 'safer sex' is meant to be relevant in all kinds of sexual relationships—homosexual, heterosexual and bisexual—be these pre-marital, marital and extramarital. But misconceptions about relationships, which require the need for precautions restricted condom use. There was lack of clarity about what constitutes 'homo', 'hetero' and 'bisexual' relationship.

Also, while publicity in the media about unsafe sex has made awareness about AIDS almost universal, it has also resulted in the apparent universal belief that condom use for protection from infection is necessary only in high risk relationship such as those with homosexuals and CSWs. Multi-partner casual relationships with girl friends and strangers are not considered unsafe. As a result condom use in these cases was less common. The other important factor was the 'gender' confusion about eunuchs. Men were unable to categorise this sexual relationship as 'high risk'. Further, many men in the slums, from low socio-economic strata were economically dependent on eunuchs.

Thus men seldom opted for condoms within marriage, for reasons other than contraception, as they perceived marital relationship as low risk for contracting any STD. This attitude while acceptable in monogamous relationship was a cause of concern if the same men continued to view this relationship as a 'low risk' despite either of the partners being promiscuous and with multiple extramarital relationships. Sex with eunuch or with other heterosexual partner, made these men vulnerable to STDs, which they could have passed on to the other partners, to wife in case of married men and to the girl friends or other women in case of unmarried men. The relationship, which is seen by men as 'low risk', thus had the potential to become passive receiver of STD or AIDS or turn into 'high risk' for the partner.

Was inadequate awareness or knowledge the main reasons for low use? Though the use of condom and non-use of condom were directly related to the knowledge about its use for safer sex, this did not always result in men using condom, or lack of knowledge did not stop acceptors.

Despite the awareness that CSWs were seen as a source of STDs or AIDS, more than half of the married men did not use condom with them. Rather a good number of unmarried men asserted that even if the condoms were not available, they would go for sex with either CSWs or the girl friend.

Thus, the awareness programme promoting condoms seems to be paradoxically responsible for its restricted use to a certain extent. In its eagerness to rush the awareness creation agenda, the programme has failed to pay attention to various details, such as, the need to promote its use in all sexual relationships, especially multi-partner sexual relationships and sexual relationships with persons of any sex, and disseminating information about steps involved in condom use. The other limitations are the absence of realistic promotion considering the capacity of the people to understand the need and the reasons for the same.

Another problem voiced by both the acceptors and the non-acceptors that merits attention is the dissatisfaction with use, storage and disposal problems. Lack of pleasure, fear of condom bursting, and embarrassment in procuring condoms from stores/depots, storing and disposing them without the knowledge of the family members continue to be concerns unaddressed by the programme, that made some men discontinue the use. This highlighted the fact that if proper attention is not paid to genuine concerns of current use, it will lead to discontinuation of condom by dissatisfied users.

A vast majority of poor, unmarried or married, whose needs were not necessarily restricted to contraception, were not the focus of the government programme. And these men sometimes being unable to access condoms resorted to 'unsafe sex'. The programme seemed to have failed in exploring alternative methods for free service delivery to those un-reached by the government programme, viz. the unmarried sexually active groups.

On the other hand, men, especially unmarried men, voiced inadequacy of their knowledge and desire for more information, from professionally qualified personnel. This seems to offer a window of opportunity to the government programme which if exploited through creation of favourable conditions, and with greater support and knowledge, would motivate men to accept condoms more readily.

9

Sexuality and AIDS Awareness among Diamond Workers

BINOD C. AGRAWAL

Introduction

All over the world, young people are at risk of getting affected by the AIDS epidemic. In India too it is found that young people in 15-45 age group are most vulnerable to be infected by HIV as they are sexually more active. Economic pressures are driving youngsters to migrate to cities for employment. Most of the migrants are young unmarried or married males forced to live alone in cities. These young men also happen to have money of their own which they can use to engage in sexual activities with commercial sex workers (CSWs) and are then likely to infect others. The present study aimed at understanding among the migrant diamond workers in Surat City, Gujarat State, knowledge of sex related issues, and their sexual behaviour. The study was to understand their awareness regarding HIV-AIDS, their media access and usage and communication needs pertaining to HIV-AIDS. With a view to attempt to design media strategy to enhance the current level of awareness.

Young people are most vulnerable to be infected by HIV as they are sexually more active. Economic pressures are driving the youngsters to migrate to cities for job and employment. Most of the young unmarried or married male migrants are forced to live alone in cities as they cannot afford to keep their families in cities. These young men also happen to have money of their own which they can use to indulge in sexual activities with commercial sex workers. The commercial sex workers, one of the target risk groups, might infect their clients, who in turn may infect others, they have sexual contacts with, in cities or back home. On this background present study aimed at understanding and analyzing the sexual behaviour, sexuality and awareness about HIV-AIDS among Diamond industrial workers.

The migrant industrial workers of Surat—the diamond workers from Saurashtra in Gujarat, were studied. Methods of data collection were mainly participant observation, indepth interviews and group discussions. Workers living in groups of 4-5 in a room were chosen and 60 such workers were studied in depth. 32 case studies, and 6 group interviews, represented by young married and unmarried respondents in the age range 17–36 years were included. The researcher first got entry in the field through local leaders and officials of the Surat Diamond Manufacturers Association (SDMA).

The education of the diamond workers ranged from VII to XII standard and they were fairly well exposed to media as radio, TV, newspapers, posters, hoardings and advertisements on buses. They often watched movies and TV in groups and liked to watch Hindi action movies with sex, serials and game shows. Their exposure to sex before migration included watching blue films, masturbation, wet dreams and premarital and extramarital sex in their native homes. In Surat, the young men were exposed to new experiences as movies, new friends, city life, staying with unrelated people, freedom, independence, own money to spend and to top them all with a spirit of adventure. After migration, they even visited the red light areas in Surat. There was no need felt as such for information on HIV-AIDS, as most of them knew the cause. All the respondents had seen advertisements on buses and hoardings about HIV-AIDS. Majority of them mentioned the use of contaminated or untested blood and blood products and use of unsterilized needle as sources of HIV. One-third of them knew infected mothers giving infection to their newborn babies. These workers become sexually active at a young age of 17-18 years. Early exposure to sex and finding the use of condom unnecessary exposes them to the risk of infecting themselves with HIV virus. The workers are willing to learn about HIV-AIDS in spite that they are superficially informed. Their need was to have people or an organization who would advise them in a friendly and non-threatening manner. To plan a communication strategy the contact points of diamond workers, need to be furnished with accessible media. Though the task of counselling is enormous, it can play an effective role in behavioural change to wean from risk behaviour.

The sexual exposure of the diamond workers, migration pattern, living conditions, lifestyles, separation from family for extended period, make them vulnerable to get infected by HIV-AIDS. The information need of the diamond workers regarding HIV-AIDS, is obvious. However, they do not perceive it as a felt need.

The Locale

Surat is one of the most important historical and commercial cities in Gujarat State founded about 500 years ago. Today, city is known for its diamond cutting and polishing industry across the world. The population of Surat, provisionally released after the Census 2001, stands at 2.8 million.

The diamond industry has attracted migrants from all over the State. The diamond workers, from Saurashtra, have a virtual monopoly on the cutting and polishing job in the industry. The migrant workers share accommodation and eat from a common mess. Twenty or odd number of people, all males, occupy a four or five storey building, each floor of which has a hall, occupied by 4-5 diamond workers. The toilets are located usually on the second and the top floors and shared by all inmates of the building. The occupants of a hall are generally from the same place in Saurashtra and known to each other. There are a number of such buildings in Varachha Bazar in Surat. The ground floor of these buildings often have shops selling tea, renting cycles and other necessities. Some diamond workers live in the factory premises that are not very different from the residential buildings. The halls in these buildings are used as work places during the day and at night the workers spread their modest beds to sleep. There are about 2,00,000 such diamond industrial workers in Surat.

Methodology

Methods of data collection were—mapping, participant observation, in-depth interviews, case studies and group discussions. The researcher first got entry in the field through local leaders and officials of the Surat Diamond Manufacturers Association (SDMA). The places where the diamond workers lived with other workers and the locations of the diamond factories were marked on the map. The study focused on the diamond workers who were not living in families, as these workers were likely to have a different pattern of sexual life. The map showed that a sizeable number of workers were living in the factories. Mapping was also used to locate the red-light areas in Surat. While there was one area, Varyavi Bazar which was a designated red-light area, there were five other places from where commercial sex workers were picked up by their clients. The mapping gave some idea of places frequented by the diamond workers.

In the first week, the investigator stayed in Surat and in the second week he moved to live in one of the buildings at Varachha road and shared a room with four other diamond workers. This facilitated observation from close quarter. Some days, the researcher went to their place of work and other days sat at the tea shop to watch T.V. with others. This anthropological participation helped to gain their confidence. He also accompanied them to red-light areas.

Interviews were conducted in Gujarati language, mostly at night, from 9 p.m. to 12 midnight with prior intimation. The interviews were unstructured and free-flowing. No notes were made during the interview. Each interview lasted about 90 minutes. The details of the interview were written down the next day. Six group interviews were also conducted. Each group had 4 to 6 respondents. Often, the participants avoided talking about themselves but talked on behalf of others. In addition, 32 case studies were made which provided details about the life of diamond workers. Key informants like auto-rickshaw drivers, restaurant owners, *pan* shop owners who were believed to be well informed about sexual activities of the diamond industrial workers were also interviewed.

Respondents' Profile

The industrial workers chosen for this study were the ones who live in Surat, leaving their families in Saurashtra. 60 diamond industrial workers in the age range of 17 to 36 years, who had migrated to Surat from Saurashtra were covered for this study. Out of the 60 respondents, 14 were under 22 years of age and 13 were between 31–36 years of age. Nineteen respondents were unmarried and 41 were married. 17 respondents had studied up to the 10th standard and 43 were educated up to the 12th standard. More than half of the respondents 33 earned more than Rs. 3,000 per month while others earned between Rs. 2,000–Rs. 3,000 per month. They belonged to a variety of castes and had migrated from Surendra Nagar, Rajkot, Jamnagar, Junagarh, Amreli, Porbandar and Bhavnagar in Saurashtra region of Gujarat. Most of them were addicted to chewing *pan masala* with tobacco. Each worker on an average spent Rs. 5-7 a day on chewing tobacco, *pan masala* or smoking *Bidi*. Nearly one-third of them had an occasional alcoholic drink, when they could afford.

A Typical Day in the Life of a Diamond Worker

Their day begins at 5.0 O'clock in the morning. After a quick round of brushing teeth, bathing, drinking tea and eating breakfast, the worker reports for work in the factory. On way to factory, they pay their obeisance at the temple. The work begins in the factory at 8.0 O'clock in the morning and goes on till 6.0 O'clock in the evening, with a usual recess for two hours. Since most of them live nearby or in the factory itself, they eat their meals and have short-nap or a chat with their friends during recess. After the day's work in the factory they wash their clothes, have a bath, gossip with friends or have a round of the market, mostly for window shopping, but occasionally to pick up their daily requirements of soap, oil, tooth paste etc. 8.0 O'clock is the supper time after which they either gossip, socialize or watch TV and finally, retire to bed some time after 10.0 O'clock.

On a holiday, they may go out for shopping, take a stroll, visit friends and relatives. They might watch a movie once or twice a month (often Hindi movies and occasionally an English movie). All know and understand Hindi and Gujarati and a few have some knowledge of English. Some young informants also admitted with embarrassment, visiting red light areas in the city in the company of their friends. After working for about eleven months, they usually take one month vacation just before *Deepawali*, to visit the family. Some go home on two-three occasions, on short trips, to help in farming activities, or to attend other religious/social rituals.

Sex and Sexuality

Much of the sexual orientation was acquired in early childhood and adolescence, mostly through observation. The younger ones and somewhat less experienced absorbed information from older friends and got ideas about how to persuade girls for sex, what girls thought about sex, and how keen girls were to have sex. By the time came to Surat, they already had acquired certain ideas of sex. The first thing they do on arrival is to take rounds of red-light area. Here they get an opportunity to experiment with sex since they have the money and there is nobody to ask, as to how they spent it. Watching blue films on videos is very common. A group of 6-7 workers, both married and unmarried, take a VCR on rent and watch blue films at some lodging place.

> Mr. A while in class IX learned that the child was born as an outcome of sexual intercourse. Though the boys and girls were segregated in school, he was always curious about girls. He

sometimes had a glimpse of scantily clad woman bathing at the village tank or taking bath in the open in the neighbourhood. Sexual arousal was common on sighting a young girl. Discussing girls was common among his friends. He occasionally masturbated and he knew some other friends were also doing the same. When slightly older, he dreamt of girls and had wet dreams. The fear of being caught and reprimand kept him away from pursuing girls. After he came to Surat for job his sexual feeling were further aroused by looking at provocative hoardings and reading pornographic magazines. The public toilets and other places were full of advertisements claiming to cure sexual disorders and he found toilet graffiti sexually exciting. Among topics of discussion, sex was one of the most favourite topics.

Experience of First Night

Married respondents were reluctant to share their experience of first night or a first few nights of their marriage. Usually, the elder brother's wife (*Bhabhi*) was the one who gave a piece of advice as to how to conduct oneself on the first night. Sharing his experience, Mr. S narrated the advice he received from his *Bhabhi*,

> "Go slow, don't scare her. Go over her body gently, caress her. Kiss her on her cheeks, lips and all over the body. When she is wet inside, push yourself gently in."

Mr. P another respondent narrated his experience of approaching the situation,

> "Having experience with other women before marriage helps a lot. When I was nineteen years old, I had first experience of my life. I was so excited and nervous that even before entering the girl I had ejaculated. However, my subsequent attempts were successful. I used to have sex with that girl almost once a week. However, she would not allow me to have sex with her from behind. When after a few years, I got married I had no anxiety of making love with my wife. However, as my wife was a virgin I could not enter her first two days. She used to cry in pain, but I persisted. Finally, I broke into her. By God! She was virgin and pure. I know how to get a woman ready for sex. I have

never used condom with my wife. There is no fun when you use condom. In the early days of my marriage, I used to have sex five times a day. I came to Surat five years ago, at the age of seventeen. I have never visited the red-light area, never masturbated or ever suffered from STD. Whenever I have urge for sex, I would go home for ten days every two months."

Pre-marital and Extra-marital Sexual Experiences

Though no one admitted visiting red-light areas, one diamond worker made a wild guess that about 20 per cent of the migrants did visit sex workers.

Mr. C said, "Occasionally five to six young men will get into a party mood. They will get drunk and talk about their sexual exploits. After the party some of them would visit sex workers."

The respondents told the researcher that since many men were working in places away from home, their wives indulged in sex with others including family members at times.

Mr. K., said, "Sex with one's own wife is routine and mechanical. My wife is not playful and adventurous. I just enter her and come out. But older women are more playful. They are so much fun. When I was only 22 years, I used to make love to a thirty-eight year old woman in my neighbourhood. Her husband was employed in Bombay. She told me her husband had a small penis whereas she found mine bigger and more robust. Despite the fact that she had two children, we enjoyed sex with each other."

Mr. X, sharing his knowledge about girl and boys said, "By the time a boy attains the age of 13-14 years he has erection... He takes to masturbation or has wet dreams. Since a girl matures about the same time and starts having her period, she feels sexy after the period. She cannot help but have sex if some young man was around. The girls also masturbate when they feel the urge."

He also said that the sexual needs of man and woman were different. A man could be aroused in no time and he would also come out in no time. However, women were slow to be aroused and could go on and on. Another respondent also said that women were sexier but could not reveal their minds. When women had opportunity they would have sex with any one.

Sex During Pregnancy and after Child-Birth

Out of 60 respondents, 41 were married. Nine of them had undergone vasectomy and wives of 11 were at various stages of pregnancy. While they saw no problem in having sex in the first four month of pregnancy, after the fourth months they exercised caution and frequency of sexual intercourse went down considerably thereafter.

According to the respondents, after the second or third delivery the sexual act was not very enjoyable. Women too lost interest and were not much fun. It was at this time that the men sought pleasure in other women or sex workers. According to one respondent, "About half of the women after their sterlization have sex with other men, since they are not worried about getting pregnant."

Early exposure to blue films, pornographic magazines, sexy movies, access to red light areas and more than anything else, lack of social control in the new place, access to cash, loneliness, lack of emotional support, access to sex workers, advertisements, movies all led one to have sex outside wedlock.

Homo-Sexuality

Informants were embarrassed to talk about their homo-sexual experiences. However, one respondent provided a vivid description of his encounter with homo-sexuals. "Two of my room mates, seventeen and nineteen years old and unmarried, I found them having sex with each other, when I suddenly opened the door". The incidence of homo-sexuality was corroborated by three other workers. According to the respondent, homosexuals did not use a condom as there was no fear of pregnancy. In Surat, the researcher observed in a stationery train in the railway yard Hijdas (Eunuchs) carrying on sexual activities. The clients included a cross-section of people—businessmen, diamond workers, policemen, students. According to a respondent, homo-sexuality was practised by several men, irrespective of their age. Seven respondents agreed having come across homosexuals at one time or other, but denied having sex with them.

HIV-AIDS Awareness

All diamond workers included in the study had some awareness about HIV-AIDS. The awareness had resulted, largely from exposure to advertisements on the buses and hoardings displayed in public places. Some awareness had come through messages on the T.V. The data presented here have been inferred from the case studies conducted for this study.

Practically, all of them had noticed advertisements on HIV-AIDS on buses 100 per cent and hoarding 88 per cent. The subject of HIV-AIDS had also been talked about among the friends, by one and all. Among sources of information, other salient ones were workers of the NGO 52 per cent, Leaflets 43 per cent, T.V. 30 per cent, newspaper 23 per cent and the posters 20 per cent. Radio had not been a significant source 7 per cent of HIV-AIDS awareness for diamond workers.

While the diamond workers were aware of HIV-AIDS, their knowledge was not precise. HIV-AIDS was termed as an outcome of wrongful sex with those with whom they are not married. Most 87 per cent of the workers described HIV-AIDS as a fatal, serious and incurable disease. Having been exposed to publicity campaign about HIV-AIDS, friends did occasionally talk among themselves about this disease. HIV-AIDS was thought to be caused by sex with 'other' women.

Table 9.1: Causes of HIV Infection

Causes of HIV Infection	*%*
Multi-partner Sex	100
Transfusion of untested blood	88
Unsterilized injection needles	57
Mother to child	32

Source: Field Investigation.

Myths and Reality

Most of them 87 per cent knew that HIV was incurable. However, eight respondents 13 per cent believed that Ayurved was a very effective system for treatment of this infection. They also believed that good diet could help in the recovery from HIV-AIDS. Most respondents 80 per cent knew that there was no vaccination which could protect one from HIV. None of the respondents believed that the disease could be cured by any magic or appeasement of a deity.

None of the respondents had ever come across a person suffering from HIV-AIDS. Seven respondents 12 per cent had heard from some acquaintance that three men in a neighbouring village were suffering from HIV-AIDS. According to the respondents people suffering from HIV-

AIDS lost appetite and the medicines did them no good. The following table gives percentage of respondents who had several misconceptions about transmission of HIV:

Table 9.2: Misinformation About Transmission of HIV

Misinformation about transmission of HIV	%
Hand shake and hugging	24
Sharing of clothes of an HIV-AIDS patient	12
Kissing	55
Sharing of soap and comb	7
Sharing an accommodation	12
Sharing of utensils	20
Bathing in river/ponds	33
Sharing the toilet	12
Mosquito and bed bug bites	37

Source: Field Investigation.

STD and HIV-AIDS

All respondents knew about sexually transmitted diseases (STD). Sexually transmitted diseases were thought to be caused by having sex with an unfaithful, sexually loose woman. A person suffering from STD was thought to have boils on his penis, he would not have proper erection, his organ would bend and he would have premature ejaculation. A person with such problems was more likely to suffer from HIV-AIDS 80 per cent. Most of them 88 per cent also believed that a woman who had sex with different men was also more likely to suffer from HIV-AIDS, than man having sex with different women.

After the Infection

A sizeable number of diamond workers 62 per cent did not feel comfortable sharing with their wives the information of their infection. They argued that if their wives came to know of their infection, they would not allow them to have sex, will desert them, will tell others and consequently, their prestige would be a stake.

Most of them 82 per cent were not in favour of isolating an HIV-AIDS patient as this was thought to cause mental torture and social stigma to the patient. Most diamond workers seemed dissatisfied with the efforts of agencies responsible for dissemination of information about HIV-AIDS. According to them, the multi-purpose health workers and the NGOs were not doing their job well. They gave some information and then disappear. The respondents felt that their life style and long work hours, did not permit them to seek information. All workers felt that they did not have adequate information and they did not know where to seek information from.

While none of the respondents admitted having been infected by HIV-AIDS, four of them volunteered information regarding their sexual problems. They felt that they were suffering from STD because they had slow erection or premature ejaculation and wet dreams. They were concerned that their penises were not straight. They had sought help from doctor/*vaidya* but after temporary relief the problem persisted. Their knowledge about STDs was inadequate. They knew that unprotected sex meant sex without a condom.

While most of them 70 per cent felt that anyone having an infection should take the treatment, 5 per cent of them told that both partners should take the treatment, 12 per cent were only for the treatment of the husband and 13 per cent for the treatment of wife.

Those suffering from STDs were very reluctant to talk about their problems. Even the doctor was consulted at very late stage. The diamond workers told that they could not talk about their sexual problems on account of shyness, fear of ridicule, and loss of prestige. Many of them would go to some doctor and quietly take medicine without telling others. However, about 40 per cent were of the view that it would be better to share the problem with some confidant like a friend or some close relative, as that would help in getting right advice and help. Though it might be embarrassing, certainly it could save one's life but 60 per cent of them were reluctant to share their problem with anyone.

Media Usage

Diamond workers were well exposed to mass media like radio, TV, cinema, newspapers and magazines since childhood. Nearly 72 per cent of them reported having a TV set back home. Invariably, all had audio cassette players and nearly half of them had access to a radio in their native places. However, no one reported owning a VCR or VCP.

Watching T.V.

In every building occupied by the diamond workers there were 2-3 T.V. sets, bought by inmates. Those sharing a room with T.V. watched, with neighbours and friends. In case, a T.V. went out of order in one room, the inmates of that room will go to watch T.V. in some other room, in the building or another building. They watched T.V. between 8 p.m. and midnight almost four days a week.

Viewing Behaviour

Most respondents invariably watched quiz programmes like 'Kaun Banega Crorepati'. While watching the programme they indulged in betting. The loser had to give others a cup of tea or *Pan Masala.* Others frequently watched programmes were soap-operas, news and cricket. There was not much inclination for watching programmes on health. 16 diamond workers 27 per cent reported watching T.V. till midnight. When they went home for vacationing they brought a VCP or VCR on rent and watched blue films in the company of their friends

Listening to Radio

One-third of them 37 per cent had radio sets in Surat. Radio was used for listening film songs, folk songs, cricket commentary and news. The respondents said that there were not many programmes regarding health, particularly HIV-AIDS on radio. Listening to radio has reduced considerably with the arrival of T.V.

Tape-Recorders

The tape-recorders were played to listen to film music and dialogues. Only 28 per cent workers had a two-in-one (a cassette player and a transistor) in Surat.

Newspaper and Other Reading

In Surat nobody subscribed to a newspaper. They read newspaper at '*pan*' shops, tea stalls or at work place. Occasionally, a diamond worker would buy a newspaper, if he was travelling. They glossed over the headlines and shared news with their fellows. If they came across news about Saurashtra or the Diamond Industrty, they read it with much interest. The respondents also read with interest, the 'question-answer' column on health related problems. Occasionally, they read articles on health and disease'. Some of them took interest in highlights about crime, sports etc. The popular Gujarati newspapers were *Gujarat Samachar*, *Sandesh*, *Gujarat Mitra*, *Channel Surat*. Only 5 per cent workers mentioned reading magazines. Religious magazines such as *'Jalaram Jyoti'* and *'Gayatri Parivar'* and *'Stri Visheshank'* were subscribed by a few of them. While going home, they often picked up some magazines on films or sports for reading on the way. They often borrowed from friends, novels for reading at leisure. 6 of them had read '*Kamshastra'* a book on sex in Gujarati. More than half of the respondents had become aware about STDs through posters and pamphlets. Some posters were also displayed in public toilets. Whenever, a respondent came across some 'spicy' piece of information in a magazine, movie, T.V. or newspaper, he invariably shared it with others. Often, after dinner, the respondents would assemble near a cinema hall and indulge in gossip about sex.

Films

Most workers viewed Hindi films, once a month. in the cinema hall. The youngsters were more attracted to highly publicized Hindi films with plenty of sex, such as *Kamsutra*, Bandit Queen, etc. There was a general liking for films stuffed with lot of violence and sex. They often saw such films more than once. Gujarati films were rarely seen (one or two in a year).

Medical Camps

Medical camps set up to educate masses were often attended for medical consultation and for getting medical help since treatment/consultation at the camps was either free or highly subsidized. Seven respondents had voluntarily donated blood, but no one had received a blood transfusion. The respondents exchanged health related information with friends and colleagues. The information was occasionally sought from health workers, nurses from the health centre and multi-purpose health workers (MPHW). For minor ailments, they bought medicines across the counter. If the medication did not give relief, then, they went to a government or a private hospital.

Hoarding and Posters

Most diamond workers were exposed to hoardings and posters related to Malaria, HIV-AIDS, T.B., Polio etc. at the bus stations, railway stations, government hospitals and octroi posts, Zila Panchayat and at the Ring Road but they had not read the messages on the hoardings.

Folk Art

While on vacation if there was a performance by some folk artists, they made it a point to watch it. They had watched Bhawai (a folk show) and participated in the fairs.

Inter-personal Communication

Almost every fortnight a health worker from Municipal Health Centre, visited their area for educating people about diseases, such as malaria and gave information about other health related issues. They also distributed medicines free of charge. If a diamond worker was suffering from any disease, he consulted the health worker for advice and treatment. Workers from Centre for Social Studies (CSS) and Surat Municipality's Health Department under Partnership for Sexual Health (PSH) visited this area once in a fortnight for counselling and for research on HIV-AIDS. The respondents rarely sought help from these counsellors out of a sense of shame or shyness. They preferred to read about their sexual health problems in the newspapers or magazines.

Communication Strategy

Till date HIV-AIDS has not acquired, in diamond workers' perception, a serious dimension. However, conditions are favourable for HIV to become a serious social and health problem among this group. Their sexual exposure in native places, migration patterns, urban living conditions, life style, separation from family for extended period make them vulnerable to get infected by HIV. A communication strategy for creating HIV-AIDS awareness and prevention will have to consider the following:

1. What is the information need of the diamond workers of Saurashtra in relation to HIV-AIDS?
2. What behaviour modifications are required in the diamond workers to protect them from HIV-AIDS?
3. What would be the appropriate channels of communication and media to pass on the required information to the diamond workers?

4. What would be the appropriate channels of communication to induce attitudinal and behavioural change for protection from HIV-AIDS?

Information Needs

There is a felt need for information on HIV-AIDS. Most diamond workers seem to know that what causes HIV-AIDS. Many of them, in their native villages, have occasional sexual encounters with their neighbours, relations and other village women and their sexual activities are further likely to continue after their arrival in Surat. From the study, it appears that many young diamond workers visited red light areas. They generally found use of condom an impediment in sexual pleasure. Their knowledge about various aspects of HIV-AIDS seemed to be incomplete. They seemed keen to learn about HIV-AIDS but felt that there is no source that would give them authentic information. They expressed need for such information.

Sustaining Awareness

The group studied here is generally aware of the causes of HIV-AIDS. Efforts should be made to sustain this awareness by giving messages repeatedly through different channels that are accessed by them. The basic content of the message could remain the same but its presentation could vary. The messages could be given through posters, hoardings, advertisements on buses and T.V. Advertisements, for sustaining AIDS awareness, should be shown intermittently in the cinema halls or AIDS related information could be given by the cable operators. Similarly, street-plays could work well in sustaining awareness. Posters and hoardings should be displayed at places frequented by the diamond workers. Leaflets, folders and booklets containing information about HIV-AIDS could be effectively used for information dissemination. Wall paintings could be another effective way of sustaining awareness.

Attitudinal and Behavioural Change

Since there is awareness about HIV-AIDS among the diamond workers, it is important to lead them to attitudinal and behavioural change through counselling and peer support. They are occasionally visited by the health staff. NGO's participation in HIV-AIDS programme needs to be strengthened with counselling to address people's problem and clear their doubts. Counselling can be complemented by supportive literature. Support groups could play an effective role in the process of behavioural modification. The major thrust of the behavioural change, should be to impress clients with the risk of HIV-AIDS through multi-partner sex. Efforts should be made to motivate the diamond workers to practice safe sex by promoting condoms.

10

Sexuality and Sexual Behaviour of Tribal Males

P.S. AGASHE

Introduction

India has the second largest concentration of tribal people in the world. Maharashtra state has about 9 per cent tribal population with 47 per cent Scheduled Tribes spread over 14 districts. Although patriarchal, tribal women enjoy better status in terms of marriage, divorce and remarriage in comparison with caste Hindu peasantry, probably due to custom of bride price, as a consideration of her labour.

Increased transportation and communication facilities including visual media, such as TV and mobile phones, have led to the exposure of tribal society to the outside world. Low agricultural productivity has resulted in seasonal outmigration of tribals to the urban area. As a result, city lifestyle is slowly invading into the lives of tribal people. Due to exposure, life style of young boys and girls has modified significantly. Tribal men who are getting exposed to the cities are at a risk of contracting STD.

Sexuality of tribals has been studied by the anthropologists in classical ethnography. However, due to risk of HIV-AIDS attributed to liberal attitude and sex behaviour, it was decided to explore the sexuality and sex behaviour of tribal men. Research was undertaken in a tribal village of Palghar district, Maharashtra State. The study village located 125 km. from Mumbai metropolitan area, was inhabited by the Ka Thakar tribe.

The issues of adultery and premarital pregnancy were adjudicated by the Ka Thakar tribal Panchayat. To regulate the sexual behaviour, Panchayat formed its own rules and regulations for betrothal, marriage, divorce, remarriage etc.

Proportion of Ka Thakar men engaging in pre and extra marital sexual activity appears significantly high. Though no HIV cases have been reported, current practices of sexual behaviour among Ka Thakars could lead to rapid spread of the disease. There is urgent need to give sex education to the tribals, especially about HIV-AIDS, to promote safe sex practices. It is recommended to undertake studies among different tribal groups with focus on male as well as female sexual behaviour.

In the recent past, process of sanskritization, westernization and rapid urbanization have triggered changes among different societies, including tribal groups, which remained geographically isolated for long periods of time. These changes have directly or indirectly affected sexual behaviour. Increased transportation and communication facilities, advancement of technology, exposure to the mass media has also contributed towards the change.

There are several reasons to study sexuality and sexual behaviour. Pelto notes that, 'practically all aspects of reproductive health; issues concerning abortion practices and abortion seeking; gynaecological problems and contraceptive practices relate directly or indirectly to sexual behaviours and practices' (Pelto, 1999).

More pressing reason for studying sexuality is the spread of Human Immunodeficiency Virus (HIV). During the last two decades, HIV-AIDS has emerged as one of the major public health problems in many countries.

Tribal communities have not been studied from sexuality point of view. Moni Nag observed that, "Anthropological studies in India have provided very little information on the sexual attitudes and behaviour of the communities studied. Remarkable exceptions are those conducted by Verrier Elwin. Almost no information is available on the contemporary situation of tribal groups" (Nag M., 1995). However, Verrier Elwin's '*The Muria and their Ghotul*' has romanticized sex.

Need for Research on Tribal Sexuality

Over the years, increased transportation and communication facilities have led to the exposure of tribal society to the outside world. Due to food security problems, tribals undertake seasonal migration to the cities for earning their livelihood (for survival according to them). City lifestyle is slowly invading into their lives. They are getting exposed to the mass media especially television channels, radio etc. Many non-tribals have also moved to the tribal areas for employment and occupations. Social contact with these non-tribals has initiated change in the tribal society.

Tribal males, who are getting exposed to the cities due to migration, are at risk of contracting STD/HIV-AIDS and spreading it in tribal area.

The study explores the sexuality and sexual behaviour of tribal males with objectives to document the emic framework of sexuality of tribal males and also to study their sexual behaviour. The study began with following research questions:

1. What are the factors that influence sexual behaviour?
2. What are the concepts of tribal males about sexuality?
3. What are the sources of information about sex and sex related issues among them?

Methodology

Sampling Frame

The study was carried out in a village located in Jawhar Taluka of Thane District (now Palghar District), Maharashtra State. The main tribe in the village was Ka Thakar, from amongst whom the respondents were selected. It was thought to explore the sexuality of Ka Thakar males from holistic viewpoint. Males in the age group of 16-45 years were selected for the study.

Since the issue under study was sensitive, only those respondents who were willing to share their experiences and were available for the interviews were selected for the study. Thus sample was purposive. In the study village there were 94 males in the age group of 16-45 years, out of which 80 respondents were interviewed in depth. Research investigator resided in the village during the study period.

In-depth informal interviews of the target group were carried out to understand the concepts about sexuality and sexual behaviour. Respondents were interviewed in one-to-one situation. Interview guide was used for the purpose.

Key informants were also interviewed to find out the general pattern of sexual behaviour in the community. Separate guide was prepared prior to interviews and wherever necessary further probing was made.

Informal Group Discussion

Late night chat with the group of respondents served as informal group discussion sessions, through which data about sexuality and sexual behaviour was collected. These discussions also provided leads for the study.

Quasi-Participant

Observation method was used to collect information about sexual behaviour of boys and girls on the occasions like traditional dances, fairs and festivals, betrothal and marriage celebrations etc.

Survey

Household survey was conducted in the village to collect the background information of the respondents. Secondary data was collected from the sources like Primary Health Centre, Sub-centre, Cottage Hospital at Jawhar etc.

Qualitative data was analysed thematically. Common themes from the data were identified and data from the interviews were grouped according to these themes.

Ethical Issues

Prior to the interview, informed consent of the respondents was taken. Respondents were assured of maintaining anonymity and confidentiality.

Findings

Profile of Respondent

Out of 80 participating respondents, 25 (31%) respondents belonged to the age grup 16-25 years while another 38 (48%) belonged to age group 26-35 years. Remaining 17 (21%) had age in the range of 36-45 years. Nearly 30 per cent were educated up to secondary (8-10 std.) level while rest of them were less educated.

Main occupation of the respondents was agriculture. All of them were engaged in agricultural activities during rainy season. Main crops cultivated were rice and ragi. Some of them also migrated to the neighnouring taluks of Palghar and Dahanu as wage labour for paddy cultivation and harvesting, while few other respondents migrated to the urban areas of Mumbai and Thane as labour relating to building construction.

Out of the total 80 males interviewed, 11 (14%) were unmarried and all of them belonged to the age group 16-25 years. 68 (85%) respondents were married while only one was a divorcee.

Tribal society has its own norms about marriage. Divorce and remarriage are relatively easy as compared to caste Hindu peasantry. Practice of serial monogamy is prevalent in the Ka Thakar tribe of Thane District. Many respondents had married more than once. One well-to-do family had polygyny over three generations.

Of the Total 69 ever married respondents (including one divorcee), majority of them, 65 per cent had married once in their life time. About 25 per cent had married twice and 10 per cent had third marriage. Thus about 35 per cent respondents had married more than once in their lifetime. Except one respondent, none of the divorced men remained single, since remarriage was not considered abnormal behaviour.

Sexuality and Sexual Practices

Construction of concept of sexuality begins in the childhood. Young tribal boys and girls get knowledge about sexuality from different sources. They learn from their peer group, elders, by listening to popular Hindi and Marathi songs, by watching television, movies and also from animal sex. Adolescent boys learn words, phrases, terminologies, concepts etc. They also become aware about their own sexuality while experiencing physical change in the body.

Due to permissible norms, general socio-cultural environment and frequent opportunity to interact with young girls, many unmarried boys engage in premarital sex.

In the study population it was found that boys got initiated in sexual activity in the age group of 11-15 years. By the age of 18 years, about 88 per cent were initiated in sexual relations. Median age at the first sexual intercourse was 15 years.

About 75 per cent males initiated sexual activity prior to marriage, mostly with the unmarried girls from the same or neighbouring villages. In most of the cases 72 per cent first sex partner was in the age group of 10-14 years, while some respondents had initiated sex with the partner in the age group 15-18 years. The average age of the first sexual partner was 14 years. Age at marriage for girls was 14-16 years and 16-18 years for the boys. Thus, there appeared a gap of 1-2 years between the sex initiation and marriage.

Premarital Sex

Tribal men have several opportunities for engaging in premarital sex activity. Various occasions are—tribal dances like *Tarpa, Gauri* etc., tribal fairs and festivals like *Bohada,* betrothal and marriage celebrations, *Urus* and *Dasara* celebrations at taluk place and at the paddy harvesting in neighbouring taluks, where they go as labour.

Sex after Engagement

Cohabitation after betrothal is allowed in the Ka Thakar community. Key informant in the village said, "Engagement means half marriage. In our community, girl can visit groom's house and may stay with the family of the boy with whom she is engaged. In the process she could start sexual relations with him."

Table 10.1: Premarital Sex

Premarital Sex	*Marital Status*			*Total*
	Unmarried	*Married*	*Divorcee*	
Yes	7	49	1	57
%	63.6	72.1	100	71.3
No	4	19	0	23
%	36.4	27.9	0	28.8
Total	11	68	1	80
%	100	100	100	100

Source: Field Investigation.

Experience of premarital sex according to the marital status has been shown in the above table. About 57 respondents 71 per cent admitted that they experienced premarital sex. Seven out of the 11 unmarried boys had experienced sex. Out of the total 68 currently married men 49(72%) reported that they had experienced sex before marriage.

Sex partners were mostly unmarried girls from village or from neighbouring villages, and separated women. Use of contraception during sex was negligible. Jeejebhoy (1996) in her review found that premarital sexual activity among adolescents from different locations ranged from 9 per cent to 41 per cent. Other studies have also reported premarital activity in the same range (Savara & Shridhar, 1994; Khan *et al.* 1998; Apte, 2000; Collumbien *et al.*, 2001; Gupta and Singh, 2002).

Though, compared to other Indian studies, premarital sex is high among Ka Thakar males, the practice has been very much prevalent among many tribal groups. Majumdar has observed that, "All over tribal India, premarital relations are generally free, and much value is not set on virginity." (Majumdar and Madan, 1976).

Extramarital Sex

Like premarital sex, extramarital sex is also very much prevalent in the studied population.

Table 10.2: Extramarital Sex

Extramarital Sex	*Frequency*	*Percentage (N=69)*
Yes	45	65.2
No	24	34.8
Total	**69**	**100.0**

Source: Field Investigation.

Sex partners reported were, separated women, divorced women, unmarried girls and married women. Very few respondents had used contraception during extramarital sex.

Various studies have reported extramarital sexual activity among males from different groups ranging from 2-16 per cent (Savara and Shridhar, 1994; Khan *et al.*, 1998; Collumbien, 2001; Gupta and Singh, 2002). Compared to these studies, figures for extramarital sex are also high for the Ka Thakar males.

While discussing the issues of adultery, L.N. Chaphekar, who studied Thakars of Thane district during 1940-45 noted that, "Adultery which is to us is a serious matter, is only a venial offence to the Thakar, or only as first step towards changing husbands" (Chaphekar, 1960). Although society appears to ignore such relationships; adultery with married woman is a punishable offence as per tribal norms. If found guilty, adulterer is punished by the village panchs.

Developing sexual relationship with partner other than wife is considered as a masculine characteristics. Ka Thakar males engage in premarital or extramarital sex for enjoyment. Following narratives give the attitude of males for engaging in the sexual relationship with the partner other than wife.

"The experience of *majja* (enjoyment) with a girl is enjoyable. Since she is new to us you get change from your daily routine and you get lot of pleasure having 2-3 *shots* (Sexual Experience) with a strange girl." (A, Married, 22 years, 7th pass). "You should test other 'machine', meaning sex with other girl/woman, it's enjoyable experience."

Extramarital sex was stopped after around 30-35 years of age for various reasons like grown up children, *ijjat jate* (image gets tarnished), pressure of wife, people would ridicule etc.

Visit to Commercial Sex Worker (CSW)

Although there was high sexual activity in the study village, no practice of prostitution in the village was reported by the respondents. Respondents did not visit CSW in city; they feared that they might contract *Garmi* (STD) from them. Narratives about the city prostitutes are given below—

> "I don't go to *Saphed galli* (Red Light area). The women there are very *Chiknya* (good looking), they wear good attractive clothes. *pun tya don nambarchya* (but they are of second quality), they do sex with anybody. Because of them, one can contract *garmi*". (A, Married, 40, Illiterate).

> "In Rabada and Thane area there is *Saphed galli*. But our tribal villagers don't go to those women. They are *Kharaab* women. Anybody young, old from any *jati* (caste) goes to them, hence they are *kharaab*. Going to them can cause *Garmi*." (L, Married, 36 years, Illiterate).

Sexual Abstinence

Ka Thakar tribe reportedly observed sexual abstinence on many occasions. Different occasions like prior to the wrestling competition, traditional rituals like *Kansaricha Vaal* and *Maulya*, as well as wife's pregnancy and menstrual periods.

Sex during menses was a taboo. There was a belief among men that sex with menstruating woman leads to disease. However different opinions were expressed by different respondents about who contracts disease, man or a woman.

Village *bhagat* (medicine man) expressed that, "Woman gets menstruation for 3-4 days. During this period if sexual intercourse is performed with her then disease known as *Ragat Pittie* is contracted by the man. The symptoms of this disease are, swelling over legs, cough, body pain and fever. It is a very dangerous disease and is not cured very easily. It is just like the chronic disease, what you call it *Kasanar* (meaning Cancer)." (T, Married, 35 years, Illiterate). Contrary to the above opinion, another respondent said, "If sexual relations are kept during *paali* (menstrual cycle) of a woman, then that woman gets the disease and not the man." (T, Married, 42 years, Illiterate). No respondent reported sex during menses except one respondent, who used condom.

Sex During Pregnancy

During pregnancy, sexual relations were continued up to 4-5 months. Twenty two year old married respondent gave the reason for observing abstinence during pregnancy. He said, "My wife is pregnant in 5th month of pregnancy. Now since one month I am not having *shots* (sex) with her. If we do sex during pregnancy, then it hurts woman and the foetus. My friend told me about it. He has two children."

Sex before *Kusti* (Wrestling)

Three respondents who used to play *Kusti* (wrestling) in their youth, observed sexual abstinence during season of *Kusti* during village fairs. They perceived that sexual intercourse had direct relationship with the energy of man. During sexual intercourse semen was lost and so also energy.

Thirty three year old wrestler narrated how he observed abstinence, he said, "When I have to play *Kusti,* I don't do sex, not even with my wife. Because, during sex, our *paani* (semen) is lost due to which body energy is reduced. During those days, I don't even talk with my wife, sleep with her, I don't work with her. If she goes to the field I stay back home, if she comes home I go out. When we sit with wife and talk with her, we develop desire for sex. If we perform intercourse, then our *panni* gets exhausted and we are remained with no energy." (D. Married, 33 years, 4th pass).

Abortion

Premarital and extra marital sex was highly prevalent in the study area. Many times it also resulted into pregnancy. In most of the cases, men disown the responsibility. They blame other male partner (of that girl/ woman) responsible for the pregnancy. They ask their partner to undergo abortion. Different terms used for abortion are *Garbharpaat, Garbha Padane, Mul Padane, Poat padane.*

Abortion pills like 'M-Forte' or 'Epi-Forte' were directly purchased from the medical store and given to pregnant sexual partner. According to private medical practitioner at Jawhar, though these drugs were banned by the government, they were easily available to the customers.

Concepts of Sexuality

Development of sexuality begins in the childhood. Children gain knowledge from various sources like peers, elders. They also learn from the life experiences. During adolescence, ideas about sexuality were shaped and were expressed through thoughts, gestures, language, attitudes and at later stage through the practices. Social and cultural environment plays important role in shaping the concepts of sexuality. It also provided opportunities for men to get engaged in premarital and extramarital sex with the girls/women.

Pubertal Changes

Pubertal changes among the boys and girls make them more aware about their sexuality. All the 11 unmarried boys who were interviewed knew the changes in puberty. They reported development of pubic hair, beard, moustache, hair under armpit and attraction towards opposite sex among the boys, while pubertal changes among girls were development of breasts, pubic hair and commencement of *masik paali.*

One unmarried respondent said, "When girls *vayaat yetaat*, (become matured), then their *aama* gets enlarged (breasts are developed) and they start getting *masik paali* (menstrual cycle) at the age of 12-15 years. *Masik Paali* lasts up to 4-7 days and comes regularly every month. Adolescent boys start getting attracted towards girls." (P, Unmarried, 17, 9th Pass).

Masturbation

Most of the boys did not report the practice of masturbation. The reason given by one of the respondent was, "We don't masturbate. We have so many girls, we enjoy sex with them, and so we don't do that, but for the boys who don't have girl friends or sex partners, they get night emissions during sleep or they also masturbate sometimes." (A, Married, 22 years, 7th pass).

Masculinity

Masculinity depends upon the number of *shots* with the sex partner. More the number of *shots* more masculine is the man. Elder men encourage young married and unmarried men to have more *shots* with their wives as well as other sex partners.

Over Indulgence in Sex

Over indulgence in sex affects the health of man and leads to loss of weight, was the feeling expressed by one respondent, "My friend got engaged and brought his wife at home. He does sex at least 3-4 times in a day. That's why his weight has been reduced by five kilos. One should not indulge into sex so heavily. It's not good for the health." (P. Married, 24 years 9th pass)

Causes of *Garmi*

Common belief among the respondents was that *garmi* was contracted, if man had sex with a promiscuous woman who sleeps with many men. Narratives of the respondents about causation of *garmi* are given below:

> "The woman who roams a lot (go to many men), she gets *paani* from many men. When we go to such woman then we contract *garmi*."(R, Married, 32 years, Illiterate). "Women from the *saphed galli get garmi* because they sleep with anybody. And if we do sex with them then we could also contract *garmi*. That's why one should not go to them." (S, Married, 33 years, illiterate).

Knowledge about HIV-AIDS

Various ideas prevailed about AIDS among the respondents. It ranged from 'no knowledge' to 'some knowledge' about the disease. Those respondents who had some knowledge, all of them believed that AIDS was spread because of women. The common belief was AIDS was a disease caused because of the *Randi baaya* (promiscuous women) as many people go to them for sex. One respondent explained it further— "*Randi Bai* receives *paani* (semen) from many people and because of that she gets the disease and then because of her, it spreads to other men. Hence we don't keep relations with such women." (D, Married, 33 years, 4th pass).

Misbeliefs about AIDS were common in the Ka Thakar tribal community. One respondent reported spread of AIDS through mouth to month contract. He said, "While doing *majja* with an unknown girl, I tie handkerchief over my mouth. I don't kiss (he used English word) such girl. *Jantus* (germs) could spread through mouth, which can cause AIDS. If I know the girl, then I don't tie handkerchief around my mouth. (M, Married, 26 years, Illiterate).

Only one respondent was able to tell about condom use for prevention of HIV-AIDS. He said, "Information about AIDS is shown on the television. Sex with a woman having many male partners can cause AIDS. One should not have relationship with such woman. Even if one wants to have relationship with her, he should use *Nirodh* (condom)". (B, Married, 23 years, 8th pass).

Conclusion

The study has shown that proportion of premarital sex and extramarital sex was very high as compared to that found among other urban and rural societies. The reason for high sexual activity among Ka Thakars lies in the socio-cultural context, which played very important role in shaping the sexuality.

In most of the tribal communities, sex is looked from healthy view point and is not considered as taboo. Sexuality is discussed freely through folk songs, stories etc. In Ka Thakar society, no restrictions were enforced upon young boys and girls. They were allowed to mix freely. Young boys initiated sexual activity at an early age. Men engaged in plural sex for enjoyment and was viewed as a change from the routine, i.e. sex with wife. Having more number of partners was considered as sign of masculinity.

Peer group influence was the most important determinant that shaped the sexuality of Ka Thakar males. Adolescent and youth were trained through cultural traditions like songs, stories, dances. They were also influenced by the mass media. Elder men encouraged young unmarried boys to engage in sexual activity. Social and cultural setting provided opportunities to Ka Thakar males to engage in premarital and extramarital sex.

There was wide gap between knowledge about contraceptives and actual practice. In spite of knowledge about contraception, most of the Ka Thakar males engaged in unprotected sex with the partner. Within marriage also use of contraception was very low.

Contact with the outside world influenced sexual behaviour of tribals. Social interaction with non-tribals and migration to urban areas changed their world view. They were getting exposed to double meaning songs, movies, blue films and pornographic books etc. Through influence of these factors they got introduced to new concepts like oral sex, anal sex, bestiality, homosexual acts, which were unknown to them. However, in spite of this exposure, their knowledge about HIV-AIDS was very limited.

Presently, Ka Thakars were engaging in sexual activity among themselves in their own area. There was no commercialization of sex among the tribals. Sex was consensual, unprotected, with multiple partners which could lead to STDs including HIV-AIDS. At present, prevalence of STDs was very low and there were no reported cases of HIV-AIDS in the taluka. Most of the respondents were not visiting prostitutes in cities. However, some respondents had reported of friends visiting prostitutes.

As an indicator of the process of development, age at marriage is increasing, age of sex initiation is showing upward trend, and premarital and extramarital activities are declining, with less number of young males engaging in the activities. Some males have reported use condom during sex with partners other than wife.

This is probably the indicator of the expanding network of Ka Thakar going beyond the traditional geographical limits of interaction, expanding the sources of information and knowledge.

11

Sexual Behaviour of Migrant and Non-migrant Youth

ABHAY M. KUDALE

Introduction

After Independence in India in 1947, industrialization and urbanization led to large-scale movements of people from rural areas to towns, and cities, and inter-country mobility (Bhende *et al.*, 1996). The emergence of rural-urban migration is important since it is the most dominant migration stream. Both the rural and urban areas face the consequences of internal migration. The rural areas lose their able bodied male youth, the most productive population group due to migration, while in urban areas migration affects the employment and wage rate, income distribution, availability of amenities, land values and urban development (IIPS, 1994).

Historically the phenomenon of migration has always facilitated the spread of any infectious disease by two ways. First, it brings more people in contact with each other and is the means whereby diseases could be carried from one community to others over considerable distances. Second, it has been a major factor in the growth of urban areas where dense population in close contact provide a favourable environment for epidemics (Caldwell, J.C. *et al.*, 1997).

In several parts of the world, geographic mobility, migration and widespread population displacement have been identified as significant risk factors in the transmission of HIV. The argument that migration is a risk factor for HIV and other STDs rests on the assumption that migrants are more likely than non-migrants to have additional sexual partners (Mark, Lurie *et al.*, 1997).

According to the National AIDS Control Organization (NACO) about 85 per cent of HIV infection in India occur through unprotected sexual intercourse. Migration of male population is one of the important factors that make India vulnerable to HIV-AIDS pandemic. Approximately 10 million people migrate per year; the most dominant migration stream is rural to urban migration and inter-state migration in search of better living opportunities. To prevent HIV infection, one of the major strategies used by the national health programmes is to facilitate behaviour change among the so-called high-risk behaviour groups through promotion of condom use (NACO, 2003). This scenario has stimulated researchers to study sexuality and sexual behaviour in the Indian context.

Various studies worldwide have documented the high-risk sexual behaviour of migrants in the cities and their vulnerability to the HIV-AIDS pandemic. Furthermore, these studies have identified situations and conditions such as separation from family, lack of support and traditional socio-cultural norms, isolation/loneliness, and a sense of anonymity that offer migrants more sexual freedom in the context of city life (Population Reports, 1996). Besides, the availability of cash, pressures of peer group and accessibility of sexual avenues have been documented to be important risk factors (Gupta, Kamala *et al.*, 2002, Apte, Hemant, 2000). These studies indicate that these factors operating in different combinations, facilitate high-risk sexual behaviour among migrants. Recognizing this fact, the National AIDS Control Programme (NACP-II) has incorporated migrants in its targeted intervention programme as one of the marginalized and vulnerable groups. Out of 680 priority targeted intervention projects taken up under the programme (NACP-II) highest numbers of targeted interventions (n = 262, 38.5%) were addressed to the single group of migrants (NACO, 2003).

Several studies have documented high risk sexual behaviour of migrants in the cities and have identified the commonly recognized risk factors like separation from family, lack of socio-cultural norms, isolation/loneliness, a sense of anonymity that offers more sexual freedom, availability of cash, peer group pressures and availability of sexual avenues at the place of migration. The studies on migrants do not document sexual behaviour of their counterparts, non-migrant village youth, at the place of origin and the factors determining their sexual behaviour.

The present study aimed at providing comparative picture of the sexual behaviour of the migrant youth to Pune city from villages in Velhe Tahsil, Pune district, with non-migrant youth residing in the villages. The study further explored the factors responsible for sexual behaviour of the groups, compared the knowledge, beliefs and attitudes regarding HIV-AIDS among migrant and non-migrant youth and also the concerns of parents of the migrant youth with regard to vulnerability to HIV-AIDS.

On an average, 14 per cent of the youth under study experienced premarital sex. In all, 26 per cent married and 14 per cent unmarried migrants had premarital sexual experiences, while only 8 per cent of married and 3 per cent unmarried non-migrants had experienced the same. Irrespective of the marital or migratory status, premarital sexual partners of the youth were girls in the neighbourhood from the same village. One-third 29 per cent of the migrant youth reported to have visited the vicinity of red light area of Pune city in connection with routine business activities or for shopping. Of these, 8 per cent reported to have had sex with CSWs. These youth had migrated at the age of 20 years and got married within 2 years of the migration. Their visit to CSW had taken place within this period of two years in Pune city.

All youth had heard of AIDS, 88 per cent knew about its incurable nature also. When questioned about possibility of getting AIDS in future; 14 per cent were uncertain and 6 per cent expressed concern that they might get it while 26 per cent of non-migrating respondents remained uncertain and 8 per cent feared about the possibility of getting AIDS. Majority of the respondents 87 per cent believed in preventive nature of AIDS and as a result 90 per cent of migrating and 66 per cent of non-migrating respondents reported to have taken precautions to safeguard themselves from AIDS.

Majority of the parents of migrant youth 96 per cent had heard of AIDS and 88 per cent of them believed that exposure to city enhanced chances of getting involved in risk behaviour. 66 per cent of the parents reported that they were concerned about recent scenario of AIDS in the city. As a result they did advise their sons to be cautious. Parents of unmarried migrants even reported making attempts of getting their sons married at an early date to prevent their involvement in high-risk sexual behaviour.

Objectives

Despite being prioritized as intervention group, the researches conducted on migrants in the cities, have been unable to adequately bring out their sexual behaviour at the place of origin before and after migration. Moreover, the sexual behaviour of their counterparts, the non-migrant village youth, residing at the place of origin, is also unknown. Keeping this in view, the present study aims at understanding sexual behaviour of migrant youth to Pune city from Velhe tahsil with that of non-migrant youth from the same area. Based on in-depth interviews conducted among migrant and non-migrant youth from Velhe tahsil of Pune district, this chapter examines the following questions:

(1) How do migrant and non-migrant youth perceive changes happening during adolescence? What do these changes mean to them?
(2) What are the methods used by these youth to develop relationships with girls in the villages or in the cities?
(3) To what extent are these youth involved in undertaking high-risk sexual behaviour?
(4) What is the influence of AIDS on the sexual behaviour of these youth?

Study Sites

The study was conducted at two different settings in Pune district. One was a rural setting comprising three villages in Velhe tahsil, around 30 kms from Pune city, as the place of origin of the migrants under study. The other was the urban setting, comprising the residential and work places of these migrants in Pune city, as the place of destination.

Methods

The study was carried out using multiple methods in a given serial order. The study began interviewing twenty-five opinion leaders to understand the causes, types, patterns, magnitude and impact of migration in Velhe tahsil. Fifteen unstructured interviews of migrant youth were conducted to find out the work patterns, friendship circle and life styles of migrants while in Pune city and back in the villages of Velhe tahsil. After analyzing these, ninety migrant youth in the age group of 15 to 35 years from three villages of Velhe tahsil were interviewed either in Pune city or during their visit to their respective villages in Velhe tahsil with semi-structured interview schedule. Fifty non-migrating youth from the same three (study) villages were also interviewed by using semi-structured interview schedule. In addition fifty parents of the migrant youth were interviewed by using semi-structured interview schedule. Lastly, ten in-depth interviews of migrant and non-migrant youth were conducted focusing exclusively on sexual behaviour and factors influencing it.

The study began with unstructured interviews of fifteen migrant youth, conducted to find out work patterns, friendship circles and the life styles of migrants during their stay in Pune city as well as during their visits to their homes in the villages of Velhe tahsil. After analyzing these data, ninety migrant youth in the age group of 15 to 30 years from three villages of Velhe tahsil were interviewed either in Pune city or on their visit to their respective villages in Velhe tahsil with the help of a semi-structured interview schedule. Fifty non-migrant youth from the same three study villages were also interviewed by using semi-structured interview schedule. During the final phase of data collection, in-depth interviews of twelve migrant and non-migrant youth were conducted, focusing exclusively on their sexual behaviour.

The quantitative data were complemented by qualitative data, which included narratives, and unstructured observations made over the course of field data collection. For quantitative analysis of coded variables, Epi Info, version 6.04 d was used. The data were read through several times and a coding system was derived from the themes emerging from the data. The data were then coded and categorized into thematic segments, which were then analyzed manually, in conjunction with the observations and field notes made during the course of data collection.

Sample Characteristics

The median age of ninety migrant male youth originating from the three study villages in Velhe tahsil of Pune District and migrating to Pune city for earning a livelihood was 22 years. More than half 54 per cent of them were educated up to high school (8th to 10th Standard), and 16 per cent up to junior college (11th-12th Standard). More than two-thirds 68 per cent of the migrants were engaged in unskilled or semi-skilled occupations such as working as helpers or salesman in shops, hotel workers, helpers in small scale industries, street vendors, office boys, milkmen etc. 17 per cent of migrants were driving auto rickshaws in Pune city. Their monthly income ranged from Rs. 500 to Rs. 10,000 (median and mode = Rs. 2000).

The median age of the fifty non-migrant youth, residing in the three study villages of Velhe tahsil was 23 years. More than one-third 38 per cent of them were educated up to high school (8th to 10th Standard), 18 per cent were educated up to primary school (1st to 4th standard). More than two-third 62 per cent of the non-migrants were involved in farming, 30 per cent were completing their education in high school and junior colleges and were also helping out their families with farming activities.

Due to involvement in the farming sector, they were unable to elaborate on their monthly income.

Migration from Velhe

Velhe town, the seat of Velhe tahsil in Pune district, is situated 35 km diversion from the Pune-Bangalore Highway (National Highway No.4), at a distance of 65 km from Pune city. In Velhe tahsil, agriculture is the main occupation and rice and ragi are the main crops. Agriculture is rain fed and the agricultural yield is inadequate to provide year long subsistence. The main subsidiary occupation is supplying milk to dairy retailer from Pune. There are no industries in the area and no other substantial opportunities for earning livelihood. In the year, 1999-2000, Velhe tahsil was labelled as the most backward tahsil in Western Maharashtra by the State government and thereby included in the list of the beneficiary areas under the "Urvarit Maharashtra Vaidhanik Vikas Mandal" (Rest of Maharashtra Statutory Development Board) which is statutory body to plan development of the backward regions in Western Maharashtra. This has prompted youth from Velhe to migrate to cities of Pune and Mumbai to earn their livelihood. Over a period of two decades, the flow of migrants from Velhe to Mumbai has been on the decline due to increased industrialization and availability of unskilled and semi-skilled jobs in and around Pune.

Profile of Migrant Youth

The dominant rural to urban migration stream from Velhe is the flow from Velhe to Pune city. This 'Chain Migration' is male dominated, single, intra-district and at a short distance. The new migrants from Velhe migrate to Pune city by taking help of either their relatives or friends, who had migrated earlier from their respective villages. The average age of the migrants has been 18 years.

In Pune, youth from Velhe earn their livelihood by working in unskilled occupations mainly as daily wage labour in vegetable markets, grocery shops, workshops, hotels and/or driving auto-rickshaws. These auto-rickshaws are either owned by them or are hired on rent on the basis of day or night shifts from other auto-rickshaw owners. There was frequent shifting or changing of occupations and/or jobs. Around two-thirds 60 per cent of the migrants in the study group had changed their occupations and/or jobs.

Thirty nine per cent of the migrants under study were married and more than three-fourths 77 per cent of them had got married after migrating. The wives of nearly two-thirds sixty three per cent of the migrants were staying back in the villages of Velhe. Forty-five per cent of these migrant youth visited their village homes every week and the remaining managed to visit them either monthly or after one and a half to two months.

Ninety seven per cent of the migrants had one or more of their relatives staying in Pune city. Sixty seven per cent of these migrants stayed at the houses of their relatives either by giving them fixed amount for food expenses or rent charges for accommodation on a monthly basis. Twelve per cent respectively stayed with their friends from the villages and at the workplaces. More than four-fifths 82 per cent of the male parents of migrant youth from Velhe visited the residential and work places of these migrants during their visits to Pune city. More than two-thirds 62 per cent of these male parents preferred to stay with their sons' at least for a night.

The monthly income of these migrants ranged from Rs. 500 to Rs. 10,000 (median and mode Rs. 2000). These youth reported sending an average amount of Rs. 1000 per month to their homes (range Rs. 250 to Rs. 4000). The major expenses reported by the migrants while in Pune city were food and rental charges. On an average, their food charges were Rs. 800 and their house rental charges were Rs. 500 per month. Their average total monthly expenditure was Rs. 1500 (range Rs. 50 to Rs. 4700). 41 per cent of these migrants reported having disposable income in their hands. Sixty per cent of them reported having savings in banks or chit funds.

These migrant youth reported having good friendship circles in Pune (average of six friends). These friends were either originally from their own or neighbouring villages and now working in Pune city or new friends from workplaces or place of residence.

Profile of Non-migrant Youth of Velhe

The youth who never migrated to any city for undertaking work before, or at the time of the study were considered as non-migrants. More than half of these 52 per cent non-migrants were unmarried. These youth stayed with their parents in a joint family, with an average of five family members.

More than four-fifths 88 per cent of them were involved in farming activities. The average land holding of families of these non-migrant youth was about 4 acres.

More than eighty per cent of the non-migrant youth had at least one relative staying in Pune city. They reported visiting their relatives or friends in Pune when they went to sell farm produce, and/or buy new clothes, farm equipments, seeds, fertilizers, insecticides, books, notebooks etc., and also for referral health care.

Due to their major involvement in the farming sector which was mainly the family owned vocation, with an annual one time income, they were unable to compute their monthly income. On an average, they reported that their families spent Rs. 1000 per month, towards purchase of grocery items other than grains and cereals, health and education-related expenses of their children and younger siblings etc. When probed regarding disposable income and savings, only one-third thirty four per cent of them reported having investing their money in banks, postal small savings schemes, chit funds etc.

These non-migrants had an average of five friends in the village. They had close interactions with their friends, who had migrated to cities like Pune and Mumbai, during their visits to their respective villages. On an average, they reported having four migrant friends. More than two-thirds 66 per cent of these youth reported that they felt bored in the villages and their means of overcoming boredom mainly included visiting friends and relatives, playing cards, watching television, and wandering around the village etc.

Typical Migrant Youth from Velhe

"Anil is 18 years old. He comes from one of the villages in Velhe tahsil. He currently works as a salesman in a utensil shop, which is located in the heart of Pune city. He receives Rs. 1700 as monthly salary. As a salesman his job involves addressing customers. He works from 10:00 a.m. to 9:00 p.m. everyday. He stays with his paternal uncle in a small and crowded slum area at the foothills of the famous Parvati hill. His uncle is married but stays alone in Pune. Earlier his uncle used to work in Mumbai in a sugarcane juice centre. Later on, he shifted his base to Pune with the help of his sister and brother-in-law and managed to get job in the utensil shop. His uncle also managed to get accommodation with the help of his villagers at the foothills of the Parvati hill, where he now resides with his two nephews, Anil and Kumesh. Kumesh who is Anil's cousin, works in an optician's shop. Kumesh is younger than Anil by one year. Anil comes from a joint family of eight members including his parents, grandparents, uncle, aunts and younger siblings. His family is primarily engaged in agriculture on a 7.5 acres of land, which is jointly owned. Some of his family members are also engaged in a small-scale business of milk distribution. Yet the income from both the sources is too meagre to support the family."

Typical Non-Migrant Youth from Velhe

"Sunil is 17 years old. He resides in one of the villages of Velhe taluka and is a twelfth standard student, completing his education in a junior college located in the neighbouring village. His college timings are from 8:00 a.m. to 12:00 noon. He stays in a joint family setup in the main settlement of the village. The family consists of his parents, uncle, aunts, grandmother, younger cousins and siblings. The main occupation of the family is agriculture; they jointly own four-five acres of land. The annual income from the agriculture is not enough for the family to sustain themselves throughout the year. Realizing their poor economic situation, his elder brother migrated to Pune city in search of a job, immediately after completing his twelfth standard education last year. Sunil while completing his education, supports his family by undertaking farm work whenever needed, taking the cattle for grazing on the hills regularly and helping the family everyday in milk distribution. Yet, his efforts are not enough and his father now expects him to migrate to Pune city after completing his twelfth standard examination, find a job and join his elder brother in supporting the family members in the village by sending them money regularly."

Adolescence

With the onset of adolescence, both migrant and non-migrant youth appeared to be more sensitized regarding their familial responsibilities and commitments. In case of migrant youth, such sensitization was reflected in their decision to move out for earning a livelihood and owning up to their responsibilities. One migrant youth while elaborating the changes during adolescence, mentioned,

> "...the first thing I realized after coming of age, is that I should go to the city and start earning money, as in farming, there is not enough production and conditions in the household were also not good." (*Unmarried, 17 years, 10th Standard, Milkman*)

With regard to non-migrant youth such sensitization was expressed by way of giving more time to share responsibilities by working on the farm. Even though they were completing their education, they tried their best to maintain a proper balance between their household and educational commitments.

The major behaviour pattern reported by migrant and non-migrant youth with the onset of adolescence, was increased attraction towards girls, nocturnal emission and masturbation.

> "From the age of 16 years, thoughts regarding girls keeps on coming in my mind, like I should have some girl who will be only mine, she should be able to give me sexual pleasure, I could marry her also, she should be there to support me."

> "...after every five, seven days I used to have 'fault' (night emission). In my dreams we feel as if we are having sexual relations with girls and in sleep only we ejaculate. After this 'fault' we do not remember the dream at all. When we wake up, due to ejaculation we have a horrible feeling. We also wonder whether our health would get deteriorated due to such ejaculations. This is not the right thing from the point of view of health." (*Migrant, Unmarried, 18 years, 10th Standard, Salesman in Utensil shop*)

> "Changes after coming to an age means starting to masturbate, developing moustache and beard and having feelings of wanting to have sexual relations with girls. Nobody told me, nor did I learn this from anybody. After erection, I felt like holding it (penis) and then started playing to take out the semen. Right from the age of 16 years I am doing this, but now I fear whether my semen would get finished or what?" (*Non-migrant, Unmarried, 17 years, 12th Standard Student*)

Thus the changes at adolescence as reported both by migrants and non-migrants covered the entire range of sexual transitions and dilemmas, usually faced by adolescent boys.

Patterns of Developing Relationships

After the onset of adolescence, both migrant and non-migrant youth reported following different tactics to approach the girls they were interested in, to persuade them to develop relationships.

> "While in school, boys will first start sending chits to the girls, they liked, stating that they love them. If the girls agreed, then boys would call them to a side and would have talks with them. From that if both of them agreed to keep relations then they would get married also. Generally such kinds of love affairs are of two kinds, one type of love affairs were aimed at marriages. Other love affairs were aimed at only friendship and would not lead to marriages. Those who have love affair aimed at marriages would generally eat and drink together, would keep sexual relations also but love affairs of friendship would never ever lead to sexual relations." (*Migrant, Married, 30 years, 9th Standard, Hotel Worker*)

Another married migrant youth while elaborating on his own experiences, attitude and behaviour at the age of adolescence mentioned that,

> "Around the age of 16 to 17 years I started coming of age, and started developing a kind of passion. Thoughts regarding sexual relations used to be always there in mind. Then I started looking to girls from that perspective, started teasing, flirting, and asking "loveship" (love relationship) to them. I was unable to sleep at night with thoughts on how to persuade this girl or that girl, how and when to meet her used to be there in the mind and then I would be unable to think and imagine regarding other things. At that time, while undertaking relations with the girls, neither there were any thoughts about the family, nor were there thoughts regarding what will happen in future then." (*Migrant, Married, 29 years, S.Y.B.A., Supervisor in Transport Company*)

One unmarried non-migrant detailing on what psyche and preparation goes behind developing a relationship with girls at the age of adolescence mentioned that,

> "Around that age after listening from their friends, boys start thinking about a particular girl. Before that unconsciously also they might have had the same girl in mind, but after listening from friends, thoughts about the girl gets fixed in their mind.

The same thing happened with me. Then, to attract that girl, I started wearing good clothing. During childhood I used to wear clothes, which were not ironed, tattered ones, but then stopped wearing those. I used to keep my hair style appropriate and started living up-to-date by observing others." (*Non-migrant, Unmarried, 17 years, 11th Standard, Farming*)

While elaborating on the steps in persuading the girl to develop relationship, one unmarried migrant youth mentioned,

"Firstly we have to make eye contacts with her and have to see whether she is giving signals to us...have to observe that carefully. If she did then either we should try to talk with her or she would try to do it. After a time we could touch her also. If she allowed us to touch then we could directly catch her 100 per cent for sexual relations." (*Migrant, Unmarried, 18 years, 10th Standard, Salesman in Utensil Shop*)

Another unmarried migrant remembering his relationship developed while in high school, elaborated another dimension in developing relationships, in which the girl took the lead role,

"She only took the initiative for approaching me; she used my cousin sister as a media to communicate to me that she loves me. We anyway used to be meeting everyday in the school, even during Diwali vacation also under the pretext of extra lectures we used to meet. I used to visit her house but while doing that, used to take my cousin sisters along with me so her family members did not have any doubts regarding us." (*Migrant, Unmarried, 19 years, S.Y. B.Com, Milkman*)

Elaborating on the methods employed by migrant youth after returning to the village to persuade the girls for developing relationships, one non-migrant youth mentioned that,

"...Youth, who are working in the cities, on their return to the village try hard to persuade one of the girls from the village. They write them chits through common friends. These boys, at night, generally bring video on rent in the villages for showing new Hindi and Marathi movies. Girls in the villages, as haven't

> seen those movies, in the hope of watching it, come there. If these boys earlier had approached and persuaded them then they signal each other and abscond from the scene. They then go either in the fields or into broken houses and have sexual relations with each other." (*Non-migrant, Unmarried, 17 years, 12th Standard, Student*)

One migrant youth elaborated on his attempts to persuade a girl in the city,

> "Here in Pune there is a girl who puts on good 'makeup' and has good 'shape' (figure) also. She comes daily to the dairy, in which I am working, for collecting milk. I would not get much time to speak with her. Once while taking a utensil for dispensing milk from her, I touched her hands but she did not react at all, she neither got angry nor did she abuse me. I felt that she was also willing and would not tell anybody about my touching her." *(Migrant, Unmarried, 17 years, 10th Standard, Milkman)*

Another migrant youth expressed his reluctance in persuading girls while in the city, by reasoning that,

> "...I did not even think about persuading any girl in Pune because of two reasons, firstly after coming to Pune I already started loving a girl from the village and the second reason is that from the behaviour of the first girl whom I loved most while in the village, I got very hurt. If I try to do something here and from that if my image gets spoiled, then the girl whom I love now would also get affected." (*Migrant, Unmarried, 19 years, S.Y. B.Com., Milkman*)

Thus, the range of methods used by both migrants as well as non-migrants for persuading the girls included dressing up well, having appropriate hair style. Then, at second level trying to approach girls, flirting, teasing them, making eye contacts, sending chits with common friends and at third level talking alone with them, touching them and if they agreed, having sexual relations with them.

Sexual Behaviour

On an average 13 per cent of the youth had experienced premarital sex, and more than three-fourths among them were migrant youth. In both married as well as unmarried categories migrant youth surpassed non-migrants with regard to their experience of premarital sex. Irrespective of the marital or migratory status, premarital sexual partners of these youth were mostly neighbouring girls from the villages. The first sexual partners of married migrant youth included village and city girls, wives and commercial sex workers (CSWs) while the first partners of married non-migrants included wives and village girls. The first sexual partners of unmarried migrant youth included village and city girls including their fiancée, while in case of unmarried non-migrants, the first partner was a village girl. This shows that with regard to first sexual partners migrant youth were ahead of non-migrants.

While elaborating on his premarital sexual relations with a girl in the neighbouring village one married non-migrant reported that,

> "...I restrict myself to one girl, I impressed her and she agreed to it. For doing this I spent seven to eight days, everyday there used to be eye contacts and exchange of signals with her. After two to three days she said yes. At that time I used to be staying at my aunt's place in the nearby village, the girl was from the same village. By watching blue films I knew how to have sexual intercourse and was not illiterate in that regard. So I went to her house and had sexual relations with her. That girl used to be staying at home and helping her family in farming. We were having sexual relations once or twice in a week, and for four to five months this affair continued. Then later on she got married, meanwhile my parents also started attempts for arranging my marriage." (*Non-migrant, Married, 25 years, 9th Standard, Farming*)

While elaborating on his premarital sexual relations, an unmarried non-migrant who had experienced the girl taking a lead role mentioned that,

> "I didn't have to do anything..., the girl came to me and she agreed to have sexual relations with me. This girl used to be from our neighbourhood, who, after a day or two, used to visit our home. Once in the afternoon when I was sleeping in the temple, she came to me and said that even after not having any sexual relations with me, her father had accused her of having

sexual relations, so she wondered why not to have such closer relations? Then in the evening, on the pretext of fetching water from village well, she came to the fields near the well and there we had sexual relations with each other. I used condom during the intercourse. After that nothing happened, as two months later, she got married with another boy and now nothing else remains to be told." (*Non-migrant, Unmarried, 23 years, 5th Standard, Wireman*)

It was also clear from the narratives of the youth that social pressures and specifically threats regarding premarital pregnancies also do determine premarital sexual relations with a girl from the village. One married non-migrant while narrating his tactics for persuading the girls mentioned that,

"...it's not that we have to sit in front of the girls for 24 hours while persuading them, even smaller impression is enough. From that signals got exchanged then one has to plan to meet at one remote site. My case was similar but I restricted myself to kissing and did not go for sexual relations. The reason for that was one of our friends kept sexual relations with a girl from a neighbouring village the girl became pregnant. Then after consulting a doctor, her family members terminated her pregnancy and 'clear'ed her. Then they married her at a distant place. But because of this event the other youth became very cautious, thinking that if in case their premarital partners became pregnant then social prestige ("*Aabru*") of their parents would be at stake and the name of the family would also get spoiled." (*Non-migrant, Married, 30 years, 10th Standard, Farming*)

One-third (29%) of the migrant youth reported having visited the red light area near Pune city. This was mostly in connection with routine business activities or for shopping. But curiosity about the red light area kept attracting them back to the area, where they would roam around with friends at workplaces or from their villages.

One unmarried migrant youth mentioned that,

"...Initially I was going to just move around in the "*gallis*" (lanes). I heard that there they beat children and snatch money from them, so firstly I was afraid. Later on one friend of mine, who used to reside in the neighbouring village, took me upstairs as he already knew which 'building' is good and which is not. Slowly and gradually I started going upstairs initially to get a feel only. There, all those women would call me by signalling and whistling. Then my friend who was experienced took me to one building where we both decided to have one girl. At that time I was afraid of getting AIDS but was unable to control myself. So I put three condoms one over the other. I was still afraid, I put on a fourth one, but because of that my penis got squeezed and during intercourse, I was unable to enjoy it, and within less than two minutes I ejaculated." (*Migrant, Unmarried, 17 years, 10th Standard, Milkman*)

Another unmarried migrant described in detail, the scenario in the red light area, and gave reasons for not having sexual relations with commercial sex workers there. He mentioned his encounter vividly as follows:

"I went to the '*galli*' along with my friends and sat outside...I did not go inside the room. I went up through the staircase, where people kept on coming. These girls were brushing them, sitting over their laps, crushing and pressing them, giving their mouths into their mouths. I did not like that scenario at all. These girls did come closer to me, but I slapped them aside. I went there (red light area) with five to six close friends, one was from my village and remaining others were from the workplace. That day, two of our friends who used to play lotteries, won a big amount that day, so they got drunk and asked us to accompany them to the '*galli*' to see what it looked like. Three of them went inside and had sexual relations. Each of them paid eighty rupees and girls made them put on two condoms while having relations. The entire scenario (at the red light area) was dirty. I had a feeling that it is not right for my friends to undertake such relations, but these decisions depend on each one's minds. My friends insisted that I also should have sex with the girls ...and were even ready to pay for that, but I said no to them and straightaway returned home." (*Migrant, Unmarried, 18 years, 10th Standard, Salesman in Utensil Shop*)

These narratives about the sexual relations described by the migrant and non-migrant youth bring out their pattern of premarital sexual relationships.

Scare of AIDS and Sexual Behaviour

Relying on their real life experiences with HIV-AIDS cases, more than half (56%) of the migrants and a little less than half (44%) of the non-migrants claimed that they would be able to recognize persons suffering from HIV-AIDS with the help of certain identified community markers like prolonged illness, severe weakness, wasting, sudden weight-loss etc. The following quotes elaborate these markers more clearly.

> "The whole body becomes weak ("*Kamkuvat*"), due to heat, pustules develop on the entire body, which later turn black. I have seen two persons having AIDS, one person used to weigh 100 kg, but after the disease his weight reduced to 30 kg, his bones also got reduced". (*Migrant, Married, 27 years, 10th Standard, Workshop worker*)

> "If one has prolonged fever and diarrhoea then within one month his hands and legs become emaciated, skin gets loosened like an empty bag. He will appear like a small child with rickets, his face will also become dry. He will not have strength or power and will be unable to take his meals." (*Migrant, Unmarried, 23 years, 10th Standard, Salesman in Hardware shop*)

> "His health went down, he was even not able to digest the food eaten by him. While walking one could observe the difference in strength..., his eyes got deeper (sunken)." (*Non-migrant, Unmarried, 16 years, 10th Standard, Farming*)

> "...would have blackened appearance, eyes become bigger, get dry and black. The body frame appears like a skeleton of bones, and the body would have no blood at all." (*Non-migrant, Married, 27 years, Fourth Standard, Farmer*)

When probed about familiar cases of AIDS deaths, 92 per cent of non-migrants and 79 per cent of migrants reported in the affirmative, referring to deaths of migrant youth in their locality, who used to work in the cities and had been labelled by the village community in Velhe as 'died due to AIDS'.

The cases of AIDS deaths reported by non-migrants mostly included migrants working in the cities as rickshaw drivers, juice bar workers and watchmen. Besides these, wives of migrants staying in the villages, who got infected from their husbands, were also reported as victims of AIDS by the non-migrants. The familiar cases of AIDS deaths reported by migrant youth were also mostly from these above mentioned professions, since these mainly constituted the community labelled cases of AIDS from their villages. In addition to these professions, they reported unemployed youth, barbers and liquor sellers in their neighbourhood in the city as the cases of AIDS deaths.

This scenario regarding AIDS appeared to create a kind of positive pressure on the sexual behaviour of the migrant youth. The rural community, mostly parents of both migrant as well as non-migrant youth had also become more alert to the HIV risk, due to exposure to urban areas. They reported undertaking actions such as getting their youth married earlier and keeping a close eye on their behaviour so as to prevent their involvement in high-risk sexual behaviour. Youth, who were also well sensitized to this scenario, were taking precautionary measures and trying to stay away from undertaking high-risk sexual behaviour.

One representative quotes of unmarried migrants summarized the situation.

> "Being human, everyone is bound to die, but in our village one person died due to AIDS and people did not even turn up at his funeral (*Maytila Aali Nahit!*). When I came to know about this, I gave up outside sex relations. Even previously I was not going to professional prostitutes but fixing things in villages, but now realizing that this also could be troublesome I stopped it completely!" (*Migrant, Unmarried, 21 years, 7th Standard, Workshop worker*)

Discussion

The present study attempts to provide a comparative understanding of a range of sexual behaviour of youth against the background of migration. The migration pattern from Velhe tahsil to Pune city is peculiar as it is male dominated, intra-district, short-distance migration resulting in frequent back and forth mobility of youth from Pune to their native villages in Velhe. This migration flow and pattern from Velhe tahsil provides the opportunity and logistics to undertake such a research of studying the sexual behaviour of migrant youth at both ends of the migration spectrum. This research site also helped in exploring the sexual behaviour of non-migrant youth from the villages of Velhe tahsil and provided insights into a range of sexual behaviour.

There is well documented evidence that sexual activity for many people begins in adolescence, even in the rural Indian set-up (Pelto, P., 2000). The present study strengthens this finding and explicitly documents the changes among migrant and non-migrant youth during adolescence. At the onset of adolescence, experiences with acts of masturbation and nocturnal emissions made youth from Velhe get concerned with the ill-effects of these experiences on their health and sexual performance in the future. This finding also supports earlier research findings on adolescents in India which have concluded that adolescents in India tend to be extremely poorly informed and confused regarding their own sexuality and physical well-being, their health and their bodies (Jejeebhoy, S., 2000; Pelto, P., 2000).

During adolescence, irrespective of the setting (rural or urban) and migratory status (whether migrant or non-migrant) the youth studied reported employing a range of methods to attract girls and draw them into relationships. The patterns of developing the relationships threw light on the degree of emotional commitments and attachments accorded to such relationships. Some of the youth were deeply involved and felt committed to these relationships and appeared to be giving thought before developing these relationships further. But a majority of these youth appeared to be developing the relationships very casually and employed different methods to persuade girls without giving much thought to its consequences for themselves, their partners' marital prospects and more so on psychosocial and sexual health.

The data on sexual relations showed two distinct patterns. The first was the sexual relations of these youth, irrespective of their migratory status, primarily with the village girls. The other was the sexual relations these youth had with Commercial Sex Workers (CSWs) in the city, particularly the migrant youth. The pattern of sexual relations with village girls appeared to be a complex mix of natural sexual urge, desire and emotional involvement of both migrant and non-migrant youth with their sexual partners in the villages and the availability of opportunities in the villages for undertaking sexual relations. This pattern of sexual relations with village girls appeared to be mostly premarital and the use of condoms during sexual relations by non-migrant youth showed knowledge, awareness and practice with regard to prevention of unwanted pregnancy and HIV-AIDS. After the gradual termination of such relations due to marriage of their sexual partners, these youth showed their sensitivity by not further complicating such relations and spoiling the marital future of their casual sexual partners. Many of the non-migrant youth preferred not to stretch their developed premarital relationships up to sexual intercourse in order to avoid the possibility of premarital pregnancies out of such relations thereby compromising the social prestige of their parents and their families.

The second pattern of sexual relations reported to be undertaken by youth migrants with CSWs, however, appeared to be of serious consequences. This pattern appeared to be also the result of a complex mix of natural sexual urge for experimentation, curiosity regarding commercial sex workers, peer influence and availability of disposable income of migrants as well as the availability and accessibility of sexual avenues for migrant youth. This pattern of sexual relations is definitely high-risk sexual behaviour. The silver lining of this behaviour is that not only does this group of migrants have sufficient knowledge regarding precautionary measures, but they also put this knowledge into practice by actual use of condoms in high-risk sexual behaviour. This acceptance of precautionary measures by migrants was also hinting towards the in roads made by the national programmes of mass awareness regarding HIV-AIDS in the migrant community.

The background of instances of community labelled AIDS cases and deaths in Velhe area had generated good awareness and sensitization regarding the association between high-risk sexual behaviour and causation of HIV-AIDS. These instances also generated concerns among parents of migrant youth and the opinion leaders from Velhe Tahsil regarding the vulnerability of their youth in the cities to HIV-AIDS and facilitated their coping mechanisms and actions to overcome these concerns. These inter and intra-dynamics provided insight into high-risk sexual behaviour of migrants.

12

Perspectives of Sexuality among Adolescent Girls

MAUSHAMI JOSHI

Introduction

Human sexuality and sexual behaviours are interrelated to a complex network of social and public health concerns. This fact has been especially highlighted by the central importance of sexual behaviours in the transmission of HIV-AIDS. The heterosexual route is recognized as the main pathway for transmission of HIV in India, as in most other countries. As a result, there is great need to understand the complex patterns of sexual behaviour in different sectors of the Indian population. Nowhere is the need for study of sexual behaviour and sexuality more important than in the adolescent population. Adolescents make up approximately 20 per cent of the total population of India, and they are at a greater risk of HIV infection than other segments of the population (Jejeebhoy 2000). Half of all new infections detected are in the age group of 15-24 years according to UNICEF India, (*Indian Express*, February 11, 2004).

The significance of behavioural factors as determinants of transmission of HIV-AIDS and other STIs has been established by many studies. Heterosexual route of transmission of HIV is recognized to be highest in India. According to a survey by UNFPA, many of the HIV infected individuals contract the infection before they are 20 years of age. Young women are biologically and socially more susceptible to STIs and, many of the STIs are asymptomatic and therefore, may remain unnoticed and untreated for longer periods of time. So far, the kind of studies that have been conducted in the area of sexuality have looked at the knowledge, attitudes and practices regarding reproductive physiology, and sexual relations (pre-marital and extra-marital), contraception, fertility, age at marriage and the first child, number of children and the like. But, there is paucity of information about how adolescent girls construct their sexuality, their perceptions about their own sexual selves, what do relations, in general and sexual in particular mean to them, their information networks and their perception about risk or vulnerability to HIV-AIDS.

Adolescence is a crucial stage in the life cycle, since young bodies are maturing sexually, developing sexual urges and interest in the opposite sex, combining with lack of information and understanding about reproduction, the risks of sexual involvements, and the specific dangers of STIs and HIV. This is also the time, during which individuals establish life styles and behavioural patterns that have profound effects on their adult careers, including aspects of sexual and reproductive health.

The past two decades have seen a very large increase in research on sexual behaviour and sexuality in India (Pelto, 2000; Verma *et al.*, 2004). A whole range of studies measuring Indian attitudes towards premarital and extramarital sexual behaviour, awareness of the risks of HIV-AIDS, and other topics, have been reported. Recent studies have also explored issues such as power relations and negotiations in marital sexual relations, domestic violence, and other issues related to women's sexual and reproductive health (George, 1997; George and Jaswal, 1995). A number of studies have focused on the sexuality, sexual behaviour and levels of knowledge among adolescents (Apte, 1997; Bhende, 1994; Jejeebhoy, 2000). On the whole the research paints a compelling picture, which shows that adolescents are an especially vulnerable sector of the population, as they indulge into sexual relations with inadequate knowledge levels. The health programmes in the country have generally not been focused on serving the specific needs of adolescents. There is a widely recognised need for programmes that can lead to significant improvements in the levels of knowledge and awareness among young people, as well as improvements in the reproductive health services available to them.

Within all populations, adolescent girls are biologically and socially most susceptible to STIs, HIV infections, and other health problems. Biologically they are vulnerable since, studies have shown that male-to-female transmission of HIV is two to four times more prevalent than female-to-male transmission (Aral, 1993). Also during the developmental stage of the cervix, (during puberty) there is greater susceptibility to diseases such as Chlamydia and Gonorrhoea. Many sexually transmitted infections are asymptomatic among the females, and may remain unnoticed and untreated for longer periods of time. Thus, adolescent girls often may not realise that they have an infection (AIDS Update, 1999). Socially the vulnerability of young girls is greatly increased by the risks of forcible sex from aggressive young men. Those risks are compounded by the serious lack of information among young girls regarding sexual matters and reproductive physiology. Adolescent girls are ignorant with extremely scanty and often incorrect information about their own bodies and sexuality. According to UNICEF India over 50 per cent of young people in the age group of 15-24 continue to harbour serious misconceptions about HIV leading to high risk behaviour (*Indian Express*, February 11, 2004). Cultural taboos and the guilt and shame associated with sexual matters and sexually transmitted infections are among the many factors reinforcing the vulnerability of young girls. Generally, parents avoid discussions of sex and reproduction with their children since "sex and puberty are considered to be embarrassing, distasteful and dirty subjects, not to be discussed with their adolescent daughters" (Jejeebhoy, 2000:75).

Since childhood, girls are socialised to believe that the most significant role for them is that of a wife and mother. During puberty, the prime focus of gender role socialisation is on virginity/chastity, which is a means of restraining and controlling female sexuality until it is channelled into marriage (Dube, 1988). Despite the ideals concerning virginity, young girls are attracted to boys, particularly when they reach puberty; and the great emphasis on romantic attachments and sexual attraction in movies and TV have added a new dimension to the conflicts between socially accepted ideals and the realities of heterosexual attractions experienced by young girls (Sodhi, 2000, 2004).

The women's health and empowerment movements have generated considerable interest in women's sexuality and gender research. In the HIV-AIDS scenario, the emphasis is given mainly to preventive efforts, which places special emphasis on the study of the 'everyday' sexuality and sexual behaviour of individuals (Oomman, 1998). Prevention of the spread of HIV and other sexually transmitted infections is possible only if intervention efforts are informed by clear understandings about the ways in which sexuality and sexual behaviours are woven into the fabric of everyday life. Much more information is needed about the gaps and tensions between culturally patterned 'ideal norms' of adolescent behaviours and the actual behaviours in different sub-groups.

Studies of the spread of HIV infections in India have noted that about 50 per cent of the infections are found in the age group of 15 to 24 years (UNFPA, 1997), and many individuals have contracted HIV infections, before the age of 20 (Population Report 1996). In addition to the dangers of HIV infections, young girls are vulnerable to a wide range of other health risks, including unwanted pregnancies, sexually transmitted infections, reproductive tract infections, as well as severe depression, anxiety, and other mental health problems.

The study attempts to understand adolescent girls' perceptions about their sexuality, their information networks and friendship patterns with boys, and their knowledge of reproductive health. The term sexuality has been operationally defined as the total sexual make-up of an individual. In addition to covering the physical aspects, it also encompasses attitudes, values, experiences, and preferences (IPPF, 1989 cited in Bhende, 1994).

The study was carried out in a slum area in Pune city. Qualitative data collection was comprised the methods as key informant interviews 7, group discussions 8 and in-depth individual interviews 50 with adolescent girls. The quantitative part comprised a survey of school girls 300 from standard 8th and 9th of the Municipal Schools near the community. The participants of the study were unmarried adolescent girls in the age range of 12-18 years.

The prelim nary findings showed that 72 per cent respondents had heard of menstruation and 65 per cent had attended menarche. Only 9 per cent were aware about relation between menstruation and pregnancy. Sources of information on contraception were TV 49.7 per cent, Posters/ Advertisements 14.3 per cent, Balwadi/Clinic 16.7 per cent, Health workers 17 per cent and Peers 24.7 per cent. Information about STDs and AIDS revealed that 54.7 per cent had not heard about STDs whereas only 28.7 per cent had not heard about AIDS. Out of the 45.3 per cent who had heard about STDs, only 4 per cent reported the correct causes of STDs. Of the 35 per cent who responded that they knew the causes of AIDS 22 per cent gave correct responses. School going girls, especially those who had attended talks in school or in the community, had better information as compared to their peers.

Perceptions of sexuality was guided by films and TV about their images of self, and their bodies. Beauty, looking attractive, and attention of opposite sex were the major concerns during this age. It was reported that 48.3 per cent of the girls had friendship with boys, and around 42.3 per cent had only acquaintance with boys in school. 94 per cent of the respondents mentioned that they were scolded by elders for talk to boys in their community. The qualitative findings suggested that girls and boys got involving in multiple relationships.

Out of the 50 respondents a majority 35 mentioned public toilets as convenient for places sexual activity. Social occasions were used to meet each other. Thus adolescent girls were aware regarding menstruation, hygiene, pregnancy and abortion largely through peers and educational programmes conducted by NGOs in the community. They had scanty knowledge regarding basic body processes and about reproductive health. More so in the case of school dropouts. The vulnerability of the study group was revealed from the lack of knowledge of HIV and contraception in contrast to romantic ideas about love with boy friends.

In my study I found that, despite the strong restrictions on heterosexual contacts imposed by their families, many of the adolescent girls were involved in 'affairs' with boys, and those relationships often led to sexual behaviours for which the girls were ill-prepared. In the study community, girls and boys enter into multiple relationships of varying nature, and physical intimacies are often a part of the relationship. These relationships begin as simple friendships and then blossom into love relationships. Both girls and boys fall in and out of love. There is considerable fluidity in these relations. Initially the girl may consider the boy to be 'like a brother/maternal uncle (*mama*) or a 'friend'. The relationship then deepens, to that of 'lover'. In the 'lover' stage the boys usually call the girls to meet at secluded places at night, such as at the public toilets, homes or secluded rooftops/terraces. The notion expressed by many of the girls in the qualitative interviews was that for love one can 'do anything'. Since the major interest of the boys was in having sex, the girls were very often drawn into sexual activity without awareness of the possible consequences. Films and TV were found to be the main sources that guide the girls' ideas and knowledge about themselves, their bodies and their relationships with boy friends.

This chapter deals with the emerging sexuality of adolescent girls and their perspectives on heterosexual relationships in a low income residential area of Pune, Maharashtra (India). The study focuses on the vulnerability of young girls in relation to the risks of unwanted pregnancy as well as sexually transmitted infections (STIs), HIV-AIDS and other health problems. Adolescent girls in low-income communities are especially vulnerable because of their involvements in heterosexual relationships, coupled with their low levels of knowledge regarding sexual and reproductive matters.

The study is intended to identify the pathways and possible guidelines for developing greatly increased sex and reproductive health education for this very vulnerable segment of the population.

Defining Sexuality

Sexuality is a multifaceted term, which includes dimensions such as the ability to maintain meaningful relationships, appreciate one's own body, interact in a healthy manner with both males and females, and express love and intimacy in ways consistent with one's socio-cultural values (Watsa, 1996). An individual's sexuality is not a constant, and continues to develop as the individual matures and enters into new relationships. Many of the changes are influenced by broader processes of social and cultural changes occurring in our local and regional communities. Kakar has written that "sexuality is a system of conscious and unconscious human fantasies, arising from various sources; seeking satisfaction in diverse ways, and involving a range of excitations and activities that aim to achieve pleasure that goes beyond satisfaction of any basic somatic need" (Kakar 1989: 21). Thus, sexuality encompasses eroticism, sexual behaviour, social and gender roles and identities, relationships, and the personal, social and cultural meanings attached to all these.

The Research Site and Data-Gathering Methods

The research was carried out in Mahatma Nagar (pseudonym), which is a low-income community in Pune city. Participants were adolescent girls in the age range of 12-19 years. The community has been predominantly a migrant population, the majority of whom have been Hindu, Buddhists (ex-untouchables converted to Buddhism). There are also a few Muslims, and other Hindu sub-castes, such as *Kannadigas* (migrants from the Maharashtra-Karnataka border), *Lamanis* (construction workers migrated from Rajasthan) and others migrated from Uttar Pradesh and Andhra Pradesh (particularly Hyderabad). There are four private clinics in the area and people also utilize a nearby private hospital (Kamal Nursing Home), and the Sonawne Hospital run by the Pune Municipal Corporation. The population numbers about 10,000 persons, as per January 2000 survey. Most of the men work in the nearby Market yard, in the vegetable, flower and fruits market, and in the warehouses where the grocery items are stored. Other occupations in which men are involved are collection of scrap, construction work as casual labourers (*bigaari*) and as other miscellaneous unskilled labour. Women work as housemaids in the nearby residential colonies and some among the middle class families. They are also involved in seasonal work, including cleaning of grocery items, such as tamarind, wheat, rice and other food grains.

Methods

The data in this study were gathered through key-informant interviews, group discussions, in-depth individual interviews and a survey carried out in three municipal schools. The respondents were adolescent girls in the age range of 12-19 years and the key-informants were community health workers, social workers, mothers and the elder sisters of the adolescent girls.

The data-gathering included a mix of qualitative and quantitative methods. The qualitative data collection consisted of ten key informant interviews, 10 group discussions and 50 in-depth individual interviews with adolescent girls. The quantitative data collection entailed administering a structured interview schedule to 300 girls studying in the three municipal schools that serve the local community. The respondents in the schools were in the 8th and 9th standards, and their median age was 14. Only a few girls in the 9th standard were 17 years of age.

The Influence of Mass Media on the Girls' Self-Images

The adolescent girls of this low income community, develop their ideas about physical appearance and self-image to a considerable extent from the mass media, particularly television. In the survey I found that 88 per cent of the girls watched TV, and approximately 50 per cent of them watched on an average 3-4 serials everyday, which amounts to four hours of TV watching per day. In addition, the girls spent a lot of time in talking about films, heroes and heroines, their clothing, and other details. The majority of the girls with whom I carried out in-depth interviews (35 out of 50) spent some amount of the pocket money given to them on waxing, eyebrows and trimming hair/haircuts. The rest of their spending money was utilised for buying imitation jewellery and cosmetics such as *bindis*, nail paints, earrings, rings and necklaces. The girls in my study expressed the widespread Indian ideal, that fair skin was equated with beauty, and thus, considerable amount of money was also spent on various creams and talc to develop fair skin.

Appearing attractive is one of the major goals of the girls, for getting a boy friend. Most of the girls said, that they got very few chances of "getting ready" (dressing up) and going out. And they make the most of it when they do get an opportunity. That is, under some pretext or the other they try going out of the house to get 'noticed'. During such times, girls heard comments from boys, such as 'Madhuri Dixit where are you going? *(Aye Madhuri Dixit kahan chali?)'*. Girls enjoyed such attention as they got it very rarely. The overall 'restrictiveness' for girls was high and affected their mobility severely. One of the narratives addressed to the investigator (*Tai*-elder sister) is as under:

> Tai ('elder sister' in Marathi) see how much dressed up this Sarika (name changed) is! [Sarikaa was wearing a white sharara (an Indian dress with a long umbrella skirt, a top and a stole) with lots of jewellery, big earrings, bangles, rings, a decorative bindi, and she had put on a lot of powder and lipstick and foot wear (chappal) with high heels]. Tai, I tell you this Sarika always gets dressed up even when she is not going out. And then you know she will keep roaming in the slum getting ready like this, under some pretext or the other. And then she keeps complaining that 'boys are always after me!' Tai, now just tell me if she will do all this '*nakhra*' (fashion) and *latak-matak* (sensous movement while walking) obviously boys will be after her! And to tell you the truth she likes all these boys coming after her. She just keeps complaining for the sake of it. Secretly she enjoys it. See how she is smiling... (Sangeeta, Age 14years).

> "Sarika: No, Tai, it is not like that. Only sometimes I get a chance to get ready and then is it not natural that I will feel like going out? So I lied to my mother and told her that we all were supposed to get ready (dressed up) and go to the Balwadi (child care centre) that's how she let me out of the house."
>
> (Sarika, Age 16 years).

These statements express a central theme in the daily lives of the adolescent girls. They are interested in being 'noticed' by boys, and hope to develop relationships, but at the same time their families put severe limitations on their movements. The girls managed to get out of the house under some pretext or the others.

When a girl attains menarche there is further tightening of 'controls' on her movements, and her parents impose an entirely new set of rules that she must comply with, in order to conform to the social norms. After reaching puberty, a girl is no longer permitted to play outside the house, and she cannot wear frocks unless it is the school uniform. Girls are strictly instructed not to talk to strangers, and any such instance is sternly reprimanded, if it comes to the attention of the parents. The following excerpt from an interview illustrates this sudden change:

> "*Tai*, when I first got my periods my mother asked me to take a bath and then gave a whole lot of instructions to me like when you are in periods don't talk to boys or strangers. Now you cannot go out and play and you have to cover your breasts, so no more wearing of frocks. Now you have become 'wise' (You have come of age.) (*Ata tu shahani jhali hai.*). And I wondered was I mad all these years?"

Many of the girls said that they felt awkward about the changes taking place in their bodies, and they received no guidance from either elders or from anyone at the school concerning the physical and psychological experiences of this transition. In the qualitative data, 35 girls out of 50 mentioned the process of growing up and the changes occurring in the body in terms such as 'strange/dirty/awkward/bad'. As one of the respondents reported.

> "I cried a lot when I saw my breasts growing. It used to hurt, and I used to feel I was better off without them." (*Savitri, Age 15*)

One of the girls mentioned:

> "*Tai*, when I got breasts I used to hate going out alone, as all the boys and men used to continuously stare at me. That is why I started going to the toilet also very early in the morning when men are not around and, therefore, I even eat less with the fear of going to the toilet at an awkward time." (*Sameena, Age 14*)

Yet another respondent indicated behavioural restrictions on her:

> "It (life) was better before I got my periods. Now I am not allowed to play outside the house, wear frocks, and even if I laugh loudly my mother admonishes me." (*Surekha, Age 15*)

One girl complained:

> "*Tai*, here in the slum people are not very good. If they see a girl and boy talking, then they immediately get suspicious and start gossiping. Therefore, my mother and my elder brother never

> allow me to go out of the house alone. Even if I am going to the public toilet, somebody always accompanies me." (*Pushpa, Age 14*)

Most of the girls said, they knew something about 'coming of age' (menstruation) before it happened to them. The quantitative data showed 73 per cent of the girls in the schools had heard something about menstruation, including something about the ritual restrictions, as well as the physiological pain. Most of them had heard that girls were supposed to 'sit aside' for four days, that they should not touch the deifies [images of the deifies in the household *puja* place] and that sometimes the stomach or lower back hurts. But very few girls knew about the actual physiological processes of menstruation, and what to do when it occurs. The following statements illustrate this point.

> "I had heard about it from my elder sister and one of my friends. But when it actually happened to me I thought that I had got some deadly disease in which I would bleed to death. Mother had gone out to work so I went to my aunt and she advised me to take a bath and put a cloth in my underwear". (*Suvarna, Age 15 years*)

> "*Tai*, you know all our neighbourhood women used to ask my mother when will Taidi become wise? (*taidi shahani kadhi honar?*). And when I got my periods for the first time I was so happy that I danced around and felt very good about it, you know...I felt like a grown up woman. Then my *mami* (aunt) and my *ajji* (grandmother) told me to put a cloth and told me that from now onwards I cannot play outside the house and should wear only '*salwar kameez*'. Till then everything was fine but when I realized that it happens every month I felt very bad and cried a lot as the restrictions on me were increasing day by day." (*Aruna, Age 16 years*)

Friendships and Relationships with Boys

Dosti ('friendship') as it is popularly known, is a milestone that marks the beginning of relationships with boys. The girls whom I interviewed in depth expressed the belief that most girls wanted to have boy friends, and that such relationships were the usual pattern in boy-girl relations, despite the efforts of the girls' parents to prevent their occurrence. The courtship usually follows this pattern.

Boy sees or notices girl. This usually happens when the girl is out running errands, or going to school or going to use the public toilets. Often small groups/gangs of boys sit at crossroads or near the public toilets and these are the places where it all begins. Boys begin by teasing the girls. Teasing is one of the most effective ways for boys to attract the girls' attention. Episodes like the ones cited below are quite usual.

If a girl is seen passing by, the boys would talk amongst themselves loudly so that the girl could hear. Comments would be made about her dressing style, hair, her looks or the way she walks. Very often the remarks would include comparisons to film heroines, which is one of the ways of flattering girls. Remarks such a *"Aishwarya Rai is going (Aishwarya Rai chali)"* or *"This one is looking like Madhuri Dixit (ye to Madhuri Dixit jaisi lagti hai)"* or *"met Madhuri Dixit on the street (Madhuri Dixit mili rastey mein)"*.

If the girl turns around to see who is making such remarks or feels like laughing at any of the comments, it is seen as a positive response from her side. Her response would lead to statements such as 'she is giving line *(line de rahi hai)*' or *patli rey or phasli rey* are used (which roughly means: 'now the girl is trapped'). Or sometimes if the girl talks back, it encourages the boys to make further comments, such as 'if I take one kiss what will you do?' or inscriptions are written with big bold letters on the common walls such as the name of the girl and *A 30 ka? 'yetis ka?* (to be read in Marathi meaning 'coming with me?') Or: *13 mera, 7 tera mera sath* ('you and I are together'), *teri meri 21, ikkis* (to be read in Hindi to mean, 'You and I kiss'). This is also one of the ways in which the boy can malign the girls' name.

Stages of Friendship and Intimacy

1. Common teasing by the boy is to sing popular film songs for the girl. Recent favourites include songs such as: *kaanta lagaa* (thorn has pricked my heart) or *and Iss pyaar ko mein kya naam doon? Bechain dil ko kaise aaram doon?* (What name should I give this love that I feel for you, and how should I give peace to my restless heart?). Another popular song is *Tum agar saamney aa bhi jaya karo laazmi hai mein tumse parda karoon* (Which roughly translates as: a girl must act shy when her boy friend is around) or one of the all time favourite song is *Aati kya*

Khandala? (Coming to Khandala for fun and frolic?)

2. The second stage, after the two have 'noticed' each other, is when the boy follows her and finds out where she lives and who her friends are. He often befriends the girl's friends and gathers information about her likes and dislikes, which school she goes to, her favourite colours and other information.
3. The next important step is that the boy attempts to get himself noticed, by loitering around her house, making comments when she passes by, singing songs and sending a message to the girl through her girl friends. Making eye contact is very important during this stage, and smiles are exchanged.
4. When the girl comes to know that the boy is continuing to be interested in her, she initially refuses all the overtures and conveys a message that she is not interested. The girls often refer to this as *latkavaycha,* (hanging, to keep on hold) which means that you should not give in easily to boys' attentions, as it diminishes one's value. After a certain period has elapsed the girl also starts smiling and would go out of the house on some pretext or the other, just to get a glimpse of the boy.
5. One of the key stages, wherein the boy makes a move, supposedly a bold one, is either to go directly and talk to the girl, or else he sends a *chitthi* [written message], through one of the common friends or through children playing around in the neighbourhood. The typical messages of such *chitthis* consist of the boy's declaration of love for the girl, and asking her reply. One of the *chitthis* shown to me by a respondent stated as follows: Pushpa I am madly in love with you. *kaho na pyaar hai—kaho na pyaar hai* (say, you also love me) with a picture of a red rose on it.

   Sometimes boys include some "blackmail" in their messages, including threats *(dhamki)* such as 'if you say no I will kill myself,' or 'I will stop coming to school,' or 'I will start drinking.' In some cases they also make threats such as "I will spoil your name in the neighbourhood so that nobody will marry you or your family will face a lot of *badnaami* (disgrace)."
6. If the relationship takes a positive turn, then the affair begins (popularly known as *chakkar* or *lafda).* Clandestine meetings are fixed by the couple at convenient places and times. The physical intimacies also follow a pattern or a sequence. Initially, the boy will hold the girl's hand or put an arm around her shoulder or waist, progressing to embracing or hugging, followed by

fondling and kissing, first on cheeks and then on lips. The culmination is, particularly as planned by the boys, is sexual intercourse. But al! affairs do not necessarily end in sexual intercourse.

Many of the narratives told to me by the girls purported to be about their girl friends, though in some cases the story was probably about the informant herself:

"You know *Tai*, these boys, they start living very smartly. Then you know they will try to make themselves seen. Like they will find out all the required information about the girl, like who are her friends, where does she live, which school does she go to, and what does she like etc. Then they start sending messages to the girl through her common friends or so that (she will know that he is interested in her). Then they (the boy) will do whatever the girl likes, wearing her favourite colours etc. And once they come to know that even the girl is interested then they send love-letters, ask the girl to go out, or meet somewhere. This is how it begins! Sometimes boys also give lots of gifts."
"Tai, you know Sunita? Her boy friend has given her a lot of gifts. What trick these boys do is, first they will talk very sweetly and lovingly with you and once their purpose is served then they leave you. *Tai*, most of the boys here do only "*masti*" (play, enjoyment) in the name of love. (*Ganga, Age 15 years*)

In the following narrative the girl tells of her own *chakkar:*

"You know Anita. She once came and told me that Ajay likes you a lot and is in love with you. So once when I was washing utensils outside my house he was standing at the terrace of the public toilet which is just opposite to my house. He was constantly staring at me so I smiled at him. After this he went completely mad and was after me (*'mag to majhya maagach padla'*). Then once I only wrote a *'chitthi'* (love letter) to him mentioning that Anita told me that you love me and that is why you follow me everywhere even to school! Is this true? Then I gave this *'chitthi'* to Anita and she gave it to him. *Tai*, you won't believe this he gave a reply to me within 15 minutes. He had written in the *'chitthi'* "Yes, Sangi, I really love you a lot (*kaho na pyaar hai—kaho na pyaar hai*). Then we started seeing each other regularly. He always used to stand on the terrace and I used to keep coming out of the house under some pretext or the other. Then gradually he started making '*isharas*' (Visual Suggestions) conveying that I should go and meet him. Once he called me near the bus stop. Since it was the first time, I was jittery and took a friend along and he had also come with one of his friends. Then he used to call me to meet very often.

Then my mother realised that I was onto something so she scolded me for being out of the house for longer periods of time. So I told him that now it was difficult to meet him. Then he got very angry with me and just stopped even looking at me. I sent a message saying that I will somehow manage to meet him. This time he called me at night on the terrace of the public toilet. *Tai*, I was so scared but had to go otherwise again he would be angry and leave me. So I told my mother that my stomach was aching and that I needed to go to the toilet. When I went there it was pitch dark as after 11.30 all the lights are off. He was waiting for me and *Tai*, you know what he did? He pulled me in his arms and was pressing my breasts and then he kissed me. I was so scared that in a hurry I pushed him and straight came home without looking back. I cried a lot that night. You know after 'it' happened I was feeling bad about the whole thing. But now I enjoy what he does.

He also gives me a lot of money to spend. He has given a lot of gifts to me like a watch, necklace, and rings. Earlier he used to give me 50 or 100 rupees, but now he just gives me 10-20 rupees. So once I asked him why now you give less money to me? To this he retorted that now you have become 'old' now I won't pamper you so much (*ata tu juni jhali ata tujhe phar laad karayche nai*).

He used to call me at different places so that people from our slum won't come to know about anything. We used to meet at the *tekdi* (hill) near the godown or the bus stop. But then later we realised that a lot of time was spent in coming and going, that's when we decided to meet at night either at the public toilet or at an open ground behind the slum. But, you know, this relationship will never work out, as my mother will never agree to marry me outside the caste. But I cannot stop myself from

> meeting him. Even if I marry I will always love him and will keep meeting him". (*Sangeeta, Age 14 years*)

Once the *chakkar* (affair) is established and the girl and boy declare their love for each other, they start meeting at isolated places. If the girl's parents are both working, there is the possibility that they can meet there; or at the boy's house. In some cases, the boy has a friend whose house is vacant and available at certain times. The areas near the public toilets also have some privacy after darkness falls. Girls who are working may find it comparatively easy to meet their boy friends. That is, they can call their lovers to the work place and then go out. As one of the respondents mentioned:

> "*Tai*, I call Shankar at the bungalow where I work, and I tell my madam that my cousin has come to pick me up and I have to go early today. Then we either go to Saras baug or we go to his laundry *(workplace),* as in the afternoon he keeps it closed, so we go inside and pull the shutters!" (started giggling). (*Nagava, Age 16 years*)

Several of the girls that I talked with admitted that 'girls are shy and will always say no' to the boy's more aggressive sexual advances. One of the respondents mentioned her own experience:

> "He had called me near the ground (an open area behind the slum) and since it was late evening there was nobody there. When I reached I asked him as to why he had called me so late. He just pulled my *dupatta* and kissed me. I got very angry and told him so. That time he sung this poem (*shayari*) for me '*Surya var aag ahey, chandra var daag ahey, tujhya cheherya var jo raag ahey to majhya premacha ek bhaag ahey*' which roughly means there is fire on face of sun, spots on face of moon, the anger on your face is a part of my love for you". (*Reena, Age 14 years*)

Since it is a belief supported by film songs that girls always say no, even when they mean 'yes,' the common pattern is that the boy will force her to engage in sexual intercourse, provided they have sufficient privacy. In some cases the girls are only vaguely aware of what the sex act actually consists of, and do not know how to protect themselves if they are unprepared for full sexual intercourse. The use of condoms or any other protection from pregnancy is of course highly unlikely in these situations. Some, but not all, of the girls are aware that pregnancy can result from unprotected sex, so they may experience acute anxieties about their sexual encounters, as in the following narrative:

> "*Tai*, some girls over here have done "everything" like sleeping together. Tai, you know Shobha has done it! She was telling me that Ajay called her near the Public Toilet at night and then he slept on her and it seems that white stuff came out from him! She was telling me when we met the next day. She was very much scared of getting pregnant! So I told her that whatever she was doing was not right! And I told her that there was no point in crying now and that she should have thought of all this before she went to meet him at night! And you know she did not get her periods for 3 months after that, so then I told her that she should go to a doctor and get herself examined. I told her to go to Dr. Pawar's clinic. But then the next day she got it!" (*Sunita, Age 14 years*)

In cases of pre-marital pregnancy, the informants reported that sometimes the boys help the girls financially to abort the child, but in many cases they just leave the girl to deal with the situation by herself. The girl either takes the support of her friends, cousin sisters or maternal aunts. In some cases, if she has no other resort, she must confide in her mother, who then takes the girl for abortion. In cases where the pregnancy has advanced and it is not possible to resort to abortion, the parents may seek to get their daughter married off to another boy in a far away village so that people don't know what has happened. Another solution is that the girl is taken to a relative's village, usually the mother's side, where the childbirth takes place, and the girl is brought back to marry. In such cases her child would be left with her mother's relatives.

Sometimes, couples elope and decide to get married. The favourite place where they can get married is at Aalandi, which is a religious place approximately 35 kilometres from Pune. The priests at the temple would solemnize the wedding. Usually the couple returns to the community after staying at a lodge or rented room for a few days. If the parents accept the marriage, the couple starts living with the boy's family. But, if they don't, then the couple must separate, and the girl is married off by their family. The following episode illustrates a not uncommon outcome:

> "I was so much in love with Amar that when he told me that we should run away to get married I readily agreed. He called me near the bus stop in the afternoon and told me not to get any bag or else people will get suspicious. We met near the bus stop and then went to the main bus station near Swargate. From there we took a bus to Amar's uncle's village. *Tai*, I stayed with him for a four and then we came back. His parents were ready to accept us but my mother refused, saying that he was from another caste. So we could not get married. Now my mother is looking out for marriage proposals for me..." (*Nehal, Age 13 years*)

Many of the love affairs are short-lived, as the boys often see these relationships as 'time pass' or *masti* (fun and frolic), just to see if they can induce a girl to have sex with them. Boys who have the means can give girls money and gifts, just to see if the girl will give in to them in the first or second meeting. In such cases the boys will profess their 'love' for a girl, but they only do that as a pretext to get a meeting with her. Some girls know that they boys are not really serious, but they will go with him nonetheless, as they feel that they are in love. In such cases the romantic fantasies from movies and TV lead girls to be trapped by the boys' statements of love. The following exemplify the transitory nature of some 'affairs':

> "*Tai*, I really loved him a lot and used to do everything in order to keep him happy, but see now he is going around with my best friend. I told her about how bad he is but she says that Ajay told her that I was just a 'game' for him and she is true love..." (*Chanda, Age 15 years*)
>
> Another girl narrated:
>
> "...there was a time when I was hopelessly in love with Suresh but after a few days I realised that he was more interested in my cousin then even I fell in love with another boy Vikram who used to sit near our house and sing love songs whenever I used to pass." (*Reshma, Age 13 years*)

One reason for the transitory nature of these affairs is, of course, that the parents will put a stop to the situation if they find that their daughter is getting involved with a boy. Quite usually the 'remedy' adopted by the families is to arrange a marriage for their daughter as soon as possible, to an acceptable husband—often someone from their home village back in Uttar Pradesh, Rajasthan, or other distant place. Both the boys and the girls involved in 'affairs' are aware that, howsoever much they may feel strong attachments to one another, their love affairs will usually be broken up by the parents through the mechanism of arranged marriages. The following narrative explicates this:

> "What to tell you, *Tai*, so many instances of broken love affairs we see here. Now see this Sukkhi, she was in love with Dilip and they were planning run away as Sukkhi's mother was not ready for the match. So she took her away to their native village and they kind of drugged her during the marriage ceremony and now see she has left her husband and has come back to her mother's place. She is still meeting Dilip. Now what will her mother do?" (*Annapoorna*).

'Good Girls' and 'Bad Girls'

It is not possible to find out how many of the girls in (affairs) Mahàtma Nagar community actually get involved in *chakkars* with boys; as such activities are strongly disapproved by the parents, as well as by others in the local community. A few respondents mentioned their fears and anxieties regarding *dosti* (friendship).

> "*Tai*, you know I find all these things very bad. My mother does not allow me to go out of the house for days together. I do not go out alone in the slum, not even to the toilet and even when going out with mother I have to wear *burkha*. Mother says '*izzat*' of a girl is like glass, even if a tiny crack develops it can be immediately seen."
>
> Another girl said:
>
> "No *Tai*, I don't like to even hear of things like these (boy friends). My mother tells me not to talk to girls who have boys as friends. You know Nagavaa. She is a very bad girl. She is always talking to boys and she just doesn't bother about what people will say! My mother and brother don't even send me to the 'balwadi' as right in front of the 'balwadi' all these *mawali* (vagrant) boys

sit. Mother says once a girl's name is spoilt it is very difficult to get her married and her sisters will also face '*badnaami*' (disgrace)."

Yet another informant expressed her ambivalence about *dosti (friendship):*

"*Tai* you know mother says the girl should be like clean washed rice (*dhutlya tandula sarkhi*). She should not talk much, always walk with her head lowered and should not take part in any kind of discussions. She does not allow me to talk to even my brothers' friends. And even I feel girls should not get involved in all this '*dosti*' and '*chakkars*' because boys do this only for time pass. But, when I hear other girls talking, I also feel that even I should have somebody who loves me or waits for me! But it is bad, right?"

The following excerpt shows how peers exert an influence on relationship:

"Oh I never thought that I will also fall in for friendship and loveship. *Tai* I am so dark but there was this boy who used to stare at me and smile or sing songs whenever I used to pass. The other day he was singing 'excuse me, *kya rey mera dil tuj pe fidaa rey*!' (my heart is aching for you). So, I told my best friend about this. Then she and a few other friends of mine start teasing me with him and then slowly you know I also developed love for him."

In the in-depth interviews, informants gave their opinions that many of the girls did develop relationships with boys, and many times these relationships led to full sexual involvement. At the same time, my informants were quite clear about local distinctions between 'good girls' and 'bad girls.' As one of my informants expressed it:

"Those girls who are bad, they roam around a lot. And they are always looking for opportunities to talk with boys. Even when they are walking their eyes are always roving. They are also seen more often on the street. Those girls who are bad are always disagreeing with their parents, and answering back."

"But good girls are those who will stay in the house all the time. They will talk properly and with respect for their elders, and are soft-spoken. They will not even look at boys, and whenever they have to go out they will not look here and there, but walk with their head down. *Tai*, I tell you that here in this slum, if young girls laugh, then people will call them names...they say, 'Girls from good families don't laugh loudly".

These stereotypic depictions of 'good girls' and 'bad girls' are very similar to the ideal roles reported in Mumbai (Bhende, 1994), Delhi (Sodhi and Verma, 1998), and other communities. The contradictions between these 'cultural ideals' and the real-life aspirations and interests of the girls are striking, and reflect an environment that is likely to produce strong psychological tensions as well as diminished self-esteem among the adolescent girls.

In the quantitative survey, I asked the girls about receiving any letters from boys, only 35 of the 300 respondents said they had received letters from boys 'recently'. On the other hand, twice that many 78 said that their girl friends had received such letters. 52 (17%) of the girls answered that they had received gifts from boys, and 48, 16 per cent said they had gone to meet a boy while accompanied by a friend. Nearly 28, 10 per cent of the girls reported that they had gone alone to meet a boy. Because of the sensitive nature of these questions, I suspect that there is very considerable under-reporting despite the fact that the girls were assured that their responses would be kept entirely confidential.

My qualitative interviews strongly suggest that considerable numbers of these adolescent girls become involved in 'affairs,' and consequently run the risks of an unwanted pregnancy as well as the possibility of sexually transmitted infections.

Lack of Knowledge about Reproductive Physiology and HIV-AIDS

Many studies, in Maharashtra and elsewhere, have documented the very serious gaps in knowledge among adolescents concerning reproductive physiology and the dangers of sexually transmitted infections (Apte, 1997; Bhende, 1994; Ramakrishna *et al.*, 2001). As pointed out in many studies, girls have much less exposure to sources of information on sexual and reproductive health matters, and consequently are extremely naïve about even the most elementary aspects of reproduction and childbirth. Although sex education is now mandated in the public schools of Maharashtra, beginning in the 8th standard, the girls in my quantitative survey exhibited very serious gaps in basic information.

On being asked about any relationships between menstruation and pregnancy, 82 per cent of girls didn't know, if any, relationship existed and only 16 per cent mentioned that there was some connection. When asked if a woman gets periods during pregnancy, 60 per cent of the girls gave a response 'don't know,' while 37 per cent gave the correct response. To the question, "how does a woman get pregnant?" only 22 per cent of the girls gave 'sexual intercourse' as the answer.

Approximately two-thirds of the girls in my survey said, they had heard of HIV-AIDS; but only one-third (105) said they knew how it spread. One, third of the respondents correctly answered that there was no cure for HIV-AIDS, but half of the girls said they did not know the answer to the question. It is clear that their exposure to information about HIV-AIDS and other sexually transmitted infections is extremely superficial, leaving them seriously vulnerable to sexual health problems.

Conclusions

As can be seen from the data, the adolescent girls in my study community are strongly affected by the romantic and sexually arousing contents of TV and movies, and many of them are involved in 'affairs' with boys. According to the discussions with my informants, they are preoccupied with the possibilities of having heterosexual friendships, and, therefore, extend considerable effort and a major part of their spending money on their appearance and dress. Their notions about love and marriage are largely derived from what they see in films and television.

The girls are caught between the strong urges and emotions of adolescence, and the controls imposed on them by their families. They express need for more information about sexual and reproductive matters, but these topics are socially sensitive, and their parents and other family members generally do not consider it appropriate to inform young girls about such things. Sex education as taught in the schools appears to come too late, and does not seem to provide much understanding or detail. Probably the teachers are reluctant to dwell on explicit details of sexual matters.

The conflict situations of these adolescent girls can have serious consequences for their mental well-being, in addition to the other health risks involved. Research among school students in Karnataka found that girls who become pregnant, or who got trapped in disapproved love affairs, often contemplate suicide as the only wayout of their impasse (Ramakrishna *et al.*, 2001). Andrew and Patel (2001) found evidence of depression and high anxiety levels among many school girls in Goa, reflecting the same kinds of psychological pressures and social conflicts. In their study 32 per cent of the girls reported that sometimes they feel that 'life is not worth living,' and nearly half of these respondents had sought help for their mental problems. Their study in Goa included adolescents from both low income and middle income families, showing that many of the conflicts and contradictions faced by young girls are not confined to low income families, but are a more general condition in both urban and rural environments. These problems seem to be more severe, however, in communities made up primarily of migrants from distant rural areas, in which both the younger generation and their parents are attempting to adapt to new social and cultural values, changing norms of sexual behaviours, as well as the marginal economic circumstances in which they live.

A study by Sodhi and associates in a low income area of New Delhi has highlighted some of the same issues that I have examined in this study. They pointed to the extreme vulnerability of young girls, and particularly the added risks posed by the parental attempts to maintain strict controls, without any increase in the girls' levels of knowledge and problem-solving skills. They summarized their findings by pointing to the needs for programmes to improve the knowledge levels and coping strategies of adolescent girls:

> "In effect, traditional strategies used to protect the girls from these modern influences (TV, films, changing patterns of heterosexual conduct etc.) render the girls more vulnerable rather than protecting them. New influences, knowledge, and coping strategies are needed for the girls, which are not being provided in the family context, and for these to be effective, the context of the family (the 'immediate environment') also needs to be addressed" (Sodhi *et al.*, 2004).

The respondents, during in-depth sessions expressed rather naive, simplistic ideas concerning their expectations about married life. They want their future husbands to love and respect them, and they frequently mentioned that they wanted their husbands to avoid alcohol, and to be good economic providers. However, given the current urban patterns of masculine expectations and sexual behaviour, the adolescent girls are in danger of serious sexual and reproductive health problems both before marriage and during their early marital life. As pointed out in a number of studies (*cf.* Verma *et al.* 2004), the adolescent boys are also lacking in information about protecting themselves from sexually transmitted infections, including HIV-AIDS. The young men's eagerness for sexual experience is not matched with sufficient knowledge of condom use and the dangers of STIs.

The study shows that the adolescent girls in low income communities are caught between the attractions of boyfriends, and the strong restrictions imposed by their families and social norms, according to which 'good girls' do not have any relationship with boys. In dealing with these conflicts, the girls have few resources of either information or social support. Programmes to improve the situations of the low-income adolescent girls will need to be comprehensive in nature. In addition to empowering the girls through increased information about sexual and reproductive health topics, such programmes should also reach the parental generation, to increase their understanding of STIs, HIV-AIDS and other reproductive health problems, and also to raise their awareness of the dangers involved in the traditional styles of parenting. A very large component in any programmes of sexual and reproductive health education, or 'family life education,' for adolescent girls, needs to focus on building their self-esteem and problem-solving capabilities, as pointed out in the studies by Bhende (1994), Sodhi and Associates (2004), and others. The schools and teachers, too, should play a larger role in providing support and counselling to adolescents of both sexes.

13

Sexual Behaviour among Migrant Hotel Workers

LOKESH GUJJARAPPA AND SANDEEP RASALPURKAR

Introduction

Social and moral values are rapidly changing in India. Majority of adolescents who become sexually active do so without adequate information about sex. In Indian culture, sex is permitted only within marriage. But, pre-marital sexual activity among adolescents and young adults is well documented by several researchers in the past decade (Apte, 1997; Abraham, 1999; Goparaju, 1993; Sharma, 1995; Watsa, 1993). On the one hand, in India, the average age at first marriage is rising, while on the other hand boys and girls are becoming sexually active at a much younger age. The median age of initiation of sexual activity was 16-17 years for rural adolescent boys and college going males (Sharma, 1995). Contact with commercial sex workers was highest among sexually active migrant rural adolescents, most of them being wage earners and somewhat economically independent. A study among the lower middle class migrant workers in four towns of Maharashtra report pre-marital sexual experience rate of 32 per cent (Savara and Sridhar, 1994). Such an exposure to high-risk sexual activity is clearly reflected in the increasing HIV prevalence in the country with adult HIV prevalence rate of 0.8 per cent.

An attempt was made to study sexual habits of urban educated Indian youth through large-scale surveys by Family Planning Association of India (1990). Studies conducted so far covered special target groups such as medical or health vocation (Divekar and Banerjee, 1992) students (Chitale *et al.*, 1992; Abraham, 1998; Rangaiyan, 1996), truck drivers, and (Singh, 1992), adolescents (Bhende, 1994; Apte, 1996). Most of these studies were focused on determining the extent of the risk of HIV infection.

The emergence of HIV-AIDS among different groups, such as, unmarried/married youth, married women, skilled/unskilled labour, businessmen, housewives, industrial/factory workers, students and hotel workers led to understanding the context within which such populations are getting engaged in high risk sexual behaviour. The need to study these groups was expressed by Nadkarni (1999). However, very few studies have been documented so far (Singh, 1992; Savara and Sridhar, 1994).

Hotel workers constitute a group of migrant workers with low levels of education. Due to group living in an urban environment they are likely to indulge in risky behaviour and become vulnerable to sexually transmitted infections including HIV. However, there are hardly any Indian studies available that throw any light on the sexuality/sexual behaviour of this migrant, unorganized group.

The present study aimed at documenting sexual behaviour of migrant hotel workers in Pune City with focus on knowledge and opinions, perception about sexual and risk behaviour. Data were collected by a survey of 100 hotel workers and eight key informant interviews. At the same time three group discussions were conducted. The respondents were chosen from the twelve hotels.

The median age of the respondents was 22 yrs and 93 per cent of them were literate. Poverty was the main reason for migration and availability of free lodging and food over and above the monthly salary was the major reason for joining the hotel industry. Most of them did not know much about STDs 81 per cent. Sex with CSWs, excessive masturbation and spicy foods were thought to be the main reasons for causation of STDs. Friends were the main source of information about STDs including HIV-AIDS followed by newspapers, television, books and lastly, a doctor. Only 15 per cent were of the opinion that STDs could be prevented and cured.

Almost all respondents had heard about AIDS caused by sexual intercourse, infected syringes and shaving blade. Infected blood and mother to child transmission were reported as the principle modes of transmission for HIV-AIDS. Misconceptions about spread of HIV-AIDS due to kissing, shaking hands, sharing clothes, sharing kitchen utensil, stepping on urine or stool, mosquito or flea bite were also reported. 82 per cent respondents said that AIDS could be prevented. 75 respondents thought that they could never get AIDS. Out of these, 58 thought that since they never had sex with CSWs, they would not get AIDS. 15 respondents out of 92 perceived that they could get AIDS. Two of them thought so due to their prior sexual contacts with CSWs, whereas the rest of them perceived it because of their ignorance about causation of AIDS.

Fifty eight per cent of the respondents reported having sexual experience with a single partner 53 per cent and the rest 47 per cent with multiple partners. Median age at first sexual contact was 19 years and in many cases, with a village girl or with a CSW 11 per cent. Out of all those who had sexual experience, 23 respondents were currently sexually active and four 17.39 per cent reported CSWs as their current sexual partners. In most instances, first sexual contact occurred before migration and was rather unexpected and unplanned. Condom use was generally found to be very low. More than 80 per cent of the respondents thought that behaviours which involved physical contact between a male and a female could be called sex. Only two of the respondents reported homosexual experience. Respondents associated the risk of AIDS, TB, oral diseases and weakness with homosexual acts. Due to lack of any formal and credible source of information, misconceptions about causation of the infection, peer interaction and pressure due to group living, lack of social control, and interplay of other predisposing and enabling factors prompted hotel workers to get involved in risky sexual behaviour.

Objectives

Increasing migration for work to urban centres have prompted more studies on studying sexual behaviour among migrant population. Lack of uniform rural development programmes in India has led to migration of male labour force into cities. Almost one-fourth of these migrants are young, single, illiterate and unskilled (FRHS, 1994). Hotel workers constitute a distinct group of migrant workers. Their age, economic independence, low level of education, group living and residence, at a place away from their family, make them vulnerable to the risk of contracting STDs including HIV. Although the priority need to study hotel workers as one of the migrant populations was spelt out, not much has been done so far. Apart from the study regarding KABP on AIDS awareness among hotel workers, no study has specifically documented sexual behaviour of hotel workers.

National AIDS Control Organization (NACO) reports that in Maharashtra, of the total persons tested HIV positive at the STD centres, hotel workers constitute the maximum 26.9 per cent. Thus, there is a need to understand the behavioural risk of hotel workers, particularly migrant hotel workers in term of getting HIV-AIDS. They are one of the bridge population and by understanding their sexuality, interventions could be planned to limit the spread of the infection to their partners. Being in an unorganised sector and out of formal set up, government programmes are difficult to reach this population. As a result, they are unable to avail the benefits of such programmes. The present study was an attempt to understand the sexual behaviour among migrant hotel workers so as to facilitate awareness building about HIV-AIDS and safe sexual practices among them.

The aim of the study was to document sexual behaviour among migrant hotel workers in Pune City. The objectives were:

1. To document knowledge and opinions of hotel workers regarding STDs and AIDS.
2. To understand the perceptions of hotel workers in terms of sexual and risk behaviour.
3. To study sexual behaviour among hotel workers, and
4. To document the antecedents of the reported sexual behaviour.

Methods

The study was exploratory and formative in nature. Apart from STD and AIDS awareness among hotel workers, data regarding sexual behaviour of hotel workers were collected using both qualitative and quantitative methods. The study was conducted in two phases. In the first phase emphasis was mainly on key informant interviews and observations to establish the context of the study and the second phase consisted of interviews with hundred hotel workers to quantify some of the findings. In-depth interviews and group discussions were also conducted.

The study was carried out among migrant hotel workers in Pune City. Prominent reason for selecting Pune City as the study site was rapid increase in HIV prevalence and inflow of large number of young people in the city seeking employment. There are a large number of hotels and restaurants in Pune City.

The permission to conduct the study was obtained from the Hotel Owners Association who expressed the need for such a study as hotel workers were getting infected with HIV. The Joint Secretary of the Association gave a consent letter, and a request letter to hotel owners, to extend their co-operation.

During first phase of data collection, the researchers contacted the owners and managers of different hotels and briefly explained to them the nature of inquiry. They were ensured about the confidentiality of the data collected and sought their oral consent for conducting the study among their employees. The researchers then contacted the hotel workers individually and asked if they were willing to participate in the study. Key informant interviews (8) were conducted during this phase.

During second phase, the hotel workers were contacted and were informed about the project. The researchers told them that the study aimed at understanding the lifestyle of hotel workers. The researchers also told the respondents that they would give them information regarding STDs and HIV-AIDS towards the end of the project.

Interviews were conducted either in the hotel or in the staff room as per the convenience of the respondents. Not all workers were able to talk or understand Marathi, the local language. Few interviews were also conducted in 'Kannada' and in 'Hindi' language. Group discussions (3) were conducted after the survey. Rapport established during the interviews helped in conducting group discussions. Group discussions were organised after the duty hours of the workers. Two of them were conducted after 11 p.m. and went up to 3 a.m., while one was conducted during afternoon hours. Each group consisted of seven to eight participants.

Data from the key informants revealed that most of the hotel workers belong to the age group of 12-30 years. Hotel workers were mostly migrants from draught prone areas. Poor socio-economic conditions forced them to migrate to cities. There were around 10-15 hotel workers working in a hotel. They either stayed in the hotel itself or in a room provided by the hotel owner. Group living was a peculiar characteristic of hotel workers. They worked in a shift of 8 hours but in most instances the timings were not fixed. Occasionally, they had to put in more than 8 hours of work. They got a weekly holiday and some free time between two shifts. Most of this time was spent either in sleeping or pursuing some other recreational activities. Some of the hotel workers were also engaged in other economically gainful activities. There was a fair degree of promiscuity among hotel workers. Factors responsible for the promiscuity that got highlighted during the discussions were lack of social and familial control, influence of mass media and economic independence etc. Hotel workers who formed a set of migrant workers were, therefore, studied to explore different factors responsible for sexual risk behaviour in terms of vulnerability to HIV-AIDS. These findings helped in designing the interview schedule for the survey.

Migrant hotel workers, for the purpose of the present study were defined as those workers who were not permanent residents of Pune City.

Hotels in Pune City were grouped under twelve different areas and approximately nine hotel workers were then randomly interviewed from these twelve areas.

During the first phase of the study, reasons for migration, socio-economic status, expenditure patterns and day-to-day activities of hotel workers were explored. The key informants were managers in hotels, waiters and a member of the hotel owners association. Expanded notes were immediately written down after the interview and subsequently translated into English. During the second phase, a survey using a pre-tested interview schedule was conducted.

In-depth interviews of those who reported having sexual relations were conducted in the second phase where, respondents were asked to narrate their sexual experiences. In all five such in-depth interviews were conducted, each spanning over three to four sessions of one to one and half hours duration. Group discussions yielded data about the reasons for premarital sex, extramarital relations, knowledge regarding causation, transmission and prevention of HIV-AIDS, perceived risk to self, homosexual relationships etc. Three group discussions were conducted each spanning 60-90 minutes with 7-8 participants in each group.

It was difficult to interview hotel workers after their duty hours because they were tired and hence reluctant to give information. It was found that almost none of the respondents were available at a time set for the interview due to extra work. On several occasions the researchers had to make 10-12 visits to a hotel to convince a hotel worker for an interview.

Some managers feared that the researchers might give information about the number of workers, their salaries, number of customers etc. to the income tax department or to the labour department, which could create problems and hence, refused permission to interview their staff.

Sometimes, there were interruptions during the interview process either by the managers or co-workers. Hotel manager sometime, visited the interview site as a result of which the respondents were unable to speak freely. It is felt that some valuable information might have been lost in the process. Some hotel workers and owners kept postponing the dates of interviews, which showed their reluctance and unwillingness to participate in the study.

The interview schedule was prepared in 'Marathi' language. It was found that not all hotel workers were able to understand 'Marathi', so the researchers had to communicate either in 'Hindi' or in 'Kannada'.

In one of the restaurants after completing the interview late in the evening, the researchers were about to be assaulted by a drunkard but the hotel manager intervened in time.

Profile of the Respondents

Background information of the respondents was obtained through a semi-structured interview schedule. Median age of the respondents was 22 years. The median age at migration to Pune was 17 years. Educational level of the respondents is given below:

Table 13.1: Educational Level of Respondents

Education	*Per cent*
Illiterate	7
Up to Primary School	9
Up to Secondary School	66
Up to Graduation	18
Total	**100**

Source: Field Investigation.

Twenty per cent of the respondents were married and mostly belonged to Hindu religion except one who was a Muslim and the other was Buddhist. Majority of them were from Maharashtra 66 per cent, around one-fifth were from Karnataka state and the others had migrated from Uttar Pradesh, Bihar, Haryana, Andhra Pradesh, Madhya Pradesh, Rajasthan, Gujarat and Kerala. One respondent was from Nepal.

Almost 50 per cent of the respondents 49 per cent were working as waiters, 22 per cent as cook, 8 per cent as manager and helpers, 6 per cent as table boys, 4 per cent were bill writers, two were barmen and one was working as a watchman. The income differed according to the cadre. Managers received higher salary ranging between Rs. 3500-4500 per month while, table boys and helpers the lowest Rs. 900-1000 per month. It was found that salaries of the respondents also varied according to the type of the hotel and their experience. 6 per cent of the respondents were also found engaged in other gainful activities such as newspaper distribution, helper to a kiosk vendors etc. 66 per cent of the respondents reported that they regularly sent some part of their earning to their families.

Activities during Leisure Time

Eighty three per cent of the respondents watched movies, mostly Hindi films. Occasionally they also viewed an English movie. 69 per cent of the respondents saw movies on the television provided by the management. 77 per cent of the respondents said that they spent time reading the newspaper, 32 per cent read novels/books. More than 50 per cent of the expenditure was on entertainment. Addiction to alcohol, tobacco and cigarette was quite prevalent.

Reason for Migration

More than two-fifth of the respondents 42 per cent reported poverty as the main reason for migration, whereas, lack of employment opportunity in rural areas was reported by an equal number. 16 per cent respondents mentioned 'attraction towards the city life' as a reason for migration. On probing further, several respondents said that since facilities such as lodging and food in addition to monthly salary was taken care of, most of them preferred to work in hotel industry.

Group living is a peculiar characteristic of hotel workers and hence to determine the extent to which it is common, the respondents were asked about their lodging 80 per cent of them reported staying with fellow workers in the hotel or in the staff room provided by the owner. Others reported staying with friends, relatives etc.

Knowledge about STDs

Only 20 per cent respondents knew about STDs. The finding is in accordance with the national statistics given by NACO where less than one-third of the sampled population reported awareness of STDs. Half of the respondents equated STDs with AIDS, while, the remaining half said that these are the diseases that spread through sexual relations with sex workers and are some kind of skin diseases. Only 17 per cent of the respondents had heard or knew of symptoms of syphilis or gonorrhoea. Causes of infection as reported by the respondents are given in Table 13.2.

Those respondents who were aware of one or more symptoms of STDs were asked about preventive measures. Most of them reported use of condom and avoiding sex with a sex worker. 88 per cent of the respondents who knew about STDs reported that STDs could be cured. Respondents said that although they were at risk of acquiring STDs they would not get infected because they did not have sexual relations with sex workers. This clearly reflects the notion among hotel workers that sex workers were the only source of STDs.

Table 13.2: Causes of Infection reported by Respondents

Causes	*Frequency (N=17)*
Sexual intercourse with CSWs	15 (88.2%)
Sexual intercourse with a person suffering from STD	13 (76.5%)
Infected blood	13 (76.5%)
Excessive masturbation	6 (35.3%)
Sex during menstruation	1 (5.9%)
Contaminated water	1 (5.9%)
Wearing wet underwear	1 (5.9%)
Sharing undergarments	1 (5.9%)
Spicy food	1 (5.9%)
Heat in the body of a woman—CSW	1 (5.9%)

Multiple response question.

Source: Field Investigation.

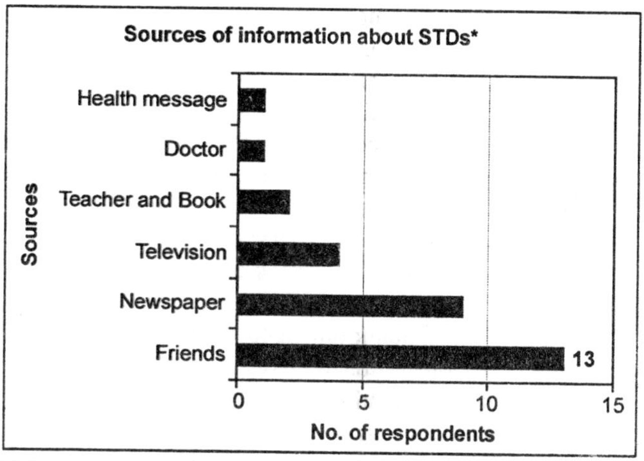

* Multiple response question.

Fig. 13.1: Sources of information about STDs

The respondents reported friends (13) as the prime source of information about STDs, followed by newspapers (9) and television (4). Two reported teachers and books as the source. One respondent received information from a health message while the other said that he had received information from an authentic source like a doctor.

Awareness about AIDS

Ninety two per cent of the respondents had heard of AIDS. Table 13.3

shows per cent distribution of responses about mode of transmission of HIV.

Table 13.3: Percentage of Mode of Transmission

*Mode of Transmission**	*Percent (N = 92)*
Sexual relations	87
Heterosexual relations	84
Infected blood	80
Infected syringes	79
Mother to child	71
Mosquito or flea bite	39
Homosexual relations	36
Kissing	31
Sharing clothes	27
Stepping on urine or stool of infected person	19
Shaking hands	17
Sharing kitchen utensils of infected person	16

*Multiple response questions.

Source: Field Investigation.

More than 70 per cent of the respondents were aware of the four modes of transmission of HIV. As compared to other migrant populations, hotel workers were well aware of HIV, which could be attributed to the availability of television and NGO interventions. Studies (Singh *et al.*, 1992) report that only 20 per cent of truck drivers had heard about HIV-AIDS. Hotel workers reported sexual intercourse with a CSW as the prime mode of transmission, a finding similar to the one by Mani (1993) and Chuttani *et al.* (1990). Misinformation regarding transmission prevailed among the respondents (as seen from the table). 21 per cent of the respondents felt that AIDS could be cured. 82 per cent were convinced about the fact that AIDS could be prevented.

Sources of Information about HIV-AIDS

The Researchers have observed that most of the hotel rooms occupied by the hotel workers were provided with a television. 64 respondents reported Television as a source of information, 60 respondents reported friends and 58 reported newspapers. 43 respondents reported health messages as their source of information on HIV-AIDS. Only a quarter of the respondents got information from medical practitioner. 6 respondents learnt about it from teachers and only one from hotel owner. Further probing revealed that these hotel workers had received this information during their school days where special programmes were arranged on HIV-AIDS. Hotel owners were also sensitising the workers about HIV-AIDS, which was mentioned by four respondents. The other sources reported were Books and Radio. More than 50 per cent of the respondents reporting TV, friend and newspapers as sources of information about HIV-AIDS.

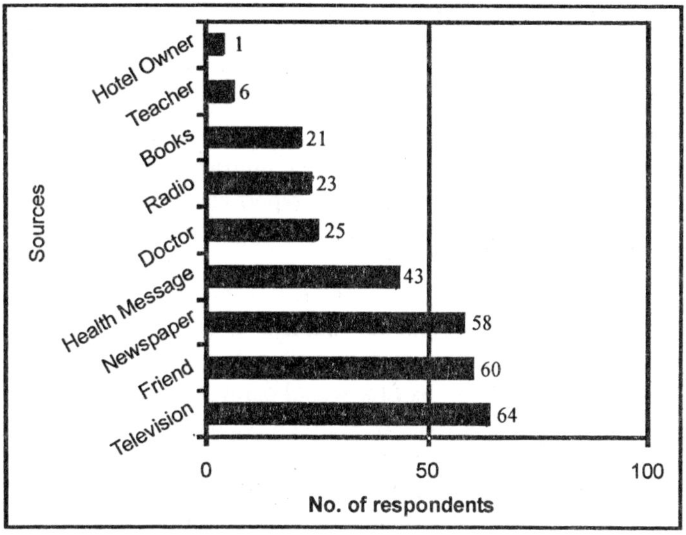

Fig. 13.2: Sources of Information about HIV/AIDS

The respondents were asked whether they thought, they were at the risk of contracting HIV-AIDS. 15 respondents out of 92, 16 per cent felt that they could get HIV infection because they had sexual relations with sex workers and there was a possibility that they could already be infected. The rest of the respondents said that they were vulnerable because the health messages said that any one could get HIV infection.

Sexual Behaviour

Ninety per cent of the respondents had information about sex related issues. While, the rest of them said they did not know anything about sex. Most of the respondents 61 per cent had received information about sex from television, cinema and videos, while 27 per cent reported self-experience or friends as a source of information. Pornographic literature as a source was reported by 58 per cent of the respondents.

Hotel workers were asked about their perception of sexual behaviour and risk behaviour. More than 90 per cent of the respondents reported peno-vaginal intercourse as sexual and thought it to be risky in terms of acquiring STDs or HIV.

Sexual Experience

Fifty eight respondents 58 per cent reported having sexual experience. A little more than half 53 per cent reported having sexual relations with one partner and the rest 47 per cent reported having sex with more than one partner. Median age at first sexual intercourse was 19 years. It was found that in the case of many respondents their first sexual experience was after migration. Studies among other migrants such as truckers, construction and furnace workers also report early initiation of sexual activity, in the adolescent age group of 15-19 years (Rao *et al.*, 1994 and Savara and Sridhar, 1994).

Of the 58 respondents, around 60 per cent reported village girls as their first sexual partners (similar findings have been reported among other groups mentioned above), 3 per cent each reported married women in the village or a relative as first sexual partner. Only 10 respondents reported having sex with a sex worker. Of those who were married 70 per cent reported wife as their first sexual partner.

The respondents reported several reasons for pre- and extra-marital sex. The reasons were: fascination of village girls towards boys returning from cities and for married women—non-availability of the spouse. Some of the other reasons mentioned were uncontrolled sexual urge, for fun, vigour of youth, natural phenomenon, love culminating into sex, psychological relief sexual hunger.

Interviews revealed that uncontrolled sexual urge was the most frequently reported reason for engaging in sexual activity. Fatigue due to busy work schedule also led to risky sexual behaviour. Beliefs about masculinity, non-availability of the sexual partner and desire for physical or mental peace were reported as reasons for indulging in sexual relations.

Suresh (name changed), age 23, working as a cook said, "I had my first sexual experience when I was in the sixth standard, a woman residing near my house, whose husband was working in the City called me and asked me to do it. I was very frightened." He further said, "Married, divorced and separated women in the villages allow boys to have sex, since they have unfulfilled sexual desires."

Nagesh (name changed), age 25, working as a bill writer said, "I had sex with my fiancée on the last day of the Ganapati festival. She went on saying no, but I insisted and managed to do it. A girl always refuses to have sex but she also has an impatient longing (*Khaaj*) for sex. Even if she denies, we should do it."

Ramanna (name changed), age 30, working as cook said, "I routinely have sex because it gives me a peace of mind after working so hard."

The respondents were asked about their current sexual partners. Out of 58 respondents who reported sexual experience, 23, 39.7 per cent were currently sexually active. The following table shows the number of current sexual partners:

Table 13.4: Number of Current Sexual Partners

Current partners	*Frequency (N=23)*
Sex worker	4
Village girl	2
Student	2
Friend + Sex worker	1
Married woman	1
Fiancée	1
Wife	12

Source: Field Investigation.

Of the 20 married respondents, only 12 respondents reported that they were currently having sexual relations with their wives.

Condom Use and Non-Use

Condom use among migrant workers studied so far has been very low (Ahmed, 1992; Mani, 1993 and Savara and Sridhar, 1994). Only thirteen, out of 38, 34 per cent unmarried respondents reported consistent condom use. Almost all of them used a condom to prevent STDs and HIV, while 25 respondents who said that they have not used a condom, reported lack of information about a condom or its availability. Some felt it unnecessary because of emotional involvement in sexual relations. Those respondents who reported having sexual relations with sex workers said that sex workers sometimes allowed them to have sex without a condom if they paid more than the usual charges.

Homosexual Relationship

It was felt that because of the peculiar living conditions, i.e. group living,

MSM activity would be prevalent among hotel workers. A study by Kulkarni (2000) reports a great deal of MSM activity prevalent in Pune City. Such behaviour mostly remained invisible because of social stigma and discrimination. Studies conduced so far report prevalence of MSM activity from 1.5–10 per cent. In the present study, only 38 respondents said that they had heard about MSM relationship. Majority of them (more than 50%) knew about MSM activity through friends and pornographic material. Only two respondents reported homosexual experience and in both the cases it was forced by a relative and by a fellow passenger. The respondents were of the opinion that hotel workers working in hotels situated away from red light area were more likely to engage in such activities as compared to those who were working in hotels surrounding the red light area. They further estimated that at least 10 per cent of the hotel workers might be indulging in MSM activity.

Discussions

Labour migration has always been a common livelihood strategy not only in India but also across the world. Poverty and lack of economic opportunity forces many to migrate to urban areas in formal and informal sectors. These migrant communities are vulnerable to HIV infections for various reasons.

Hotel workers, yet another group of migrant workers, although similar in terms of the socio-economic characteristics, has a peculiar feature of group living. Most of the hotel workers in the study had migrated during adolescence and hence were out of formal schooling. Most of them 66 per cent had studied up to 7th to 8th standard. Being unmarried and exposed to all urban evils, it is likely that they would go astray as reported by more than half of the respondents who were sexually experienced. Lack of awareness, lack of social control, availability of money and freedom to spend it and peer pressure creates a suitable environment for risk behaviour.

Hotel workers did not know much about STDs but the awareness of AIDS 92 per cent was much higher than that of national average 76 per cent as reported by NACO (NACO website). Even then misinformation was prevalent. Although, hotel workers were aware of the preventive measures, beliefs, peer pressure and pornographic literature, prompted them to engage in risky sexual behaviour.

The first sexual encounter was usually after migration and during adolescence. Not many 10 per cent reported CSWs as their first sexual partners. More than 50 per cent reported village girls as their first sexual partners. It thus becomes necessary to chart the sexual careers to understand the routes of spread of the epidemic.

Only 22 per cent of the unmarried respondents who reported sexual experience consistently used condom with their partners in a six-month recall period. Lack of information about how to use it, where to procure it and a belief regarding no need of a condom in an emotional relationship (with fiancée, friend and sex worker) hindered the safety of the respondents in terms of HIV infection. Although 92 per cent of the respondents felt that peno-vaginal intercourse as 'the real sex' it was ranked as the behaviour with highest risk in terms of acquiring STDs including HIV.

Because of the sensitive nature of inquiry about MSM activity and lack of time, the researchers were not able to get more information on this issue. However, the respondents did not deny MSM activity among the hotel workers working in hotel situated away from the red light area.

In order to promote awareness about risky behaviours and to promote condom use, an aggressive campaign by the government and NGOs in the City is required. Increasing HIV incidence rates in the City and also in the rural areas demand an increase and interactive HIV awareness programme, which would focus on the clients of sex workers, migrants in particular. Groups like those of hotel workers are hard to reach and hence government programmes should have a built-in element of flexibility to reach these populations. Studies have shown the peer education strategy does work best in these types of settings and awareness levels could be raised to mitigate the spread of the infection.

14

Coping with Stigma among PLHA

JYOTSNA BAPAT

Introduction

In the context of the risk of pandemic of HIV, there emerged a need to explore not only sexuality and sexual behaviour of high-risk groups but also the socio-cultural context of the transmission of HIV and particularly the role of social and historical factors, which shape and sustain the transmission of HIV. Due to the stigma and fear of social isolation associated with the disease, many HIV positives do not reveal their status and continue to infect other innocents, especially the wife. In this context, it was felt necessary to focus on the social behaviour of the HIV positive people and see whether positive people have modified their sexual behaviour and make use of the information published through mass media to prevent transmission.

The study was conducted by one time interviews of positive persons at testing and counselling centres located in various part of Mumbai. In all 5 such centres were selected for patient contact. Total 39 in-depth interviews were carried out during the study period. The responses of the persons were analyzed using qualitative analysis techniques while responses to the information management strategies were put in relevant categories and the findings were reported in tabular form.

The total of 39 positive persons interviewed were between 25 to 35 years of age and 7 of them were females, who were married or widowed Among males, 13 were unmarried. All the positive men were from skilled labour force and few were white-collar workers from service industry, and their income ranged from Rs. 2000-6000 per month. All of them reported HIV positive status within the last one to six years time. All men reported visiting CSW before marriage. All of them were referred to the Centre by health care professional.

Frequently used strategy by positive persons (29 patients) while dealing with family and kin was to form a core group of confidants, including wife who protected their disease identity from others. None of them revealed their disease status to the employers, except 6 who were forced to undergo test by their employers. Most of them reported to have taken or taking Ayurvedic medicine and avoided going to the government hospitals as they received discriminatory treatment by staff and doctors.

The results highlighted the major concerns of the positive patients like job security, and dependence on family for care. Positive people suggested to have support groups and more holistic information on HIV, and awareness campaigns to face the stigma and fear of social isolation despite education.

In India HIV transmission is mainly through heterosexual contact. The research on HIV in India, like other developing countries, points to the need to focus on four areas: poverty, productive employment, social integration, and implementation (Godwin, P., 1997). The issue of social integration, given the stigma, therefore, becomes an important area for intervention. Existing government health care systems do discriminate the PLHA (Persons Living with HIV-AIDS) and there are reported instances of social isolation of the families of PLHA (personal interview: January 8, 2000, Dr. Shirgopikar, FADA). There are increasing problems of violence mainly against PLHA (Trivedi, D., 1995) and women (Bhagat, R., 1997), everyday care (Bharat *et al.*, 1992) affordable health care (Personal interviews of PLHA), discrimination in health care delivery even in government hospitals etc due to stigma attached to the disease.

State Policy

Government of India is committed to accelerating the pace of activities for prevention and control of HIV-AIDS pandemic (Planning Commission 1997; MAP 1994; NACO 1997, Salunke, S.R. *et al.,* 1998). Given that the average life expectancy after infection is 7 years, concern over depleting population stock and especially productive labour of India, is a major motivation for the state action (Sethi and Carter, 1996; Peter Goldwin, 1996).

The attitude of the state towards the spread of HIV can be summed up as 'private moral intolerance'. Over time there is increasing emphasis on spread of knowledge and thus avoiding misconceptions and therefore, stigma associated with the disease. The government has adopted a policy of involving Non-Governmental Organizations (NGOs). The NGOs are encouraged through Government funding, to set up and run various support groups, undertake rehabilitation efforts, counselling and testing centres etc. In addition, treatment in government hospitals is available to the people living with HIV-AIDS (PLHA).

All this interest and research related to HIV epidemic has led to creation of exclusive centres for treatment. This may have been a bureaucratically rational strategy to ensure funds earmarked for HIV-AIDS are not diverted to other purposes but has resulted in discrimination and stigma towards the PLHA. The new language resulting from the research has created a new category of people called 'vulnerable populations', or people involved in 'high risk' behaviour. The dominant discourse in the public domain such as the press and the mass media and government documents portrays People Living with HIV-AIDS (PLHA) as minority street people abandoned by family and friends, commercial sex workers and their clients, drug addicts, gay communities etc. in short social deviants (Schiller, N. *et al.*, 1994) living on the margins of society. But the fact is the entire population is a 'vulnerable population' from HIV-AIDS perspective.

New Morality and Stigma

The focus here is on the social behaviour of positive people. Given the perception of PLHA as social deviants, the state in the absence of known treatment for the disease and no known form of control of the disease, expects certain behaviours from them. PLHA are expected to avoid 'risky behaviour' and are considered to be 'vulnerable population'. Both the terms, vulnerable groups and high-risk behaviour are biomedical terms but have now gained social meanings different from that originally intended (Schiller *et al.,* 1994). In India vulnerable group is categorized as people involved in multiply sex partners or those who visit commercial sex workers or those who have sex with people who have multiple sex partners. The 'risk behaviour' in this context is having sex without using condoms. These were socially considered as permissible behaviour and most males visited commercial sex workers before marriage or experimented with drugs and other form of sexual behaviour in their adolescence or early adulthood is a norm where compensation for the sexual favour is in the form of gifts or cash. For long term extra marital sexual relations there is usually a more sustained social and economic provisioning for the partner and the child born to them. These same behaviour patterns are considered now as uncommon deviation from the 'new' norm.

This new norm is the sexual behaviour considered as ideal by a traditional society, namely monogamy. At this stage there is no cure for AIDS. At the same time the normative expectations from an AIDS patient is negation of 'normal' life, i.e. sex, wife, children, family life are denied to him. The message he gets is there is no cure for it once he gets it, and it is only a short time before he dies. In the meantime altruism should motivate him to become an ascetic. Normative expectation of 'asceticism without reward' is a new morality imposed on him. This new set of normative expectation has not been fully incorporated in the society. A necessary condition for social life is sharing of a single set of normative expectation by all participants. These norms are sustained because social behaviour rules associated with these norms are incorporated in the society. When the rules breakdown, restorative measures or damage control measures for victims (provisioning) exist in society. Thus for a rule to be fully incorporated in a society, there has to be checks and balances in place, so that when rules are broken there are restorative mechanisms or damage control measures available to the person who is responsible for flouting it, so that his victim (usually his wife and children) does not suffer. The evolution of damage control mechanisms in the form of social legal and economic provisioning for the 'victims' of PLHA is evolving albeit very slowly due to stigma attached to the disease. So the perpetrator cannot resort to them, nor is a social control agency in place to perform this. Legal provisions are just a beginning towards the development of damage control mechanisms. The perpetrator in this case PLHA acts rationally by flaunting the normative expectations of this 'new' morality, as there are no punitive measures. He gets to leading a normal life and have someone to take care of him, towards the end of his life. Hence, the new rules of 'safe sex', no children within marriage for PLHA are flouted, as is evident by narratives of PLHA during their personal interviews with the researcher.

The concept of deviation is the bridge that links the study of stigma to the study of the rest of the social world. The concern for ordinary deviation from the common social norm is important. Experimenting with drugs by teenagers or experimenting with sex by adolescent and young adults is historically considered ordinary deviations from the common norm. The threat of AIDS as a fatal disease makes this 'uncommon deviation.'

It would, therefore, be of interest to know whether people have modified their sexual behaviour norms in the light of HIV epidemic? Do people actually behave as per the government expectations? Do they voluntarily test for HIV-AIDS? Do they reveal their status to their sexual partners? Do they seek treatment where possible? These are important questions, but the focus of the study is, given the stigma attached to the infection how does a PLHA cope with it or in other words what strategies does a PLHA use, in everyday life to try and lead as normal a life as he can.

Experience of Stigma

When a person is referred to and AIDS Testing Centre (ATC) there is already enough knowledge in the society about the HIV-AIDS epidemic that being declared positive is like being called a 'leper' in the past. The implication of the HIV status being known to the person's neighbours, relatives and especially in-laws for a woman, and employer is 'a death sentence'. There are enough 'stories' floating about HIV-AIDS and its spread that is enough to treat him as a social outcast. Stories of denial of access to public facilities like toilets, water and schools are common. Women and especially widows of persons who have died of AIDS typically suffer more than men. A woman, who is detected to be HIV positive in the husband's house shared by her in-laws, is expected to leave his house with at least the nursing child and go back to her natal home, if the husband is dead. Older children are taken care of by the husband's family. If she continues to stay she is not allowed to enter the kitchen and forced to confine herself to a room without proper treatment. She is usually economically dependent on her husband. The husband, if alive, rarely rejects her and continues to visit her at her natal home.

Study of Stigma

Given the stigma experienced by PLHA the main objective is to understand how this information about his/her positive status is managed by Persons Living with HIV-AIDS (PLHA) in the two distinct contexts: socio-cultural settings and economic relations concerning work environment.

Stigmatization can be removed by reform and structural institutional changes. The role of social policy is to create a just society through purposeful government intervention, promote entitlements instead of charity for PLHA (Merton, R., 1984) through regulations. After all it is the Market and not welfare ethics that perpetuates the system. Therefore, the cycle of stigma and loss of productive labour force can be destroyed through creation of social safety nets and social provisioning that is practical.

What is stigma? Society establishes the means of categorizing persons and the complement of attributes felt to be ordinary and natural for members of each of these categories. Social settings establish the categories of persons likely to be encountered. When a person comes into the presence of another, first appearances are likely to enable individuals coming in his contact to anticipate his category and attribute, a 'social identity' and 'social status'. Each of us living in a society, depend on these anticipations that we have, transforming them into normative expectations, and finally, righteously presented demands. When a person is reduced in our minds from usual to a discounted one there is a stigma, especially when there is a discrediting effect.

There is always fear in the mind of a person suffering from stigma, that others will disrespect him because of something he shows or discloses about his reality. He is always insecure in his contact with other people. 'I am inferior. Therefore, people will dislike me and I cannot be secure with them.' The stigmatized individual feels unsure of how other 'normal' members of the society will identify him and receive him. This discrepancy spoils his social identity. It has the effect of cutting him off from the society, he stands a discredited person facing an un-accepting world.

Whether it is a visible mark or an invisible stain, stigma acquires its meaning through the emotions it generates within the person bearing it and the feeling and behaviour towards him of those affirming it. These two aspects of stigma are indivisible since they each act as a cause and effect of the other. Based on case studies of various stigmatized individuals Goffman (1964) generalized their behaviour and created a framework that details six conceptual techniques of by a stigmatized person. These are: denial, avoiding detection, concealing, creating a core group of confidants, lie about the condition by passing it for something less significant and finally 'coming out' in the open with it (D'Souza, D., 1992). These generalization are based on studies of physical handicap and diseases suffered by people. Thus, the observations and the conceptual framework is too general and needs to be context specific and operationally defined.

Techniques of Information Management

The operational definition of the strategies was created after some preliminary interviews with PLHA at AIDS Testing Centres (ATCs) in Mumbai and analysis revealed five of the six techniques mentioned earlier were used by PLHA. The operational definition strategies used for coping with the stigma associated with HIV-AIDS by PLHA are:

1. **Denial:** The very first strategy is denial. But for the present study we cannot consider this strategy as the persons who have come to the ATC have already accepted their positive status and cannot deny it to the interviewer either. One often comes across person at the ATC who are still denying their disease but then they are in no state to talk about either themselves or about the disease. Therefore for practical reasons we have dropped this information management strategy.
2. **Avoid detection:** Avoiding testing for HIV to the extent possible is a strategy used by a few people coming to the ATC and was manifest by people not turning up or refusing to collect their reports, even when they are were referred by their physicians.
3. **Concealing:** There is enough awareness about the disease that once infected people know they have it, they hide it from every one. Two persons chose to go back to his village, others chose not to tell anyone their discredited status so that they can lead a normal life.
4. **Create a core group of confidants**: A widely employed strategy is to handle the risks of being discredited is, by dividing the world into a large group to whom PLHA tells nothing and a small group to whom he tells everything and relies on their help. The intimates not only help the discreditable person but they serve as a protective circle, allowing him to think he is more fully accepted as a normal person than in fact is the case. Those who share a particular stigma can often rely upon mutual aid in 'passing' in a society. Most persons told only select kin persons usually including the spouse. Only a few in the initial stage do not tell their wives. These are the only people who take the patient to treatment when ill and on whom the patient depends for help and support.
5. **Lie about the disease:** passes it for less stigmatized one. A most people use this as a technique for dealing with neighbours that it is something else usually T.B. and not AIDS.
6. **Come out:** reveal the status and network to create support group. Tell anyone that cares to ask and publicize it, like the one PLHA

who is used by the medical doctor in the Salvation Army Centre to convince the patients that having the disease is not the end of life. This is especially the technique of the MNP+ support group encourages. But in most cases it was a forced 'coming out' as the employer forced the employee to undergo annual medical checkup including that for HIV and the medical record is used for not re-employing the person. Especially for the labour markets in the Middle-East this is a requirement for long term (more than one year) contact for skilled labour.

Having established that the five techniques exist among the positive people, the next step was to identify which of these technique is predominantly used in which of the context by positive people.

Context

Persons Living with HIV-AIDS (PLHA) at least at the initial stage of being positive do not look any different from non-positive people and live in the same society. Therefore, the family, the kinship groups, the social worlds and the economic world are the same for positive people. These are identified in the following manner:

1. **Immediate family:** with whom the social and physical space is shared by the PLHA on a day-to-day basis. These include the nuclear family and the joint and extended family with whom they live and share spaces.
2. **Immediate neighbourhood:** where the physical space is definitely shared by the PLHA on a daily basis. These are people living in the surrounding areas other than the family whom they share some public spaces everyday. They may or may not choose to have face to face interactions with each and everyone but do have a few people with whom they choose to interact socially at formal levels.
3. **Relatives and friends:** who may or may not share the physical space, as in urban areas but are part of the shared social space either as kinship members or by association. These are extended kinship ties and voluntary associations with friends. These are people with whom the PLHA has face to face interactions and meet at social occasions.
4. **Work area:** as the physical space shared with co-workers with

whom there is a professional contact and where economic activity takes place.

These are not water tight compartments of interpersonal relations bur determine the dominant types of relationship of the PLHA with them.

Having established the conceptual framework we then proceeded to interview various positives persons in order to get answers to the four main questions:

1. Irrespective of the context of interaction between the PLHA and others, which is the most frequently used techniques of information management by PLHA?
2. Which is the most frequently used technique specific to the context?
3. Which is the least frequently used techniques irrespective of the context?
4. Which is the least frequently used technique specific to the context?

Locale of Study

The research involved enquiry into the sexual history and sexual behaviour of the people and as such a very difficult and delicate issue to talk to strangers. The added complication in this was the enquiry into a much publicized and stigmatized disease. Any discussion about this in public places is a taboo. Therefore, it was very essential to look for a social space where the PLHA felt secure and was willing to talk to the researcher (Pelto, P., 1995). The PLHA feels very vulnerable and uncomfortable about talking about the question related to getting the disease. Therefore, it was decided that a testing counselling centre would be a good point of entry for interviewing PLHA whose positive status is already known.

Mumbai city and its suburbs were selected as a place for the study. It is a capital of the state of Maharashtra and is an urban metropolitan centre. As such there is a lot of industrial activity and a lot of migrant labour working in the city. There are also better treatment facilities run by government agencies both municipal as well as state government, for general medical treatment and for AIDS Treatment and Counselling (ATC centre). It is naturally divided into island city, the western and central suburbs and each of these parts host unique socio-economic profile of its residents. The government institutional health facilities are well spread out. There is enough NGO activity in the city. All this made it an ideal locale of study.

Selection of Centres

Universe of study is not all the patients in Mumbai, but those who are coming to the counselling centre. There are a total of 29 HIV-AIDS counselling centres established by various NGOs and the governments where free testing a counselling facilities are offered to the person who comes for testing. All the centres are located within the Mumbai Municipal Council limits were visited personally and facilities and information about the centres and their functioning was recorded. Among these the AIDS Research and Counselling (ARCON) run centres are only six. Three of ARCON centres and two privately run ATC, each representing the geographic spread of the BMC limits, were covered in the study. One of the centres was affiliated to the hospital and is also offering a treatment facility for AIDS patients. Given the stigma, repeat interviews with PLHA were not possible, therefore, the sample size as doubled from 15 to 17 to 39 to compensate for it.

Typical Situation

We visited one centre once a day after consulting the technical person in charge of the centre for a convenient day when we could meet the PLHA and when they were likely to be in the talking mood. Having established a time we would go and wait at the counselling centre. As and when a PLHA completed his consultation with the technical person, the technical person would introduce the researcher and ask if s/he would be willing to talk to us. If they were willing we would introduce ourselves and explain the nature of our research. The casual conversation mode was adopted for data collection. Very often the conversation meandered to topic not directly relevant to the research. We had to gently steer it to the topic of our choice. We stated with question of the onset of the disease what were the various stages and steps taken by the PLHA before the information about the positive status was revealed to him. We then asked PLHA how may people he had told about this he would usually list out the names and relationship to them. We would ask him to narrate if possible how did he break the news to the very first person he ever told and how and so on. We would ask him, what does he tell his neighbours friends other distant relatives and at place of work when he is absent from work or has stopped going to work etc. Finally, it always ends with him asking us if we know of some one who can make him 'from positive to negative'. Only three out of 39 respondents could be interviewed twice in the same premises and so a consistency check could be done to a limited extent. No one was willing to give their address or work place and as they were all afraid that we may come and visit them at these places. Most begged us not to do so.

Data Collection

Data was collected from face to face interactions using a partially structured schedule at the counselling centre. The interviewer memorized the schedule, so that the interview took the form of a conversation. The PLHA are already under tension and feel very vulnerable. We initially tried to record their conversation after taking prior permission. But, we seemed to intimidate them and they gave very limited responses. We, therefore, quickly abandoned the attempt and documented the conversation immediately after the interview, through recall.

Method of Analysis

The data collected was in a qualitative form and we then converted it into categories of responses and have reported the quantified profile of the positive people interviewed for the research. This procedure of data collection and analysis, therefore, took up much more time than anticipated. The qualitative responses to the information management strategies were put in relevant categories and the findings are reported in the tabular form.

Table 14.1: Age and Sex Composition of the Sample

Age	*25-30*	*30-35*	*35+*
M	14	14	5
F	6	1	0

Source: Field Investigation.

The profile of the total of 39 PLHA interviewed for the present study indicates that they were all between 25 to 35 years of age. This is confirmation with the state findings and therefore the concern about the depleting stocks of human population.

Only 7 out of 39 were females and all were less than 35 year of age. All others were males. All the women who came to the centre were either married or widowed, while 13 men were unmarried. All the men were representing skilled labour force and a few were white-collar workers from service industry. These were men gainfully employed in professions such as electrician, cobblers, rickshaw drivers, drivers, dairy business, cooks etc. They all drew a salary between Rs. 2000 to 6000 a month. About eight of them were self-employed people. All of them reported to have positive status within the last one year to six years time. No one reported to have positive status more than 7 years even when they all had children older than 7 years. All the men reported visiting CSW before marriage.

At the centre in the western suburb the profile of the PLHA indicated that they were skilled labour force earning an average of Rs. 3500 to 5000. A month most of them had learnt about their positive status just one or two years ago. This could be because the centre was also new. But, one person who knew of his positive status seven years ago said he was asked to come here by the doctor who was treating him because this place was providing free medicines.

At the government hospital based centre the persons visiting the centre had known of their status for six years and more. Most of them were menial workers on daily wages or subsistence wages. Some were coming for treatment to the centre from out-stations.

The centre located in the southern tip of the city had people who were mainly young and single males in their late twenties some even aspiring to go abroad.

The central suburbs and central city location attracted people from a specific ethnic group. People belonging to the same ethnic group operated these centres.

The Strategies Used

Matrix indicating different information management techniques used in different contexts.

Table 14.2: Role of Information Management Techniques

	Avoid detection	*Conceal*	*Core group*	*Lie*	*Reveal to all*	*Sample*
Family	1	6	29	3	0	39
Friends/relatives	4	17	10	8	0	39
Neighbours	2	26	1	10	0	39
Workplace	9	19	0	5	6	39
Total points	**16**	**68**	**40**	**26**	**6**	**156**

Source: Field Investigation.

Most and Least Frequent

The most frequently used technique by PLHA in all circumstances is concealing (68 points) the second most frequently used strategy was forming a core group of confidants who protected them from the other (40 points). Lying about the disease and passing it for less stigmatized one was the next most frequent strategy (26 points). Avoid detection by permanently migrating to the village or not collecting the reports of the test were the strategies used by some PLHA (16 points). Coming out and voluntarily disclosing the information about the infection and the least used strategy (6 points). Except for one, the employee through compulsory annual medical checkups including HIV, forced all these disclosures.

Within Family

Within the family the most frequently used strategy is forming a core group of confidants usually including the wife who help them deal with the outside world. 29 out of 39 PLHA use this as a strategy in the context of family. Only two respondents had not as yet informed their wives. Even when wives have been forced to leave their home by their in-laws they rarely leave their husbands and continue relationship with him sometimes even clandestinely. This reveals that rejection by family members, due to the stigma attached to the disease, is least feared by the PLHA.

This was followed by concealing of the status (6/39) one person avoided detection by leaving the city. The never used technique, is come out and admit to all members of the family.

Among Relatives and Friend

Among friends and relatives concealing is the dominant strategy followed by 17/39 people. This is followed by core group of confidants among friends and relatives followed by 10/39. Lieing and passing the disease for a less stigmatized one is used by 10/39 people and avoiding detection by severing contact is adopted by 4/39 people. No one came out and revealed to all their relatives and friends their discredited status.

With Neighbours

Among neighbours concealing the infection was dominant technique adopted by 26/39 people. Only one person trusted his neighbour enough to form with them a core group of confidants. 10/39 lied to the neighbours about their illness and 2/39 left the place of stay. No one came out and revealed to all their neighbours their status.

At Workplace

In work place forced detection and revealing of status is least common 6/39 person's status revealed to fellow workers because of the employer forcing such a revelation on the employee. Concealing is the highest technique used by 19/39 people. No one used the core group formation technique at the work place and interestingly 9/39 people chose to avoid detection by never returning to the work force at all. When ever possible the self-employed small business men hand over their business to some relative to run it and casual labour uses this strategy in providing the employer with a substitute and receives a 'rent' in return.

Agenda for Action

There are three distinct policy implications of the research findings. As mentioned earlier norms related to social behaviour including sexual behaviour are sustained because social behaviour rules associated with these norms are incorporated in the society. When the rules breakdown, restorative measures or damage control measures (provisioning) for victims exist in society. Thus for a rule to be fully incorporated in a society, there has to be checks and balances in place, so that when rules are broken there are restorative mechanisms or damage control measures available to the person who is responsible for flouting it, so that his victim (usually his wife and children) does not suffer. The evolution of damage control mechanisms in the form of social, legal and economic provisioning for the PLHA and their dependents is evolving over the past decade. Strategies to reduce social stigma by making more information and knowledge related to AIDS and HIV is being made available to people at large through various mass media as social provisioning is already underway. Strategies to protect legal rights of PLHA and their dependents by moving the courts for human rights violation is the form of legal provisioning available to PLHA. More recently attempts to involve the kinfolks that the PLHA trust into the care of dependents of PLHA even before they are terminally ill in Uganda is one such example of economic provisioning using existing socio-cultural practices.

The present finding indicates that the dominant coping strategy of PLHA is concealing followed by forming a core group of confidants to ensure that he can lead as normal life as possible, it is time that policy research focused on finding ways to facilitated the latter tendency and reinforce it with formal rules. If each of them have a core group of confidants they can identify and trust, then this group should be involved in place of employment (if possible), medical treatment of PLHA, in more informed responsibility towards the people left behind by PLHA and better preparing and involving them for inevitability of death of PLHA, through support group activities. Identifying the kinship networks of PLHA and involving them in more ways to re-enforce rules for medical, social, legal and economic provisioning will have to be the future agenda for research.

SECTION II

Gender and Sexuality

"Sexuality is not a mere categorical concept but encompasses several dimensions such as sex, gender identities and roles, sexual orientation, eroticism, pleasure, intimacy and reproduction. Sexuality is experienced and expressed in thoughts, fantasies, desires, beliefs, attitudes, values, behaviours, practices, roles and relationships. It is seen as a dynamic concept influenced by the interaction of biological, psychological, social, economic, political, cultural, ethical, legal, historical and religious and spiritual factors." (SIECUS, 2002; WHO, 2002)

The term gender is widely used in social science research and now also in public health or medical research. Concepts of sex and gender have become central to the understanding of health and illness and also for the utilization and effectiveness of health services. In patriarchy, male gender can be an advantage in the context of health, since it is likely to give the individual man greater power, wealth and status than a woman in a comparable social situation. Similarly, sexuality is also largely learnt, rather than something purely innate of which we become aware. Furthermore, for both biological and social reasons, sexuality is learnt very differently according to one's gender and socio-cultural context. The way feminine and masculine sexualities develop is largely in the context of the separate socio-cultural worlds which boys and girls grow up with.

Several studies have highlighted the relationships between gender and sexuality, but most of them have narrowly focused on fertility and factors that would promote use of contraceptives. These studies have extensively used survey research and have not considered social context within which the decision is taken. Social expectations linked to gender influence how women and men behave and this includes their sexual behaviour, attitudes and feelings. The proponents of women's empowerment fear that if women could not make free and informed choices about sex and reproduction, gender equality would not be achieved. The right to make decisions and to access information and services relating to partnerships, marriage, sexual relations and the bearing of children-free of coercion, violence and discrimination—are fundamental to women's equality and well-being. Besides, having choices in the sphere of sexuality and reproduction can empower women to pursue other opportunities and to participate in social and economic life outside the home.

It is with this background that four research studies are presented in this section. The first study looks into college students' ideas and opinions about construction of sexuality while the next chapter looks into gender construction in rural areas. Male involvement in family planning issues is another study which enriches our understanding about gender relations, roles, cultural expectations and behaviour in the context of sexuality.

15

Construction of Sexuality among Male College Students

RAM D. GAMBHIR, SAJU JOSEPH AND SHANTANU OZARKAR

Introduction

Apocalyptic advent of HIV-AIDS and failure of family planning programmes forced investigators to look into the issues of sexuality and sexual behaviour which otherwise were considered too private and sensitive for research (Vance, 1991: 875; Zeidensteine and Moore, 1996: 1).

Detailed review of literature shows that, in scientific literature, terms such as sex, sexuality, sexual behaviour, sexual experience and sexual contact have been used interchangeably (Chandiramani *et al.*, 2002: 8; Hilber and Colombini, 2002:1). Further, biological determinism viewed 'sex' as given and natural distinction, ignoring the cultural influence. Thus the concept of sexuality has often been narrowly used to mean sexual behaviour, particularly coital behaviour alone.

As a result it is expected that, sexuality and its social construction would differ in urban, rural and tribal settings due to the different socio-cultural and economic forces operating there. Characteristics of tribal communities such as group orientation, strong kinship bonds and obligations, labour intensive agrarian economy would strongly influence notions of sexuality, and one would expect presence of traditional attitude towards and values regarding various aspects of sexuality. In the rural context, sharply defined gender roles and dominant male sexuality may be the norm. Whereas in urban setting, various factors and forces have initiated a process of redefining sexuality and gender roles and associated attitudes, beliefs, practices and perceptions.

Fresh impetus to review and reconsider our ideas about gender and sexuality comes primarily from two sources, one being the practical need of health services programmes and the second the feminist scholarship and activism. Sexuality, gender roles and power were hardly the considerations in the health programmes (Zeidenstein and Moore, 1996:1). However, the centrality of 'gender' and 'sexuality', in addressing various issues of AIDS and STDs, population control and family planning and reproductive health has been recognised. Now the real challenge lies not only in understanding the complexities and dynamics of gender and sexuality, but to successfully incorporate them into health programmes. This had led to dramatic increase in gender and sexuality studies among researchers and programme managers. Feminist efforts, on the other hand, led not only to review earlier theoretical contentions but also contributed to the conceptual refinement and clarity (Vance, 1991). As a result, newer theoretical orientation and perspectives are brought to bear upon our understanding of gender and sexuality. They are no more viewed as biologically determined, naturally given, but rather as social constructions, emerging from the interplay between culturally constituted ideas and subjective meanings.

In the light of the above considerations the present study focused on sexuality and its variable construction in three cultural settings among college going male youth. The study explored cross-cultural differences in the specific aspects of sexuality—images of man and woman, gender roles, eroticism, sexual acts and associated values and beliefs. The study is underway and the sample was drawn from college going male student population in three settings as Urban Setting: Pune City, Rural Setting: Kalwan, Nashik District and Tribal setting: Rajur, Ahmednagar District. Pune City is known for its cosmopolitan, urban nature, Kalwan, which is relatively isolated and with much less urban influence exhibits rural culture and Rajur is predominantly a tribal cultural area. One college from each of the three settings would be selected for the study. Sampling frame consists of undergraduate students between 18 to 24 years of age. Further, a few students will be identified for in-depth qualitative study.

The present study draws upon the social constructionist perspective to examine changes in the attitudes and perceptions regarding sexuality among college going youth in the context of changing social reality in India. There is now common talk of gender discrimination, gender equality and women's rights. Spread of education among women and changing social aspirations among both men and women, are affecting traditional male and female segregation. The stereotypic gender roles are being questioned. Economic and career pressures are causing women to seek employment and work outside homes and men to share household work. Has this initiated a process of rethinking about gender and sexuality, and reorganizing associated attitudes, beliefs and perceptions particularly in the younger generation of college students? This study explores the changes in the specific aspects of sexuality—images of man and woman, gender roles, eroticism, sexual acts and associated beliefs and values.

Conceptualising Gender and Sexuality

Previous explanation stemming from biological approach viewed gender roles and sexuality as naturally given. Khanna and Price (1994) point out that, "One view of sexuality, derived from Western thought, sees it as determined by our sex and reproductive physiology. The acceptable and 'natural' face of sexuality is represented by the adult, preferably married, able-bodied, heterosexual couple, in which man and woman have different roles and modes of behaviour, which are predetermined by their biological sex. In this analysis, women are viewed as inferior, but are held responsible for male sexuality, which is thought to be more aggressive and often uncontrollable." This essentialist view, however, fails to explain historical and cross-cultural variation in the expression of sexuality. So also while admitting the influence of culture in shaping sexuality, the perspective that culture determines sexuality is unacceptable. Vance (1991) says, "the cultural influence model recognises variations in the occurrence of sexual behaviour and its cultural attitudes, which encourage or restrict behaviour, but not in the meaning of behaviour itself." As Courtenay (1999a, 2000) points out from own earlier work, "... men and boys are active agents in constructing dominant norms of masculinity. This concept of agency—the part and producing effects in their lives—is central to constructionism." Thus, a given gender system or sexuality is the result of interplay between culturally constituted ideas and subjective meanings mediated by factors such as power relations, age etc.

In more objective terms, as Gokova (1998) puts it, "Gender refers to widely shared ideas and expectations (norms) about women and men: ideas about "typically" feminine and masculine characteristics and abilities and expectations about how women and men should behave in various situation. These ideas and expectations are learned from families, friends, opinion leaders, religious and cultural institutions, schools, the workplace and the media. They reflect and influence the different roles, social status, economic and political power of women and men in society." Therefore,

"Gender is constructed from cultural and subjective meanings that constantly shift and vary, depending on the time and place" (Kimmel, 1995). Dixon-Mueller (1996: 139-140)? identifies four dimensions of sexuality—sexual partnerships, sexual acts, sexual meanings, sexual drives and enjoyment, which are arranged along gender lines. Operationally sexuality includes, "sex, gender identities and roles, sexual orientation, eroticism, pleasure, intimacy and reproduction. Sexuality is experienced and expressed in thoughts, fantasies, desires, beliefs, attitudes, values, behaviours, practices, roles and relationships. While sexuality can include all of these dimensions, not all of them are always experienced or expressed. Sexuality is influenced by the interaction of biological, psychological, social, economic, political, cultural, ethical, legal, historical and religious and spiritual factors" Hilber and Colombini, 2002; WHO 2002). Therefore, "...sexuality is a social construction of a biological desire; it is multidimensional and dynamic" Zeidenstein and Moore, 1996: 2). Thus for instance "...social construction approaches adopt the view that physically identical sexual acts may have varying social significance and subjective meaning depending on how they are defined and understood in different cultures and historical periods" (Vance, 1991). Gender and sexuality are thus fluid and dynamic constructs.

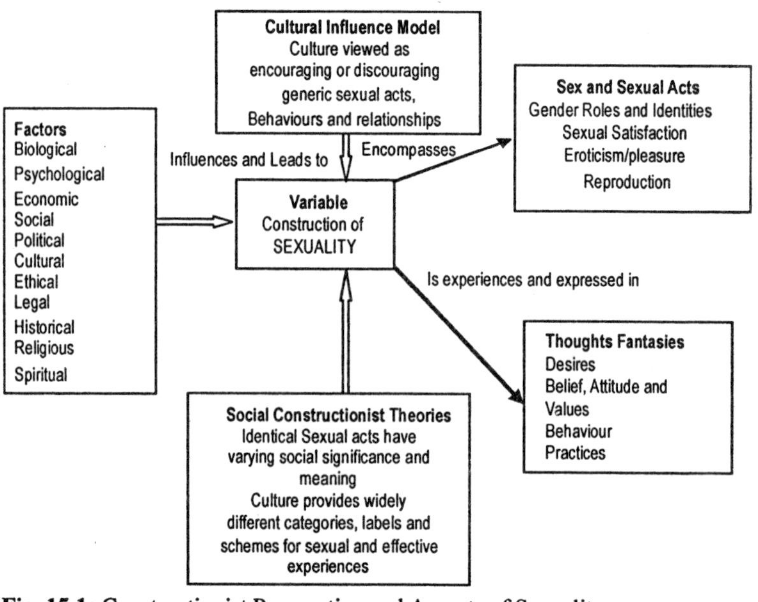

Fig. 15.1: Constructionist Perspective and Aspects of Sexuality

Though analytically distinct, gender and sexuality are closely connected. Vance (1991) suggests that, "...Sexuality and gender are separate systems which are interwoven at many points. Although members of a culture experience this interweaving as natural, seamless, and organic, the points of connection vary historically and cross-culturally. For researchers in sexuality, the task is not only to study changes in the expression of sexual behaviour and attitudes, but to examine the relationship of these changes to more deeply-based shifts in how gender and sexuality were organised and interrelated within larger social relations." Zeidenstein and Moore (1996: 2-3) make the same point. They say that, an individual's subjective experience of sexuality, "... is mediated by biology, gender roles, and power relations, as well as by factors such as age and social and economic conditions. Perhaps the most profound societal influence on an individual's sexuality comes from prescribed gender roles—the social norms and values that shape the relative power, responsibilities, and behaviour of women and men. Since gender roles typically support an imbalance of power between men and women, and individual's experience of sexuality is likely to express that imbalance."

Methodology

Study Population

Male students from two colleges, one located in a predominantly tribal village (Rajur, District Ahmednagar), and the other located in a rural area (Kalwan, District Nashik) from Maharashtra, were selected for the present study. The survey was conducted in the classrooms to achieve maximum response rate. A total of 311 students, 158 from tribal society and 153 from caste groups, were thus incorporated in the study. After the survey, 13 youth (6 tribals and 7 from caste groups) were selected for in-depth interviews. This selection was based on the willingness shown by the youth to be the part of qualitative study.

Procedure

In each college, male students were segregated from female students and were taken to a separate classroom. Nature and importance of the study was explained to the respondents. They were provided with consent forms in which they were informed that their participation was voluntary and that they were free to leave the study at any point of time if they wished so. They were also assured that the data would be kept confidential. No names or other identifying information was obtained from the students. After the survey, a few respondents were interviewed.

Questionnaire

In order to obtain data on the selected aspects of sexuality, a mix of quantitative and qualitative tools was used. The data was primarily collected using a structured questionnaire, which was supported by a few qualitative in-depth interviews. The questionnaire had five sections seeking information on Media Behaviour, Gender Roles and Images, Eroticism and Preference for Sexual Acts and Associated Values and Beliefs. The questionnaire was translated to Marathi, the local language and medium of instruction. Both, English and Marathi formats were made available to respondents. Table 15.1 contains the description of the questionnaire.

Table 15.1: Description of the Questionnaire

Section	*Contents*	*Youth were asked to*
Profile of the respondents	Age and tribal or rural background faculty, place of residence, family income etc.	State factual information
Gender roles and stereotype	15 items describing routine duties and roles performed in household (e.g. cooking, minor vehicle repairs etc.). 22 different professions (e.g. Accountant, Nurse, Nursery Teacher, Civil Engineer etc.) 39 personality traits (e.g. Shy, Talkative, aggressive etc.).	State which jobs/professions/ traits are appropriate for men, for women or for both
Values and Beliefs: Social Behaviour	25 statements (e.g. on opportunities in education, jobs etc.)	State whether agree or disagree or are unsure
Values and Beliefs: Sexual Behaviour	40 statements (e.g. Pre-marital sex, Extra-marital sex etc.)	
Sexual Acts and Meanings	35 acts (Kissing, Peno vaginal intercourse etc.)	State whether find them erotic or not

Source: Field Investigation.

Interviews

A few of the respondents who had filled in the questionnaire earlier were further selected for the interviews. Inventories from the questionnaires were used to find out their own rationale and logic for the beliefs and opinions that they had expressed. The respondents explained their views using examples, narratives, phrases, and analogies; which were noted down immediately.

Analysis

Simple frequency tables and percentages were drawn for tribal and caste populations separately. χ^2 test was performed to seek significant differences between the two populations. The responses to questions on eroticism and preference for sexual acts were analysed using Multidimensional-scaling technique.

Findings

In the first section, findings on gender stereotypes as seen from personality traits, roles and duties in domestic and professional spheres, ascribed typically to men and to women are presented. It also includes findings on behavioural norms and expectations. In the second section, findings on sexual acts and associated meanings are discussed.

Gender Stereotypes

Personality Traits

In every society, while describing general personality of men and women a number of traits are used. Certain traits are considered to be typical of either men or of women. These stereotypic images of men and women are socially constructed and commonly held regarding their innate qualities and nature.

It is seen from Table 15.2 that respondents from tribal community view certain traits more associated with women than men. The traits they consider typical of women are theatrical, gullible, secretive, talkative, compassionate, soft spoken and shy. Respondents from the caste community too consider these traits typical of women, however, they add two more traits—emotional and traditional to the list. In the view of tribal youth, both these traits are seen both in men and women.

Table 15.2: Personality Traits Primarily Considered to be of Men and Women

Traits	*Caste*						
	Seen in Men		*Seen in Women*		*Seen in Both*		N =
	Freq.	*%*	*Freq.*	*%*	*Freq.*	*%*	
Traits seen in Women							
Secretive	33	23.1	67	46.9	43	30.1	143
Gullible	32	21.2	72	47.7	47	31.1	151
Traditional	32	22.2	59	41.0	53	36.8	144
Emotional	17	11.3	75	49.7	59	39.1	151
Talkative	15	9.9	103	68.2	33	21.9	151
Soft spoken	14	9.8	85	59.4	44	30.8	143
Compassionate	13	8.6	78	51.3	61	40.1	152
Theatrical	38	25.2	64	42.4	49	32.5	151
Shy	1	.7	138	90.2	14	9.2	153
Traits seen in Men							
Aggressive	113	75.8	13	8.7	23	15.4	149
Bold	111	73.5	6	4.0	34	22.5	151
Strong Personality	111	74.0	4	2.7	35	23.3	150
Willing to take risk	105	70.0	10	6.7	35	23.3	150
Sportive	99	64.7	3	2.0	51	33.3	153
Dominant	94	63.1	12	8.1	43	28.9	149
Playful	77	50.7	15	9.9	60	39.5	152
Easygoing	77	53.1	15	10.3	53	36.6	145
Independent	74	49.7	12	8.1	63	42.3	149
Conceited	70	47.3	39	26.4	39	26.4	148
Flatterable	59	40.4	55	37.7	32	21.9	146
Self-reliant	41	27.0	32	21.1	79	52.0	152
Traits seen in both Men and Women							
Openness	54	35.5	35	23.0	63	41.4	152
Reliable	53	35.3	25	16.7	72	48.0	150
Leadership ability	50	33.1	8	5.3	93	61.6	151
Jealous	41	28.7	47	32.9	55	38.5	143
Gentle	38	25.0	22	14.5	92	60.5	152
Acceptance of faults	36	23.8	43	28.5	72	47.7	151
Analytical	32	21.6	37	25.0	79	53.4	148
Understanding	32	21.1	36	23.7	84	55.3	152
Moralistic	32	22.1	22	15.2	91	62.8	145
Loyal	31	20.5	37	24.5	83	55.0	151
Ambitious	27	17.8	17	11.2	108	71.1	152
Tactful	23	15.0	47	30.7	83	54.2	153
Competitive	22	14.5	20	13.2	110	72.4	152
Intelligent	20	13.2	20	13.2	112	73.7	152
Cheerful	14	9.3	51	33.8	86	57.0	151
Honest	18	11.8	20	13.1	115	75.2	153
Loves Children	1	.7	51	33.6	100	65.8	152
Religious	5	3.3	58	38.2	89	58.6	152
Self-reliant	41	27.0	32	21.1	79	52.0	152

(Contd.)

Traits	*Tribe*						
	Seen in Men		*Seen in Women*		*Seen in Both*		*N =*
	Freq.	*%*	*Freq.*	*%*	*Freq.*	*%*	
Traits seen in Women							
Theatrical	31	19.9	63	40.4	62	39.7	156
Gullible	30	20.0	82	54.7	38	25.3	150
Secretive	28	18.9	62	41.9	58	39.2	148
Talkative	18	11.4	91	57.6	49	31.0	158
Compassionate	11	7.1	77	49.7	67	43.2	155
Soft Spoken	7	4.6	81	53.6	63	41.7	151
Shy	3	1.9	138	89.0	14	9.0	155
Traits seen in Men							
Strong Personality	120	77.9	5	3.2	29	18.8	154
Aggressive	110	71.0	12	7.7	33	21.3	155
Bold	107	68.6	5	3.2	44	28.2	156
Dominant	88	56.8	24	15.5	43	27.7	155
Sportive	86	55.1	4	2.6	66	42.3	156
Willing to take risk	83	52.5	20	12.7	55	34.8	158
Conceited	73	48.0	38	25.0	41	27.0	152
Playful	73	47.4	13	8.4	68	44.2	154
Reliable	64	41.3	32	20.6	59	38.1	155
Traits seen in both Men and Women							
Independent	67	42.9	20	12.8	69	44.2	156
Easygoing	61	40.7	18	12.0	71	47.3	150
Flatterable	57	37.0	37	24.0	60	39.0	154
Openness	53	34.6	31	20.3	69	45.1	153
Jealous	52	35.1	26	17.6	70	47.3	148
Leadership ability	49	31.6	20	12.9	86	55.5	155
Self-reliant	44	28.2	23	14.7	89	57.1	156
Loyal	43	27.4	36	22.9	78	49.7	157
Understanding	41	26.3	41	26.3	74	47.4	156
Traditional	38	25.5	45	30.2	66	44.3	149
Gentle	36	23.4	21	13.6	97	63.0	154
Competitive	36	22.8	11	7.0	111	70.3	158
Acceptance of faults	35	23.0	46	30.3	71	46.7	152
Analytical	34	22.2	25	16.3	94	61.4	153
Tactful	32	20.3	56	35.4	70	44.3	158
Moralistic	31	20.4	23	15.1	98	64.5	152
Ambitious	30	19.0	20	12.7	108	68.4	158
Honest	27	17.2	24	15.3	106	67.5	157
Emotional	25	16.3	61	39.9	67	43.8	153
Cheerful	20	12.8	61	39.1	75	48.1	156
Religious	19	12.0	40	25.3	99	62.7	158
Intelligent	17	10.8	13	8.3	127	80.9	157
Loves Children	3	1.9	55	35.0	99	63.1	157

Source: Field Investigation.

The tribal respondents listed down nine traits, which according to them are predominantly seen among men, whereas, respondents from caste community listed down eleven traits typical of men. The tribal respondents viewed the trait 'reliable' as that of men whereas in the view of caste community, it is seen among both men and women. Three traits—easy going, independent and flatterable, are seen as typical of men by respondents from caste community but, are attributed to both men and women by the tribal respondents. Thus, there is agreement between both the groups upon eight traits that are commonly seen in men. These traits are strong personality, aggressive, bold, dominant, sportive, willing to take risk, conceited and playful.

Large numbers of traits are viewed as common to both men and women as these traits, according to the respondents, become apparent in the behaviour of men and women in different contexts. For instance, women tend to be very analytical (critical) when it comes to buying clothes while men may display the same quality when it comes to money matters or purchase of agricultural implements. Both may display 'leadership ability', 'understanding', and 'tact' in different contexts. The stereotypic image that emerges from these depicts women as comparatively weak. She is also seen as gullible at the same time secretive and skimming.

Youth thus agree on what are considered to be typically feminine and typically masculine characteristics. These characteristics point to the dominant social norms of feminine and masculine behaviour. They are made meaningful in assigning social roles and duties to men and women.

Gender and Household Duties

In the general view of the youth (Table 15.3), core household duties such as cooking, washing, cleaning and child rearing continue to be women's domain. While giving bath to children and changing their diapers are women's jobs, looking after studies and their general care are responsibility of both the parents. Similarly buying grocery and vegetables can be anyone's job. Though pressing cloths is a job to be done by either of them, quite a few see it as men's task. Vehicle and electronic repairs are men' jobs.

Women, according to youth, are "...taught cooking and other household chores at an early age and they often volunteer for it. And hence, they are best at it." Further women are "by nature loving and caring" and thus, can handle children better. This "affection leads them to change the diapers without hesitation and shame", whereas "men find those tasks embarrassing and shameful".

Table 15.3: Household Duties Considered Appropriate for Men and Women

Household Duties	*Caste*							*Tribe*						
	Appropriate for Men		*Appropriate for Women*		*Appropriate for both*		*N =*	*Appropriate for Men*		*Appropriate for Women*		*Appropriate for both*		*N =*
	Freq.	*%*	*Freq.*	*%*	*Freq.*	*%*		*Freq.*	*%*	*Freq.*	*%*	*Freq.*	*%*	
Cooking	0	0	107	72.8	40	27.2	147	1	0.7	96	64.9	51	34.5	148
Changing kids' diapers	0	0	118	80.3	29	19.7	147	1	0.6	107	69.0	47	30.3	155
Cleaning utensils	0	0	126	85.7	21	14.3	147	1	0.6	130	83.3	25	16.0	156
Giving bath to children	3	2.0	105	70.9	40	27.0	148	2	1.3	112	73.2	?9	25.5	153
Taking care of children	3	2.1	49	33.6	94	64.4	146	4	2.7	37	25.0	107	72.3	148
Sweeping house	4	2.6	88	58.3	59	39.1	151	0	0	79	52.3	72	47.7	151
Washing clothes	4	2.7	115	78.2	28	19.0	147	1	0.7	112	74.2	38	25.2	151
Minor electronic repairs	120	80.5	4	2.7	25	16.8	149	131	86.8	2	1.3	18	11.9	151
Minor vehicle repairs	129	86.6	6	4.0	14	9.4	149	132	88.0	3	2.0	15	10.0	150
Cleaning the household toilets/bathroom	7	4.8	52	35.6	87	59.6	146	5	3.3	57	37.5	90	59.2	152
Looking after sick people in the family	11	7.5	13	8.9	122	83.6	146	11	7.3	11	7.3	129	85.4	151
Helping children in studies	20	13.6	16	10.9	111	75.5	147	16	10.6	14	9.3	121	80.1	151
Buying vegetables	35	23.2	13	8.6	103	68.2	151	24	16.1	12	8.1	113	75.8	149
Ironing clothes	50	33.8	8	5.4	90	60.8	148	57	37.3	11	7.2	85	55.6	153
Buying grocery	64	43.0	4	2.7	81	54.4	149	49	32.2	7	4.6	96	63.2	152

Source: Field Investigation.

Men are seen to be stable and more adept to perform tasks that involve certain skills and risks. As one respondent puts it, "Electronic and vehicle repairs involve certain risk, which women can not handle. Also vehicle repairs involves physical labour which women can not undertake, thus it is men's job."

Helping children in their studies and looking after them is the responsibility of both the parents but things such as giving bath to them are a woman's job. Youth also note that certain tasks such as upbringing of children demands attention from both, "Children's education and socialisation ('*Sanskar*') are responsibility of both, mother and father." Similarly, looking after sick person in a family is everybody's responsibility while, "Buying grocery and vegetables can be done by anyone who is free."

It can be seen that certain tasks are seen to be of women due to their 'inherent' or 'natural' qualities of affection, love and care. Similarly men's stable, physically strong nature qualifies them to perform certain tasks.

Gender and Profession

A large number of youth, both from tribal and caste communities, consider professions of nursing and nursery teacher more appropriate for women (Table 15.4). They think that women naturally possess qualities required for these professions. One of the respondent said "Woman has an entirely different mentality, she is soft (Komal), she is understanding, she is loving, she is caring...these qualities are naturally embedded in them, women can understand people better, they can understand sick people's pain and with their talk they can reduce their pain." Similarly one respondent mentioned that women posses the qualities to become teachers in nursery schools: "It's a job where care, love and affection is needed more...in case of small kids it is very necessary. Males by nature are short tempered though they love and care. They don't have that patience which women have". Professions like electronic engineer, civil engineer, politician, business and mechanic, which need skills and technical know-how, skills to deal with people and certain degree of physical strength were considered typical of men. As one respondent puts it, "Women who plan to be in politics won't be supported by their families. Women do not know many things and their information gathering resources are very bad. These are qualities of men. Many a times women don't understand easy things in life, how can they then understand complex game plans of politics."

Table 15.4: Professions Considered Appropriate for Men and Women

Outside Duties	*Caste*							*Tribe*						
	Appropriate for Men		*Appropriate for Women*		*Appropriate for both*		*N =*	*Appropriate for Men*		*Appropriate for Women*		*Appropriate for both*		*N =*
	Freq.	*%*	*Freq.*	*%*	*Freq.*	*%*		*Freq.*	*%*	*Freq.*	*%*	*Freq.*	*%*	
Nurse	0	0	122	81.3	28	18.7	150	0	0	130	85.0	23	15.0	153
Nursery Teacher	0	0	95	62.9	56	37.1	151	1	0.6	107	69.0	47	30.3	155
Politician	75	50.3	0	0	74	49.7	149	79	51.0	1	0.6	75	48.4	155
Secretary	72	48.3	14	9.4	63	42.3	149	86	55.8	12	7.8	56	36.4	154
Office/Hotel Receptionist	74	51.0	15	10.3	56	38.6	145	90	58.8	7	4.6	56	36.6	153
Civil Engineer	84	55.6	2	1.3	65	43.0	151	95	62.5	1	0.7	56	36.8	152
Electronic Engineer	99	66.9	1	0.7	48	32.4	148	104	69.8	1	0.7	44	29.5	149
Mechanic	130	86.1	1	0.7	20	13.2	151	118	77.1	3	2.0	32	20.9	153
Business	77	51.7	1	0.7	71	47.7	149	70	44.9	3	1.9	83	53.2	156
Doctor	1	0.7	0	0	151	99.3	152	7	4.4	0	0	151	95.6	158
School Teacher	8	5.3	6	4.0	137	90.7	151	9	5.8	5	3.2	141	91.0	155
Professor	9	5.9	1	0.7	142	93.4	152	21	13.5	0	0	135	86.5	156
Fashion Designer	9	6.0	54	36.0	87	58.0	150	7	4.6	68	44.4	78	51.0	153
Lawyer *	10	6.6	1	0.7	140	92.7	151	26	16.7	0	0	130	83.3	156
Computer Engineer	16	10.5	5	3.3	131	86.2	152	20	13.0	1	0.6	133	86.4	154
Vegetable Vendor	23	15.3	19	12.7	108	72.0	150	22	14.7	16	10.7	112	74.7	150
Cleaner/Sweeper *	30	20.7	33	22.8	82	56.6	145	16	10.4	39	25.3	99	64.3	154
Accountant	34	22.7	3	2.0	113	75.3	150	47	31.1	5	3.3	99	65.6	151
Clerk	41	27.0	7	4.6	104	68.4	152	49	31.6	5	3.2	101	65.2	155
Bank Manager	50	32.7	2	1.3	101	66.0	153	68	43.6	2	1.3	86	55.1	156
Agriculture **	63	41.7	1	0.7	87	57.6	151	26	16.8	0	0	129	83.2	155
Architect	62	42.2	4	2.7	81	55.1	147	66	43.7	11	7.3	74	49.0	151

*: χ^2 significant at 5 per cent level **: χ^2 significant at 1 per cent level

Source: Field Investigation.

Interestingly more than half of the respondents in both group stated that job of receptionist in hotels and office are more appropriate for men. They think that, as hotel receptionist; women are vulnerable to sexual exploitation. Besides they are required to work in night shifts, which is risky. Popular image of hotel/office receptionist in Hindi movies is often negatively projected. At times it shoes women as morally loose, liberal and sometimes she is innocent victim who may be coned or sexually molested. Even otherwise, working as receptionist is not seen as honourable and respectful profession.

Comparatively a large number of professions are seen appropriate for both men and women. These are the types of jobs, which are confined to office work and are perceived as not involving intense physical activity. Besides it is widely experienced that women have successfully taken up many of the professions, which were earlier monopolized by men. Women doctors and teachers is not uncommon in towns and villages. Youth consider certain professions like doctor, school teacher, professor, computer engineer and vegetable vendor as appropriate for both. Professions like lawyer, cleaner/sweeper and agriculture are considered appropriate for both the genders, there is a significant difference in choices between the two groups. Majority of the respondents from both the groups think that both men and women can take up fashion designing; many consider it more appropriate for women as if women have natural flair for it. Both men and women contribute to the agricultural activities. Therefore, perhaps it is considered as appropriate for both. As compared to the youth from the caste communities, a higher number of tribal youth think that both men and women can undertake it. Traditionally tribal societies have been characterized by relative lack of division of labour and subsistence economy, which affect their views. In the caste societies, however, with relatively sharply defined male-female segregation and division of labour (women confined to household duties and man primarily as bread winner) many youth consider agriculture as men's domain.

Thus, traditional notion of masculine and feminine qualities, which are believed to be inherent, are made meaningful in considering various jobs as appropriate either for men or for women. However, a large number of jobs are considered appropriate for both, since women have been successfully working in diverse fields.

Gender Practices

Youth think that just as boys, girls should be allowed to have a career and not remain confined to household. Girls can hold important positions in different professions. They also insist that equal preference should be given to the education of both the boys and girls even if money is scarce. Thus many think that like boys, girls too, should attain a certain level of education. Further, they expect both, husband and wife, to earn for the household. Youth do not see sharing work in the household to be less manly (Table 15.5).

Although youth show such liberal attitude in many respects, a significant number of youth from both the groups consider it important to have a hold over wife. Some even agree to man beating his wife if she disobeys him.

Sexual Behaviour

Values associated with Women

Traditionally, women are expected to be more virtuous. This is reflected in the belief that woman's chastity and virginity prior to marriage is not only a matter of her individual pride but also of her family. This belief is strongly held by youth. (Table 5). Many respondents agree that virginity is more desirable in case of women than men. However, equally large number of them are undecided. A small minority approves that men could have premarital sex, while a majority of youth do not approve this idea. This may be due to the dominant value that expects both, men and women, to remain chaste (Table 15.6).

A large number of respondents believe that men and women should have their spouse as the sole sex partner. However, the traditional permissiveness and tolerance for men's deviations from norms of sexual behaviour and restraint on women's behaviour is clearly reflected in the data. Youth from both the groups seem to think that one can understand if man indulges in extra marital sex but women should not. At the same time, having multiple sexual partners is not viewed as a sign of manliness nor it is considered as natural for men.

Thus, the ideology reflected in these responses stresses on virginity of both men and women but more so for women. It emphasises on monogamous sexual relations, while women are expected to follow the norm more strictly than men.

Gender and Beliefs about Sexuality

Many youth agree that girls are attracted towards boys who are manly (Table 15.7). More respondents from caste community than tribal think

Table 15.5: Gender Practices

Practices	Caste							Tribe						
	Approve		Disapprove		Can't Say		N =	Approve		Disapprove		Can't Say		N =
	Freq.	%	Freq.	%	Freq.	%		Freq.	%	Freq.	%	Freq.	%	
Boys should be allowed to decide when they want to marry	116	75.8	25	16.3	12	7.8	153	110	70.1	37	23.6	10	6.4	157
Girls should be allowed to decide when they want to marry	112	73.2	29	19.0	12	7.8	153	109	69.0	40	25.3	9	5.7	158
Boys can select their own wife	132	86.3	15	9.8	6	3.9	153	133	85.3	11	7.1	12	7.7	156
Girls can select their own husband	122	80.3	20	13.2	10	6.6	152	121	77.1	23	14.6	13	8.3	157
When money is scarce and family cannot send all children to school boys should be sent before girls	25	16.3	106	69.3	22	14.4	153	33	21.0	110	70.1	14	8.9	157
It is important for woman to finish her education before marriage	103	67.3	38	24.8	12	7.8	153	113	72.0	28	17.8	16	10.2	157
It is important for man to finish his education before marriage	129	84.3	17	11.1	7	4.6	153	131	82.9	18	11.4	9	5.7	158
Both wife and husband should earn for the family	127	83.0	18	11.8	8	5.2	153	136	86.6	15	9.6	6	3.8	157
Boys should spend as much time as girls on household duties	76	50.3	55	36.4	20	13.2	151	70	45.2	67	43.2	18	11.6	155
Men who do household works like washing clothes, cooking, cleaning etc. are not manly	25	16.4	100	65.8	27	17.8	152	32	20.5	103	66.0	21	13.5	156
Boys may have a career while girls should look after household	25	16.3	121	79.1	7	4.6	153	23	14.6	127	80.4	8	5.1	158
Like men, women should have same rights to hold important while working outside	130	85.0	13	8.5	10	6.5	153	136	86.6	16	10.2	5	3.2	157
It is important for husband to have hold on his wife	87	57.6	42	27.8	22	14.6	151	100	63.3	41	25.9	17	10.8	158
It's OK for husband to beat his wife if she disobeys him	76	49.7	59	38.6	18	11.8	153	71	45.5	59	37.8	26	16.7	156
Wife should always follow instructions given by her husband	68	44.4	67	43.8	18	11.8	153	62	39.5	78	49.7	17	10.8	157
Husband should seek advice from wife but he should be the final decision maker	79	51.6	57	37.3	17	11.1	153	84	53.2	61	38.6	13	8.2	158
Husband should be the major breadwinner in the family	22	14.7	119	79.3	9	6.0	150	21	13.4	122	77.7	14	8.9	157

Source: Field Investigation.

Table 15.6: Values associated with Women

Values	Caste							Tribe						
	Approve		Disapprove		Can't Say		N =	Approve		Disapprove		Can't Say		N =
	Freq	%	Freq	%	Freq	%		Freq	%	Freq	%	Freq	%	
Female's chastity is pride of the family	144	95.4	5	3.3	2	1.3	151	144	91.7	9	5.7	4	2.5	157
Virginity is more desirable in woman than man	70	46.7	18	12.0	62	41.3	150	65	42.8	21	13.8	66	43.4	152
Woman should satisfy man's all sexual desires	112	75.2	15	10.1	22	14.8	149	97	62.6	29	18.7	29	18.7	155
It is 'OK' for man to have extra-martial sex	62	41.6	57	38.3	30	20.1	149	71	46.1	56	36.4	27	17.5	154
It is 'OK' for woman to have extra-martial sex	14	9.5	124	83.8	10	6.8	148	13	8.5	126	82.4	14	9.2	153
Man should have his wife as the sole sex partner	128	83.7	20	13.1	5	3.3	153	131	84.5	20	12.9	4	2.6	155
Women should have her husband as the sole sex partner	140	92.1	5	3.3	7	4.6	152	138	89.6	11	7.1	5	3.2	154

Source: Field Investigation.

Table 15.7: Gender and Beliefs about Sexuality

Beliefs	Caste							Tribe						
	Approve		Disapprove		Can't Say		N =	Approve		Disapprove		Can't Say		N =
	Freq	%	Freq	%	Freq	%		Freq	%	Freq	%	Freq	%	
Youth who are not attracted towards girls are not manly	35	23.3	81	54.0	34	22.7	150	39	25.7	79	52.0	34	22.4	152
Girls are attracted towards boys who are 'manly'	104	68.9	17	11.3	30	19.9	151	85	54.8	35	22.6	35	22.6	155
Women like men to be rough and strong in their approach	13	8.6	99	65.6	39	25.8	151	17	11.0	77	49.7	61	39.4	155
Large breast of woman are sexually attractive to men	120	80.5	10	6.7	19	12.8	149	86	57.0	33	21.9	32	21.2	151
For men it is difficult to control desire for sex	58	38.4	66	43.7	27	17.9	151	59	39.6	66	44.3	24	16.1	149
For women it is difficult to control desire for sex	75	50.7	34	23.0	39	26.4	148	64	42.4	40	26.5	47	31.1	151
Women have stronger sexual desire than men	110	72.8	6	4.0	35	23.2	151	105	68.2	9	5.8	40	26.0	154
Men have more sexual desire than women	56	36.6	54	35.3	43	28.1	153	44	28.2	69	44.2	43	27.6	156
Women are difficult to satisfy sexually	49	33.6	43	29.5	54	37.0	146	55	35.5	49	31.6	51	32.9	155
Large penis is of great importance to women's sexual satisfaction	86	56.2	32	20.9	35	22.9	153	67	42.7	37	23.6	53	33.8	157
Man with larger penis has more sexual capacity	36	23.7	55	36.2	61	40.1	152	28	18.2	59	38.3	67	43.5	154

Source: Field Investigation.

so. At the same time, not feeling attracted towards girls, does not make a boy less manly. However, such boys may be targeted and ridiculed. This was witnessed when respondents were filling up the questionnaires for this study. Youth often asked us, "...That boy doesn't even look at girls...how can he fill the questionnaire about sex?" Although youth say that women are attracted towards manly boys, they do not like them to be rough in approach. In their view, girls expect qualities of love and understanding. Majority of the youth say that large breast of women are attractive to men sexually. They also think that men with larger penis are more capable of satisfying woman's sexual desire. However, larger penis does not mean larger sexual capacity.

When it comes to sexual desire, respondents stated that as compared to men, women not only have stronger sexual desire, but also find it difficult to control.

Sexual Acts and Their Sexual Meanings

Sexual acts and associated eroticism, which constitute an important dimension of sexuality, are explored in this section. A list of 35 different sexual acts was provided and youth were asked to state whether they consider the acts as either erotic or not erotic. Their explanations for the responses were sought through interviews. The quantitative data reveal as to how many of the respondents considered each of the acts as erotic or otherwise, and nothing beyond. Interviews, however, revealed that people tend to group sexual acts into different categories such as 'acts that increase passion', 'dirty acts', 'acts expressive of love and affection' etc. Thus youth seem to have seen the acts not in isolation but in relation to each other as reflected in such categorisation. In order to explore the possibility of identical patterns in the quantitative data, multidimensional scaling analysis was performed and a two-dimensional solution was plotted. What emerged was a number of clusters of sexual acts, which matched with those revealed in the interviews (Figure 15.1).

The responses from both the groups did not significantly differ except for a few and hence the data was pooled together for multidimensional scaling (MDS) analysis (Table 15.8 and Table 15.9).

The MDS plot for eroticism (Figure 15.1) shows two major sections divided by the slanting line 'pq'. To the right of this line are four clusters, A, B, C and D, whereas to the left of it are two small clusters E and F. Acts 1 and 19 and Acts 7 and 3 are outliers in relation to others, in right and left divisions respectively. Table 15.8 and Table 15.9 show actual

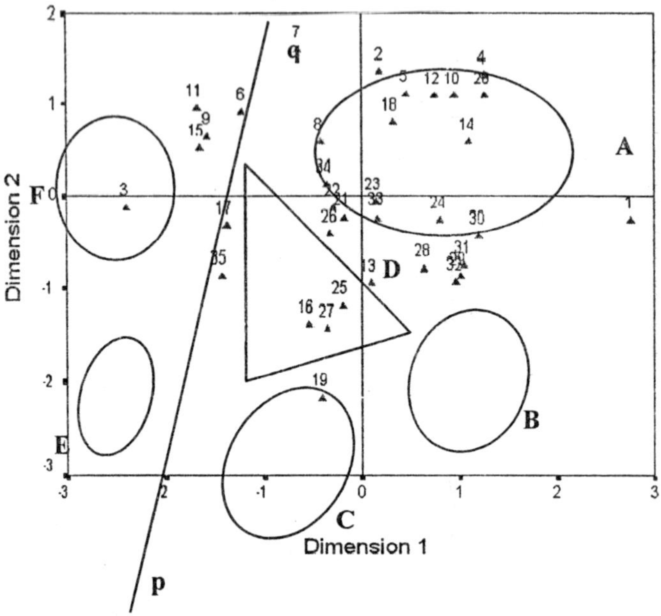

Note: Numbers indicate the serial numbers for the acts shown in **Table 15.8 and Table 15.9.**

Fig. 15.1: Two-dimensional MDS plot for erotic acts

frequencies for these acts, which are arranged according to the clusters seen in the MDS plot.

Clusters A and D besides others, include certain kissing acts. In cluster A, man and woman kissing partner's eyes, nose and earlobe are listed, while in D kissing navel, lips and deep kissing are mentioned. These acts (cluster D) were termed as 'acts which increase the passion' ('Sex wadhavtat') by almost all the respondents. They preclude lovemaking, "...begin lovemaking, and then step by step go to kissing on lips and then the real thing...this gives more pleasure (*Sukh*)."

Not many find kissing acts in cluster A erotic. As one some respondent said that "when you have lips and cheek to kiss, why kiss nose and eyes? I don't feel like doing these as I don't feel sexually aroused by these acts." One of the youth said that he would not allow his wife to these acts as "...these acts don't have direct effect on intercourse."

Thus, youth seem to make a distinction between locations on body for kissing. Certain locations (cluster D) are preferred over others (cluster A) as they positively relate to sexual desire. As a result, these

Table 15.8: Erotic acts Arranged According to Clusters in the MDS

Act No.	Sexual Acts	Erotic		Not Erotic		Can't Say		N =
		Freq.	%	Freq.	%	Freq.	%	
	Cluster A							
2	Sucking the fingers/toes of woman	73	23.7	165	53.6	70	22.7	308
4	Kissing eyes of woman	122	40.0	131	43.0	52	17.0	305
5	Kissing nose of woman	69	22.8	167	55.3	66	21.9	302
10	Kissing the earlobe	108	35.4	123	40.3	74	24.3	305
12	Woman kissing nose of man	88	30.3	124	42.8	78	26.9	290
14	Women kissing eyes of man	127	42.2	111	36.9	63	20.9	301
18	Woman kissing/sucking chest of man	160	52.3	75	24.5	71	23.2	306
20	Woman kissing man's earlobe *	104	34.1	130	42.6	71	23.3	305
	Cluster B							
24	Kissing on cheek	239	78.6	46	15.1	19	6.3	304
28	Looking at woman's breast	167	56.8	70	23.8	57	19.4	294
29	Woman playing with man's hair	152	49.8	92	30.2	61	20.0	305
30	Playing with hair of woman *	161	53.1	91	30.0	51	16.8	303
31	Woman caressing man's face	165	55.2	83	27.8	51	17.1	299
32	Caressing woman's face	191	64.3	64	21.5	42	14.1	297
	Cluster C							
13	Intercourse of Penis-Vagina	207	68.8	42	14.0	52	17.3	301
16	Man initiating sex	149	50.3	60	20.3	87	29.4	296
25	Caressing woman's buttocks	180	59.4	68	22.4	55	18.2	303
27	Looking at woman's buttocks	138	46.2	87	29.1	74	24.7	299
	Cluster D							
8	Kissing the navel *	148	48.5	100	32.8	57	18.7	305
21	Deep kissing (French kiss) **	172	56.6	97	31.9	35	11.5	304
22	Kissing/Sucking breast of woman **	192	64.2	65	21.7	42	14.0	299
23	Kissing on lips	251	82.0	35	11.4	20	6.5	306
26	Caressing woman's breast	218	72.4	41	13.6	42	14.0	301
33	Hugging	241	79.3	42	13.8	21	6.9	304
34	Woman sucking the fingers/toes of man	93	30.7	148	48.8	62	20.5	303
	Outliers							
1	Holding hands	169	54.9	102	33.1	37	12.0	308
19	Woman initiating sex	139	46.0	69	22.8	94	31.1	302

*: χ^2 significant at 5 per cent level **: χ^2 significant at 1 per cent level

Source: Field Investigation.

acts are distinctly placed from each other (Fig. 15.1). These views are reflected in quantitative data (Table 15.8).

Cluster B contains the acts of kissing the cheek, looking at woman's breast, men and women playing with partner's hair and caressing partner's face. These have variable meanings in the view of youth. Looking at women's breast while waiting for bus at bus station could be casual and unconscious. So also playing with female friends' hair could be a playful act. One respondent says "I do it all the time with my girl...it happens unconsciously as a time-pass activity when we are talking." Another respondent said, "When husband sneaks from behind and kisses his wife on cheek, while she is busy cooking, she feels very happy... such acts increase and sustain the love between husband and wife." These acts thus are contextually viewed as expression of love and affection or unconscious actions. They could be erotic in a situation but devoid of any sexual meanings and eroticism in another. As one respondent puts it, they "symbolise emotions of love" (*Bhavanatmak Prem*). It is generally experienced that pecking of cheek, caressing face or ruffling of hair can happen in other social relations; among mother and children, friends and siblings. This fact may explain why they are contextually viewed as expressions of love and affection, unconscious acts or erotic. Whatever the context, youth seem to approve the practice of these acts (Table 15.8).

Cluster C includes 4 acts—peno-vaginal intercourse, man initiating sex, caressing woman's buttocks, and looking at woman's buttocks. Cluster D, besides kissing acts which respondents find erotic, include caressing woman's breast and hugging. Youth seem to see these acts as central in sexual relations. They see peno-vaginal intercourse as the 'sex' and 'the most important thing!' As one respondent noted, "We do all other things for this only!!" One respondent equated acts of kissing and caressing to trailers of movies. He says, 'we watched the trailer and now this is the real movie! Watching only trailer and not the movie is not good! (Laughs).' Similarly kissing woman's navel can be a passionate act, "woman's navel is deep...it is good to kiss it." Hugging, kissing on lips and kissing and caressing the breast are favoured by majority of youth. They say, "hugging automatically occurs when you start it". Further quite a few equated kissing on lips with 'real sex' by saying that "kissing on lips is as good as real sex...when boys don't get to do it (referring to peno-vaginal intercourse) they do this!"

Caressing breasts is generally seen to be most erotic, "Breasts are meant to be caressed, otherwise what is their use?" One youth spelled the degree of erotic nature of the act by saying that "this act is so erotic ('*Bhari*') that some boys ejaculate while squeezing girls breast...since men do not have such a soft part, they like to get hold of these balls whenever they get the chance...they find it very erotic." However, significantly lesser number of tribal youth shares this view. A tribal youth stated, "Breasts are mother's place...(they symbolise motherhood). Then caressing and kissing her breasts or even looking at girls breasts...it can not even be thought of." Breasts may be associated with motherhood and close mother—child relation.

Youth thus see various acts of cluster C and D as those which *'increase the passion'* and peno-vaginal intercourse as *'the sex'*. These acts received highest positive frequencies and, therefore, reflect general acceptability and desirability.

Holding hands, one of the acts listed, is commonly experienced by the members of a society. Siblings hold hands while road-crossing and friends while talking. It could be a protective gesture or a gesture of affection or an unconscious act depending on the context. It is a general act devoid of any sexual meaning. Therefore, it is an outlier. None of the youths interviewed said much about it.

Table 15.9: Non-Erotic Acts Arranged According to Clusters in the MDS

Act No.	*Sexual Acts*	*Erotic*		*Not Erotic*		*Can't Say*		*N =*
		Freq.	%	Freq.	%	Freq.	%	
	Cluster E							
17	Getting masturbated by woman	128	43.5	75	25.5	91	31.0	294
35	Woman caressing man's buttocks	136	45.2	81	26.9	84	27.9	301
	Cluster F							
6	Man kissing genitals of woman *	111	36.0	123	39.9	74	24.0	308
9	Woman kissing buttocks of man *	117	38.6	98	32.3	88	29.0	303
11	Man Masturbating Woman	112	37.0	81	26.7	110	36.3	303
15	Woman kissing the genitals of man	127	42.2	92	30.6	82	27.2	301
	Outliers							
3	Kissing buttocks of woman	149	48.5	95	30.9	63	20.5	307
7	Anal intercourse	75	25.2	96	32.2	127	42.6	298

* χ^2 significant at 5 per cent level **: χ^2 significant at 1 per cent level

Source: Field Investigation.

Clusters E and F are located to the left of the line 'pq'. Acts in cluster F in general are not much favoured. These acts generate feeling of repulsion. In respondent's view, genital area is dirty. One respondent said that "this is the place from where we defecate and urinate, so it has to be dirty and kissing there can lead to disease and infection". Another said, "These acts are exotic and are shown in English BP's (Blue Print, or

Blue Films) only. They show these acts as they have to do something different from normal." Other youth said that "girls have her periods and all. So many times they have some or the other disease there, so kissing genital area is so dirty that I cannot imagine that!" Apart from this, certain acts could be problematic, as one youth pointed out, "kissing buttocks is so awkward physically! We are kissing on the cheek and lips and all from the front and then suddenly how do we turn and kiss the buttocks? (Shows action by hand and laughs)". However, many find it erotic to kiss woman's buttocks and woman kissing the genitals of man, but not the other way round. Similarly, 'dirtiness' of the vagina does not mean that peno-vaginal intercourse is also 'dirty'; one respondent said, "...That the act is for reproduction...everyone has to do it."

Anal intercourse (act 7) lies at a distance from other acts. The least number of respondents find this act erotic. Many were undecided perhaps because they could not understand the formal words describing the sexual act. Most of the time people use colloquial terms while talking about genitals and describing sexual acts. Youth have cited different reasons for not favouring it. Besides it being 'dirty', youth also said that anal intercourse "...is not natural" and that "it can lead to medical problems. I have read so in one sex education book". Another youth mentioned "it is shown in BP (Blue Films) but in reality if you ask a woman that 'I want to screw your ass' ('*gand maraychi*') then she will definitely say no...she will not accept it."

Comparatively, many accept act of masturbating the partner though a quarter could not say anything about it. This was also reflected in the interviews. Almost all the respondents asked the researchers the same question; "if the boy and girl are naked and are in position to masturbate each other then why not directly have sex?" Another respondent said, "I don't get it! When they can have real sex, why do all this?" More respondents prefer act of woman masturbating man. However a few prefer it other way round perhaps because it is erotic or out of consideration for woman's sexual satisfaction as this youth pointed out, "sometimes men squirt faster and the woman remains unsatisfied. At that time putting fingers is OK so that she also gets satisfaction. People from my parents' generation would come home after work, have sex and then go to sleep. Men hardly bothered whether woman is satisfied or not. We now think of the satisfaction of both man and woman. This act can be done in such situation."

Thus some acts are favoured by youth either because they 'increase the passion' or because they 'express emotions of love'. Certain other acts not favoured by respondents as they are seen as repulsive and unnatural. Body parts associated may be seen as 'dirty' and may be 'disease spreading areas'. A few acts were seen as 'causally happening' for 'passing time'. Such acts are contextually understood and may not be loaded with sexual tones all the time.

Discussion

This study, mainly sought to understand changes in the attitudes, beliefs and perception related to gender and sexuality among the college going youth; and to understand the sexual acts and their meanings from the social constructionist perspective.

The youth from both groups, tribal as well as rural, did not show distinct patterns of beliefs and perception in the context of the subject matter of the study. The tribal youth involved in the study were from Kokana and Mahadeo Koli tribes. For quite some time now both the tribal communities have adopted many elements of the dominant cultural tradition of Hinduism. Among all the tribes in the State of Maharashtra, they are considered as 'advanced' and are way ahead of other in terms of participation into the modern processes of politics, education and occupations. Thus on the folk–urban continuum, both are closer to rural-urban, rather than to the folk society. This could be the predominant cause for the close similarity in their attitudes, beliefs and perceptions.

Gender and Sexuality

Indian society has patriarchal system. "In a patriarchy, roles are allocated not only in accordance with biological functions (procreation), but are ascribed according to the values prescribed to males and females" (Dagar, 1998:22). Thus women are confined to domestic sphere—child rearing and household work and men to social. Besides roles allocation (men to dominating and controlling functions and women to supportive functions) certain norms and values along with beliefs and practices promote the man-woman superiority-inferiority, relationships.

Youth under study hold on to various patriarchal values and beliefs. Certain attributes of women such as compassionate and soft-spoken seem to go with their roles as mother and caretaker. Similarly attributes such as aggressiveness, boldness, will to take risk; go with man as the provider. However, more numbers of positive attributes are assigned to men than to women.

These variable attributes of men and women are made meaningful by the youth in determining what household duties and professions are considered appropriate for men and for women. Only two household duties—minor electronic repairs and vehicle repairs were primarily seen as men's duties. Similarly only two professions—nursery teaching and nursing were primarily attributed to women. The reasons were obvious. The repair work involves certain amount of risk, skill and labour. Women on the other hand are inherently loving and caring.

The youth uphold the value of fidelity—being faithful to one's husband or wife. They think that men have better control over their sexual desires while women do not. At the same time, men are fallible to the charms of women enticers, and therefore perhaps youth are more tolerant of husband's infidelity. This is often depicted theme both in Hindu mythology and Hindi movies. Similarly they express strong belief in the value of female chastity and purity prior to marriage, but the same is not applicable to men.

Although the youth subscribe to various values and beliefs of patriarchy, they are more flexible when it comes to economic and educational spheres. They disapprove of discriminative practices of confining girls to household duties and giving preference to boy's education. They think that both men and women have equal rights to important professional positions, choose marriage partners and decide when to marry. They believe that earning for the family is the responsibility of both and not merely of husband. Conversely men should share household responsibilities. Today in India, even in the rural and tribal communities, a substantial number of girls go for higher education and obtain degree. Women work in private firms and government offices and a few obtain professional degree and practice law or medicine, which were earlier seen as men's domain.

Thus, at the larger societal level, girls' education is gaining acceptance for variable reasons such as, a stop-gap arrangement till marriage, boys expecting their prospective wife to be closer or at par with their educational qualification or girls themselves aspiring for education and career. Besides, women are increasingly being called upon to earn and augment family income. It is in this context that youth show attitude of gender equity in the limited sphere of education and occupation. Again it is the same context in which they think that men should contribute to household duties. However, they do not expect men to perform those duties, which are inherently associated with women. Similarly, men and women both are called upon to earn, but their primary roles with associated social values have remained unchanged and responsibility of earning woman towards household chores remains undiminished.

Here, is the situation of cultural lag where certain practices have altered without significant changes in the cultural ideas and values. As compared to its ideational aspects the material aspect, of culture changes at a faster rate, necessitating change in the former sooner or later to resolve the dissonance between the two.

Sexual Meanings

Discussions among peers, media such as movies, books, television, pornographic movies, conscious and unconscious process of enculturation, and even personal experiences in a case of few, are among the most important factors responsible for shaping the sexuality of youth.

Individual sexual acts are grouped together and are assigned categorical meaning such as dirty and repulsive, expression of love and affection, and passion increasing acts. It seems that acceptability or non-acceptability of sexual acts and associated eroticism or non-eroticism arise not from the physiological nature of pleasure alone, but are influenced by cultural ideas and values.

In the Hindu view, genital and anal areas are considered both polluting and dirty. They are associated with the physiological acts of urination and defecation, which cause pollution. Further women in general and menstruating women in particular cause pollution. Such cultural notions mark certain body parts either as completely dirty (e.g. anal area) or dirty in certain context (e.g. vulva for oral stimulation but not for peno-vaginal intercourse) or totally dirty during menstruation. Sexual acts associated with these body parts are rendered dirty and repulsive.

At the same time, certain body parts figure more importantly in the cultural perception of female beauty, body aesthetics and sensuality. Indian literature is replete with metamorphic descriptions of female beauty involving lips, hair, naval and breasts. Sexual acts associated with these body parts are more acceptable to the youth. Acts such as kissing lips or naval or caressing breasts are arousing. But this alone does not make them acceptable. The value that practicing them increases the passion and thus adds to the pleasure of both men and women is the equally important reason for their acceptance. They are important, perhaps next only to peno-vaginal intercourse in the sexual relation.

Different individuals, with subjective bias view certain acts as erotic or non-erotic and unnecessary, as they do not directly impact sexual intercourse. Identical physical acts may be viewed either as erotic or as asexual and mechanical (holding hands while talking) or merely as expression of love and affection depending upon the context and persons involved. They have varying social significance and meaning in different regions and ethnic groups.

Culturally constituted patterns social contexts in which acts occur, people involved and subjective feelings, together provide a framework within which individuals construct variable meanings of sexual acts. Sexuality is thus a socio-cultural construct.

16

Gender Construction and Rural Health

AARTI NAGARKAR

Introduction

Gaps in the availability of information on women's lives are now beginning to be filled, with the United Nations leading the way (United Nations 1991; United Nations, 1995; WHO, 1992a; UNDP, 1995 and 1997). However, much remains to be done if the database for health-related policy making is to be improved. In particular, there is a need for the development of appropriate indicators combining biomedical, epidemiological and socio-economic data to monitor the changing state of women's and men's health around the world. Research which takes account of gender has to consider the differences between women's and men's roles and responsibilities, their knowledge base, their position in society, their access to and use of resources and the social codes governing female and male behaviour. Strategies to improve women's health need to be grounded in a rigorous analysis of the whole range of their productive and reproductive activities and of the way, these change across the life span. Femaleness can no longer be equated with motherhood and the scope of health research needs to shift accordingly. We need to know much more, for example, about the risks women face through their work, both in the home and in the workplace.

Until recently, few researchers had examined the risks of domestic work. As interest in the issue grows, new techniques are now being devised to get inside the 'black box' of the family (Dwyer and Bruce, 1988; Kabeer, 1991). Time-budget studies for instance have used a variety of strategies to estimate who does what in the home and to assess the impact of this on gender differences in well-being (Khander, 1988; Leslie, 1989). Related work has explored the relationship between women's patterns of energy consumption and the volume of their household work (Ferguson, 1996; ICRW 1989). Studies are also needed to assess the labour intensity of specific tasks and the need for development of methods to ascertain these, which would allow a more accurate estimate of the health risks involved for both women and men. More research of this kind is urgently needed to explore the health implications of household labour in a variety of different settings.

Numerous studies have reported gender differences in the social relations and its impact on morbidity and mortality (Fuhrer and Stansfeld, 2002). Studies have also shown that cultural norms and sanctions at the community level, and socio-demographic characteristics at the individual level, influence women's productive and reproductive roles in the household and work place. Social capital, roles, psycho-social stresses and resources, health services, and behaviours mediate social, economic and cultural effects on women's health outcomes. Inequality between and within households contributes to the patterning of women's health (Moss, 2002).

Over and above, most important determinant is social and cultural practices relating to women's position in Indian society which directly affect their ability to care for their health. This is especially so in regard to reproductive health. Women's dependency on men, their lower level of education, limited access to resources, and lower economic status is enhanced in the area of health care, particularly in their capacity to protect themselves from sexually-transmitted infection (Black, 1992).

Increasingly, it is being recognized that cultural values and the status of girls and women in society are important aspects of the AIDS problem. AIDS is a development and gender issue (Seidel, 1993). Social inequality between men's and women's roles and positions is cited as being most responsible for the spread of HIV-AIDS in India (Balaji, 1994). Thus women's problems in reproductive health and reproductive rights in relation to gender were discussed extensively in many studies which in many ways reflect deep-rooted cultural beliefs about gender relations (WHO, 1998).

The basic hypothesis of the study is that women's health needs and status, in the course of the life cycle, extend beyond reproductive/fertility issues and they are shaped by the status of women in the society. Therefore, present study aimed at understanding the construction of gender and its impact on health of women and men in the society with specific reference to women's access to and control over economic, education and social aspects in comparison with men belonging to the same society.

Significance of Study

This study explores the plural ways in which gender influences health status at the micro-(household and individual) levels. Operationally this study aimed at identifying the position, role, and participation of women and men in the social, educational and economic field and its influence on health. Data were collected using combination of tools and techniques in a village in Pune District of Maharashtra.

The difference in the status of men and women was observed in the attitudes, perceptions expressed during in-depth interviews. The trend of amniocentesis to detect the sex of the fetus was also noticed which reportedly has begun recently. The gender construction initiates at the age of 2-3 years by re-emphasizing traditional gender roles and is continued throughout. Young men, many a times took their own decisions to migrate in search of jobs. Younger women's mobility was severely restricted. The elderly men and women were engaged in work associated with farm production activity and they remained vital decision-makers at domestic levels too.

Reproductive health problems such as menstrual irregularities, white discharge, problems regarding contraception, and backache were reported by 30 per cent of women, while genito-urinary problems were reported by 8 per cent of men. Very few women were aware about HIV-AIDs while most of the men had heard about HIV but had no knowledge of its transmission and prevention. Often men controlled the cash, and decision regarding treatment type and time. Cost of travel, economic loss due to absence at work, family adjustment and pharmacy expenditure played a major role in determining the final decision regarding treatment.

Low self-esteem limits women's ability to make demands, and this was reinforced by embarrassment, if the problem was one that was tabooed. Lack of education, restricted mobility, and attitude of entire society contributed to lack of self-confidence resulting into absence of timely care. Presence of a trained health worker in the village would help in reducing the burden of illness and health care cost.

Methods

Data were collected using combination of various data collection methods such as semi-structured interview schedule, in-depth interview guide, observation guide and number of participatory methods. The study was carried out in a village in Pune District of Maharashtra covering the population of 1209 from 225 households where majority belonged to a dominant caste Maratha and a few 12.8 per cent were from Scheduled Caste category. Though majority of the families reported agriculture as a primary source of income, nearly one fourth of the families also reported one of the members in public or private service.

The following indicators were used in the present research to understand gender construct. Role and status in the family, level of literacy, extent of mobility, access to information, access to public health services, availability of economic alternatives, cultural barriers to women's decision making powers and independence. Information on these indicators were collected with the use of multiple techniques.

Enculturation in Gender Roles

The construction of gender and associated roles and statuses were reflected through attitudinal and behavioural differences observed from the birth of an individual. Fertility of married daughter-in-law being the focus of the family, a large number of traditional practices were associated with pregnancy and delivery. Pregnancy carried numerous food and behavioural prescriptions and proscriptions. The practices were re-iterated in daily food preferences. Amniocentesis trend was also introduced recently.

Coincidently number of boys under five years of age was more (64) in comparison with girls (50). The overall sex ratio of the population was 972, which was equal to Rural Maharashtra (972) but more than all India (933/1000) figure. Total number of females in early childhood (5-9 years) and adolescent age group (10-19 years) were less than boys in the same age group. Underreporting may also be a possibility.

Birth of a son was celebrated in a flashy way which would incur expenses up to Rs. 2500 on a feast, while in case of a birth of a baby girl, celebration (naming ceremony) was restricted to a small group of close relatives.

Gender roles were introduced quite early at the age of 3 or 4 years. Girls of that age were initiated in the domestic work like lifting used plates, washing them, arranging utensils on the kitchen rack, carrying a small bucketful of water from well etc., while boys of the same age were busy playing with sticks and stones. They were not introduced to any work apart from occasional help in fetching water. When such issues were raised in the group discussion, they unanimously agreed with the difference in the treatment but also mentioned, "....why one should ask boys to do household jobs? They won't be able to perform such type of work while they are young. Moreover, how can they do this job when it is meant to be performed by only female? It's their age to play...." This showed that the gender roles were strongly engraved on their minds.

It was also observed that an Anganwadi in the village was running for past several years. The nursery rhymes recited in Anganwadi, re-emphasized the traditional gender roles. Few of such lines from the songs are mentioned below:

> "mother goes on farm and father goes to market,
> mother goes to fetch water, cooks food and serves father and her children
> mother makes *chapatti* while father eats the *chapatti*
> Elder sister takes care of the younger, while elder brother goes to school.........."

Impact of gendered socialization was observed in the behaviour of the children during play time as well. Young girls imitated the role models of their mothers. Doll's play as socializing technique has been cited in sociology text books.

Adolescent girls and boys rarely mixed with each other and they usually forms separate, gender specific, groups. Adolescent girls as well as boys faced problems associated with lack of information particularly because of lack of scientific sources of information and communication with those who know 'more'.

Adolescent girls mentioned that discussion on their problems related to menstruation, and growth of secondary sex characters. Many adolescent girls were expected to do the household jobs and assist their parents at work in agricultural fields. The school going adolescent girls also participated in the domestic chores like cooking, washing clothes, cleaning utensils, fetching water etc. They complained of lack of time for studying which was reflected in their scholastic performance. Eventually, they would get dropped out of the school and concentrate more on the domestic duties.

Adolescent boys were often asked to focus on studies and were given every opportunity to participate in extra curriculum activities, picnics, hobbies etc. too. They further mentioned that their parents did not expect them to participate in day-to-day agriculture activities. Lending a hand during planting and harvesting season was appreciated.

The important event between 15 to 25 years of age was marriage, where family members dominated the scene. The average age at marriage for females was 15 years while 20 years was reported for males. As a wife, she was expected to serve by cooking food, efficiently performing reproductive duties along with productive work participation. While adult man as a husband or father of young kids, rarely participated in child rearing or domestic chores but focused more on productive work.

The free listing and pile sorting data on gender role revealed the traditional division of labour as well as change in the role expectations prevailing in the study area. Young adult (16 to 22 years) male respondents expected their female counterparts to get involved in domestic work as well as develop their ability to work outside, if required. Encouraging response was noted for women's participation in the political field. As seen in Table 16.1 below, female respondents emphasized productive role of males and did not expect males to participate in day-to-day domestic work but only occasionally. Female respondents expressed that apart from routine domestic work, women in the family should be encouraged to opine on matters like taking loan, health care and marriage choice. They further reported that they should be allowed to move freely with their husbands like going for a movie, participating in the village festival and if required work in a public or private enterprise.

Table 16.1: Perceived Division of Labour in the Village

Sorted for	*Sorted by*	
	Young adult Males	*Young adult Females*
Male	Farming—Ploughing, harvesting, husking. Decision making in buying and selling of agriculture produce, choice of clothes etc. Occasionally taking part in childcare.	Farming as main activity should participate in sowing, weeding, manuring etc. Decision making—marketing, food items, gifts, choice of clothes, health and marriage. Participate in works, like fetching water, child rearing, cleaning, cooking etc.
Female	Fetching water, cleaning, cooking, and washing clothes, utensils. Taking active part in politics. Can be involved in paid work (non-farm) if educated. Decision making—marketing, food items, gifts etc.	Farming—sowing, weeding transplanting (paddy), cooking, cleaning, washing clothes and utensils. Service. Taking active part in politics. Decision making—marketing, loan, purchase of food items, gifts, choice of clothes, health care and marriage partner choice.

Source: Field Investigation.

Participation in Economic Activities

The predominant occupation was farming along with dairy as subsidiary occupation. Eighty-nine percent of the population was involved in farming. Women too were engaged in family farming. Eighteen per cent of the population was in the low-income category where their per capita daily income was less than Rs. 50, while 24 per cent were in high income category earning Rs. 100 per capita per day. The wages paid per day ranged from Rs. 50-75 for men and Rs. 25-35 for women.

On an average, women were engaged in paid work for 180 days in a year. Their total contribution to the family income was 40 per cent of the total income of the family during that period. In spite of that, females had limited access to economic resources in terms of cash available to handle for domestic or personal use. Their mobility was also restricted because of traditions as well as lack of cash at hand. Their participation in relation to major purchases or economic dealings was limited.

The decision taken by male member in the family usually husband or father-in-law was considered as 'appropriate'. The female respondents mentioned during group discussion, "since man in family is more exposed to the world (*jasta jag pahile asate tyani*), they are the better judges of the time." Middle aged and older female respondents did not express any discontent for not being included in economic decision making. However, they expressed their desire to get included in the decisions pertaining to other crops (other than main crop) like oil seeds, vegetables, pulses to be taken, variety of seeds to be purchased etc. They thought that if they were consulted and allowed to purchase vegetable seeds from the market, that would have generated some income for them, especially fast cash at disposal.

Table 16.2 given highlights some of the economic indicators used to calculate Gender Development Index. As seen from the table, women's participation in the work was similar to that of men but the economic returns were much less. Control over resources was calculated using the formula given in India's GDI report of 1997.

Work Load

Detailed noting of day-to-day activities and time spent on each of the activities was noted and analyzed for adult males and females of several households. Nearly 75 per cent of the adult females worked for 18 hours a day as compared to 13 hours by males in the same household. On an

Table 16.2: Economic Indicators Across Gender

1.	Work participation rate	For Male For Female	97% 98%
2.	Percentage of non-farm workers among main workers	For Male For Female	14% 2%
3.	Percentage of agricultural labourers among marginal/ subsidiary workers	For Male For Female	3.5% 3.7%
4.	Agricultural wage rate per day	For Male For Female	Rs. 50-75 Rs. 35-40
5.	Control over resources	For Male For Female	Rs. 5820/person/annum Rs. 2940/person/annum

Source: Field Investigation.

average, men spent 2-3 hours on watching television and almost equal time on chatting with friends, while women spared 30 to 50 minutes on watching television, and equal time spent cn interacting with neighbourhood ladies. Women's day was much longer and resting time was much less as compared to men, in the same age group. The analysis of the timeline exercise is shown in Table 16.3 which disclosed the fact that men and women participated in the productive activities and women provided equal amount of time in a day for working on own farm or outside. However, the value for their labour was negligible as compared to men. Working on own farm was often considered as an essential part of their duties.

Table 16.3: Time Line Analysis of Division of Work

Type of Work	*Males (hours)*	*Females (hours)*
Productive Work	7	7
Domestic Work	1	8
Leisure time	4	2
Personal activities	2	1
Total hours spend working	**14**	**18**
Sleep/Rest	10	6
Total Hours	24	24

Source. Field Investigation.

Educational Indicators for Males and Females

The overall literacy rate was 58 per cent in the study village. The illiteracy among females was more 42 per cent as compared to males 18 per cent.

The proportion of females receiving primary and secondary education was less 54.5 per cent as compared to males 73 per cent. Female children were largely kept devoid of higher education for economic reasons and the roles they were expected to play in adult life. Young girls contributed substantially to domestic chores and often not able to attend school which resulted into high drop out rate for girls especially after 7th or 8th grade. Women were confined to household jobs for which education was not considered as necessary qualification. Highly educated (up to graduation) males and females were considered as an economic liability at the time of marriage, as amount of dowry needed for educated groom was more. Educated girl though desired by marriageable young man; his family often thought it as 'inviting trouble'. They feared that the educated daughter-in-law would not obey the orders and respect the elders at home. The strong influence of socially "ideal" gender roles was observed resulting into lack of education among young girls. People failed to understand the importance of education which is often indirect and subtle. Hence, it was not considered as a priority for girls and illiteracy was more among women. Due to social customs and societal pressure, the marriages were often decided 1-2 years after attaining puberty which in turn was considered as a major hindering factor for pursuing higher education (after 10th grade) by young female respondents. Analysis of the secondary data is provided in Table 16.4 below. Total literacy rate, middle level and higher schooling rates were much less for females as compared to males. School attendance rate for girls was considerably low as compared to boys of the same age group. Illness, domestic work, and other unforeseen incidents restricted girl's attendance at the school. Moreover, the lack of importance of the education, and apathy towards girl's education was one of the significant reasons for such a scenario.

Table 16.4: Literacy Indicators Across Gender

1. Literacy rate for age group 7 and above	For Male	82%
	For Female	58%
2. Percentage of population completed middle level education	For Male	53%
	For Female	36%
3. School attendance rate for age group in 6-14 years	For Male	97%
	For Female	59%
4. Percentage of students appearing for 10th Board Examination	For Male	29%
	For Female	7%

Source: Field Investigation.

Health Problems among Men and Women

The general pattern of health problems among men and women was related to their culturally prescribed productive roles. Almost 20 per cent of men reported musculoskeletal problems like shoulder pains, back pain, joint pains. They accorded these problems to the type of work like ploughing, carrying load, husking etc. Among women, reproductive health problems such as, menstrual irregularities, white discharge, contraception problems, and backache were reported by 30 per cent of women, while genito-urinary problems were reported by only 8 per cent of men. The illnesses among women were hidden and were kept secret for several days. Women's health status and health seeking behaviour, as recorded through the case histories, reflected both, their lower social status and their lack of decision-making power. Often men controlled the cash, making it difficult for women to pay for health care or for transportation costs as facilities were far away. Lack of education contributes to lack of self-confidence resulting into lack of timely care. Nearly 78 per cent of men and 98 per cent of women were found to be underweight for height. The data was collected immediately after plantation season. Since majority of them were agriculture workers, they were involved in the planting operation extensively during monsoon.

Access to Health Care Resources

The results suggested that women often lacked access to health facilities and services. Women suffered more illnesses than men but used health services less. There were many reasons why women were unable to access health care, even in times of great urgency. Health services sometimes were unavailable or there was no transport available to take the patient to the hospital. Restrictions on the mobility, economic dependence on men and carelessness due to low self-esteem made women access health care facilities. Cultural sensitivities were another major constraint. Women's health problems received a lower priority, where the treatment of men's illnesses was considered more urgent due to their position in the family. Lack of access to health care thus negatively affected the health of women, in both direct and indirect ways.

It was reported that 80 per cent of the men took treatment when sick while only 42 per cent of women took treatment. 47 per cent of men preferred to take treatment in private hospitals as compared to 23 per cent of women. For many women, multiple visits were impractical, and often acted as disincentives to her seeking health care. This was evident from the 'no treatment' rate among women 58 per cent and men 20 per cent. Those who could not reach the health facility due to restricted mobility and economic compulsions took resort to local remedy or continued to suffer. Men mentioned that perceived severity, economic conditions and lack of time to spare for treatment prevented women from taking any treatment. The average delay in taking treatment among men was 24 to 36 hours as compared to 48 to 72 hours among women.

It was revealed that institutional delivery was not considered as a part of normal practice but they visited hospitals in case of emergencies. In younger generation, women preferred to conduct deliveries in the hospitals.

The shortage of trained health personnel at the peripheral level was also a serious constraint. In circumstances, where female health workers were not available, treatment by investing travel cost, work cost, family adjustment and pharmacy played a major role to determine the final decision and many women went ahead without care in order to avoid this. The opportunity costs of medical treatment were greater for a woman. A number of examples were recorded especially at the time of plantation and harvest. Non-availability of a male member (due to heavy work load during harvest season) to accompany her resulted into worsening of the conditions. They demanded a trained health worker in the village to reduce the burden of illness and health care cost. There emerged number of situations where due to lack of immediate first level care, led to delay in approaching the PHC and resulted in aggravation of the illness.

Discussion

As seen from the review of literature, practical gender needs are usually derived directly from men's and women's existing gender roles and reflect their responsibility for the well-being of their families. Most health related development initiatives are designed to meet practical gender needs, leaving the strategic gender needs unattended.

However, policies that reflect women's strategic interests go a step further changing their basic conditions. These policies also challenge existing gender roles and stereotypes, transforming women's situation with respect to men. It is still important that women's practical needs are met but this alone will not transform their situation. Making it easier for a woman to get a job, for instance, may simply increase her overall burden of work if there is no associated change in who does the domestic labour.

Thus policies designed to meet women's practical needs must also take their strategic interests into account if they are to be of lasting benefit. For this to happen, women themselves and men need to be actively involved in their development and implementation. These principles have emerged as the foundation for the 'gender and development' approach but they also need to be applied in the planning of health services. Unless these broader contextual issues are carefully elaborated and woven into the implementation process at all stages, the resulting policies will not be sensitive to the different circumstances and needs of women and men in their approach or equitable in their effects.

Cultural factors play a major role in shaping the socio-economic profile of the women. Some traditional beliefs and societal pressures disadvantage women. In spite of constitutional guarantees for women's rights and equal status, discrimination is visible in many areas. Gender stereotyped roles assigned to girls and women often placed restrictions on women's behaviour and their mobility outside the home. Conditioned by society to believe that a woman's role was mainly reproductive, girls were often married early, even below legally sanctioned age. Early marriages mean early pregnancies and therefore higher maternal morbidity. The association of various factors affecting health is given in Fig. 16.1.

Women's health was influenced by the patriarchal social structure and numerous of cultural traditions, customs, attitudes, and subordinate status of women in the society. As a result, they were given the role of 'maintainer' which included unpaid domestic work and other allied duties to support family economy. In consequence, they were found to be deprived of opportunities in education and economic field. They did not get access to outside world and information, due to restricted mobility and illiteracy and lack of decision making power for themselves. Hence, it can be argued that the status of women in the society is one of the crucial determinants of their health. Due to re-emphasised cultural traditions, structural position and lack of opportunities to develop, women developed low self esteem, lack in assertiveness, and lack of control over resources leading to suffering and delayed treatment which affected their health negatively. At the same time, non-availability of the direct and emergency transport facility, costs involved and other socio-cultural constraints; timely availability of health worker or personnel was a felt necessity. However, in general, access was related to woman's social status in addition to level of income, and decision-making power within the family.

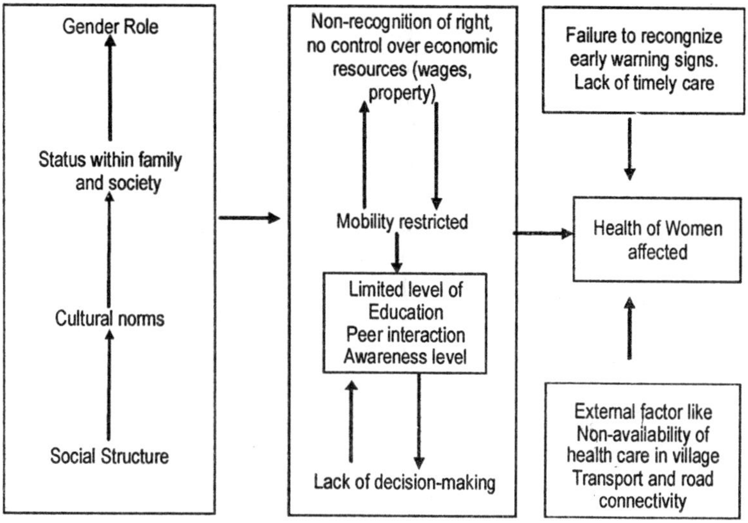

Fig 16.1: Role of various factors in determining gender role and health behaviour

Conclusion

There have been numerous critiques posted against the prevailing paradigm of research on gender and health, dominated in the latter part of the twentieth century. One of the documents highlights the role of history and need for contextualization while putting evidence for gender differences (Hunt Kate, 2002). In this chapter it was attempted to show that, even within a relatively confined geographical locale, over a relatively short period of time, with the use of selected indicators, gender construction process could be explored.

Indicators pertaining to economic resources, education, demography, and health were used for understanding the construction of gender. These indicators suggested that 'females' when labelled as 'women' must restrict their own desires and mobility and allow 'men' to make decisions which may affect their lives totally and intensely. The contribution they made to the society was often neglected being 'reproductive' that is 'unpaid' in nature. This and such ideas are deep rooted in the culture and social structure.

However, a minute change reflected in the opinions and attitudes of the young generation was also noticeable. A study focusing on more qualitative indicators should help in bringing out these positive trends in relation to women's status. Nonetheless, present study observed change though restricted to a few households where men in those households were more proactive and positive in contrast to the traditional image. Thus, the study reaffirms that possible solution is involvement of men in the empowerment of women to achieve gender balance in the society.

17

Male Involvement in Family Planning Decision Making

ANJALI GANPULE

Introduction

National Family Planning Programme at the national level was committed to promote Small Family Norm and legislated to support population control and development programmes. The data from National Family Health Survey, 1992-93 showed that in Maharashtra total unmet need for fertility regulation was 26.3 per cent (IIPS, 1994).

Considering the gaps in the previous programme, in April 1996, emphasis was put on needs of the clients and increasing male participation in the use of family planning methods (Ministry of Health and Family Welfare, 1997).

In the patriarchal society of India, generally men make the decisions. The issues related to child bearing and caring are still mostly considered as 'women's affairs'. These thoughts deep-rooted in our society deprive men from reproductive health information and services and gradually made men to look at the reproductive issues as women's domain.

Better knowledge and awareness regarding family planning aids the couple to make choice of the contraceptive to be used to plan their family. Husbands were provided counselling services for adoption of the contraceptive methods from the health workers.

Inter-spouse Communication

A couple needs to have interaction and communication, as it is a catalysing and motivational force for joint decision making. A study was conducted in all Indian states on 6300 males and females revealed that inter-spouse-communication was a better predictor of family planning practice than other background characteristics (Bhatia, J., 1980).

Status of the Spouse

The fertility decisions depend on the social, economic, educational, cultural status of the couples, all of which are interrelated and decide how the couple will deal with the situations.

Kar (1971) in his study has observed that education and socio-economic status are the important determinants of the fertility decisions.

Fertility Preferences

A couple's decisions related to the number and sex composition of the children take place in the span of 7-8 years of marriage.

A Study in rural Maharashtra illustrated that, the husbands and wives have different interests in childbearing decisions (Jejeebhoy, S., 1989). Individual motivation was more important for positive male participation in family planning rather than choice of method (Karra, M., 1997).

Son Preference

Although the aspects of 'modernisation' are found to affect the traditional norms in the case of the family size (Sidramshettar, S., 1993), they affect the couple's decisions related to the sex composition of the children.

The traditional concept of continuation of the family name (*Kul*) with the birth of a male child is deep rooted in the Indian culture that reflects in the son preference lowering the status of a female child. There are several studies; in urban and rural India has found that, the decision regarding adoption of a contraceptive method is strongly associated with sex composition of the children. There is a strong son preference that affects the couple's decision (Vlassoff, C., 1990; Khan, M.E., 1990; Asif, R., 1994; Tripathy, S., 1994; Rajan, S., 1996).

Data regarding the number of male and female living children of the men who had undergone vasectomy clearly show the preference for male children in a study carried out during Vasectomy camps organised in Maharashtra (Dandekar, K., 1980).

In addition to the gap between desired and present number of children and the sex composition of the family there are various other aspects that affect decisions regarding adoption of a method.

Acceptance of Family Planning Measures

The attitudes of the spouses, especially of the men, towards a method can affect the choice of a method. A hospital-based study in Cuttak on 500 women showed that unwillingness of the husband for the female sterilisation was a reason for non-acceptance for the method (Tripathy, S., 1994). There are couples who go for repeated induced abortions, either as a method of contraception or as an escape from a female child (Jamshedji, A., 1990).

Type of Family

The communication and decision making regarding the reproductive issues does not limit to the couple but extends to the other family members. The favourable opinion of family members regarding reproductive health services was found to have an influence on these decisions (Khan, A.G., 1997). A study in Tughlakabad in 1995 showed that the family members play a major role in couple's decisions regarding fertility (Shyamini, K.A., 1995).

A study of 250 currently married women from nuclear and extended families in a fishing community found that communication does not limit to spouses but extend to the close kin of the couple. The overall trend observed in regard to the decision-making process as a consistently higher frequency of joint decisions by both the spouses followed closely by collective decision involving kin and husband-dominated decisions in that order (Murthy, R., 1986).

Poffenberger (1969) undertook an early exploration of husband-wife communication and its relationship to family planning in an Asian setting in India. Second, as socio-economic differentials in fertility decrease individual factors in decision-making attain increasing explanatory power.

We need to understand whether it is an expectation regarding involving men in sharing responsibilities, is it involvement of men in making decisions with a better concern for women's health and reproductive rights, or is it involvement that will allow women to equally participate in decision-making. Studies have shown that in addition to couples, family members participate while making decisions and in implementation of the decisions made (Khan, A.G., 1991; Shyamini, K.A., 1995). How a family setting affects a couple's decision-making is also an essential component that should be studied.

We need to know how a couple understands male involvement in decision-making as well as in sharing responsibilities; what is the role of family in the entire process. Thus, in the present study the researcher has studied the influence of the type of family on male involvement in decision making regarding family planning among Brahmin couples in Pune City.

In most of the studies on different aspects of reproductive health, the data were collected only from the female respondents. The review of studies done on couples and reproductive health outcomes examine the effectiveness of interventions that target couples compared with those that target only one partner. For couple's statements about reproductive events, studies throughout the world typically show identical reports less than 90 per cent of the time. While study male involvement it was thought necessary to understand from both the spouses regarding the factors that they gave due consideration while making the family planning decisions. The data were collected conducting individual interviews of the spouses. The last two chapters are devoted for data presentation and discussion regarding decision-making process of couples and change in male involvement as per the type of family.

Need for Male Involvement in Decision Making

Decision-making process regarding reproductive health issues has been of interest to several researchers over the last five decades. A few studies have focused on the decisions made regarding family planning, reproductive morbidity and mortality, whereas others have documented on factors influencing these decisions. Involvement of spouses in decision-making and in the execution of decisions made has also been the focus of a few studies.

Despite the differences in terms used, they highlight the current need to study men's perspectives in improving a couple's health.

Meaning of Terms using in the Study

Male Involvement

For the present study, the male involvement was considered in form all the direct and indirect actions of husbands in decision making related to planning the family and in execution of the decisions made.

Family Planning

The issue of family planning covered in the study involves decisions and related actions concerned with

- Number of children,
- Sex composition of children,
- Spacing, and
- Failure of a method, if any.

Types of Family

A joint family set up includes a couple with their child/children and parent/s of the husband staying together in a house that has common kitchen. A nuclear family set up includes a couple with their child/children staying together in a house with their distinct kitchen.

Decision Making Process

This involves a study of different steps of decision-making (Initiation, Communication, and Discussion) in consideration with the underlying situations and implementation of the decisions.

Present Study: Characteristics

In the present study the researcher has studied the influence of the type of family on male involvement in decision making and implementation of the decisions regarding family planning including abortion as also adoption of a child. The present study was carried out among 50 Brahmin couples; 25 couples from joint families and 25 having nuclear families with at least one child. The couples were selected from Shaniwar Peth, Narayan Peth and Sadashiv Peth, that have predominantly been the traditional, residential area of Brahmin families at Pune city. Interviews of three practising gynaecologists, from the same area were conducted to know about their opinions and experiences regarding male involvement in family planning.

Among the respondents, the median age of husbands was 35 and 32 for wives. Couples in both types of families were married for an average of eight years. Almost 90 per cent of the respondents had studied at least till graduation. About 60 per cent of the female respondents were involved in an economically gainful activity. The monthly income of the couples was between Rs. 15,000 and Rs. 25,000 per month.

The resources available (such as time, manpower and etc.) to the couples differed with the type of family and this had an influence on the decisions regarding timing and number of children. About 40 per cent of the respondents belonging to joint families and 50 per cent of nuclear families had spontaneous discussions regarding family planning. In few families, either wife or husband initiated such discussions. In nuclear families, despite participation of both partners in decision making, the wives were found to make final decisions in most instances, while in joint families, husbands were found to finalise the decisions. More than 50 per cent respondents from both types of families reported a good inter-spouse communication.

In both types of families, doctors were reported to be the first preferred source of information followed by friends, relatives, books, TV, newspaper and magazines. The use of contraceptive methods to delay first pregnancy were condoms and birth control pills. A few couples accepted a combination of condom and safe period. The condom acceptance was found to be greater in comparison to the other methods in both types of families. Of the 5 couples from joint families and 12 couples from nuclear families who had 2nd child, after a gap of 3 to 5 years, more than 50 per cent relied on CuT as a spacing method. The male respondents had greater preference to have only one child in comparison to the female respondents in both types of families.

Although, all couples achieved desired number of children, 60 per cent had not yet discussed about permanent contraception and continued to rely on temporary contraceptives. Of the remaining, 20 per cent women from joint and 28 per cent from nuclear families had undergone tubectomy. In general, the condom was used for contraception rather than for protection from any infection. A very few couples reported to be vulnerable for HIV-AIDS.

In the present study, male involvement was understood as "all the direct and indirect actions of husbands in decision making related to planning the family and the use of a contraceptive method." The study looked at the ways in which reproductive decisions were made and the context that influenced these decisions. Men's health status and behaviour affect women's health and reproductive health consequently of the couple. All methods of family planning and most methods of STDs and HIV prevention are traditionally labelled either as male-only or female-only methods. Considering only female or male is not an adequate approach to reproductive health issues.

The Objectives of the Study

1. To study the decision making process of couples in relation to planning their families in a joint or nuclear family setting.
2. To study the practices of couples following the decisions made in regard to planning their family in a joint and nuclear family setting.
3. To study male involvement in the couple's decision making process, with respect to planning their family and an influence of joint and nuclear family setting on male involvement.

Knowledge and awareness of spouses regarding family planning help them in making an informed decision. The type of family has a bearing on decision making due to resources available with them such as, time, labour, moral support etc. The type of family also affects space available and privacy required for inter-spouse communication.

In the present study, the researcher has studied the influence of the type of family on male involvement in decision-making and implementation of the decisions regarding family planning as also adoption of a child, among Brahmin couples in Pune City.

Research Design

Sampling

The present study was carried out among 50 Brahmin couples from Pune City. The couples were selected from three areas that has predominantly been the traditional residential localities of Brahmin families. The election data provided information about name, age, address and type of family of residents in the study area. The couples thus identified were sorted on basis of their type of family (joint/nuclear) and place the residence. Further, proportionate sampling was done and the couples were surveyed. During the survey, couples who had at least one child were informed regarding the study topic.

The sample covered 25 couples belonging to joint families and 25 couples belonging to nuclear families having at least one child. This helped the researcher to get data on the process of decision making of couples in both the family settings.

The respondents were informed regarding individual interviews of both the spouses. The couples who were ready for the interview were included in the study. As per the convenience of the respondents, timing of the interview was fixed.

Interviews were tape recorded with permission of the respondents. Interviews were conducted in houses of the respondents, but in a separate room.

Ethical Consideration

Researcher took verbal consent of the respondents and assured anonymity of their names. Interviews were tape recorded with permission of the respondents.

Limitations of the Study

The method of sample selection limits scope of the study because, only a specific segment of population was covered. The reference group belonged to a specific stratum. Thus, there is possibility that, the study sample represents only a segment of the population that has similar socio-economic and educational, cultural background of the reference group.

Tools and Techniques

Both, qualitative (Key informants interview with gynaecologists, in-depth interviews husbands and wives) and quantitative (survey) methods were used (*see* Table 17.1).

Three-fourth of the couples consulted a doctor after conceiving their first child, half of the first pregnancies were planned, and couples had used a spacing method. Out of these a few couples experienced failure in use of a method. In addition, the female respondents are cautious while making decisions, such as, selection of the spouse, childbearing etc. A few husbands willingly use condoms whereas a few prefer to accept a rhythm method.

Response of Doctors

All three gynaecologists mentioned that percent of couples accepting vasectomy, as a permanent method is very less. When a couple makes decision of planning first baby, child bearing is given first priority. Maximum couples desire two children but most of the couples restrict

Table 17.1: Research Findings

Background Information	*Nuclear Family*		*Joint Family*	
	Husband	*Wife*	*Husband*	*Wife*
Median Age	36	32	35	31
Mean age at marriage	28	24	26	24
Education				
Twelfth	–	2	3	3
Diploma	2	–	–	–
Graduation	21	17	10	16
Post Graduation	5	6	12	6
Occupation				
Business	16	3	10	9
Job	9	13	15	6
House wife	–	9	–	10

Source: Field Investigation.

family size to one child, considering factors such as, economic considerations, career of wife etc. Although there are indirect pressures from elders regarding having the first child immediately within first year of marriage, the decision is made exclusively by the couple. All three doctors expressed need for Training to boys and girls from adolescent period regarding family life.

Decision Making

Several studies have identified that, better socio-economic, educational and cultural status helps an individual in making informed decisions in regard of reproductive health matters and execute them. Gender relations also influence decision making and implementation of the decisions made. In the present study, the researcher has studied the decision making process of Brahmin couples in Pune city. As most of the couples 80 per cent, currently belonging to nuclear families were living in a joint family set-up for first five years after they were married, they had an experience of making decisions in both scenarios, namely joint family set-up and nuclear family set-up. Couples in both types of families were married for an average of eight years. More than 80 per cent couples had an arranged marriage. The mean age difference between spouses belonging to joint families was 3.6 years and in couples belonging to nuclear family it was 4.3 years. The median age at marriage for female respondents in both types of families was 24 years. For the male respondents belonging to joint families the median age at marriage was 26 years and for those belonging to nuclear families it was 28 years.

Decision-Making According to Family Type

Although the respondents belonged to a similar background, the family settings in which they made their family planning decisions were different. The resources available (such as time, labour etc.) to the couples differed with the type of family and this had an influence on the decisions regarding timing and number of children.

Only three couples belonging to joint families and a couple belonging to nuclear family reported participation of family members in decision making. A male respondent belonging to joint family said, "In joint families, parents being more experienced suggest different options to solve any problem. Experience is an important factor that helps in decision making."

In addition to moral and physical support, the respondents reported that elders in joint families helped in inculcating moral values (*Samskara karane*) in children. Physical and moral support of parents was not always available to couples belonging to nuclear families. An influence of the type of family was remarkable in regard of the decisions related to childbearing. 13 couples belonging to nuclear families said that their parents took care of their children. A few of wives left their job since they neither had family support nor were they ready to keep their child in a crèche.

In spite of the fact that couples belonging to joint families had family support, a very few of them preferred joint families. Main reasons reported by the respondents for preferring nuclear family set-up in comparison to joint family set-up were, lack of privacy and pressure of presence of family members while making decisions in joint families.

A husband currently belonging to nuclear family but who had lived in a joint family said, "the basic demand of nuclear family setting is that the wife should have some role in decision-making. As she takes the active role, automatically, men's monopoly in decision-making reduces. In joint families, there is a hierarchy. A couple cannot make mutual decisions all the time in such a set-up."

Despite having a separate room, 16 per cent of the couples belonging to nuclear families and 40 per cent, couples belonging to joint families mentioned that they discussed family planning outside their homes. In a joint family, a couple had to take into account suggestions of family members as also their convenience. The respondents belonging to nuclear families also found it convenient to discuss this issue outside the house.

About 40 per cent of the respondents belonging to joint families and 50 per cent of those who belonged to nuclear families had spontaneous discussions. In few families, wives initiated such discussions while among the rest, the husband initiated such discussions. Respondents from both types of families were asked regarding participation of husbands in decision-making and sharing responsibilities. In nuclear families despite participation of both partners in decision-making, the wives were found to make final decisions in most instances.

Inter spouse Communication

More than 50 per cent respondents from both types of families reported a "good" inter-spouse communication. 36 per cent respondents belonging to nuclear families and 28 per cent respondents belonging to joint families reported that it was "ok".

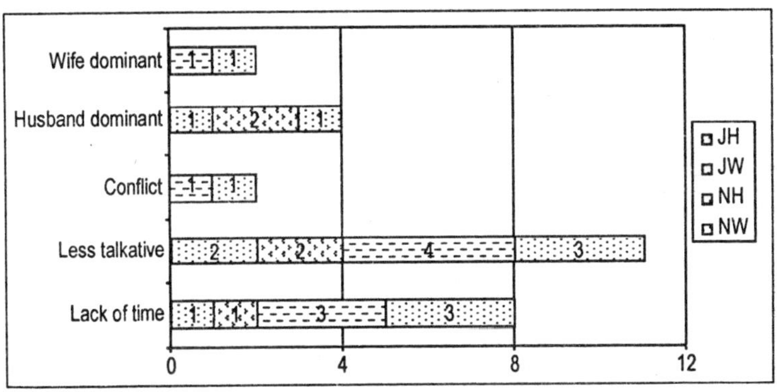

The remaining respondents reported that their inter-spouse communication was not satisfactory. The reasons for non-communication and less inter-spouse communication, as reported by the respondents by nuclear families (28%) and joint families (20%) were, dominating or introvert nature of a spouse and lack of time either due to workload or due to their social activities. Only one couple belonging to nuclear family had age difference between the spouses more than 7 years. They reported it to be the reason for non-communication among themselves.

The major reason for this was lack of the time spent by men in sharing the family responsibilities.

A wife from nuclear family responded, "My husband wants me to make such decisions in which he will not have to work as he has no time to spend for family matters."

A husband belonging to joint family said, "I have experience that females cannot make correct decisions. Their considerations while making a decision are restricted to their family set-up."

Twenty four per cent respondents from joint families and 40 per cent respondents from nuclear families reported husband's participation in sharing responsibilities.

A few respondents reported male involvement through certain indirect actions. A female respondent belonging to nuclear family while reporting about the care taken by her husband during the first pregnancy said, "My husband used to remind me to take the medicine." About 36 per cent respondents belonging to joint families and 24 per cent belonging to nuclear families reported no husband's participation in sharing responsibilities. The remaining respondents from both types of families reported a partial participation of husbands, i.e. when wives occasionally asked for it.

Only three women belonging to joint families and six women belonging to nuclear families expressed need to involve men not only in decision making but also in sharing the responsibilities. 36 per cent respondents belonging to nuclear families and 28 per cent respondents belonging to joint families reported that it was 'OK'.

The reasons for non-communication and less inter-spouse communication, as reported by the respondents by nuclear families 28 per cent and joint families 20 per cent were, dominating or introvert nature of a spouse and lack of time either due to workload or due to their social activities. Only one couple from a to nuclear family had age difference between the spouses more than 7 years.

During the period of eight years of marriage, almost all of the couples have made their decisions regarding family size, composition and spacing.

Table 17.2 shows different sources of information from which couples sought information regarding issues of family planning.

There are different sources of information from which couples sought information regarding issues of family planning.

A very few (3 to 4) couples from both types of families mentioned that they talked about when to have first child prior to marriage. More than 60 per cent couples discussed within first 10 days of marriage about the issue of timing of the first child and spacing method to be accepted or not. The decision regarding contraceptive method was made considering

Table 17.2: Different Sources of Information Sought by Couples

Source of Information	*Nuclear Family*		*Joint Family*	
	Husband	*Wife*	*Husband*	*Wife*
Doctor	18	17	20	17
Friends	5	12	5	9
Relative	1	1	3	4
Books	1	–	3	4
Wife	3	–	3	–
TV, Paper, Magazines	3	2	–	1

Source: Field Investigation.

the suggestions from doctor.

More than 80 per cent of the couples belonging to both types of families had their first child within first two years of marriage. The contraceptive methods accepted between marriages to first child were condoms and birth control pills. A few couples accepted a combination of condoms and safe days. Four wives from nuclear families and three wives from joint families required treatment for conceiving their first child.

Decision to Start a Family

Almost 90 per cent of the female respondents belonging to both types of families had gone to natal homes for first delivery. Although, none of the family members directly participated while making decisions regarding timing of the first child, suggestions from them and, from friends and relatives pressurised the couples to have their first child within first two years of marriage. Two to three couples belonging to joint families had a child immediately within first year of marriage because of the desire of bedridden mother-in-law. The fear and stigma of infertility almost forced the couples to make such a decision.

A female respondent who had the first child within first 2 years of marriage said, "The elder women from my family used to advise me to have a child immediately after marriage." The reasons reported by the remaining couples for delaying their first child were, to gain an economic stability, pregnancy wastage, treatment required for conceiving their first child. A very few couples (2-3) belonging to nuclear families delayed their first child by one year due to career of wives whereas, in case of others it was given second priority.

Most of the respondents made the decision regarding having/not having second child immediately after birth of the first child. The couples wanted to have two children either as they felt that the first child would be lonely or as they desired to have two children. The main reasons for not having second child were economic considerations, career of wife and for population control.

Two to 3 couples from both types of families had not a made firm decision regarding having or not having the second child, even after 3 to 4 years of the birth of first child. The five couples belonging to joint families and 12 couples belonging to nuclear families, who had second child, took a gap of 3 to 5 years in between their first and the second child. Out of these, more than 50 per cent couples relied on CuT as a spacing method. Other contraceptive methods accepted were condoms and birth control pills.

Planning the Family

There was a difference between the desired and actual number of children in both types of families. In joint families, 64 per cent husbands and 44 per cent wives expressed the desire where as, 80 per cent had only one child. Whereas in nuclear families, 36 per cent husbands and 32 per cent wives expressed the desire and 52 per cent couples had only one child.

The male respondents had greater preference to have only one child in comparison to the female respondents in both types of families.

Most of the couples desiring two children wanted to have one son and one daughter. A very few couples (3 to 4) openly reported preference for a male child. Two husbands belonging to joint families had sough Ayurvedic treatment for having a male child.

Although, all the couples have achieved desired number of children, 60 per cent have not yet discussed about the permanent method to be accepted and were currently relying on a temporary contraceptive method. Out of the remaining, 20 per cent wives belonging to joint and 28 per cent wives belonging to nuclear families have done tubectomy. Only 2 husbands belonging to joint families have done vasectomy. 3 couples belonging to nuclear families did not accept a permanent method because temporary method was comfortable for them.

Eighty per cent of the respondents from both types of families selected a method of contraception as guided by the doctor. 70 per cent to 80 per cent wives belonging to both types of families had a normal delivery. None of the couples had induced abortion as a spacing method. Up to 20

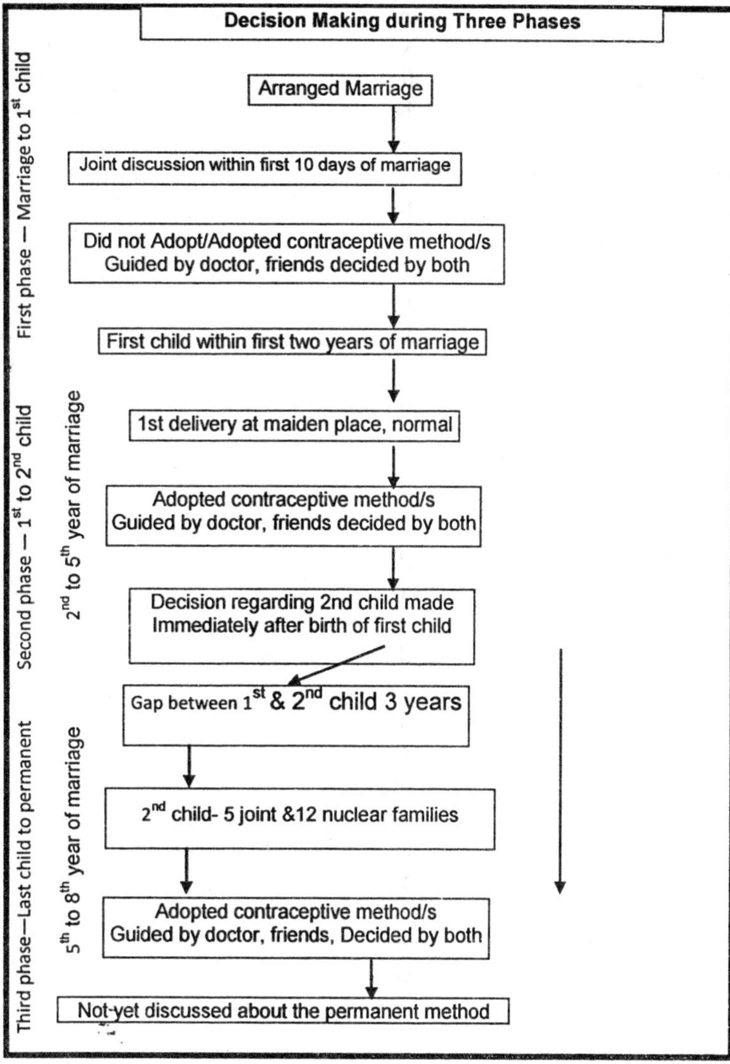

per cent respondents reported a history of pregnancy wastage prior to and after having a child. Almost 40 per cent respondents from nuclear families reported pregnancy wastage prior to having the first child. The couple although desired two children decided not to have the 2nd child as there was risk to life of the mother.

More than 40 per cent husbands from joint families and 50 per cent husbands from nuclear families accompanied their wives during antenatal check ups. While, a few husbands accompanied their wives only 2 to 3 times. Up to 40 per cent husbands from joint families and 32 per cent, husbands from nuclear families were informed by the doctor about care of wife to be taken during pregnancy.

A husband reporting need for information to be given by doctors said," They should involve the husbands. In addition, if husband is present at the time of the delivery then it may affect the decision regarding the next child. "Among the couples belonging to joint families' acceptance of a spacing method was grater during marriage to the first child where as the number of nuclear couples accepting a method during 1st to 2nd child was greater.

Majority of the couples in the first phase, i.e. marriage to first child decided to have the first child within first 2 years of marriage. The decisions in second phase regarding having or not having a second child differed as per the type of family and desires of the spouses. In spite of having more constraints for managing child bearing responsibilities, the preference for having the second child was higher in nuclear families.

Following are some of the decision trees followed by a few couples. They show that though the decisions implemented in the two phases were similar in many couple, sometimes the process of making these decisions differed as per the situation.

Among the couples, belonging to joint families' acceptance of a spacing method was grater during marriage to the first child whereas the number of nuclear couples accepting a method during 1st to 2nd child was grater. The overall trend showed that in all phases except from marriage to first child, the female acceptance of a contraceptive method was greater than that of the males.

If we look at the overall decision-making pattern of the respondents we find that the respondents followed the steps shown in the diagram were followed.

Majority of the couples in the first phase, i.e. marriage to first child decided to have the first child within first 2 years of marriage. In the last phase, most of the couples have not yet discussed the issue of adoption of a permanent method.

The decisions in second phase regarding having or not having a second child differed as per the type of family and desires of the spouses. In spite of having more constraints for managing child bearing responsibilities, the preference for having the 2nd child was higher in nuclear families.

Six couples belonging to joint families followed the decision tree-1. All the couples made the decision regarding not having the second child. In four couples belonging to joint families, only the husbands made the decision.

A nuclear couple followed the decision tree-2. Out of the two couples belonging to nuclear family set-up in one family the wife had experienced pregnancy wastage twice prior to birth of the second child. The husband decided to have the second child that was not desired by the wife. This made the wife to make decision to go for a permanent method.

A couple belonging to nuclear family had twins followed the decision tree-3. Considering the risk to wife's life, the husband decided not to have 2nd child although the wife desired it. The decision regarding permanent method to be accepted was made by both as guided by doctor.

In a few cases the pregnancy wastage was a factor affecting the decision regarding total number of children. As we can see in the decision tree-4, In a couple belonging to nuclear family there was pregnancy wastage prior to and after first child.

Three couples belonging to nuclear families and two couples belonging to joint families followed the decision tree-5.

Out of the three couples from nuclear families who had 2nd children, all had different reasons for having the 2nd child. In one couple, the spouses wanted to have a male child, one couple did not make any decision while the remaining one couple desired to have 2 children.

Out of the two couples from joint families, a husband from one family desired to adopt the second child. The decision tree-6 shows decisions of a couple belonging to joint family. It clearly indicates that bad communication affects the reproductive decisions of a couple.

Decision making of Couples regarding Adoption of a Child

The issue of adoption was studied on two couples, one belonging to joint and one belonging to nuclear family.

A Case of the Couple One

The couple had a love marriage. At the time of marriage, the husband was 21 years old and the wife was 18 years old. The husband had a married elder brother who had one child. The wife had a working mother. At the time of marriage the couple was not economically settled. They were away from their family as the husband got a job out of Pune. The couple decided to use a spacing method. The family members were not informed about this decision. After this incidence, the couple planned to have a child after a year's gap. From then onwards the wife experienced habitual spontaneous abortion (5-6 times). The couple sought treatment by from 2-3 doctors. After that, the husband got a job in Pune, where they stayed in a joint family. In Pune, the couple also tried child bearing treatment of a few doctors that did not suit the wife.

During a family function in the night when all family members were together, an elderly female relative of husband talked about a couple who had adopted a child and suggested the similar option to the couple.

The wife had thought about adoption of a child prior to marriage when she was experiencing the life without her father's support. The husband also knew about thoughts of the wife regarding adoption of a child.

He had no problems in adopting a child.

After the whole family discussed the issue, the couple found family members were supporting acceptance of the option of adoption of a child. While deciding about whether to adopt a male or a female child, the husband desired to have girl child. The wife wanted to adopt a male child. The wife got convinced with this thought and the couple made the decision of the adoption of a girl child.

The couple is now staying in a nuclear family set up. The wife said that her decision regarding having an induced abortion would have been different if it would have been made in a joint family set-up.

The Case of the Second Couple

In this couple, the husband was a medical doctor and was having a general practice. The wife was a homemaker. They were staying in a joint family-set up and belonged to the economically well to do family. After marriage, the wife underwent habitual spontaneous abortions for 3-4 times.

Friends, family members and doctors who were close family friends suggested the option of adoption of a child. The wife was ready for it, as she had seen a family who had adopted a child. There was complete physical and moral support of the family members that was reported by the couple to be the important factor in such a decision.

After studying these two cases, we find that whether a joint or a nuclear family set up, the support of family members play an important role in decision-making. Both the spouses need to participate completely in the decision-making, as otherwise, the decision cannot be executed.

Involvement of men in responsibility sharing and decision-making was studied to know whether couples are able to make an informed decision regarding their reproductive health.

While studying these aspects reproductive rights with a special concern to male involvement, couples from both joint and nuclear families were studied.

The individuals at the every level, i.e. at the society level, family level and couple level were involved in the process with different strength and influenced the decisions differently.

Not every couple in the study followed each step of decision-making. A few directly made the decision without any discussion whereas a few spouses discussed the issue with family members, relatives, other members in society, such as doctors, friends and then made the decision.

In a few cases, decisions needed modification according to situation. For example, when there was pregnancy wastage, couple again had to make decisions regarding child bearing and spacing.

The factors at the family level were most immediate ones affecting decisions of a couple. At the family and kin level, suggestions of the relatives and family members directly put pressure on couples to make decision regarding their first child. Whereas, the factors at the society level although were not immediate, had a bearing on couple's decisions.

A decision-making process of family planning in the present study was a study of; decisions of a couple regarding planning their family; Implementation of decisions and role of spouses in it; Change role of the spouses as per the type of family in decision making and implementation.

The family planning decisions of the respondents, made during the eight years period of marriage until now can be divided in three phases.

A couple had to implement the decisions in these three phases made either individually or jointly. It was also essential to study the individuals involved, other than the spouses, in the decision-making and implementation because as they undoubtedly influenced the decision-making. One of the important factors was the type of family the couple belonged to.

In a very few critical situations, such as whether to abort an unwanted and unplanned child, a couple needed and sought support from the family members. Otherwise, whether a joint or a nuclear family there was in general no direct interference from family members in decision-making. In joint families, this support was taken for granted whereas the couples belonging to nuclear families had to ask for it. The family planning decisions were made independently by the couples but considering the resources available to them.

Male involvement in decision-making and sharing responsibilities was analysed based on following aspects.

When percentages of couples belonging to joint and nuclear families were compared with regard to type of discussion they had, 10 per cent more couples from nuclear families were found to have mutual discussions.

It was found that the percentage of husbands' participating in sharing responsibilities was greater by about 20 per cent among couples belonging to nuclear families in comparison to the couples from joint families. The couples belonging to nuclear family set-up could ask for a support from other family members only in case of an emergency.

Ten per cent more husbands belonging to nuclear families accompanied their wives during antenatal check ups.

If we look at the decision making of the couples, in general we find that whom so ever, whether a man or a woman, does not make reproductive decisions unless it is forced by situation on them. At the time of the first child, there were social forces that pressurised the couple to prove their fertility. Desires of the couples or failure of a contraceptive method made a couple to think about the decision regarding second child.

One of the male respondents talked about the similar trend. He was belonging to nuclear family and was socially active. Spouses sought reproductive information related very specific aspects of reproductive health.

Conclusion

The study among the families from Brahmin caste groups, who are considered referral groups, with educated women provide insight about the empowered women and liberal families with communication and decision making as equal partners. Similar studies in different regions, different linguistic caste groups would throw light on the concept of *varna*, caste and family as units of social organisation. Family Planning has been a nodal health programme, which became politically significant. The answer was sought in female literacy and women empowerment with a decisive voice in family decisions.

18

Menopause as Multivariate Issue

AARTI NAGARKAR

Introduction

Menopause is one of the most significant events in a woman's life and brings in a number of physiological changes that affect the life of a woman permanently. There have been a lot of assumptions about the symptoms that appear during the period of transition, that is from pre-menopausal to post-menopausal period. About 130 million Indian women are expected to live beyond the menopause into old age by 2020. Hence, it becomes a major issue of concern for the researchers working on women's health. Menopause is emerging as an issue owing to rapid urbanization, changing life style and increased longevity among urban Indian women, who are evolving as a homogeneous group (Kaulagekar, 2010). Previously, menopause was presented as a medical condition with its associated body changes described as symptoms in need of treatment (Jones 1997). In last two decades, research on menopausal symptomatology has focused on identifying symptom groupings experienced by women as they progress from pre-menopausal to post-menopausal status. Health concerns of menopausal women include vasomotor symptoms, urogenital atrophy, osteoporosis, cardiovascular disease, cancer, psychiatric symptoms, cognitive decline, and sexual problems. However, it has been difficult to distinguish between symptoms that result from loss of ovarian function and those from the aging process or from the socio-environmental stresses of midlife years. However, most remain ignorant of the short and long term implications of the morbid conditions associated with middle and old age, due to lack of awareness, unavailability and ever-increasing cost of the health care (Avis, Stellato, Crawford *et al.*, 2001).

Cross-cultural studies have documented wide variations in the symptoms, perception and reporting by women from different ethnic origins (Richters, 1997). Several studies have indicated that Asian women's experience of menopause is different and it affects them differently (Lock, 2002). Cultural explanations of these differences need to include many factors including beliefs and attitudes to menopause and the social status of middle aged and older women (Lock, 2005). Women reported to appreciate menopause in developing countries and especially in India (Kaulagekar, 2011). Iinformation on menopausal symptoms and the way women chose to treat these symptoms is essential for designing appropriate delivery of health care services and ensures easy transition to old age. Therefore, the present study was aimed at documentation of menopausal symptoms and experiences of women undergoing menopause, their coping, mechanisms, and attitude and support of the family, as reported by women between 40 to 55 years of age.

Method

Total 156 middle income urban respondents were included in the study who were selected purposively from five different electoral wards where predominantly middle-income groups reside. The final analysis is based on the sample of 156 respondents who responded to all the questions.

In the first phase, data were collected with the help of a pre-tested questionnaire. The questionnaire along with the letter of introduction and instructions to fill the questionnaire was given to the respondents. The questionnaire was provided in languages—English as well as the local language, Marathi. Words and phrases used were locally understandable and at the same time acceptable. The options of responses in the closed ended questions were made as exhaustive as possible to make every response fit in the given categories.

In the second phase, in-depth interviews of respondents who had experienced the complete cessation of menses for last five years were taken. It helped in gaining holistic and detailed information (with relatively less recall bias) on individual experiences, subjective description of the severity of the symptoms, communication with, and support available from spouse and other family members, coping strategies adopted, attitude towards menopause etc. Quantitative data analysis was done with the help of software while in-depth interviews analyzed thematically.

Background Characteristics of the Respondents

Of the 156 respondents majority of the subjects were married 89.8 per cent, remaining were either single or widowed. Many respondents were housewives 67 per cent and the rest who were employed worked mostly in private companies. Same number of the respondents were graduates and remaining 33 per cent had completed secondary education or couple of years of college. Two-third of the respondents were staying in the nuclear family setup.

Age at Menopause

Approximately 60 per cent (N = 93) of the respondents were in post-menopausal stage and majority (N = 76) of them had experienced it naturally. Total 17 respondents reported surgical menopause. Therefore, the mean age at menopause was 45.8 years (±4.3 SD) for all subjects, while for those experiencing naturally, mean age at menopause was increased by 3 years (48.3 years ±1.9 SD). Majority (74.4%) of the respondents were aware about the symptoms and changes during menopause. Friends, colleagues, and relatives were the chief sources of information. Magazines and media proved to be the main sources of information for 14 per cent of the subjects.

Attitude towards Menopause

Attitude towards menopause was studied to explore the prevailing concepts and perceptions about menopause. A mixture of opinions and attitudes was observed in the process of data collection.

Many respondents associated menopause with gained respect and 'promotion' to the status of senior member in the society, even though it occurred when they were in late forties. Though not much change in the role within the family and outside the family was noticed, they felt change in their status through the attitude of their own self. The psychological state of fulfilment filled their minds and collective expression of that was seen from their reactions.

First reaction after the attainment of menopause was recorded during in-depth interviews, 'freedom from monthly ritual'. Almost all post-menopausal respondents, with the exception of sixteen, 'felt relieved' as they got rid of monthly cycles, associated menstrual irregularities and some socio-religious restrictions.

Since majority 86 per cent of the respondents had fruitful reproductive years and marital relations, menopause was welcomed and showed positive attitude. Maintaining self-confidence, positive thinking, satisfaction with achievements and current life events, regular exercise for physical fitness were some of the aspects that the respondents thought were important in accepting menopause as a natural life event.

Few expressed feeling of 'emptiness' (vacuum). They felt that 'something is missing'. Some of the reactions can be summarized as, "......well! Natural cycle has to stop at some point of time". Some felt that their feminity was affected because of menopause. They missed their menstrual cycle and felt as if something was missing in them (*kamtarta aali*) or had a feeling of emptiness (*pokli nirman zali*). They believed that monthly cycle would clean their body of 'dirty blood'. Getting rid of impure blood refreshed and revitalized their body. They felt that their importance was decreased (*kamipana yeto*), (*mahatva kami hote*) and that they were of no use (*nikami janavate*). They associated menopause with loss of feminity (*stritvavar parinam hoto*). Decreased physical capacity, loss of interest in social life, lack of sexual interests, loss of stamina, feeling of being old, feeling depressed about being of no use were associated with menopause.

Symptomatology

A wide range of symptoms were attributed to menopause. Like many researches carried out earlier, it was difficult to distinguish between symptoms that result from loss of ovarian function, hormonal imbalance and those stemming from aging process, or socio-environmental stresses of the mid-life years. There is a wide variation in the frequency with which women from different ethnic groups, different socio-economic and educational backgrounds report the occurrence of symptoms. The variables that affect the menopause experience are different in the urban and rural population.

Graph 18.1 shows various menopausal symptoms reported by the subjects. In the study 21.15 per cent reported no menopausal symptoms. Majority 70 per cent were in pre-menopausal stage. On an average, each respondent noticed four symptoms. The most frequently reported symptoms were—irritability 48 per cent, nervousness 43.08 per cent, hot flushes 38.2 per cent, and aching joint and muscle discomfort 35.8 per cent. Every third subject reported irritability or nervousness, anxiety, and mood swings. Nearly 15 per cent reported vasomotor symptoms, like hot flushes and night sweating which were frequently accompanied by insomnia, palpitation, and breathlessness. Response to the questions on urogenital problems was very low, frequent urination 22 per cent, vaginal dryness 17 per cent, and reduced sexual desire 16.3 per cent mentioned together only by 13.10 per cent. Huge majority 42.2 per cent reported non-specific somatic symptoms like headache 26.8 per cent, tingling sensation 22.7 per cent, along with specific changes like facial hair growth 9.7 per cent, and sudden weight gain 20.3 per cent. Origin of most of the somatic symptoms can be accorded to various other factors. Of the 123 subjects reporting one or more symptoms, merely 67 (54.5%) took treatment for the relief. Among them, only 29 subjects relied on modern medicine while the remaining 38 subjects resorted to alternative therapies.

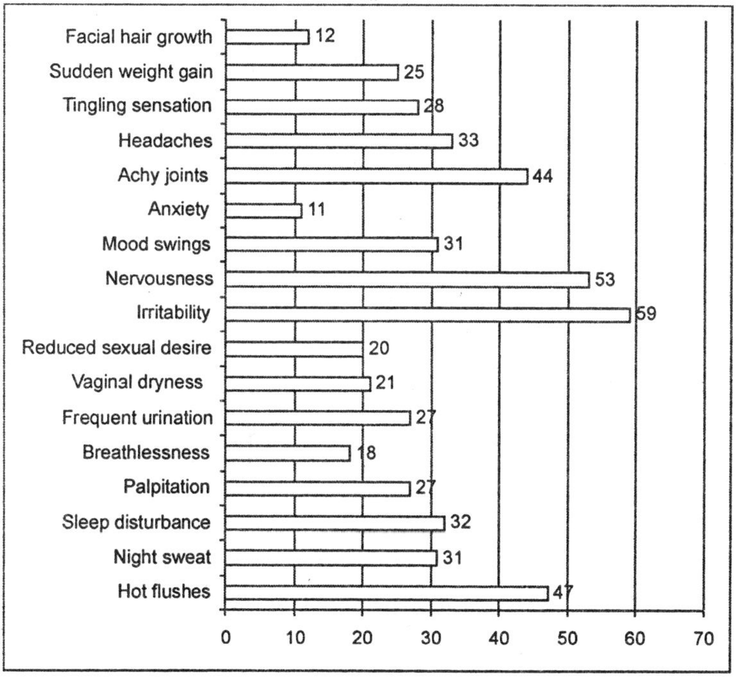

Fig. 18.1: Frequency of Symptoms of menopause

Source: Field Investigation.

Distressing Symptoms

There were 21 symptoms identified as distressing symptoms. The symptoms included achy joints, headache, as it affected their physical health as well as functional status. They further mentioned that "not being able to walk freely, work to the full capacity due to these pains" were matters of concern. Respondents narrated their experiences during in-depth interviews. Some of them had a traumatic menopausal phase. Hence, the final relief was appreciated, while some passed through this phase instantly without much annoyance. A respondent housewife and mother of three children, who had described a difficult eight-year menopause transition that started at the age of 42 years. "Just before my menopause I always had this feeling of drained out. My periods were very heavy and would last for several days. I suddenly became old and lonely. I would feel depressed and would cry for no apparent reason. I wanted to fight and shout and yell but could not do it. However, now that I am on the other side, I finally feel very fine about myself. What I went through was unexpected. I wish nobody goes through such horrible feeling. Today, I am very happy that I am on the other side."

Irritability was reported more frequently as 'distressing' symptom because it disturbed not only mental peace but also the relationship with family members and other people around. This was accompanied by the other psychological symptoms like mood swings, mental instability, nervousness, loneliness, and headaches. A respondent mentioned "I have recently celebrated 25th marriage anniversary and throughout I was very happy and had very enriching life experiences. However, menopause has changed my attitude and nature. I am very irritated all the time. My relation with husband and my children and, in fact, even with other relatives has changed to a great extent. I get irritated with small things and my husband complains that I pick up a fight over very insignificant issue. There is a change in our marital relation and I cannot stop thinking about it, neither can I bring any change in my mood or the way I feel and think."

Physical symptoms like hot flashes and sweating during night was reported to be disturbing as it created physical discomfort and resulted into sleepless nights. Disturbed sleep was troublesome, especially it affects energy and enthusiasm and daily activities. Other physical symptoms believed to have resulted into lack of confidence and lack of initiative reflecting in inefficiency at workplace. Having no one as friends or relatives to speak on these issues was more problematic to some, than the actual symptoms.

Thus, respondents mentioned that menopause affected their mental stability and physical capacity. Indecisiveness, lack of confidence, anxiety about any new thing, lack of initiative, and fear of failure stopped them from taking various decisions. Struggle with own mental happenings and coping with changed temperament made them more tense. They found it difficult to accept that their behaviour was dependent on the hormonal imbalance during menopause. Lack of awareness and information led to confusion and resulted in squandering time on home remedies, religious and spiritual solutions to their problems.

Support and Heath Seeking during Menopause

The study began with the assumption that the support available to woman depends on the severity of the problems faced. It was revealed that 62 per cent of the respondents discussed their physical as well as psychological problems with their husbands. Among those who discussed, nearly 50 per cent mentioned that their spouse reacted 'positively' to their menopause. 'Positively' was interpreted as "being aware of the condition, sympathetic and caring enough to offer domestic and financial help." Remaining mentioned that their spouse and family were indifferent, meaning they did not show any concern and did not participate in the discussion. In majority of the cases, remaining family members were least considerate and did not provide any assistance, physical or mental support. Yet it was also mentioned that presence of a 'grown-up' daughter provided them a supportive environment to discuss their matters. Communication with spouse, discussion with friends, neighbours and colleagues helped them to relieve the 'tension' experienced during distressful moments. It was also observed that nearly half of the respondents accepted their experience as part of their womanhood. Nearly 40 per cent relied on modern medicine and were consuming prescribed vitamin supplement, pain killers and other medicines. Four respondents were using hormone replacement therapy (HRT). Rest relied on the alternative therapies to modern medicine. A few practised *yoga* postures and took nutrition advice. One-third of those with 3 to 5 symptoms did not take any treatment. Of the remaining two-thirds, 50 per cent selected alternative therapies. Help from modern medicine was sought by majority of the respondents reporting more than ten symptoms. Inability to participate in routine activities and in family and social life was considered as an indicator of the severity of the problem. Majority 76 per cent opined that menopause being a natural event in life course; no treatment was needed, but a treatment to get relief from unpleasant somatic symptoms was considered vital for quality of life.

Conclusion

Although the Western culture views midlife women's changing body weight and associated changes in the appearance as process of ageing, Indian women experiences are different. In this context, the researcher would like to draw attention to the studies done in recent decade by experts from sociology and anthropology. They have investigated menopause and stated that attitude towards menopause, views on femininity, and changes in physical and emotional health attributed to menopause, can be viewed from a cultural perspective. According to Crawford (1984), body is a cultural object, which provide us with a powerful medium through which we interpret and give expression to our individual and social experience. Bodily states are key markers manifesting the social definitions of the self, role, normality and abnormality. It is called as a powerful source for metaphor (Crawford, 1984). Similarly, social construction of menopause in Indian context provide a sense of relief to the respondents. Getting old was interpreted in more positive manner as one gaining status and authority within the traditional age stratified society. The cultural context made suffering and pain of menopause easier and provided positive outlook in the minds of the respondents about midlife changes. Many women reported, what anthropologist Margaret Mead identified as 'postmenopausal zest' (Klatz and Goldman, 2003). This sense of well-being, individuality, and positive attitude towards new roles in life drives women into the rewarding period of their lives. Majority of the post-menopausal women reported positive attitude towards menopause, which may indicate that once women had gone through menopause they found it to be less troubling than they anticipated earlier in life.

Opinions expressed about loss of femininity, distressing symptoms or appreciating menopause, were all part of individual's own environment and no generalization could be made from experiences of few women's. Thus the study suggests looking at menopause from women's perspective. Women's perspective is embedded into social, cultural and personal environment. Changing urban environment may add to the existing anxieties of urban women. This calls for widespread awareness about physiological and psychological changes among menopausal women, irrespective of their socio-economic environment.

Lastly, considering Indian women now normally live about 10 per cent to 20 per cent of their lives in the post-menopausal state, it is imperative that the public health care system gears itself to meet the challenge posed by the health needs of post-menopausal women. The public health care system has typically concentrated on women of child-bearing age. Once women move out of this bracket, they receive less attention and are forced to seek care from private health care sector. Creativity and empowerment could enhance and express more positively in the post-menopausal stage of life.

SECTION III

Reproductive Health

Ensuring universal access to reproductive health, empowering people to exercise their right to reproductive health, and reducing inequities are central to the development goals globally. This was recognized more than 15 years ago at the International Conference on Population and Development (ICPD) in Cairo and was reaffirmed when universal access to reproductive health became a target of the sustainable development goals. Reproductive health research gained impetus only after International Conference on Population and Development (ICPD) called on countries to provide a full range of sexual and reproductive health services to the citizens. Largely these services or sexual and reproductive health programmes contain five main components; maternal and newborn health; family planning; prevention of unsafe abortion; management of reproductive tract infections (RTIs) and sexually transmitted infections (STIs), including HIV-AIDS, and promotion of sexual health.

"A little was known about women's reproductive health problems in India and South Asia until the landmark report a few years ago. Bang and colleagues found very high rates of untreated gynecological problems in their study population in an eastern Maharashtra rural region (Bang *et al.*, 1989). Various surveys of gynaecological morbidity in India and other South Asian populations demonstrate the pressing need for much greater attention to gynaecological morbidity in the primary health care system" (Pertii J. Pelto, 1996).

The increasing number of researches on reproductive health revealed that women's health in general and reproductive health in particular is largely influenced by the political and economic factors and is embedded within specific social relations and cultural context. These contexts are important in any health promotion programme and especially of HIV-AIDS programme aimed at behavioural change. While research on sexuality and sexual behaviour is considered to have policy implications, in regard to HIV-AIDS, research on reproductive health and contexts is also required to make these policy and programmes work at the community level. Research driven policies and programmes could be more meaningful, since these are based on a better understanding of human behaviour in the wholistic perspective of bio-socio-cultural contexts.

Within the mainstream reproductive health literature, the understanding of the role of culture in influencing behaviour has been largely explained by number of theoretical frameworks. For example, diffusion theory framework within reproductive health holds that the most important source of behaviour change is the spread of new ideas. Normative behaviour framework focuses on empirical and descriptive accounts of culture as norms, about how, when, and why people choose to use norms to legitimize behaviour or when and why they adopt strategies which challenge taboos and contradict social norms. Whatever is the framework, many research studies have mentioned that women face several barriers, at personal and socio-cultural level, as well as, at the level of health services and policy, which influence reproductive health and eventually affect sexual health of both men and women.

In this section, results of four different research projects are presented briefly. These projects addressed reproductive health issues and the results have programmatic implications. For example, pathways leading to reproductive tract infections among rural women provide deeper understanding of the reproductive health issues of adolescent girls as well as commercial sex worker. The study about health behaviour during pregnancy and post partum period among urban high caste women, reproductive concerns of adolescent girls and even commercial sex workers who become mothers and have concerns beyond sexuality are critical issues which need comprehensive policies and decentralized mechanisms of implementation, not limiting to OPD visits at the Primary Health Centres.

Reproductive Health Issues are not illness issues to be dealt as curative services but are an integral aspect of socio-cultural, psychological, economic aspects impacting the biology.

Chapters in this Section provide a panorama of reproductive health concerns of the cross-section of women's groups.

19

RTI and Genital Hygiene

BHUPALI MHASKAR AND KALPANA MUTATKAR

Introduction

The reproductive morbidity in developing countries forms a greater burden of ill health, i.e. 36 per cent for women of the total disease burden compared to 12 per cent for men (The World Development Report, 1993). The reproductive morbidity accounts for major causes of death and disability among women especially during reproductive years and accompanies throughout her life. During her life span, a woman may experience obstetric, gynaecological or contraceptive morbidity. Reproductive morbidity refers to conditions of ill health related to the reproductive process during and outside the child-bearing episode and occurs due to dysfunction of the reproductive system and its organs. It includes morbidity, which is a consequence of reproductive behaviour including sexual behaviour.

Studies from Bangladesh, Egypt, Nigeria and Karnataka, India, have all documented significant increased levels of reproductive morbidity among women (Dixon Muller Wasserheit, 1991; Germain *et al.,* 1992). These studies illustrated the need for the provision of appropriate medical care to respondents' problems and have emphasized the need to use local terminology and probing for the problem due to presence of embarrassment.

Studies on reproductive morbidity are no longer confined to clinic-based population but have been studied in various rural and slum communities. The thrust on ethnographic research on women's health has led to study in detail the various aspects of reproductive morbidity.

Most of the community-based studies in early 1990s have focused on self-reported morbidity. In some studies, women's self reports were complemented with clinical and laboratory data and the degree of correlation between women's perceptions of morbidity and medical definitions of pathology were examined (Koenig, *et al.*, 1996).

All community-based studies of gynaecological morbidity in India indicate a considerable burden of Reproductive Tract Infections and Sexually Transmitted Infections-RTIs/STIs, underscoring the development of need-based interventions and show the variation in the perceptions of women about the genital tract symptoms, which they experience. There is little data as to how women perceive the body changes and symptoms of the disease and how these changes get reflected in their treatment seeking behaviours (Garg, Sunila, *et al.,* 2000).

Reproductive Tract infections can present symptomatically as vaginal discharge, vulvo vaginal itching, genital ulcers, low backache, pain in lower abdomen and pain during sexual intercourse. If untreated they can cause serious complications among women like Pelvic Inflammatory Disease, cervical cancer and adverse outcome of pregnancy such as foetal wastage, low birth weight, congenital infections, and ectopic pregnancies. There is evidence that RTIs increase women's vulnerability to HIV-AIDS. Early detection, diagnosis and treatment are cost effective and beneficial to patient (S. Pachauri, 1994).

Reproductive Tract Infections have been largely ignored because of the widespread belief that they rarely result in severe morbidity, the assumption that their diagnosis and treatment is too expensive, as also the belief that RTIs occur among sexually promiscuous adults. RTIs are a biological problem in a web of psychological, economic, political and social factors that foster spread and must be addressed it RTIs are to be brought under control (Germain, A., 1992).

Women face more risk because of their reproductive biology. RTI related symptoms like white discharge, burning maturation, vulval itching is considered as a source of shame and guilt by the average Indian woman. They are rarely reported even to women members of the family, much less to the health care practitioner. (Dr. Apte, Trasi Reshma, May 2001). Reproductive health is a sensitive issue and there is a "Culture of Silence". Symptoms related to reproductive tract are simply not discussed (Dixon-Mullar, Wasserheit).

It is known that the perception regarding health; illness, disease and care seeking are deep rooted in culture. They stem from a mix unique of cultural context and a gender biased reality. So, it is necessary to understand women's reproductive health needs as part of bigger picture with her poor household status, her lack of decision making power, minimal control over finances, unequal division of labour and resources and oppression by a patriarchal society.

The risk factors for RTIs can be grouped into personal hygiene practices, socio-economic status, sexual behaviour and iatrogenic factors. Studies show that "RTIs contribute significantly to the burden of reproductive morbidity in women and poor women may be at increases risk because of unhygienic management of menstruation" (S. Pachauri, 1994). In Indian study by Bhatia and Cleland (1195) it was reported that women with poor personal hygiene and unsanitary household conditions were more likely to have gynaecological problems. The study done by Sunila Garg in Delhi, mentioned that socio-economic conditions, personal hygiene habits like daily bathing, washing genital parts, changing undergarments, bathing during menstruation, type of pad used etc. have significant correlationship with high prevalence of RTIs (Garg, Sunila *et al.*, 2000).

Several research studies on RTI related issues have also shown that there is a need to design studies that would look at socio-economic, behavioural and bio-medical causes of reproductive ill health (Jejeebhoy, 1996; Poornima Mane, 1992; UNFPA). Understanding of health behaviours related to RTIs/STIs are less which apart from accessibility and affordability are also influenced by factors such as assessment of personal risk, recognition of the significance of symptoms and the importance of early treatment. The major determinant and pathways of RTIs in Indian context have not been investigated in detail (UNFPA).

Most of the community-based studies in early 1990s have focused on self-reported morbidity and perceptions of women complemented with clinical and laboratory data. Several critiques on RTI related studies have shown that there is need to design studies that would look at socio-economic, behavioural and bio-medical causes of reproductive ill health. A very little understanding of some of the aspects of RTI, like iatrogenic risk factors, health behaviour for RTIs, and assessment of personal risk has been gained over the years. There is need to study and make valid assessment of the load of RTI due to iatrogenic causes, and treatment seeking behaviour and the range of factors that influence them. A very little understanding of health behaviour related to RTIs/STIs, which apart from accessibility and affordability are influenced by various factors such as assessment of personal risk, recognition of the significance of symptoms and the importance of early treatment. The major determinants and pathways of RTIs in Indian context have not been investigated in detail.

The present study has been designed to understand socio-cultural and behavioural causes of reproductive ill health. The study conducted in rural Maharashtra tries to explore women's perceptions and experiences regarding RTIs and the correlation of symptoms with personal menstrual and genital hygiene practices.

Methodology

The study was conducted in 5 villages of Velhe block of Pune district in Maharashtra, India. The data collection was done through Focus Group Discussions (FGDs) and semi-structured interviews. There were 778 ever-married women in the age group of 15-49 years in these 5 villages from which the study sample was derived.

The first phase of data collection was FGDs of village women. Three FGDs of women from the age specified groups were conducted for identification of their personal and menstrual hygiene practices, their concepts about symptoms, causation and ethno-pathways of RTIs, and the relationship of hygiene with RTIs. Each FGD was in three sittings each. The age groups were (15-30, 30-45, 45 + years of age). A total of 8-10 women from five villages participated in each Focus Group Discussion. Same women attended the three sittings in each FGD.

In the second phase, a total of 342 women out of 778 women who volunteered to participate in the study were interviewed with the help of semi-structured interview schedule. The interviews were directed to explore the habits about personal hygiene, menstrual hygiene and the presence of symptoms suggestive of RTIs out of 342 women, 171 women, i.e. 50 per cent reported to have some symptoms suggestive of RTIs while the remaining 171 did not report any symptoms. A comparison was made between both these groups to document the correlationship between the hygienic practices with that of symptoms suggestive of RTIs.

The personal hygiene habits included bathing habits like frequency, use of soap, use of towel/cloth, washing of hands after defecation and urination etc. The genital hygiene included cleaning of genital area, use of soap, practice of removal of public hair and also the hygienic practices after sex. The menstrual hygiene included practices to manage menstrual flow, the type of pads used, the cleanliness of pads etc.

After conducting the interviews, in the third phase three FGDs were conducted again for further clarification of concepts found in the first phase and second phase of data collection.

Findings

General Information about age, education, type of family, family size, living area, and availability of water and bathrooms were noted to understand the prevailing hygienic practices and the constraints and limitations to follow the correct practices.

The median age of 342 participants was 30 yrs. Out of 342 women, 51.9 per cent of women were in the age of 21-30 yrs, 34.1 per cent were in the age group of 31-40 yrs., 10.6 per cent were in the age group of 41-49 yrs and 3.5 per cent were in the age group of 15-20. Regarding literacy, 43.14 per cent of the respondents were illiterate, 21.9 per cent had completed primary and 22.7 per cent secondary level of education. 11.5 per cent had studied up to higher secondary and graduation level. Regarding type of family, more than half the respondents 66.7 per cent were staying in joint families. The average household size was of 6 persons. Regarding the space in the house, 42.1 per cent of families had two rooms, 37.1 per cent had three rooms and 20.8 per cent had single rooms.

Cleanliness of house was studied as one of the important hygienic practices. Cleanliness was assessed by the presence of clean floor and cleanliness of the area around the house. 91.2 per cent of respondents had kept their houses clean.

The availability of water was studied as an important determinant to observe hygiene. Water source for 223, 65.2 per cent families was well water whereas for 119, 34.8 per cent families it was from bore well. It was also observed that only 48 per cent of families have access to bathrooms while 52 per cent had no bathroom.

Self-reported Morbidity

Morbidity as reported by individual woman was noted through structured interview schedules. Table 19.1 shows the distribution of women with different complaints. 171 women out of 342 reported symptoms suggestive of RTIs and probably needing investigation and if necessary, medical attention. These self-reported complaints were mainly of white discharge, white discharge with vuval itching, pain in lower abdomen, low backache, burning in maturation and menstrual problems.

Table 19.1: Frequency of Women with Self-Reported Symptoms Suggestive of RTIs (N = 342)

Self–Reported symptoms	*No. of women*	*No. of women*
Only while discharge	64 (18.7%)	105 (61.4)
White discharge with vulval itching	21 (6.1%)	
White discharge with itching and swelling	9 (2.6%)	
Yellowish, grayish discharge	1 (0.3%)	
Watery discharge	1 (0.3%)	
Foul smelling discharge	1 (0.3%)	
Red discharge other than menstruation	4 (1.2%)	
Low backache and white discharge	4 (1.2%)	
Low backache when no menstruation	31 (9.1%)	
Pain in lower abdomen when not in menses	2 (0.6%)	
Pain in lower abdomen and other	6 (1.8%)	
Menstrual problems like irregular, scanty, heavy etc.	8 (2.3%)	
Burning in urination	14 (4.1%)	
Pain while urination	3 (0.9%)	
Genitals itching without discharge	2 (0.6%)	
Total	**171 out of 342**	

Source: Field Investigation.

It is seen that out of 171 women 105 (61.4%) were suffering from white discharge of different types with or without associated symptoms. 17 (5%) women also had urinary complaints suggesting clinical help. Only having low backache was reported by 31 (9.1%) of women.

Personal Hygiene

Practices like bathing daily, cleaning and wiping the body dry and changing menstrual pads were some of the commonly followed practices by majority of the respondents. However, practices like daily change of undergarments, cleaning of genital area and sexual hygiene were some of the less common practices. Total 342 women were interviewed (Table 19.2).

Water scarcity was highly significant (p = .000003) as 120 (35.08%) women reported water scarcity and out of these 67 per cent had symptoms as compared to 40 per cent women who had symptoms but no scarcity suggesting that adequate water is the important requirement for personal hygiene.

It is seen that 98.5 per cent of women were bathing daily and 92.8 per cent of these were taking bath with only water. 50 per cent women who bathe daily with only water had reported symptoms suggestive of

Table 19.2: Corelation of Habits: Personal Hygiene and Symptoms Suggestive of RTIs

Habit of personal hygiene	*Total no. of women with %*		*No. of women with self-reported morbidity with %*		*No. of women who have not reported any symptoms with %*		*P-Values*
Source of water							
Well water	223	65.2	117	52.46	106	47.53	0.25
Tap water	119	34.76	54	48.6	65	58.5	—
Water scarcity							
Yes	120	35.08	81	67.0	39	32.5	.000003
No	222	64.91	—	—	—	—	—
Cleanliness of house							
Yes	312	91.22	152	48.71	160	51.28	0.16
No	30	8.78	19	63.33	113	6.66	—
Bath							
Daily bathing	337	98.5	168	49.85	169	50.15	1.0
No daily bathing	5	1.4	2	40.0	3	60.0	—
Use of only water for bathing	371	92.7	161	50.78	156	49.21	0.07
Use of soap for bathing	16	4.7	4	25.0	12	75.0	—
Wash genital parts during bathing	328	92.7	163	9.69	165	50.31	0.78
No washing of genital parts	14	4.09	8	57.14	6	42.86	—
Washing genital parts							
Once	303	88.6	156	50.48	150	49.50	0.8
Twice in day	25	7.3	10	40.0	12	60.0	—
Wiping body							
Yes	305	89.18	143	46.88	162	53.2	0.001
No	37	10.08	28	75.67	9	24.32	—
Use *sadi* for drying body	162	47.36	64	39.5	98	60.5	—
Use towel/cloth for drying body	143	41.81	79	55.24	64	44.75	0.008
No drying of body	37	10.8	—	—	—	—	—
Daily wear of panty	281	82.16	113	40.21	168	59.78	—
No daily wear	61	17.83	58	95.09	3	5.0	—
Changing undergarments							
Yes	97	28.36	33	34.02	64	5.97	—
No	245	71.64	138	56.32	107	43.68	0.0003

Source: Field Investigation.

RTIs whereas 50 per cent women had no symptoms. Use of soap was reported by only 4.7 per cent. Among these, 25 per cent of women had symptoms while 75 per cent had no symptoms. Cleaning genital area with water was common during bath among 88.6 per cent women. Out of 328 women who washed genital area during bath, 49.69 per cent had symptoms as compared to 50.31 per cent of asymptomatic group. Among the symptomatic group 50.48 per cent washed genital area once in a day as compared to 40 per cent who washed twice in a day. This shows the beneficial effect of genital cleanliness.

Proper drying of body is an important practice to avoid humidity, which might predispose to infections. 47 per cent women were using *sari* where as 41 per cent were using common towel to dry the body and 10 per cent used nothing for drying body. Statistically significant difference ($p = 0.001$) was found between those who dried body after bath and those who did not wipe the body dry after bath. 46.88 per cent women of symptomatic group had practice of drying body as compared to 75.67 per cent who did not dry. Similarly the proportion of symptomatic women using own towel/sari (39.50%) was less as against 55.24 per cent of the same group who were sharing a common towel. This shows importance of proper drying of body with one's own sari/towel and shows that practice of using common towel is not desirable.

While exploring the practices regarding the use and change of undergarments, it was revealed that practice of everyday use of undergarments was reported by 281 (82.16%) of women where as 61 (17.83%) women did not use them daily. It was found that there is a high statistical significant difference ($p = 0.0000$) between those who used undergarments daily and those who did not use. Daily use of underclothes is important as shown in the symptomatic group where 40 per cent of users and 95 per cent of nonusers had symptoms. Statistical difference ($p = 0.0003$) was seen among those who change the undergarments daily and who do not change. 97 (28.36%) of women changed undergarments daily whereas majority 245 (71.64%) did not change. Among those who changed 34 per cent have reported symptoms suggestive of RTIs while a larger proportion of women, i.e. 56.32 per cent had symptoms who did not change.

The above results about practices show that women follow the practices but do not do so in hygienic way perhaps because of lack of awareness about the scientific and health aspects of each practice.

In the asymptomatic group, water scarcity was reported by lesser number of women. Though proportion of daily bathers and with water was almost same, use of soap was more during bath, washing of genital area was more common, drying of body was practiced more and with separate cloth. Similarly wearing of undergarments was more, changing them was also more among women who have not reported any morbidity.

Menstrual Hygiene

Menstrual hygiene is an important aspect of women's reproductive health during her reproductive years. There are different practices followed by different communities. Many of these practices are traditional practices being followed for generations. They are mainly influenced by social, cultural, spiritual and economic factors at household level. They are also influenced by availability of adequate water, bathrooms and awareness and degree of cleanliness at individual family level. Table 19.3 has shown some of the menstrual hygienic practices observed during the study.

Table 19.3: Correlation of Menstrual Hygiene and Symptoms Suggestive of RTIs

Habit of menstrual hygiene	*Total no. of women with %*		*No. of women with self-Reported morbidity with %*		*No. of women without symptoms %*		*P. Values*
Bathing during Menstruation	336	98.2	167	49.70	169	50.30	0.68
No bathing during menstruation	6	1.8	4	66.66	2	33.34	—
Use of menstrual pads							
Yes	339	99.1	168	49.55	171	50.45	0.24
No	3	0.9	3	100	—	—	—
Changing Pads							
Once in a day	214	62.57	145	67.75	69	32.24	—
More than once in day	125	36.55	23	18.4	102	81.6	0.000
No reply	3	0.8					
Washing of genital parts while changing menstrual pads	252	73.68	93	36.90	159	63.09	—
No washing	90	26.32	78	86.67	12	13.33	0.0000
Washing genital area while changing pads							
With only water	231	67.54	93	40.26	138	59.74	0.0006
Soap	21	6.14	—	—	21	100	—
No reply	90	26.31	—	—	—	—	—
Washing menstrual pads							
With water	287	83.92	149	51.91	138	48.08	
Soap	52	15.20	19	36.53	33	63.46	0.05
No replay	3	0.98	—	—	—	—	—
Drying of menstrual pads							
In sunlight	142	41.52	65	45.77	77	54.22	—
In shadow outside house	149	43.57	64	42.95	85	57.04	0.00003
Inside house	51	26.31	42	82.35	9	17.65	—
Storage of menstrual pads							
In house	106	30.99	55	51.88	51	48.12	0.0
In cow shade	236	69.01	116	49.15	120	50.85	—

Source: Field Investigation.

It is seen that out of 342 women, 98.2 per cent took bath during menstruation whereas only 1.8 per cent of women do not take bath. Use of menstrual pads was seen among 339 (99.1%) of women. 214 (62.57%) of women change pads once in day while 18.4 per cent changed more often. More women, i.e. 67.75 per cent of those who changed pads only once showed symptoms as compared to 18.4 per cent of the same group who changed pads more than once. A statistically significant difference was found ($p = 0.000$) among those who changed menstrual pad once in a day with that of those who changed more often. 73.0 per cent of women while changing pads took perineal wash as against 26.32 per cent who did not take. It was seen that nearly 37 per cent of women who took wash had symptoms as compared to 86.6 per cent who did not take was and had symptoms showing that perineal wash is beneficial. Statistical significant difference ($p = 0.000$) was found between practice of perineal wash and no wash. Similarly statistical significant difference was also found between women who use only water as compared with soap users (p-0.0006).

As regards cleanliness of home-made pads, it was seen that nearly 84 per cent of women washed menstrual pads with only water and 15.2 per cent of women used soap. 52 per cent of those using only water had reported symptoms suggestive of RTIs as compared to 36.5 per cent of women using soap. Practice of drying menstrual cloth showed that 41 per cent of women dried washed pads in sunlight, 43 per cent dried them in the shadow and 14 per cent dried inside house. When not in use the pads were stored on a loft inside the house by 106 (31%) women and in cow shade by 236 (69%) of women. Statistical significant difference ($p = 0.0003$) was found among those who dry pads in sunlight with that of those who dry in shadow and those who dry inside house. Being considered unhealthy and polluting, menstrual cloth is not supposed to be touched by others.

In the asymptomatic group, it was found that more number of women, i.e. 81.6 per cent were changing pad more often and 63.4 per cent were using soap to wash pads. Perineal wash while changing the pads was also practiced more 63 per cent.

These quantitative results about menstrual hygiene support the qualitative data, which limits the hygienic practice during menstruation. Though changing menstrual pads depends on the menstrual flow, more frequent change is seen to be better.

Genital Hygiene

The habits regarding the cleanliness of the genital area were studied. Genital/perineal area has outlets for urine, stool and menstrual discharge and prone to cross contamination. The practices studied included washing practices after defecation, urination and sexual contact. Practice of removal of pubic hair was also explored.

Table 19.4: Corelation of Habits: Genital Hygiene and Symptoms Suggestive of RTIs

Habit of genital hygiene	*Total No. of women with*	*%*	*No. of women with self-reported morbidity*	*with %*	*No. of women without symptoms*	*%*	*P. Values*
Way of washing anus forward to backward	27	7.89	8	29.62	19	7.38	0.04
Backward forward	315	92.11	163	51.75	152	48.25	—
Washing hands after defecation with							
Only water	303	88.6	159	52.47	144	47.53	0.001
Soap	35	10.2	8	22.86	27	77.14	
No reply	4	1.16	—	—	—	—	—
Awareness about Hygiene after sex	32	9.35	10	31.25	22	68.75	—
No awareness	310	90.65	161	51.93	149	48.07	0.04
Washing Genitals after sex	73	27.14	20	27.40	53	72.60	—
No washing	269	78.66	151	56.13	118	43.87	0.000024
Washing genitals							
Only water	68	19.89	18	26.47	50	73.52	—
Soap	5	1.46	2	40	3	60	0.8
No reply	269	78.66	—	—	—	—	—
Urination after sex	75	21.93	13	17.33	62	82.67	—
No habit of urination	267	78.07	158	59.18	152	40.82	0.0003
Removing pubic hair with blade	240	70.2	117	48.75	123	51.25	
Ash	102	29.9	54	52.94	48	47.06	0.5
Frequency: once in a month	243	71.1	129	53.08	114	46.92	
More than once in a month	99	29.0	42	42.42	57	57.58	0.009

Source: Field Investigation.

Hand washing after defecation is an important hygienic practice. 303 (88%) of women washed hands after defecation with only water and 35 (10%) used soap. 27 (7.89%) women mentioned the practice of forward to backward way of washing anal area after defecation. 52.4 per cent of women with symptoms had reported washing hands with water as compared to 22.86 per cent of women who washed with soap. A highly statistical significant difference (p = 0.001) between those who used water for washing hands after defecation and those who used soap.

The way women wash anal area was also explored. 92 per cent of women wash with backward to forward movement of hands and 51.75 per cent of them had reported RTI symptoms. Compared to this, 70 per cent of asymptomatic women had the habit of washing from front to back showing statistical difference of (p = 0.04). It suggests that the washing practices after defecation if correctly followed can prevent faecal contamination of lower part of vagina.

Awareness about sexual hygiene, cleanliness of genital area after sex and urination after sex were the practices reported by women. Regarding awareness about hygiene after sex 90.65 per cent had no awareness. Out of these 52 per cent had symptoms (p = 0.04).

It is seen that a large number of women 78.66 per cent did not take wash after sex while few women 27.14 per cent reported washing. Smaller percentage of women 27.4 per cent who washed genitals after sex had symptoms suggestive of RTIs as compared to a large number of women 56.13 per cent who did not wash. Statistical significant difference (0.00002) between the two groups was seen. The beneficial effect of wash was reflected, as 72.6 per cent of women who practiced washing of genitals were asymptomatic.

Urination after sex was another practice reported by nearly 22 per cent of women and 78.6 per cent did not practice. Out of those who were not following this practice 59 per cent of women had symptoms as against 82.6 per cent of asymptomatic women who were following the practice. Statistical significant difference (p = 0.003) was found between those who had habit of urination after sex and those who did not have this habit. 17.33 per cent of those who had habit of urination after sex, reported symptoms suggestive of RTIs, whereas almost 59.17 per cent of women reported symptoms suggestive of RTIs who do not have this habit.

Cleanliness of perineal skin by practice of removing pubic hair was seen to be a common practice followed by 70 per cent of rural women with blade and by 30 per cent women with ash. This practice did not have statistical different between symptomatic and asymptomatic group.

It is seen from the above analysis that drying of body, use of undergarments, changing undergarments, frequent change of menstrual pads, and some other practices have direct relationship in reducing the risks for RTIs. Analysis of quantitative data about the practices followed by rural women for personal, menstrual and genital hygiene shows that the practices are followed due to lack of awareness, scarcity of water, cultural norms and beliefs. There are some practices about sexual and genital hygiene, which have not been reported in earlier studies but are found to be influencing predisposition to RTIs. This being an explorative study, the practices are only studies and evaluated in view of self-reported morbidity.

After exploring the personal, menstrual and genital hygienic practices and its correlation with symptomatic and asymptomatic respondents, it was necessary to understand socio-cultural aspects and women's perceptions about their own body image, menstruation, concept of purity etc. and the causation of the most common symptoms related to RTIs like white discharge. The health seeking behaviour and the linkages from menstruation to RTIs were studied. This was done through focus group discussions.

Perceptions about Body Image

Discussion about their own body image included their perceptions about different parts of the body, their location, functioning, and the interrelationship with other organs. Women mentioned: "the body starts from mouth from where we eat, drink, followed by neck which has two tubes meant for eating and drinking, and the other for breathing. Further down come breasts, which have a purpose of nourishing child by producing milk. Then there is actual stomach, small and large intestines for digestion, storage of food and rectum to store undigested food and urinary bladder for storage of urine. Woman's abdomen at its lower end has two holes, for urination, and the other for child birth and for menstrual blood to come out."

Concept of Menstruation

Menarche symbolized the attainment of physical maturity and ability to bear child. There was no other purpose ascribed to it. The attainment of menarche was considered to be associated with biological maturity and hence women becoming capable for marriage and reproduction. *Pali* is the local word used for recurring monthly menstrual cycle. It is supposed to start between the age of 12-15 years.

Concept of Normal Menstruation

Normal menstruation was described, as a four-day's cycle with scanty flow on first day, which progressively increased and stopped on fourth day. Any pattern other than this is considered as abnormal menstruation. Women perceived that at the time of menstruation the mouth of uterus open through which blood was discharged. There is pain in low back because blood vessels and muscles are stretched to push out the blood. It is considered that during menstruation heat is released from body.

Concept of Purity and Pollution

There is a tradition of isolation of women during menstruation. Preparing food; touching to *Chula* (hearth, stove) and idols of deities, is not allowed during menstruation. Earlier there was a practice of not taking bath during menstruation as women were isolated and almost treated like untouchables. After the menstruation was over, women were supposed to take head bath on fourth day and then only they were considered as pure and allowed to touch and move around.

The process of menstruation is correlated with expulsion of dirty blood from body and led to segregation of women as ritual pollution. As menstrual blood is considered dirty and impure, its regular expulsion is considered necessary. It is believed that only after its expulsion the body can be healthy otherwise it could lead to morbidity.

The phenomenon of menstruation was associated with taboos and restrictions in various spheres of life, e.g. work, bath, sex etc. Avoidance of sex is the most important taboo as it is considered to have harmful effect on man and woman's body. The menstrual blood could be subjected to black magic. It is considered that the blood could transmit infection to man.

A woman who is menstruating should not enter inner rooms like kitchen, dining, bed room as she is impure. On fourth day of menstruation, after taking head bath, woman could enter all rooms and perform normal functions. The practice of taking head bath is that usually normal menstruation lasts for 4 days. The day of head bath is decided by cultural norms.

Concept of Hygiene

It was believed that menstrual flow should be managed with great care and cleanliness, because women perceived that poor hygiene could lead to acquisition of some kind of infection. But, it is actual practice, they were not able to maintain hygiene due to water scarcity, non-availability of clean cloth, inability to wash cloth. Cloth was the cheapest preferred material to use as pads during menstruation.

There was no concept of hygiene immediately after sex but next day early in the morning, women took head bath and then entered in the kitchen. It is considered proper to be clean and pure after having sex.

Concept of RTIs

The discharge other than menstruation was considered as white discharge. Before menstruation, women get white discharge, which was considered as normal as it gives signal that a woman will get menses within 3-4 days. After menstruation also, for the next 1-2 days there is some discharge, which is considered as normal. Other than this, whenever there is discharge it is always considered as abnormal. There are different types of RTIs causing white discharge yellowish, grayish and foul smelling discharge; white discharge with itching, burning and pain during urination, pain during intercourse, etc. The progression and severity of discharge was perceived only when the quantity of discharge increased to the extent of soiling of underclothes and interference in daily activity. Women said that white discharge was most common among women but sometimes it was quite serious, as it led to cancer of the uterus and finally death. They said that some women were aware of this fact these days and, therefore, took treatment. Occasionally there was red discharge and which could be distinguished from menstrual blood.

White discharge had no ill effect on the ability to conceive. Women said that even if a woman had white discharge there was no problem in getting pregnant and having a baby. Women admitted that if a woman was scared of death due to discharge, only then does she take full treatment. Some of the causes of symptoms suggestive of RTIs, as per the respondents mentioned in focus group discussions were heat, sex with more than one person, weakness, poor personal hygiene, mental tensions, stress, over sex etc.

Ethno-Pathological Pathway for Discharge as Symptom of RTI

Different perceptions were communicated by women about the origin of white discharge.

- Due to consumption of 'hot' categories of food (the food which is heat producing in body, according to Ayurveda), women may suffer from white discharge. The process of causation of discharge due to 'heat' was mentioned. "When a woman inhales any 'hot' food, 'heat' generates in her body, which goes to stomach. Since, stomach and uterus are attached to each other, it get transferred to uterus. The white solid substance, present in uterus melts, and the sticky semi solid substance comes out of genitals."

- Over sex leads to white discharge. Extra quantity of semen comes out of woman's body as white discharge.
- Only women suffer from white discharge and not men. A man does not suffer from white discharge because his organs are outside while a woman's organs are inside her body. During sex, man's organ is inside woman's body only for a while, and that is why there are less chances of him being infected (Cross-sexual transmission).
- When a man has sex with a woman, 'heat' from his body is transferred to woman's body through semen and she suffers from white discharge because of 'heat'.
- Due to sexual intercourse during menstruation, man's 'heat' goes into woman's body. As a result, more 'heat' generates and this 'heat' affects uterus and thus a woman suffers from white discharge.
- If a man has sex with a woman suffering from white discharge then and then only he may suffer from *Garmi* (STD).
- Because of weakness, uterus shrinks and becomes weak but its mouth remains open and white discharge flows out from there and comes out through the vagina. White water is formed in the lower abdomen.
- Blood becomes thick and flows out as white discharge.
- Weakness and stress are probably the psychological manifestations of depression, which physically manifest as white discharge in due course.
- Some parts during pregnancy and abortion get decayed inside the uterus. All those decayed parts are mixed with other fluids from uterus and the dirt comes out as white discharge.

Many of their beliefs are based on ethno-anatomical and ethno-physiological notions about the structure and function of the body. These notions have a bearing on treatment seeking and consequently on the reproductive health of women.

While attempting to understand the ethno-pathology of RTIs, commonly manifested as white discharge, weakness, stress, tension and increased body heat came out as major 'perceived' causes. Similar perceptions have been documented in a number of other studies from different states in India. It seems that 'weakness' is a 'feminine expression' of women's inability to cope with the situation. The most common concerns of people in this regards are weakness, fear of heart attack, health of genital organs, loss of semen and nocturnal emissions.

Treatment Seeking Behaviour

Several reasons for women not seeking treatment or delaying the treatment or for non-compliance of the treatment for RTI related symptoms were reported through individual interviews and group discussions. The reasons included early recurrence, fear of stigmatization, non-availability of lady doctor, inaccessible health facility, no priority to one's health facility, no priority to one's health, poor communication between husband and wife, non-availability of services, money problem, limited mobility etc. women generally tell husbands and mothers-in-law who are the heads of family and the decision makers about their problem especially when they cannot manage on their own. The decision makers take decisions and decide whether to go for treatment or not. It takes almost a gap from 8 days to one month for a woman to go for seeking treatment. If the clinic is far, it is difficult to get time to go for treatment by losing one-day labour. Respondents mentioned that money was required for treatment. Non-availability of money to seek specialist care leads to seeking treatment at public hospitals where presence of male doctor and non-availability of female doctor equals to having no treatment at all. Women generally prefer lady doctor for treatment because, for white discharge, a woman had to be examined internally and women do not prefer a male doctor for gynaecological check up. Women generally go to a general practitioner.

Home Remedies for Gynaecological Morbidity

The home remedies that were available for white discharge were consumption of white hibiscus flowers fried in Ghee (made from cow's milk), eating of curd, keeping cotton soaked with curd in vagina. Curd treatment was said to cure white discharge.

Consequences of RTIs

Respondents mentioned that uterine cancer and hysterectomy were the main consequences of RTIs. The worst effect that concerned them was that a woman could become infertile. They reported that if symptoms were not treated in time, it leads to all the above ill effects. They said that with prolonged white discharge, the woman gradually losses all her energy and subsequently faces death.

Conclusions

The present explorative study has shown that there is association between some of the personal, menstrual and genital hygienic practices and symptoms suggestive of RTIs. Every culture has some kind of norms and regulations for women. A norm about hygiene, which directly relates to concept of purity and pollution, is applicable to married women in India. Thus, it is necessary to have comprehensive understanding of cultural norms of personal hygiene habits.

The scientific facts about each hygienic practice needs to be documented and evaluated in the background of specific culture, to label it as safe practice for attainment of reproductive health including general health. Self-reported morbidity of women also needs further exploration through clinical support and laboratory investigation for confirmation of infections or other causes of women's ill health. Timely medical care can save a large number of women from reproductive morbidity. Similarly, utilization of local remedies for treatment of RTI related symptoms needs scientific (evidence) validation.

The exploration of concepts reported by women on different issues like body image, menstruation, RTIs, hygiene, purity and pollution through qualitative data has reflected the need of generation awareness among women regarding their health issues. Breaking the 'culture of silence' and early diagnosis of women's problems is important through availability of treatment at the village level. Issues like preference for women health care providers, encouraging effective communication between providers and clients, partner treatment, and improving access to and utilization of Reproductive Health Services present at the Government health facilities under the RCH programme need attention.

The area where there is hardly any data about the ethno-pathological pathways needs to be studied in detail. The presence of micro-cultures which have their own belief systems within the larger cultural framework need to be identified and studied. For example, the different responses received through three different groups from the same cultural set up justifies the need for such steps. Findings of such studies may be useful in only a given socio-cultural context and may not have a high level of generalization, but this in itself is an important issue for designing location and community specific interventions.

20

Reproductive Health Issues of School Going Adolescent Girls

SUSMITA BHATTACHARYA

Introductior

In recent years there have been increasing number of studies of adolescent, both in and out of school, particularly focused on their vulnerability to sexual health problems and the increased spread of HIV infections in the very young age group in India (*cf.* Andrew and Patel, 2001; Bhende, 1994; Sodhi *et al.*, 2004; and others). Adolescent has been defined by World Health Organization (WHO) as the period of life spanning the ages between 10 and 19 years. It is a period of transition from childhood to adulthood. It is also a time of emotional and physical turmoil as individuals begin to mature sexually and seek some measure of autonomy in coping with the world outside the home. Also, it is the period of greater exploration of social relationships, including heterosexual contacts, in preparation for assuming roles as economically productive and socially responsible adults. As pointed out by reports of the UNFPA (1997) and Population Report (1996), approximately half of HIV infections in India are found in the age group of 15 to 24 years, so adolescents are particularly at risk of AIDS, in addition to the risks of other sexually transmitted infections. In India, women are particularly vulnerable to HIV because of less access to information. A recent study has reported that only five per cent of women in India have full and adequate knowledge concerning prevention of HIV infections (Sambamoorthi *et al.*, 2004).

Amongst adolescents, girls constitute a particularly vulnerable group. The gender biases in the social system, the lack of adequate education, poor economic opportunities, and (usually) early marriages, put them at a greater risk of sexual and reproductive morbidity. Also, the stressful phases of life events such as menarche, menstruation, pregnancy and teen-aged motherhood are likely to produce tremendous psychological stress for adolescent girls. Healthy coping responses of adolescents depend on complex factors, including socio-economic status, home and neighbourhood environments in which they live and grow, and increasingly the opportunities for adequate schooling and adult employment. In India until recently, programmes for women were mainly focused on the reproductive functions, in the form of antenatal and maternity care. In the past few years, there is a change in focus, to include reproductive health, including health of adolescent girls, but so far these programmes have had only limited scope.

During the past decade, there has been a large increase in studies of sexual and reproductive health in India, particularly as a response to the growing concerns about the HIV-AIDS epidemic (Pelto, 2000; Verma *et al.*, 2004). The new research also reflects the influence of the Cairo Conference of 1994 (International Conference on Population and Development). Recent studies focused on the sexual and reproductive health of adolescents are practically unanimous in noting the following:

(a) Extremely low levels of information among adolescents about sexual and reproductive health matters, especially concerning sexually transmitted infections.
(b) Much lower levels of information among adolescent girls than among boys of the same age groups.
(c) Lack of information about reproductive processes and contraception among both females and males, thus leading to inability to avoid unwanted pregnancies.
(d) Lack of any information or 'forewarning' concerning menarche and menstruation among pre-menarche girls.
(e) Extreme reticence on the part of parents to give any guidance or information concerning sexual and reproductive matters to their children.
(f) Great desire for more information about menstruation, reproductive processes and sexual matters among adolescents, both boys and girls.

Some studies have noted high levels of anxiety and other mental health problems among adolescents (Andrew and Patel, 2001;

Ramakrishna, 2001). These studies point out that some of the high levels of anxiety arise from the 'air of mystery' surrounding sexual and reproductive matters. The general low level of information available to adolescent girls about menstruation is often accompanied by unhygienic standards of personal care during menstruation, which is associated with reproductive tract infections (Narayan *et al.*, 2001)

Adolescent girls living in low-income communities and families are at greater risk of dropping out of school, thus adding to their isolation from effective information sources. In place of schooling and reliable knowledge sources, adolescents are found to rely heavily on mass media, particularly television and movies, for their information about sexual and reproductive matters, as well as other 'facts of life.' Concepts of heterosexual relations and family life are coloured by the romantic and unrealistic images portrayed in movies, television programmes and TV advertisements, thus further contributing to serious deficiencies in information for coping with the increasing complexities of their life situations.

In Indian culture, as in most of the rest of the world, matters of sex are not discussed openly, especially within families. Parents do not instruct their adolescent children about sexual and reproductive matters, and the prevailing social norms are in favour of 'shielding' young girls from information about such matters, as they are regarded as immoral and 'dirty' (Jejeebhoy, 2000). Thus the cultural expectations do not recognize that knowledge about sexuality is necessary for the sexual and reproductive health of women.

If the parents are unwilling to instruct their children, especially young girls, about sexual and reproductive matters, then another source of sound information should be in the education system. In the past 10 years, the State of Maharashtra has instituted a programme of reproductive education ('family life education') that begins in the 8th standard of the public school system. It is to be hoped that gradually the education system will play a larger role in preparing young girls (and boys) for adult life. There are now signs that families in the urban sector, even in low-income communities, are placing a higher value on education for all children as an essential prerequisite for getting satisfactory employment and (especially for girls) assuring satisfactory marriage alliances.

This study focuses on the complex interrelationships among the schools, adolescent girls, and their levels of reproductive and sexual health knowledge. It appears that many changes are occurring in urban populations, in terms of attitudes toward the schools, the changing patterns of employment opportunities, as well as the expectations of adolescents concerning future careers in employment and family life. This study is intended to explore the ways in which these developments impinge on aspects of reproductive health in the school-going age groups.

The Study Site and Population

The study was conducted during the period from March to December 2003, in a low-income locality of Mangalwar Peth in Pune city. The community is located near a main road, and the lanes and by-lanes have many shops as well as some small-scale industries that manufacture paper boxes, incense sticks and other products. The basic amenities are provided by the Pune Municipal Corporation. The area has electricity, safe drinking water supply, and public toilets, for which each household reportedly contributes a small amount (about Rs. 20 per month). The housing conditions are very poor, as about 90 per cent of the houses are one-room tenements. Most of the houses do not have separate kitchen or bathing facilities. Some of the dwellings have a 'mezzanine' floor, or loft, usually built after a son's marriage, to provide the new couple with privacy to sleep at night. The local people refer to it as a *mala*. The surrounding area is dirty, open air defecation by children is a common practice, and garbage is dumped indiscriminately in various open areas.

A large municipal school for girls is located about a kilometre away. Education is free up to the 12th standard, including free provision of school uniforms and books. In addition, there are private schools in the area, although very few families could afford to send their children to those institutions. Health care facilities are provided by the Pune Municipal Corporation, which runs a dispensary and a nearby maternity hospital. The government medical college hospital is just one kilometre from the study area.

Data-Gathering Methods

Our data-gathering strategy included a blend of qualitative and quantitative methods. In-depth interviews were conducted by the two female principal investigators. Each of us has a medical degree, with a public health background and several years of experience in community-based research. Four female field workers who had long experience of working in a health centre in the study area were also trained in various methods used in data collection.

The adolescent girls are extremely shy about discussing anything about reproductive health and sexuality, but with careful probing and continued discussion, we found that the girls would 'open up' and talk about sensitive topics. Perhaps the fact that our identity as doctors helped the girls to be more forthcoming in talking about sex and reproduction. Of course, we had assured them that everything they said would be kept completely confidential, and they were also assured that their participation was totally voluntary.

In addition to individual interviews, we also conducted eight focus group discussions with adolescent girls, to understand their feelings and perceptions. Themes for discussion were selected from topics encountered during the in-depth interviews. Several informal group discussions were also held with the mothers of adolescent girls, to understand their perspectives on the problems involved in bringing up adolescent daughters in this social environment.

Data were also collected through an essay competition, in which girls wrote on topics such as: 'My ideas of a happy family' and 'Story of a young girl'. Girls wrote about their dreams and hopes. This was to encourage them to express their opinions freely, and also to encourage them to overcome shyness in giving interviews. We gave prizes for the three best entries. A competition was held to judge the girls' health awareness. A question paper with 25 items was given to participants. The questions were simple, objective, and related to health matters of adolescent girls. The participants were grouped into 12-14, 15-16, 17-19 years age groups. The top three papers in each group were given prizes. We involved parents, health care providers, community leaders in these programmes.

Quantitative Survey

The semi-structured interview schedule was administered to our total population of 323 adolescent girls. The interview included information on socio-demographic background, substance use by the girls and other family members (including alcohol use by the father), menstrual history, awareness of the legal age for marriage, and knowledge about contraceptive methods. Awareness about HIV-AIDS was also included in the interview schedule, as well as questions about any complaints suggestive of reproductive tract infections. Girls who reported any reproductive tract problems were referred to the government hospital. Interviews were taken at the urban health centre in the area.

In addition to the interviews and group discussions with adolescents and their parents, we also interviewed key informants, particularly women in the *mahila mandals* of the community, persons in local NGOs, *anganwadi* workers, as well as teachers and the principal of the school. We felt that discussions with community people enhanced our acceptance in the community, and also contributed to our framing of appropriate questions for the quantitative survey. Informed written consent was taken from the parent or guardian of the adolescent respondents.

Education and Occupations of the Parents

There are very large differences between the parents and the adolescent girls in their educational levels. As shown in Table 20.1, 42 per cent of the mothers and 17 per cent of the fathers had never been to school. Of those with some education, 37 per cent of the mothers and 53 per cent of the fathers had had five years or more of education. In contrast, Table 20.3, shows that all but 9 per cent of the girls have already attained five years or more of schooling. These data, and interview materials presented below are an indication of the greatly increased levels of education in the younger generation. Many of the parents were from remote villages where there were very few opportunities for education; and the mothers, especially, had been married at an early age, so their chances of getting education were very limited.

Table 20.1: Educational Status of Parents

	Mother (%)	*Father (%)*
Not available (separated)	14 (4.3)	63 (19.5)
Never been to school	135 (41.8)	54 (16.7)
4th standard or less	55 (17.0)	35 (10.8)
5-10th standard	110 (34.0)	150 (46.4)
Above 10th	9 (2.8)	21 (6.5)
Total	**323**	**323**

Source: Field Investigation.

The data in Table 20.2 show that most of the parents of adolescent girls in this low-income community are employed, although at quite low levels of income.

Table 20.2: Occupational Status of Parents

	Mother (%)	*Father (%)*
Not available (separated/diseased)	15 (4.6)	66 (20.4)
Unemployed or 'housewife'	191 (59.1)	23 (7.1)
Labourer/maid servant	105 (32.5)	104 (32.2)
Service	12 (3.7)	130 (40.2)
Total	**323**	**323**

Source: Field Investigation.

Table 20.2 shows that approximately one-third of both mothers and fathers are employed as wage labourers (males) or domestic servants (females). The other major category of employment for the males is in service occupations such as *chowkidars* (watchmen), peons (attendants) in business enterprises, and other low-paid jobs. In 20 per cent of the families the father was absent, due to desertion of women or death. In those cases, the female heads of households had to work outside the home to support their families.

Adolescents and Schooling

Table 20.3 shows the education levels of 323 respondents. 85 were in the early adolescent group (10-14 years) and 163 were in later adolescence, aged between 15 to 19 years.

Table 20.3: Educational Status of Adolescent Girls

	10-14 yrs	*15-19 yrs*	*Total (%)*
Presently in school	62	77	139 (43.0)
Presently out of school	21	163	184 (57.0)
Distribution by Educational Level			
Never been to school	1	17	18 (5.6)
4th standard or less	3	7	10 (3.1)
5th-7th standard	28	55	83 (25.7)
8th standard	38	47	85 (26.3)
9th-10th standard	13	85	98 (30.3)
11th-12th standard	—	24	24 (7.4)
Above 12th standard	—	5	5 (1.5)
Total	**83**	**240**	**323**

Source: Field Investigation.

As we see in Table 20.3, a little less than half of the girls were still in school. It is unfortunate that about one quarter of the girls in the younger age group had already dropped out of school. There were 17 older girls who had never been to school. However, they could write and read as they had been taught by their siblings, and also by NGOs that had conducted literacy classes in the community.

Table 20.4: Educational Status of the out of School Girls

	10-14 yrs	*15-19 yrs*	*Total*
Never been to school	1	17	18 (9.8)
4th standard or less	3	7	10 (5.4)
5th-7th standard	13	52	65 (35.3)
8th standard	4	40	44 (23.9)
9th-10th standard	—	42	42 (22.8)
11th-12th standard	—	5	5 (2.7)
Total	**21**	**163**	**184**

Source: Field Investigation.

Table 20.4 shows that among the older age group, 53.4 per cent (87 girls) had studied up to the eighth standard or higher. They are a reflection of the newer trends in favour of basic education for the girl children.

Reasons for Dropping Out of School

Although it is generally believed that parents and other family members are the main persons responsible for girls dropping out of school, about 20 per cent of the girls said, they left school because they were not interested in pursuing further education. The large number 37 per cent of girls who gave no reason for leaving school undoubtedly also included many who were "bored with school," or felt that further education was unnecessary. Table 20.5, below, gives the distribution of reasons reported by the girls were no longer studying.

Table 20.5: Reasons for Leaving School

	10-14 yrs	*15-19 yrs*	*Total (%)* *N = 184*
No reason given	10	58	68 (36.9)
No Interest in school	3	34	37 (20.1)
Family reason	7	56	63 (34.2)
Reached the perceived optimal level	1	3	4 (2.2)
Others	0	12	12 (6.5)

Source: Field Investigation.

According to our discussions with the girls and adult key informants, the reasons for dropping out of school are often complex, with both personal and family factors mixed together. Poverty is often cited as one component, but lack of money is generally a very minor factor in urban schools of Maharashtra, since almost all the school expenses, including books and school uniforms, are provided by the government. If students are unable to afford the bare essentials of paper, pencils and stationery, donations are available at the school, so that even those items could be provided to the student. On the other hand, poverty can force the mother and other members of the family to go for employment outside the home, so young girls may be required to stay home to do cooking, laundry and other chores for the family.

Parents' Attitudes towards Schooling for Girls

A major reason often given by parents for taking their daughters out of school is their fear that the girl will become involved with boys and thus 'spoil' her chances for a good marriage, thus doing damage to the family honour (*izzat*).

"Ladki log par nazar rakhna padta, colony ke ladke bekaar hai, koi unch neech ho gaya to badnami hoti hai" (We have to keep an eye on the girls. Boys are bad, and if something untowards happens there will be bad name.)

For some families the focus on protecting the girl and the family from *badnami* (bad reputation) is combined with the old-fashioned view that education for girls was an unnecessary waste of time and money.

"Mulila shikwun kaye karayche, pudhe ghar an mul baghayche." (What is the use of educating a girl? She only has to look after home and children.)

In the households where the mother is working, the school-aged girl is likely to be kept home to do household work and take care of younger siblings. Also, in some cases illness of the father or mother forced the girl to drop out of school. On the other hand, some of the mothers who worked told us that since they worked outside they felt insecure to leave an adolescent daughter at home alone, as school is a safer place and it also keeps the girls busy so they don't 'waste their time gossiping.'

Failure in school was another reason for parents to take their daughters out of school. If a girl failed in examination, the fathers sometimes took that as a signal that the girl should be taken out of school to help at home. Thus, we found cases of girls who wanted to continue in school, but the parental attitude was responsible for her dropping out of school. Some of the mothers said "what will be achieved by giving higher education to daughters. There are no jobs for them." Some of the mothers stated that the boys in the community did not have education beyond 10th standard, so there was no need for girls to get that much education. One of the common themes in this, and other communities, is that husbands should always have more education than their wives. Otherwise there will be conflict in the family.

There are, families where both the daughter and her mother are powerless to change the situation if the father had decided to take the girl out of school. However, real 'anti-schooling' attitudes are no longer common in the urban communities, and women are not nearly as powerless as they are reported to have been in earlier decades.

In group discussions with the mothers, it turned out that most of them felt that education up to the 8th or 10th standard was now essential for girls. There is a growing recognition that girls can get somewhat better employment if they have more education; and some mothers expressed the idea that girls need to know more about the world around them, and must be able to go out to employment if their marriage fails. Also they said that more families with boys are insisting that their sons marry educated girls. Some Muslim mothers told us:

"Aajkal ladke wale puchte, ladki padhi kya, Koran padhti kya, anpadh ho to pasand nahi karte." Now-a-days the boy's family asks if the girl is educated, and can read Koran. If not, the girl is rejected for marriage alliance.

Girls' Perceptions of Education

As pointed out above, some girls were bored with school, and dropped out as they could see no purpose in continuing. As might be expected, girls who did poorly in school were generally more likely to have negative feelings about continuing.

In some cases the girls (and boys) drop out of school because of prolonged absence from the school. We found that in one sector of the local community where most of the parents had their roots in Bihar, children were sometimes taken on extended visits to the village, because of family social obligations such as death of a relative, or a wedding. After an absence of several weeks from the school the girl may have had serious difficulties in "catching up" or adjusting to the situation, and thus did not return to school. In some cases school going children were taken to their natal village for harvesting or other agricultural work for long periods of time. Such absence were an additional cause for terminating their education.

Failure in school examination was a serious demotivating factor for girls. If a girl failed in school, and her friends promoted to the next standard, she was likely to drop out of school—not only due to the loss of contact with her friends, but also with the sense of shame due to failure.

During group discussions, we asked girls whether an increased level of education would increase their chances of getting better marriage partners, in better families. The girls replied that it hardly mattered. The boys and their families only appreciated a beautiful face, they said. On the other hand, some of the girls were quite clear that lack of education would bring serious hardships in marriage and other aspects of adult life. There were instances in which girls argued vehemently with their parents to allow them to continue studying. Some of the girls mentioned that they had seen the consequences of poor education in their older sisters or other relatives and friends, and they wanted to avoid those problems.

In our discussions with the girls, we found that many of them did not have clear and realistic perceptions of the connections between more education and getting higher employment. Some of the girls said they wanted to become doctors or lawyers, but they did not realize that such ambitions could only be fulfilled if they achieved excellent school records, and studied for requisite period.

The majority of the girls felt that the optimal level of education for them would be the 10th or 12th standard. They felt that women with that level of education would have higher status and somewhat better possibilities for satisfactory employment. We felt that the girls who had more education, communicated more freely and openly, compared with their less educated peers.

Aside from the attitudes towards schooling among the girls and their parents, it must be noted that the quality of education in the public schools, including the one in this community, left much to be desired. Some of the key informants, and several of the school girls, commented about the poor quality of teaching, and the lack of commitment on the part of the teachers. Both the school curriculum and the way it was taught were seen to be uninteresting to the girls.

Despite the various negative feelings about schooling, the changed attitudes about the importance of education are clearly evident. The most telling evidence of this change in attitudes is the fact that nearly 50 per cent of the girls in the 10th standard are attending tuition classes after school. Since the tuition classes cost the families approximately 100 rupees per month, this represents a major commitment for the girls' education that was largely absent a decade earlier.

In our key informant interview, the principal of the school emphasized the positive changes that had occurred in attitudes towards education over the past decade. Although according to her, about 10 per cent of the girls enrolled in 5th standard will not reach the 10th standard, the majority of families were quite supportive of the girls' education. Even though the great majority of the girls were from quite low socio-economic status, parents are willing to continue the education of girls even when they failed in their examinations. She told us that she had seen many cases in which the parents continued a girl's education even if she failed twice in a particular class.

A key informant (*anganwadi* worker) told us that not a single girl from her area had left school before tenth standard. She said that if a girl stops going to school due to family problems, the school teacher visits the parents and motivates them to continue their daughter's education. This has brought about a definite impact on the family life of girls, as none of the girls from her *anganwadi* area was married before the age of eighteen years. However, this was somewhat of an exceptional situation, as the area has a higher per cent of educated mothers.

Does Poor Education Affect Reproductive Health?

Education levels can be related to reproductive health and health care seeking in many ways. Women who are literate can, of course, learn a great deal about health issues from printed materials, and regardless of the meagre levels of health education usually found in the school system, some knowledge of reproductive health issues is gained by girls who continue in school. In addition, more education helps girls to absorb and understand materials presented in television broadcasts and other channels of information. Some studies of health-seeking behaviours have found that women with more education are more assertive and sure about asserting their rights to health care, and are listened to with more respect in their families.

Menarche and Menstruation

For young girls, menarche is the first major challenge and awakening, concerning her reproductive functioning. In India, as in many other countries, the onset of menstruation very often comes as a rude shock, as girls are usually not told anything about this basic physiological process beforehand (George, 1994; Narayan *et al.*, 2001).

Among the girls in our sample, the average age at menarche was 12.9 years, with a standard deviation of 1.8 years. However, 29 girls had menarche before 12 years and 45 reached menarche after 14 years of age. It was noted that mothers were anxious about the girls coming of age at the 'proper time,' and when it was delayed beyond 14 years they were quite worried. The attitudes and beliefs about these matters were strongly affected by neighbours and relatives. They discussed about who had come of age (*shahani jhali*) and thus contributed to the concerns of the parents. When we interacted with adolescent girls in school, some girls approached us and said "my friend has not yet got her menses, where she should go for consultation?" On other occasions, mothers of girls also approached us for medical advice. As is usual in the Indian context, most of the girls had not been told anything about menstruation before it happened to them.

Table 20.7: Source of Information Prior to Menarche

Source	*Number (%)*
Doctor	8 (2.5)
Teacher	64 (19.8)
Mother	29 (9.0)
Friends	9 (2.8)
Others	16 (5.0)
No knowledge	197 (61.0)
Total	**323**

Source: Field Investigation.

As we see in Table 20.7, most of the girls (61%) reported that they received no information about menstruation until it happened to them. At the school where most of the girls studied, the 7th standard girls are given information about reproductive health, including sessions on menstruation and hygiene through lectures and demonstrations. This is arranged by school authorities with a non-government organization. As seen in the table, half of those girls who received some information prior to their own menarche, received the information from school. Very few mothers told their daughters anything about it. When asked, some of the mothers said "why to tell, she will come to know when she gets it." They were clearly not comfortable in discussing the issue in the family situation.

Menarche was described by the girls as a traumatic, negative experience. The memory was vivid. Many of the girls said that they cried for many days at the time of menarche. A frequent statement was, "I was unable to understand what was happening to me. I was also scared to see blood on my clothes. It was so embarrassing." The mother was identified by the girls as a main provider of support, after that initial shock. They were pacified by their mothers and learned that *streechya jatila changla aste* (it is good for women). It was evident in the group discussions that the daughter's menarche was a happy event for a majority of the mothers. They felt happy that their daughter 'has grown up.' However they also felt insecure, as they expected that their daughter would now be troubled, teased or lured by boys, and hence there was an extra need to protect her.

A minority of the girls 36 per cent reported health problems with menstruation, of which the most common complaint was lower abdominal pain 30 per cent. In addition to the discomfort and embarrassment suffered by many of the girls, they found themselves subjected to a variety of ritual observances, as well as new restrictions on their freedom of movement outside their homes. Although the observance of menarche among different groups in Pune is not nearly as elaborate as among the Tamil people in south India (Narayan *et al.*, 2001), nonetheless some groups in Mangalwar Peth carried out modest puberty rituals. The girls reported that in some cases the rituals from their mothers' native villages were followed. Among migrants from Solapur and Karnataka, for example, the girls were asked to sit in the corner of the house, and were not allowed to touch things. Their mothers arranged small functions to which they invited women from the neighbourhood and close relations. The girl was given a new *sari* and (in some cases) *a salwar kurta*. The invitees also brought gifts and sweets. Some of the girls disliked the menarche rituals, as they felt embarrassed to be publicly labelled as 'available for marriage'. They said it made them feel like 'sex objects'.

Most of the girls said, they used home-made pads during their menstrual periods. However, 28 girls 9 per cent reported use of store-bought sanitary pads. It is interesting to note that in some schools of the area teaching about reproductive health, including menstrual hygiene, is presented by companies that market commercial sanitary pads. Most of the girls, however, could afford to buy those products.

Reproductive Functioning Among Married Adolescents

Out of our sample of 323 girls, 70 (21.6%) were married. About half of them stayed in joint families. Although all the girls and their mothers were aware that the legal age for marriage was 18 years, they were married before the legal age was reached. It appeared that in many cases the parents felt that it was their 'duty' to get their daughters married soon after menarche. The girls reported that they were not consulted about their choice, and they agreed that their parents were in the best position to decide about their future. On the other hand, practically all of the girls wished that they had not been married at such a young age. In 27 cases (39.5%) the girl was married to a consanguinal relative, such as a cross-cousin.

All the married girls said that they had no knowledge about sexual relations prior to their marriage. In many cases, once the marriage was fixed, young women and relatives in the neighbourhood gave the girl some hints about physical intimacies with the husband. One girl said her aunt told her, "give what your husband wants. All men want it." Another girl said that after coming to her husbands house, women folk explained her that she should not cry if her husband comes close to her [has sex with her], "otherwise the entire neighbourhood will rush to our house."

In the group discussions, the mothers said they felt too embarrassed to talk about sex and sexual relations with their daughters. Some said that the girls will learn all this automatically. They commented that "now-a-days girls are *shahani* (smart), they know all. They know about it from friends, neighbours and television shows."

Fertility Decisions and Contraceptive-use in Married Adolescent Girls

Among the 70 married adolescents, 30 had one child, 10 already had two children, and one girl had three children. Six of the girls were pregnant at the time of the interviews. As is typical of newly married couples, especially in low income families, there was no use of contraception before the birth of the first child, as the family expected the girl would become pregnant and produce offspring soon after marriage. However, all the women who already had a child wanted to use a contraceptive. Some of them said, they did not want another child, as one child is enough. Others wanted a second child only after a gap of five years. They said, they obtained information about contraceptives from the health centre and from the hospital. A few of them said that they had discussed contraceptive-use with their husbands, yet only 20 of the women had ever used any kind of contraceptives.

There were many obstacles to the use of contraceptives, even among girls who were aware of their availability and wanted to avoid pregnancy. In some cases, the mother-in-law was against any use of contraception. In many cases, the acute lack of privacy in the tiny one-room homes, made it very difficult for the girls to discuss and negotiate with their husbands about the need to limit or delay their pregnancies. Various negative attitudes about IUDs and oral contraceptive pills are quite prevalent in the community, and the women come to hear about individual negative experiences. For example some of the young women believed that oral contraceptive pills caused bleeding, 'drying up' of blood, and black circles around eyes.

Although the role of the mother-in-law was seen as negative regarding contraception, in many cases, one girl described that her mother-in-law took her to the health centre and helped her to obtain oral pills. Another described that her mother-in-law instructed her son to tell her that "you are very young, so let us postpone the birth of our second child."

In the quantitative survey we found that very few of the younger girls had ever heard of family planning methods (only 14 out of 83), and less than one-third (75 out of 240) of the older adolescents had any knowledge of contraception. This lack of knowledge about family planning methods, of course, places the unmarried girls at severe risk of unwanted pregnancies if they got involved in 'friendship' relationships with boys. Lack of adequate knowledge also contributes to the inability of the married girls to adopt appropriate family planning strategies, despite the fact that all the girls who already had children expressed a desire to avoid pregnancy.

Knowledge About HIV-AIDS

Among the younger girls, under age 15, 70 per cent had no knowledge of HIV-AIDs. The older girls were somewhat better informed, but only slightly more than half (56%) had some knowledge of HIV-AIDS, including the information that the disease is spread by sexual contact. 53 (22%) of the older girls had knowledge of all the main means of transmission of HIV, indicating that they had received some direct instruction about the AIDS epidemic. These data show that the girls are, on the whole, seriously lacking in vital information about sexually transmitted health problems.

Summary and Conclusions

The girls who dropped out of school were usually married early, many before the legal age of 18. They were more likely to be married into a family where the boy had less education, less income and a larger family. In those situations, the girls often totally depended on their mother-in-law for support and had to accept her decisions. The young daughter-in-law seldom had any money of her own, and her young husband (if he had any income) did not share his money with her, but gave part of his earnings to his mother.

A very serious gap in knowledge among under-educated girls is concerning reproductive processes in general, and specifically lack of awareness and understanding of contraceptive measures. In addition to lack of knowledge, the less educated girls, tended to show less confidence in asserting what information they had about family planning. As a result, the married teen-agers had dismal use of contraceptives, even although all the married girls with children expressed a desire to avoid pregnancy, at least for some years.

The lack of awareness about HIV-AIDS among many of the girls, especially the girls with less education, is particularly serious. Pune City is an area with relatively higher rates of HIV infections, and STIs are also prevalent in the urban population. Therefore, young girls need to learn about protecting themselves from sexually transmitted infections, in addition to avoiding unwanted pregnancy.

The positive side of this research is the evidence that a great many low income families in Pune City have adopted positive attitudes towards education for their girl children. The adoption of 8th to 10th standard as an educational goal for girls indicates very large changes in attitudes about schooling. That trend is further highlighted by the fact that approximately half of the girls in 10th standard are enrolled in tuition classes as well. These changes will, in time, help to raise the levels of awareness of reproductive health matters in the community, particularly among vulnerable young women. At the same time, the growth of interest in more education for the girl children calls for increased efforts to improve the school curriculum, including the presentation of practical reproductive and sexual health teaching. Those developments in the school curriculum are an essential part of the campaign to reduce the spread of HIV-AIDS and other sexually transmitted infections in our society.

Conclusion

This study examines the role of schooling at the public schools on reproductive health and other characteristics of adolescent girls in a low-income community in the Mangalwar Peth area of Pune City.

The data-gathering included both qualitative and quantitative methods. Key informant interviews were conducted with teachers, the school Principal, *anganwadi* workers, and NGO workers in the community. Focus group discussions were held with groups of adolescent girls, and groups of mothers. Essay 'contests' were held, in which the girls were asked to write about 'My ideas of a happy family' and 'Story of a young girl.' These methods gave us more insights into the ways in which the adolescent girls looked to their future in terms of marriage, family and other aspirations. A quantified survey was carried out with a total of 323 girls, which included all the adolescent girls, both in school and out of school.

Our data show that the girls have very weak knowledge and understanding of sexual and reproductive health matters, and they are, therefore, vulnerable to many health risks including unwanted pregnancies, sexually transmitted infections, and other problems. The adolescent girls who are already married are lacking in effective knowledge about contraception, although practically all of them wish to limit family size.

A very positive finding in our study is the clear evidence of increased value placed on education by the girls and their parents. It appears that the prevailing attitude in the community is that education at least up to 8th or 10th standard is regarded as a 'must,' for girls.

21

Reproductive Health Practices among Urban High Caste Women

AARTI NAGARKAR

Background

Reproductive health is concerned with the health of both men and women. Since women's reproductive role is more marked than men's, reproductive health becomes more important to women. Reproductive health is to a large extent a reflection of women's status and relative power. Reproductive health is influenced as much by biological factors as by cultural practices, customs, social structures, gender relations, educational and economic systems. While reproductive health refers to the physiological process of reproduction, it has been studied in their social, cultural, political and economic context to an extent, by reproductive health policy makers and other health care professionals. Many quantitative studies have proved useful in the understanding of the prevalence and incidence of discriminatory health practices affecting women, behavioural issues of concern, roles of each gender, thereby helping to identify significant areas of intervention. Understanding social-cultural practices of the population was necessary to improve the well-being of women. All such studies have taken place in the global context or in the context of policy framework. It was necessary for them to understand the links between culture, gender and reproductive health as they are vital for any intervention programme.

However, in this chapter, attempt has been made to offer observations concerning the antenatal and postnatal care practices and changes therein of a particular caste group in India. High caste, that is, Brahmin group is selected for the study since the concept of Sanskritization, put forth by M.N. Srinivas (1956) explains that lower caste groups aspire to rise high in the caste hierarchy by emulating customs, ideology, life-style, values etc. of higher caste people. However, culture is dynamic and often changes with various forces. Several studies document health behaviour and practices of lower caste groups but not particularly the high caste Brahmin women. Hence, present study attempts to present concepts and practices related to reproductive health among Brahmin women.

The present study uses anthropological perspective to understand the practices and influence of culture and cultural change on the reproductive health practices of women belonging to higher caste. The study is grounded in Ruth Benedict's theory (1934) on development of cultural pattern and its reinforcement through cultural constraints. "These patterns are learned and get reflected in behaviour as cultural rule. When members differ from these rules or norms as a response to changed situation, they have individual reasons for that. These reasons become a range of acceptable behaviour in a cultural pattern within that social situation." In the present research, study of personality, as unfolded through life histories, facilitated the understanding of influence of primary groups (family, kinship), cultural processes (enculturation, modernization) and interaction between the two. Life histories have been used to draw broader correlation and generalization about the specific culture of the members.

Abraham Kardiner and Linton (1956) offered an approach, which looked at individual members within a society and then compared the traits of these members in order to achieve a basic personality for each culture. The notion of basic personality structure places a focal point of culture integration as common denominator of the personalities of people who participate in culture. It also attempted to comprehend the causal relationship between culture and personality (Toren, 1996:144-5).

The present chapter has focused on the practices related to antenatal care and post-natal care and relate them with the cultural pattern of reproductive health behaviour among high caste Hindu women.

Methods

Data collection were done in the city of Pune in Maharashtra, India. The purposive sample was drawn from the predominant Brahmin locations from the research site. Life histories were collected from twenty six respondents. The data collection focused on cultural concepts and practices with reference to pregnancy, delivery and post-partum care and contraception in their social context. The life histories were constructed based on the narratives obtained through repeated interviews with the selected respondents and their relatives. They were selected on the basis of their willingness to participate in the study as well as those who fulfilled the inclusion criteria. Analysis of life histories proved helpful to comprehend the entire issue of reproductive health behaviour and ascertain changes therein, in the context of culture. The analysis of data, on *a priori* themes, helped in comprehending interplay between culture and human action to reveal the cultural patterns of behaviour.

Findings

The following description is based on the 'most observed' pattern of behaviour based on the analysis of the data.

In the context of present study, concepts and practices related to pregnancy have included methods of identification of pregnancy, ideas about foetal growth and all those customs and norms prescribed by culture regarding diet, behaviour and reasoning behind each one of them.

Antenatal Care

Symptoms like vomiting, fatigue, heaviness, increase in sleep, and more importantly missed menstrual cycle were considered as identification symptoms. Young respondents, after recognition of symptoms, confirmed pregnancy by visiting the doctor. Some of the common conditions observed during pregnancy were very well recognized and categorized as early or late conditions and were linked with the stages of foetal development. Nausea, vomiting were early symptoms while acidity, exhaustion, weakness, in the last trimester were due to the fast rate of growth in foetus at that time. Apart from fetal growth and full term pregnancy, safe and normal delivery were some of the major concerns expressed during pregnancy. They feared cesarean delivery because of the side effects like obesity, functional decline and sometimes other complications involving bladder etc. Therefore, care during pregnancy was considered as important objective of the mother.

Practices Observed for Healthy Pregnancy

All cultures have certain beliefs about what facilitates a healthy pregnancy and its outcome. These practices have continued by women irrespective of their awareness about modern practices. Most of the practices are associated with pregnancy aimed at welfare of foetus and the woman. In the context of present study, care during pregnancy includes norms pertaining to food and behaviour and certain rituals.

A ritual called *athangul* is performed during 8th month of pregnancy. The ritual had significance in the life of a family for two reasons; its perceived role in determining sex of a foetus, especially to beget a son and for the protection of the unborn child.

All respondents expressed desire to have healthy pregnancy as per the beliefs and practices of their culture. They mentioned that the said traditional prescriptions and proscriptions have been necessary for normal and easy delivery. It has been observed that respondents follow many ayurvedic concepts like 'heavy and light' food, 'hot and cold' food. As a general rule 'light and cold' food was preferred in pregnancy while 'hot and heavy' food was avoided. Chilly, spicy, stale and non-vegetarian food, eggs, papaya, pineapple, sesame, mango, dates, were avoided because these foods generate heat in the body, which might lead to an abortion. While 'cold and light' food items like curd, buttermilk, butter, warm milk, rice, sweet fruits, apples, green leafy vegetables, were consumed during pregnancy. The term 'light' meant those foods, which were easy to digest and helpful in easy bowel movement. Prescription and proscriptions of various foods were for averting miscarriage, abortion and for facilitating optimal foetal growth. These practices were adopted as recommended and reinforced by kin, especially elder female members of the family, peers, and were adopted as the way of life.

The behavioural restrictions during pregnancy were accepted and followed dutifully for the sake of welfare of a foetus. The normative pattern included avoiding the lifting of heavy objects, work that increases weariness, avoid using red coloured clothes as these clothes might attract evil eye, avoid excess sleep and emotions such as anger, jealousy etc. Oil massage was also proscribed, as also avoiding cutting, cooking, and other such practices during solar eclipse, since these practices in some way were believed to affect physical and mental growth of the foetus.

Post Partum Care

Post-partum period, according to the respondents, was 45 days. All restrictions, prescriptions were followed faithfully for the minimum period of one and quarter of a month. The end of the period was often marked by a visit to the temple of a deity. During that period, traditional norms about food, and behaviour were reportedly observed. During this period, complete rest, massage and bath, consumption of special foods (listed in

Table 21.1) and breastfeeding were focused activities. Compliance with these food and behavioural norms were expected to avoid lactation and health related complications such as lack of breast milk, stomach ache etc. affecting the baby and the mother.

The concept and practices of postnatal care were reported to have modified in terms of addition of regular medical check-up in the clinics, use of nutrition supplements, and no restrictions on movement.

Practices Observed for Health during Post-Natal Period

Various norms surrounding diet were reported during in-depth interviews. Energy dense food items were prescribed and consumed. The prescribed staple diet during post-natal period was milk and milk products, rice, *moongdal, chapati* or *bhakari*. The special food items were prepared using some of the perceived 'hot' foods like fenugreek seeds, garden cress, acacia gum, saffron, almonds, dry dates powder, clarified butter, poppy seeds etc. These special preparations were considered as essential to gain strength and improve lactation. These items and their properties are listed in Table 21.1. Vegetables like brinjal, potato, beans were avoided because they result in stomach ache and flatulence in infants. Certain milk products like curds was avoided being 'cold' and many other 'heavy' items like fried foods, preparations of horse gram flour avoided to prevent diarrhoea, indigestion and other digestive system related problems. It was believed that the foods consumed by mother transformed into breast milk. The breast milk carries the properties of foods to infant. Hence lactating mother is advised to follow these norms. The cognitive thought process behind the prescription re-establishes the concerns for the newborn and highlight the importance placed on the reproductive role of the mother.

As illustrated in Table 21.2, numerous behavioural restrictions were imposed during post-partum period. Objectives of the post-natal behavioural restrictions were replenishing lost energy, strength and nourishment of an infant. It is believed that the labour pains and the process of delivery of a baby takes away energy from organs and taking care of each body part is necessary for better health in middle and old age. Respondents reported that they were often advised to take complete rest and not allowed to move out of their room except occasionally. Earlier, they were restricted to keep mother and baby away from evil eye and any contagion that other people might transmit during interaction. Oil massage and use of soft bed were prescribed to reduce muscular pain. Maintaining

Table 21.1: Traditional Food and Their Perceived Utility during Post-Partum Period

Food Item English names	*Food items Marathi names*	*Period of supplementation*	*Perceived benefit*
Ligusticum Trachyspermum	*Owa*	One and quarter month	Relieves stomach pain, Helps in digestion
Almond	*Badam*	One and quarter month	Galactogogue, strength
Beatle leaf	*Pan*	One and quarter month	Improves Digestion, Rich source of calcium for bone health
Clove	*Lavang*	One and quarter month	Usually given with betel leaf to alleviate *kapha*. Antiseptic
Black Pepper	*Miri*	Two weeks	To alleviate *vata*. Useful in Dyspepsia
Acacia Gum	*Dinka*	One and quarter month	Galactogogue Strength, removes waist pain, wound healer, useful in uterus contraction
Garden cress	*Ahliv*	One and quarter month	Galactogogue Gaining strength and energy
Saffron	*Keshar*	One and quarter month	It helps in uterine problems, normal menstruation, intestinal antiseptic, alleviates *kapha* and *vata*.
Poppy seeds	*Khaskhas*	First seven days	Generates heat, improves milk secretion, useful for lactation
Dry Dates	*kharik*	One and quarter month	Strength to reproductive organs, useful in menstrual regulation
Dry ginger	*Suntha*	One and quarter month	Protects infant from cold, Improves digestion, useful in gastric pain
Dry coconut	*Khobra*	One and quarter month	Improves lactation, energy
Clarified butter	*Ghee*	Three months	Energy, strength essential fatty acids helps to make hormones needed for breastfeeding

(*Contd.*)

Table 21.1: *(Contd.)*

Food Item English names	*Food items Marathi names*	*Period of supplementation*	*Perceived benefit*
Asparagus Racemosus	*Shatavari*	During lactation	Galactagogue, and strength
Fenugreek seeds	*Methi beej*	One and quarter month	Galactagogue, avoids inflammation, heals wounds, used in dyspepsia
Asafetida	*Hinga*	Daily	Relieves stomach pain
Jaggary	*Gul*	One and quarter month	Strength, warmth, useful for regaining waist strength
Garlic (chatuny)	*Jasun*	Three months	Antiseptic, removes infection, useful in respiratory problems
Milk	*Dudh*	Three months	Improves milk secretion
Vermicelli	*Shevai*	One and quarter month	Soft, light for digestion
Millets	*Kulith*	One and quarter month	Strength, energy
Cereals	*Bajra*	Initial 2 weeks	Easy to digest, source of energy
Rice (and ghee)	*Tandul*	Everyday in both meals	Easy to digest, soft and good for health
Semolina	*Rava*	Initial two weeks	Energy, strength

body temperature using warm clothes, covering ears, feet was also considered necessary. The same concept was reinterpreted in terms of modern life context and respondents were advised to avoid watching television, video, and reading or straining eyes, needlessly. Hot water bath, use of warm clothes, has been deliberately suggested since they help in alleviating *vaat*. Formation of *vaat* was considered harmful because it leads to health problems later on in life. Use of fomentation was indicated since it helps in contraction of uterus, and acts as a sanitizer. Here again the indication of reinterpretation of practices according to the changed context has been seen.

Table 21.2: Behavioural Norms Observed during Post Natal Period

Behavioural Norms	*Reasons*
Rest	To regain strength and lost energy
Oil Massage	Relieves muscular pain
Hot water bath	Alleviate formation of *vata*
Hot Fomentation	Helps in contraction of Uterus, disinfectant
Use of warm clothes	Alleviate formation of *vata*
Use of Soft Bed	Comfortable and relaxing
Restriction on mobility	To avoid evil eye and infection
Avoid visitors	To avoid evil eye and infection
Avoid watching TV, reading	To avoid strain on organs

There have been exceptions to these norms. Some respondents started going out before completion of one and quarter of a month, for various reasons. One of the reasons was medical emergency, shopping for the baby or for oneself, and some other familial reasons. The difference in the pattern of behaviour was also seen in the nuclear and extended type of family. Degree of adherence to these practices was related to the seasonal variation. Those who delivered in summer reported to have avoided fomentation, oil massage, because those practices created health problems like boils, rash on the skin etc. Some of them consulted medical professionals who advised them to stop the traditional practices to avoid complications.

Discussion

The traditional practices and the changes therein can be looked in the context of historical processes and development in the caste group. The caste group, Brahmin, was exposed to various processes of change like Westernization, modernization, for a long period of time. Changes in the role of women with increased levels of education and participation in the family economy made it necessary for women to adopt new lifestyle and accept changes. The traditional practices associated with antenatal and post-natal period promoting their health and efficiency as an active member of the family were retained. Their health carried a functional value for them. At the same time, due to small family norms, babies became precious. The thought that children should not die or suffer from any handicap prompted them to adopt all those practices, which promote, maintain and restore health. Hence, the time tested traditional practices to promote and maintain health were accepted, obediently.

Many practices related to behaviour, food prescriptions and proscriptions are also found in the traditional Ayurveda texts. This is what Redfield referred to as 'great' and 'little' tradition, two traditions being interdependent they have long interacted with each other and continue to do so (Redfield, 1956:72). Although respondents were unable to explain the exact mechanism by which these food items respond in the body or bring adverse health outcome, they were aware of the practices and have also followed them. The interaction between little and great traditions continued although changes in the diet pattern and life style has changed. The astounding amount of similarity with the great tradition can be explained further. Knowledge regarding health was learnt through the process of enculturation and socialization. Traditionally, only Brahmins had access to knowledge of Indian traditional medicine, Ayurveda, which is the 'great tradition' of Indian medicine enshrined in the Vedic texts, and written in the scholastic, classical language. The practices related to health were followed for centuries; they are transmitted from one generation to next in the process of enculturation. The respondents adopted those practices, which they thought useful for their health as well as for the health of their infants.

We also observed changes in the traditional concepts with the changing context. The obstetric care, described in Ayurveda has six objectives; they are wound healing, gaining strength and energy, alleviation of *vaat*, increase in appetite, increase in lactation, and health of uterus. In the popular culture, lactation holds the central position and all practices and reinterpretation are in terms of 'good' or 'bad' for lactation.

According to Ayurveda, the post-natal care was based on the concept that period is divided into three stages, the first stage of ten days after delivery, second up to one and half month and last till resumption of menstruation. It is believed that needs of the women in these three stages differ considerably, hence different norms with regard to food and behaviour are prescribed. During first stage the lady is referred as *vrani*, wounded, so foods that promote healing of a wound were prescribed. In the second stage lactation and contraction of uterus were considered as main goals. No such restrictions are put forth in the third stage which, may vary from 6 months to 18 months.

Ayurveda prescribes certain behavioural and food restrictions because it is believed that woman who had given birth have lot of 'emptiness' in her body because of expulsion of the foetus and placenta. Uterus takes time to regain its own size. According to Ayurveda, balance of *tridosha,* is necessary to maintain health. Emptiness provides space for *vaat*. Secondly, foods, which produce *vaat,* may vitiate it to cause various health problems. It is further mentioned that diseases occurred during postnatal period, are not easy to cure due to lack of strength (*dhatukshaya*) in the body, and weakness (*daurbalya*). Hence, very strict code of food is to be observed.

The obstetric care, described in Ayurveda has six objectives; they are wound healing, gaining strength and energy, alleviation of *vaat*, increase in appetite, increase in lactation, and health of vagina and uterus. Here one finds that the emphasis is given more on the women's health while in popular culture lactation was emphasized.

Use of modern medicine and inclusion of modern medicine practices in the routine antenatal and post-natal care practices was observed extensively. One way of interpretation of the use of combination of the practices (traditional and modern) was because modern care was unable to offer alternative to the traditional practices (like oil massage, special diet etc.) which they believed to have positive impact on the health of the mother and child. However, there were certain modifications to suit the present requirements. In some cases, the modern scientific explanation behind the practices was sought and modifications were done using technologically advanced methods. Special preparations like clarified butter, dates, *ahliv* and *dinka laddus* were consumed not as a part of the diet but as the medicine. These food items were often preferred over synthetic nutrition supplementation. The contradictory prescriptions between modern care and traditions confused respondents, which led to discontinuation of certain practices. However, many respondents adhered to the traditional practices because of the perceived advantages. According to them the traditional practices were personalized, emotionally gratifying.

Researcher also observed contradictory behaviour. Those who were following traditional practices very dutifully, also consulted modern medicine for any trivial health problem. Such contradiction could be perhaps because the 'causation of disease' is a matter of attitude and ideas, which is a hard core of cultural philosophy. While action/behaviour that is treatment, is a matter of soft core of culture. Because health is an aspect of culture, the change in soft core like seeking modern services was easier as compared to the change in ideas, attitude. Secondly, traditional practices were followed because of perceived positive health effect and modern curative services were utilized because of the value placed on the restoration of health of women and children.

Health is an aspect of culture and hence is a matter of change with the change in the culture. Elements or traits, which make up cultural pattern, are not just a random assortment of customs. There exists coherence and a kind of a specific relationship between all aspects of culture. They function in a desired orientation in the cultural system. Health, like economic, social and political aspects, too, is an aspect of culture. Health has its own philosophy or identity as a uniform unit, however, they all show some congruity to have common pattern. This is integration of culture; which shapes its members' personality, attitudes and ultimately behaviour. Reproductive health behaviour, thus, can be considered as a result of enculturation process, which unconsciously drives individual to perform conformingly as a member of the culture. The individual range of conscious acceptance or rejection of certain aspects of the culture expands and this may induce culture change.

22

Reproductive Health Issues of Sex Workers

SUSHMITA BHATTACHARYA AND GEETA PARDESHI

Introduction

Reproductive health issues of sex workers are given very little thought in any of the health programmes or services. Some efforts by government and non-government organisations to provide medical care or welfare services are insufficient and inefficient.

The HIV-AIDS epidemic in India has brought about a concentrated focus on sex workers as major partners in the spread of infection. Many government and non-government programmes are devoted to the promotion of condom availability and use in red light areas, and raising awareness of HIV-AIDS prevention among sex workers and their clients. Previously the sex workers were a hidden sub-population that seldom drew any public attention. However, the past few years have seen a wide range of media publicity concerning sex worker organizations in Kolkata, Kerala and elsewhere; harassment of sex workers by police and others, and many related topics (*cf.* AIDS-India Forum 2003, 2004; BBC 2003; Deutsche Presse Agentur 2002). On the other hand, very little attention has been paid to the health status and health needs of sex workers. Except for the focus on HIV prevention through condom use, the sex workers, whether in brothels or other venues, remain a marginalized population in terms of health care, including reproductive health.

Since sex workers have children, they have needs in relation to contraception, antenatal care, child birth and post-partum services. These issues are given very little attention in any of the health programmes or services. Sex workers are more vulnerable to sexually transmitted diseases (STDs) and HIV-AIDS, yet little is known about their contraceptive use and treatment seeking behaviours. A high prevalence of HIV amongst sex workers is reported in many places of the country, but the illness behaviour, care seeking and coping processes are not a focus of the various studies.

Present study explored the various reproductive health issues of brothel based sex workers in a red light area of Pune City. A cross-sectional study was carried out with purposive sampling of brothel based sex workers. 60 sex workers were interviewed with the help of semi-structured interview schedule, out of which 25 were *devdasi* from Karnataka, 20 women were from Nepal and the remaining 15 from various other states. Many of the *non-devdasis* were completely alienated from their families, while the *devdasis* maintained good relationships with their parents and other relatives in their home villages.

Around 40-50 per cent of their income comes back to them, which they spend to meet daily needs, addiction and buying condom. Out of 60 respondents, 49 had experienced one or more pregnancies. They reported a total of 102 pregnancies of which 59 resulted in live births 57.84 per cent. Of these, 38 live births occurred in relation to sex work, while 21 births occurred in a marital relationship outside of sex work. Most of those pregnancies outside of sex work occurred before the woman entered into the profession. Many of them received some antenatal care, which consisted of two or three visits to the doctor for check-ups, injection of tetanus toxoid and some tablets or tonics. On an average they continued the sex work till the fifth month of pregnancy. Pregnant sex workers suffered from frequent morbidities due to poor environment, poor nutrition, and neglect. The proportion of hospital deliveries was more in cases where the pregnancy resulted from sexual contact with customers. The *devdasis* in most cases (13/25) went back to their home villages and were helped by their mothers. Eight out of 40 deliveries were caesarian sections. The costs of pregnancy ranged between Rs. 1000 to Rs. 1500 for normal vaginal delivery. The women who had caesarian section had to spend between Rs. 10,000 to Rs. 20,000. Five sex workers gave histories of postnatal complications.

33 of these pregnancies (45.28%) ended in induced abortions. A majority of the abortions, (30%) were in the first trimester. Most of the abortions were conducted in the local private hospitals. 8 women reported that they had undergone two or more abortions. Out of 33 MTPs, in four instances, post-abortion complications were recorded. The cost varied from hospital to hospital, ranging from Rs. 250 to Rs. 1500 for first trimester MTP.

Nearly, 27 (45%) respondents reported ever having complaints of vaginal discharge and 26 (43.6%) respondents had complaints of ever suffering from burning micturition and had pain in the lower abdomen. The respondents have many misconceptions regarding the cause and effect of STDs. They do seek treatment from the local health services. Majority of the sex workers suffered from anaemia because of poor diet, poor antenatal care and high incidence of infections due to poor sanitation and personal hygiene. More than half, (32%) sex workers consumed less than 60 per cent of the standard dietary allowance.

We found that the sex workers are seriously lacking in information and practices regarding contraception, and they have many problems with unwanted pregnancies, including repeat abortions, problems in child birth, and related matters. As expected, the women have a high general awareness of the risks of HIV infections, and they profess to 100 per cent condom use. However, on probing, condom use is found to be less than 100 per cent due to a number of circumstances, including special cases such as 'regular partners,' with whom condom use is much less. Symptoms of possible STIs are common among the sex workers, for which they generally seek treatment from the private practitioners in the area.

Our study shows that there are major gaps in the reproductive health knowledge and practices among the brothel sex workers, and there is acute need for improved programmes to provide better general health services, including more effective counselling.

Objectives of the Study

This study is an exploration of the reproductive health needs and problems among sex workers in a brothel area of Pune City. Our other study (given in this book as Chapter 5) has examined the general situations and practices of sex workers in the brothels, with particular reference to condom use by different kinds of clients and partners. In that study we found that, despite the widespread awareness of condom use, there were still many situations in which condoms were not used, particularly with the 'regular partners' of the sex workers. We also found evidence of serious gaps in reproductive health care of the sex workers.

Objectives of the Study

- To explore the various reproductive health issues among brothel based sex workers in Pune City.
- To learn about the sex workers' awareness of contraception, STDs and HIV-AIDS.

- To understand the reproductive behaviours of the sex workers, including information about wanted and unwanted pregnancies, abortions, childbirth, and care-seeking for reproductive problems.

Various studies have reported that sex workers are mostly illiterate, and have very little power to protect themselves from various health problems and exploitation (*cf.* Nag, 1996). In our Brothel study, we found that the brothels in Pune City could be divided into two categories, middle level and lower level, on the basis of the furnishings, types of clients, and usual costs per sexual services. In middle level brothels, sex workers have a cleaner environment and earn better. There are brothels where a particular linguistic group, or sex workers from a particular region, are in the majority. In some cases, these ethnic minority sex workers face special problems, as they often have little ability to communicate with the general social environment in which they are living.

In the past few years, there have been major efforts by governmental and non-government organizations to promote awareness about STDs and HIV-AIDS, and to promote condom use in the brothels. Treatment facilities for STDs are available in the Municipal Corporation dispensary located near the red light area. Also, there are many private practitioners in the vicinity of the brothels that provide treatment for reproductive health problems, as well as other health care services.

Research Design and Data-Gathering Methods

Data in this study were gathered through in-depth interviews with an opportunistic sample of 60 sex workers, recruited from several different areas of the brothel district in the city. We tried to get a wide variation in the background characteristics of the informants, as well as variation in the types of brothels where they work. In depth interviews were aided by use of pictures to elicit answers in sensitive areas of inquiry, and we used a '*bindi* technique' to try to get accurate information on numbers of recent clients, and the specifics of condom use and non-use.

At the beginning of this research we had meetings with a prominent NGO leader, who is chairperson of the *Akhil Budhwarpeth Devdasi Sangatana* NGO, and who has been working in the area for over a decade. The NGO works mainly for the welfare of sex workers in the areas of condom promotion, awareness, as well as guidance for health care. This NGO has 10 peer workers who have had previous experience of sex work but presently are not in sex business. These peers were sensitized about the objectives and nature of our study, and they helped us in recruiting sex workers to be interviewed. Although our research team was somewhat known too many of the brothels due to our previous research, we found it useful to take the help of the NGO peer workers for approaching the sex workers for interviews. In many cases, both the sex workers and their *gharwalis* (brothel-keepers) were suspicious of our research, but they trusted the NGO workers.

The in-depth interviews were conducted by two research workers (principal investigator and co-investigator), both female doctors. After consultation, it was decided to hold the interviews in a room provided by the NGO, which was located in the brothel area. Researchers and the NGO peer workers visited the various brothel houses and communicated the purpose and nature of the proposed study to the brothel owners and sex workers. We included sex workers from five different locations in the brothel area. We tried to include sex workers of different age groups, different linguistic groups, different states of origin and different types of brothel. All sex workers willing to participate were included in the study. We did not, however, include any 'floating' sex workers who do not reside permanently in the brothels, and we also excluded the managers or *gharwalis.* Interviews were conducted in the language preferred by individual sex workers. As the researchers speak Marathi, Hindi and Kannada, we asked the sex workers which of these three languages they preferred. The interviews generally lasted about one hour. Interviews were conducted between 11:30 am and 1:30 pm, as the sex workers told us that after 2:00 pm they take their afternoon rest.

A total of 60 sex workers were interviewed, 25 were from Karnataka, 20 women were from Nepal and the remaining 15 categorized as 'others'. Seven were Marathi, five from Andhra Pradesh, one from Goa, one from West Bengal and one was from the Lambani migratory ethnic group. We used a semi-structured interview format to collect the data. Information regarding age, education, native place, parental support, marital status, habits were collected. Information about dietary patterns was collected, including cooking practices, expenditures on food, and other information about daily activities. Our questions also probed about their awareness of contraceptives and contraceptive practices. Information about their awareness and perception, treatment seeking practices were collected in relation to STDs, and other conditions/diseases like tuberculosis, jaundice, skin infections and other such morbidities.

It was observed that the respondents were hesitant to answer direct questions, so we used sets of picture cards to elicit some types of information. For example, for a question concerning contraception, we prepared a card depicting a woman standing by the side of a man and put the question in this form: "This is a woman, Kavitha, from this area, and she comes to you for advice that she does not want a baby. What will you advise so that she can avoid pregnancy?" Picture cards were also used to ask questions such as: "If a woman is HIV positive, can her baby get infection, and if yes, then "what in your opinion should be the action in such a situation?"

We used a new approach, which we referred to as the *Bindi* technique, to collect information about the numbers of clients, and condom use. We first asked each woman to tell how many clients she had on the previous day (or latest day of sex work) and condoms used, and we recorded her answer. Subsequently, we gave her a card approximately 4 inches by 5 inches, and gave her two packets of red *bindis* and two packets of maroon coloured *bindis*. We asked her to stick one *bindi* for one client and accordingly explained that the total number of *bindis* should be equal to total number of clients. We asked her to place a red *bindi* if the client used a condom during sexual contact and a maroon coloured *bindi* if he did not. She was left alone and after sticking the *bindi* on the card, she was asked to put the card in a closed box. The main purpose was to help her to overcome inhibitions related to verbal questioning and minimize social desirability bias in relation to reporting of risk behaviours.

Reproductive history was taken using a 'time line method,' with menarche as the starting point (on the paper) and child births as anchor points. Detailed notes were taken during each interview. We also used a tape recorder for group discussions and interviews with some key informants.

The Characteristics of the Sex Workers

The data in Table 22.1 show that the median age of our respondents was approximately 30 years. The majority of the Nepali and the 'other' category of sex workers reported themselves to be married, whereas the women from Karnataka, most of whom were *devdasis,* were mostly unmarried. They were also older than the other two 'ethnic' categories, as they were mostly in their thirties.

The Karnataka group had the highest number of unmarried women because 16 of them were *devdasis.* 34 women were married, many of

Table 22.1: Social and Demographic Characteristics of the Sex Workers

Characteristics	*Ethnic Category*			
	Karnataka *N* = 25	*Nepali* *N* = 20	*Others* *N* = 15	*Total* *N* = 60
Age (years)				
Less than 20	0	1	1	2
20 to 29	9	12	7	28
30 to 39	16	6	6	28
40 or above	0	1	1	2
Marital Status				
Ever married	7	16	11	34
Unmarried	18	4	4	26
Length of stay in Pune brothel (years)				
Less than 5	4	8	6	18
5-10	9	9	5	23
More than 10	12	3	4	19
Median Age at entry to sex work (years)	20	19.5	19	19

Source: Field Investigation.

them at a very young age, at about 12 or 13 years. These women were mostly deserted by their husbands, had been widowed, or they left their conjugal home because of severe oppression or violence. A majority of the sex workers had been in the brothels for more than five years.

All except three women were illiterate. The three said that they had gone to school for two to three years.

Reasons for Entering Sex Work

Table 22.2 shows that the largest category of explanations was a failed marriage, often involving alcohol use and serious physical abuse by the (former) husband. The other large category was the special situation of the *devdasis*. Only seven women reported that they had been 'trafficked'- lured or abducted into sex work. Even among the Nepali women, only four women said they were trafficked.

The Special Situation of the *Devdasis*

The *devdasis* in our sample are a special category, as they represent the continuation of the centuries old tradition of dedicating young girls to

Table 22.2: Explanations Concerning Entry to Sex Work

	Karnataka (N = 25)	*Nepali (N = 20)*	*Others (N = 15)*	*Total (N = 60)*
Devdasis	16	0	1	17
Lack of economic support	3	4	2	9
Unhappy marital relationship	4	12	6	22
Lured/Abducted	1	4	2	7
Widowed	0	0	3	3
Rape Victim	1	0	1	2

Source: Field Investigation.

the service of the gods. As per tradition *devdasis* were mainly attached to major temples, where they 'attended gods' as persons, danced and sang before them, and like the servants of an earthly kind, bestowed sexual favours on the courtiers whom he favoured—in this case, male worshippers who paid generous fees to the temple (Nag, 1996:53). The *devdasi* system is now much diminished, as the state governments have enacted laws forbidding the dedication of girls to the gods in this manner. However, in some communities, in some castes, the tradition still continues, particularly in northern Karnataka. In certain families, selected girls are dedicated to the goddess, *Yellama,* through a special ritual. When the girl comes of age the ideal is that she develops a stable relationship with a man from the same or neighbouring village, who then supports her and her family. The relationship with a man is socially and ritually recognized, but is not considered 'marriage'. In some cases girls are offered to the god or goddess to overcome some evil influence, or as an offering in the case of serious illness.

In the drought-prone, poverty-stricken villages in parts of northern Karnataka the *devdasis* seldom find any stable relationships with males, so often their only recourse is to resort to sex work. The *devdasis* are often recruited to the brothels of Mumbai, Pune and other cities. Compared to other sex workers, they are much less stigmatized, and they usually maintain good relationships with their natal families and home villages. In times of need, particularly in child birth, the *devdasis* could return to their families for support, and their older children were generally taken care of by their family members.

Unlike the other sex workers, *devdasis* can go out and beg to augment their income. Some of the *devdasis* beg for food and money on their special days, which are Tuesdays and Fridays. They wear a symbol referred to as a *moti*, which is hung on a thread around the neck, identifying their special status as 'married to the God'. They were referred to as *Jogtin* or as women with *moti* in the brothel area.

Contraception—Awareness, Use and Problems

When we asked the women about their knowledge of contraception, some of them replied that they need not know about other contraceptives, as "we won't get pregnant because we are always using condoms." All of the women were aware of the use of condoms for avoiding pregnancy.

However, the sex workers were not very well informed about other methods of birth control, and they were also shy to discuss these matters. To overcome their shyness we introduced the topic using a picture card, about which we asked them:

> "Suppose the woman seen in this card is a sex worker. She gets many customers. What she should do if she does not wish to become pregnant?"

In addition to the mention of condoms, a few women mentioned that they knew someone from their brothel who was taking small pills, white in colour, which were available in medical shops, clearly referring to oral contraceptive pills. However, we quickly found that, other than condoms, very few of the 60 respondents had used any other temporary methods of contraception.

Table 22.3: Use of Contraceptives (ever used)

Contraceptive Techniques	*Ethnic Category*			
	Karnataka N = 25	*Nepali N = 20*	*Others N = 15*	*Total N = 60*
Oral Pills	8	1	2	11
IUD	2	0	0	2
Tubectomy	6	0	4	10
Total	**16**	**1**	**6**	**23**

Source: Field Investigation.

Thirty one women knew about oral contraceptives. They could identify the packet of oral pills, but only 11 (mainly from Karnataka) said that they had ever used them. Three women said, they were using them. One of the respondents stopped oral pills because her friend told her that it could cause cancer and one discontinued its use as she had excessive menstrual bleeding. Many of the women appeared to believe that taking an oral pill gave protection for that day, just as a condom protects for a single act.

The intrauterine device (copper T) had been used by two women at some time in the past. Seven women said that they heard about *Tambi* (local name for copper T) or they knew that some women got a spring fitted in uterus. Both the women who had used a copper T had it removed within two to three months, as they had excessive menstrual bleeding. Intra-uterine devices are generally not recommended for use by women involved in multi-partner sexual relations.

A total of ten women had undergone a tubectomy operation. Six of them were from Karnataka and four belonged to the 'other' category. Only one Nepali sex worker had ever used any kind of contraceptive. None had undergone tubectomy. All the women with tubectomies said they themselves had decided about the operation. Some of them had to go against their mothers' wishes when they decided to undergo tubectomy, having only a single child, or being without a male child.

Condom Use

Condom use is, of course, a central issue in the brothels, primarily for the prevention of transmission of HIV and other sexually transmitted infections. However, most of the sex workers are aware that fully consistent condom use would also protect them from unwanted pregnancies. All the 60 study respondents mentioned rather eagerly that they used condoms regularly. A number of reasons were given for using condoms. A majority of the women overtly or covertly mentioned AIDS. A few, however, could not name the disease. Some of the women said they used condoms to save their lives (*jaan bachna hai to logao, sharir accha rehta hai)* and to prevent sexually transmitted diseases. A few of them had misconceptions regarding the role of condoms, thinking that they could also prevent the spread of cough, cold, tuberculosis and complaints such as pains in the limbs.

Some respondents said that they used condoms with every client. They said that they return the money and drive away customers if they refuse to use condoms. Many said they would not take customers without condoms even if lakhs of rupees were offered (*Hazar devo, lakh devo, bin nirodh kunalach baswat nahi*).

When asked about the sources of condoms, some women said they get them free of cost, but others said they have to buy them. Condoms are available free of cost from the government operated local centres. Many sex workers said they buy condoms from the local NGO peer workers. They buy a red box that contains 20 packets of condoms, which costs 50 rupees. Some brothel owners buy the boxes and sell the condoms to the girls as and when they need them. Other women get condoms from the van operated by an NGO, which comes regularly to the area and distributes condoms free of cost. Three to five packets of ten condoms are given every alternate day. In some cases the women have to buy condoms from nearby shops, when government supply falls short, or when better quality condoms are needed. One woman said she asks her customers to get the condoms.

The *gharwali* seems to play an important role in condom use. Some *gharwalis* were reported to be strict regarding condom use, while others were less interested. In majority of the cases, the brothel owner advises the women to use condoms and if the customer refuses to use condoms she forces him to go away. We enquired with a sex worker as to how a *gharwali* comes to know whether a condom is being used or not. She answered:

> "We take condoms from the boxes in the outer room. If we do not take the condoms and yet entertain a customer, the *gharwali* immediately suspects that condoms are not being used and questions us about it."

The commonest condoms were *Nirodh* (government produced). Durex and Kohinoor were other names mentioned by respondents. Nearly all respondents said they used two condoms per customer. Some reported using three or even four condoms. This is because they fear that a single condom can break or tear. According to practically everyone in the study group, the use of condoms had increased in the past four to five years. A box costing fifty rupees could last from 3 days (for some women), to 3 months depending upon the number of customers they entertain. If they have many customers, the box of condoms lasts for less than a week. A majority of the respondents said the box lasts for one to one and a half months.

Though the women were adamant about condom use, the history of pregnancies, MTPs and STDs indicate that there are still lapses from universal condom use. The most usual lapse from condom use was with the man *yaar* with whom women had a steady, long term relationship.

Often the *yaar* would refuse to use condoms. Some other clients were reported to remove the condom after the lights were switched off. Other exceptions occur. One respondent said that there are customers who stay throughout the night, and pay large amounts (up to Rs. 350). These men often refuse to use condoms. Sometimes there was no stock of condoms in the brothel.

Data from Questioning using the *Bindi* Technique

In order to obtain a more accurate appraisal of condom use, we used the technique described earlier, in which the women marked the numbers of clients on cards using *bindis.* The results from this data-gathering technique were somewhat different from the answers given in direct questioning. In direct questioning, 60 respondents reported a total of 98 clients, whereas the numbers increased to 127 when the *bindi* technique was used. Also, instead of 100 per cent condom use, the *bindi* method revealed six non-condom events in the most recent encounters. We feel that the data using the *bindis* gave a realistic picture.

Issues Related to Pregnancy and Child Birth

In the reproductive histories we found that 49 of the 60 women had experienced one or more pregnancies. They reported a total of 102 pregnancies of which 59 resulted in live births 57.84 per cent. Of these, 38 live births occurred in relation to sex work, while 21 births occurred in a marital relationship prior to sex work.

Table 22.4: Pregnancy and Outcome

	Ethnic Category			
	Karnataka N = 25	*Nepali N = 20*	*Others N = 15*	*Total N = 60*
Ever been Pregnant (In sex-work)	17	11	7	35
Total Pregnancies (In sex-work)	40	15	18	73
Pregnancy Outcome				
• Live birth	23	8	7	38
• Still birth	2	0	0	2
• Abortion	15	7	11	33
Age at first Pregnancy				
• Mean	18.33	19.35	18.09	18.6
• Median	16.5	18.0	18.0	18.0

Source: Field Investigation.

In more than 70 per cent of the pregnancies resulting in live births, sex workers said that they wanted a baby. In three pregnancies the women did not want a child, but they failed to get an abortion done, as they approached the doctor too late and the doctor refused to take the risks of terminating a late pregnancy. Table 22.4 also shows that there were nearly as many induced abortions as live births as outcomes of pregnancy.

There was considerable ambivalence among the women, concerning having children, in part, because of the negative environment of the brothels, and (frequently) negative attitudes of the brothel owners regarding children. However, a majority of the women wanted a child for future support. One of the sex workers commented:

> "Don't we need some one of our own? If I have a child he will look after me in old age. When I die who will do my last rites?"

Some of the women cherish a hope that their child may give them an opportunity to get out of the brothel and out of sex work. Women usually started thinking about having a child after some years in the brothels.

The sex workers' first pregnancies in the brothel environment were the most problematic, because of the woman's insecure economic situation and the negative attitudes of the *gharwalis*. Since the first pregnancy usually occurred within the first year or two in the brothel, at that time the women were still under 20 years old and attractive, and hence they were valuable income-earners for the brothel-keepers. In eight cases the woman complied with the *gharwali's* insistence that the pregnancy be aborted. In 28 of the total of 33 reported MTPs, the woman had no living child at the time of the abortion.

In all the data about child births and abortions, the *devdasis* show up as somewhat different from the other women. For them having a child was a desired outcome, and they generally had support from their families. Table 22.6, shows that most of the Nepalis and 'other' sex workers, chose abortion for their first pregnancies, but the Karnataka women, especially the *devdasis,* generally went for abortions only with their later pregnancies. Only one-third of their MTPs were for the first pregnancy (in the brothel), while almost all the MTPs (six out of seven) among the Nepali girls for the first pregnancy (Table 22.5).

The pregnancy terminations were mostly carried out by private practitioners in the brothel area. Only five women (mainly *devdasis*) reported that they went to government facilities, where the MTP procedures were supposed to be free of cost. The costs of MTP varied

Table 22.5: Patterns of Abortions (In the Sex Work Environment)

Characteristics	*Ethnic Category*			
	Karnataka *N* = 25	*Nepali* *N* = 20	*Others* *N* = 15	*Total* *N* = 60
Total Pregnancies	40	15	18	73
Abortions	15	7	11	33
Mean age at first MTP (yrs)	21.5	18.6	16.2	19.7
Mean age at all MTPs (yrs)	22.3	18.1	16.9	19.5
Median duration of Sexwork at first MTP (yrs)	3 yrs.	1 yr.	Before 1 yr.	
MTP at first Pregnancy	5	6	4	15
MTP without a living Issue	10	7	11	28

Source: Field Investigation.

considerably from one hospital to another, ranging from 250 to 1500 rupees. Second trimester MTPs were much more expensive, as the hospitals charged 2500 rupees for the procedure. However, there were only three such cases. Eight women in our sample reported more than one abortion, thus compounding the risks to health, as well as the costs.

Pregnancy and Child Births

As shown in Table 22.5, a bare majority of pregnancies, 52 per cent in our sample resulted in child births. Most of the women said that they received antenatal care during their pregnancies. They usually made two or three visits to the doctors for check-ups, tetanus toxoid injections, and some tablets or tonics. The women continued their work, on average continuing for the first five or six months of pregnancy. Several women said that they stopped work when they felt 'the movement inside their abdomen.'

One woman told us that she worked until the eighth month of pregnancy. She said, "I used to get one or two customers everyday." In answer to our question, she said that some customers like pregnant women, but some of them, after seeing a pregnant sex worker, used to go away after giving some money. She said:

> "I did not take *phaltu satavnare* (cheap, troublesome) customers.
> I took care that no pressure would fall on my stomach."

Childbirth and Economic/Social Costs

The economic burden of pregnancy and childbirth is, of course, much higher than the costs of abortion. The costs include the medicines, doctor's fees, examinations such as blood tests and sonography, and costs of hospitalization. The direct costs ranged between Rs. 1000 to Rs. 1500 for normal vaginal delivery. The women who had caesarian section had to spend between Rs. 10,000 to Rs. 20,000. The money for a normal delivery could be managed if she had good earnings prior to pregnancy, particularly in case of a planned pregnancy. However, in case of complications or caesarian delivery they had to borrow from the brothel owner at high interest and thus ended in debt. Indirect costs were also incurred in the form of lost earnings.

In most cases the sex workers had their child births in the hospitals in the Pune area. The exceptions are mainly among the *devdasis,* who usually went to their home villages in Karnataka, where some of them had their deliveries conducted at home by their mother or other elderly relative, or the local *dai.* A few had hospital deliveries in a nearby health centre or in a private hospital in their home area.

Table 22.6: Place of Delivery and Sources of Support during Pregnancy and Child Birth

Characteristics	*Ethnic Category*			
	Karnataka	*Nepali*	*Others*	*Total*
Place of delivery				
• Hospital	17	6	6	29
• Home	8	2	1	11
Support Received				
• Parents/Relatives	12	1	0	13
• Male	4	2	2	8
• Others	1	5	1	7
• No support	8	0	4	12

Source: Field Investigation.

Table 22.6 shows that only the Karnataka sex workers, mostly *devdasis*, received support from parents and other relatives during their pregnancies. In many cases the *devdasis* returned to their natal homes in the later stage of pregnancy, and some of them stayed back in their home villages for some months post partum. Return to their home villages was hardly possible for the Nepali women, partly due to distance, but also because of lack of social support from their families. On the other hand, the Nepali women had some support from among their peers in the brothels, including the Nepali *gharwalis.* The 'other' category of sex workers in general had very low levels of social support of any kind.

In addition to the lack of social, emotional, and financial support experienced by many of the women, they also had unusual numbers of costly caesarian deliveries (8 of the 40 deliveries). In those cases the woman was hospitalized for 10 days on an average, and two of them had post-operative complications, so they were in hospital for 20-22 days, with medical bills of about Rs. 20,000. Two women said they had been advised by doctors to have caesarian deliveries, but they declined. In the cases of high hospital costs the women ended up owning large sums of money to their *gharwalis.*

A 22 year old Lambadi woman narrated her experiences in detail. She was orphaned in childhood, and entered sex work at the age of 18 years. She wanted to have a baby because she wished to have some one of her own. After becoming pregnant, she visited a doctor after two months and subsequently four times. She had undergone sonography thrice, once to know whether the baby was male or female. When asked, 'why you did this?' She simply said, 'all women do this.' She went to her village near Hyderabad to her grandmother, and had a caesarian delivery in a private hospital. There she told the doctor that her husband was in another town, in order to avoid discrimination. She was hospitalized for seven days and the bill was Rs. 15,000. She managed most of the money through loans from her brothel owner, but could not clear the entire amount. The doctor said the birth certificate for the baby will be given only when she pays the balance due of Rs. 1500.

After delivery, some of the sex workers returned to sex work in 2-3 months. They received very little post-natal care after discharge from the hospital. They went to the doctor only if they had fever or pain in abdomen. 56 workers gave histories of post-natal complications. Three had fever, one reported severe post-partum mental problems.

Thirty one women reported that they were supporting their family financially from their earnings, but only 13 women received some support during pregnancy and child birth from their mothers or other relatives. 9 women said, they had a regular male partner *yaar,* but those male partners provided very little support to pregnant sex workers. They usually stopped seeing the women after learning about pregnancy. On the other hand, two of the respondents received significant support from their regular male partners. In these cases, the men had consented to having the baby. In one case, the *yaar* took the pregnant sex worker out of the brothel, hired a room and looked after her needs. In a few cases, the brothel owner or other sex worker accompanied the pregnant sex worker for check ups and for the delivery. If the brothel owner was supportive, she instructed other women from the brothel to help the pregnant sex worker.

Where are the Sex Workers' Children?

The brothels in many ways are very unsuitable places to raise children. Many of the brothel-keepers have negative attitude towards children. There is very little extra space or play area for children. Consequently, only very small children are kept in the brothels.

After child birth, the women did keep their babies with them, as almost all the babies (33 of 38 reported births) were breast-fed. 12 were breast-fed for over one year; and another 12 were breast-fed for six to twelve months. Most of those with longer breast-feeding were the children of the Karnataka women.

Of the 38 reported births, 6 died in the neonatal or infancy period. Although this is a very small sample, it indicates very high infant mortality. Some of the babies were undoubtedly of low birth weight, but we do not know the causes of death, as all of the deaths occurred several years earlier, as reported during study.

Twelve children (all aged less than five years) were staying with their mothers in the brothels. Another 13 were in hostels, all of them more than five years of age. A majority of the older children of women from Karnataka stayed in their native villages and were looked after either by parents (especially mother) or other relatives such as sister or brother. These women who kept their children in the village or in a hostel told their children that they were working in the city as maid servants or in shops. They never bring those children to see the brothel areas.

Sexually Transmitted Diseases

When enquired about symptoms suggestive of sexually transmitted diseases, 27 (45%) respondents reported complaints of vaginal discharge and 26 (43.6%) respondents had at some time experienced burning urination and had pain in the lower abdomen.

The complaint of burning urination was described as (*pishap karte samay jalan/aag aag hona*). Many respondents felt that too much heat in the body causes burning urination, and they said it was also caused by eating 'hot' food items such as *roti* (wheat bread) and non-vegetarian foods. Some felt that drinking excessive quantities of tea, could also cause the symptoms. Some thought that they might get that condition from standing for long hours in the sun in the afternoon, trying to solicit customers. This explanation appeared rational, as they could become dehydrated standing out in the heat of the day. Some burning sensation during urination could result from dehydration.

The women said, that they cleaned their genitals with dettol and water in case of such complaints. Many said they visited the doctor. The doctor usually gave an injection and prescribed drugs. The consultation fees were Rs. 50 and the drugs cost an additional sum of Rs. 50.

Awareness about HIV-AIDS

The sex workers in general were aware of HIV-AIDS. All except six respondents said that condom use prevented AIDS. A few women knew about HIV and the difference between infection and AIDS. These were women who either worked for some NGO or had attended meetings organized by NGOs on occasions such as World AIDS Day or World Women's Day. These women could also tell about other modes of transmission of HIV, including blood transfusion and use of infected needles. Many of the women told us that AIDS was a new illness (*bimari*), dangerous disease (*Khartarnak bimari)* that it was invariably fatal, and they knew of some women from the area who died due to AIDS. But they said they knew of no one from their own brothel who had AIDS.

We used pictures to elicit their knowledge and attitudes about mother to child transmission of HIV. We showed a picture of a pregnant woman sitting in a clinic, being told by the doctor that she was HIV positive. Then we showed two cards—in one the HIV positive woman was walking towards an MTP centre, in the other she was going towards a maternity home. We asked, which of these options, the woman should choose. We found that 43 of the 60 women knew about mother to child transmission of HIV, while 13 said they did not know and the other 4 said such transmission did not occur.

Concerning the action to be taken in that situation, 20 women said that they would advise an abortion, 11 advised continuation of pregnancy to term, and 25 women could not specify any advice.

Experiences of Illness

Several women reported respiratory ailments and body aches; four spoke of current menstrual problems. A surprising number 15 said they had 'jaundice' in the past, though none were currently suffering from any signs of hepatitis. The typical history was abrupt acute onset with deep jaundice and the woman was ill for 15 days to one month. All 15 said that they went to an indigenous doctor who treated *kamini* or *kavil* (jaundice). The treatment was 'magical,' using a special sort of thread, and no medications of any kind.

All except five respondents who reported an illness in past or present, visited doctors for treatment. It was found that in the area surrounding the brothels, there are many private medical practitioners. The sex workers went to them whenever they were sick, and the doctors usually gave one or two injections and tablets for three to five days. They charged between Rs. 40 to Rs. 50 per visit. 12 of the women said they visited a government hospital or dispensary for treatment of their illnesses.

Although there are government and private health care providers around the brothel area, the sex workers do not receive any health education, counselling or advice for preventing illness or protecting their health. They also receive little or no counselling about prevention of pregnancy. The only instruction or advice given by the health care providers is 'use condoms'.

Summary and Conclusions

This study has explored a range of issues concerning reproductive health among sex workers in brothels in Pune. Although it is not possible to do a random sampling of the women in Pune brothels, we feel that the data in this study provide important perspectives on the reproductive and sexual health needs of this population.

All except two of our respondents were above the age of 20 years. The younger sex workers were closely guarded by brothel owners, fearing that they might try to escape, and the owners felt that the younger girls would be taken for questioning, to find out if they were minors. All except three women were literate and were from socially and economically marginalized rural families.

Our findings showed that the *devdasis* are a special group within the brothels. The *devdasis* are less stigmatized by their families and their home communities. They have stronger social supports than other sex workers, particularly in relation to pregnancy and child birth. In contrast, the women from Nepal had less support from their families due to the distances from their native villages. The mixed group of sex workers, from Maharashtra, Andhra Pradesh and one or two from other states, appeared to be the most marginalised, with the least contact with either natal families or brothel based support groups. As social support is a key factor in health and disease, lack of social contacts further accentuates the vulnerability of these sex workers.

In general, the women wanted to have children, especially after they were a little older, but most of the pregnancies were unintentional. Young girls who had recently entered sex work, because of their ignorance and vulnerability, were especially likely to became pregnant and had to undergo abortions. It appears that in most cases, the doctors who provided abortion services were qualified medical practitioners. However, we also noted that there was lot of exploitation of the sex workers. They were never informed about contraceptive use, so they had multiple abortions. That lack of information definitely put them at greater risk of post-abortion complications and subsequent infections and morbidity.

Although we found that pregnant sex workers received some antenatal care, it was far from adequate, considering the extra risks to which they were exposed. Many of the sex workers delivered in hospitals. Caesarian deliveries were common, and in several cases they had a prolonged stay in hospital due to complications. All these caused a high economic burden on the sex workers, as they usually borrowed money from brothel owners and ended up seriously in debt.

We found that use of contraceptives other than condoms was low. Condoms were used by all women, most of the time. However in our previous project in the same area, 18 per cent of the clients of sex workers reported that they never used condoms. The large number of pregnancies among the sex workers point to the fact that condom use was not sufficient for effective contraception, due to large number of sex acts with high probability of conception.

Availability of contraceptives was not a problem. They had access to IUDs and oral contraceptives at government run hospitals located in the area. Some of the NGOs who provided health care also distributed contraceptives, like oral pills free of cost. However the women received almost no counselling or other useful information about contraceptive measures.

The sex workers who are at greater risk of reproductive tract infections, and repeated abortions, also contribute to infertility in this population. The children of sex workers are marginalized, and their upbringing need special attention.

There is a need of a comprehensive health care service for these women, which should have general health care, maternity services, contraceptive services and treatment of STIs and RTIs. Information, education and counselling should be an integral part of health care. Promotion of good nutrition, hygiene and use of available health services are also necessary. For all these health services, intersectoral co-ordination is needed. The social welfare, health department, as well as non-government agencies should come together to develop comprehensive plans for an integrated health care system for the sex workers. We feel that the issues brought forward in our study are multidimensional, with components of physical morbidity, mental ill-health, as well as socio-cultural and economic problems.

Epilogue

I

One would have never thought that sexuality, sexual behaviour and reproductive health issues would become dominant researchable areas in bio-medical and bio-socio-cultural domain. Next to hunger, sex is a biological instinct. Both these instincts and urges are essential for biological survival of an organism and that for the species. However human species have tried to organize and institutionalize these instincts into plurality of acquired behavioural patterns, as aspects of respective cultural and social systems.

Human societies have been familiar with sexually transmitted diseases (STD) for a considerable period. We have also been familiar with reproductive health issues, focusing on fertility, reproductive morbidity, wastage expressed as miscarriage and abortion. Everything was taken in a stride as biological issues, including genetic factors. Coping mechanisms were evolved in traditional medical systems by way of preventive measures and promotive norms and practices, which were culture specific of various ethnic groups.

The key theme has been stability and equilibrium to adjust with plurality of diversities. The rules of endogamy, exogamy, polygyny and polyandry, hypergamy and hypogamy; coping practices like levirate, sorrorate, preferential cross-cousin mating etc. organized sex unions by institutionalizing marriage and family. These have been permissible normative sex liaisons. However, widowhood, desertion or divorce, migration, mobility for trade, and nerve-raking wars with risk of death, led to sex gratification outside marriage, forcing women to face economic, social, psychological and biological miseries. Possessing fertile land and women, or capturing them for affluent comforts, designed the historical rule of kings and empires. Enjoying sex with multiple partners had been an indicator of feudal aristocracy. Alternative way has been commercial sex, which developed into brothels.

Sonagachi brothels in Kolkata and Kamathipura brothels in Mumbai were initiated by the British to comfort their troops. At Pune, brothels were catering to the affluent decadence of Brahmin rulers, not very far from the seat of power at Shaniwarwada. The decadence has been portrayed in a famous play, 'Ghasiram Kotwal'.

However, there was a marked difference between the entertainers, such as dancing girls or *nautch* girls as the British addressed them and the commercial sex workers referred to as prostitutes. The dancing girls and singing girls would give entertainment performances at the festive occasions of birth and marriage. Customers could also visit their places (*Kotha*) to watch dance and enjoy music, as people visit dance-drama theatres. The dancing girl could be adopted as a mistress with a live-in relationship with client-patron, giving birth to a child and looked after financially by the biological father.

There have been occasional liaisons of what is termed as adultery or lesbian/gay relationship. All such sex diversities were ignored and tolerated in societies, until HIV and AIDS were identified as communicable and fatal morbidities.

It was believed that HIV originated in Africa supposedly due to liberal attitude to sex relationships in tribal communities all over. The papers in a special issue on AIDS in a scientific journal like 'Social Science and Medicine' hinting a racial angle, was publicly reprimanded by Charles Leslie, editor of Medical Anthropology section of the Journal, at the Amsterdam Conference, bi-annually organized by the Journal. I was present on the occasion. Simultaneously, the feminist movements and other events like ICPD in 1994 at Cairo, focused attention on safe motherhood and child survival which could be generalized as focusing on empowerment of women.

In India, the massive population control programme was sought to be operationalised through vasectomy camp-campaigns as permanent contraception, which failed miserably due to political overtones triggered by targeted approach, deviating into irregularities, 'castrating' the unmarried youth.

The abolition of feudal institutions like princely states and *zamindari*, incongruous with electoral democracy, took away the patronage to dance and music as an entertainment profession, which incidentally got embedded in Bollywood. The kind of traditional dancing labelled as *Nautanki* or *Lavani* has become 'Item Song' in Bollywood. Currently in the market, there are brothels without the art performances of dance and music. The mobility which enforced absence from family for a long duration, such as by truckers, opened the avenues of *Dhaba* culture which satisfied the dual biological urges of hunger and sex, at a reasonable price. The young sales representatives of commercial companies, who are mobile and reside in lodges, also indulge in risk behaviour. At the Dockyard area at Mumbai, in the vicinity of Dockyard Road railway station, there are hotels where rooms could be hired on an hourly basis.

The risk of HIV pandemic required preventive measures such as the use of condom and microbicides. Condom sought to be popularized earlier as a contraceptive was being promoted for safe sex, to prevent HIV. Considerable research has been underway to develop microbicides as a woman-centric gel which a woman could use to protect herself from getting infection, even within marital relationship. However, research also brings out that married women could not use microbicide without the knowledge and consent of their husbands, for fear of allegations of adultery or infidelity, if found out, during penetrative sex. A microbicide with dual function to act as a contraceptive as also to prevent HIV infection has been discussed as an ideal. Different kinds of condoms are widely advertised with a message that its use would not diminish sex pleasure. Simultaneously, aphrodisiacs are also widely advertised being manufactured by branded pharma industry. It is thus quite clear that the privacy of sex has considerably diminished, as it is openly discussed in the public domain, as also widely advertised in print and visual media.

There have been gossiping debates as to who transmits HIV to whom, between man and woman. Due to multiple sex partners for living, as an occupation by CSWs, either voluntarily or forced due to trafficking, the needle of suspicion is on the CSW. However, from where does the CSW gets infection?

Since culture and lifestyle which were traditionally co-terminus, got separated due to multiplicity of occupations necessitating mobility and migration, risky sex behaviour received a spurt in growth. It was thus necessary to document the variety of risky sexual behaviour for different ethnic and occupational groups. Sexual behaviour which has been protected for centuries by 'culture of silence' being intensely personal, could be unfolded only with the use of qualitative research tools and techniques, to unravel the socio-psychological processes. Anthropologists who claim to have fine tuned qualitative methods were not so far going beyond ethnography of culture of isolated communities focusing on religion and kinship.

The Ford Foundation in India took initiative to enhance the capacity building of researchers in the universities and NGOs to undertake research on Sexuality, Sexual Behaviour and Reproductive Health. Some of the books edited by research-administrators like Saroj Pachauri (1999), Joel Gitteisohn *et al.* (1994), Radhika Ramasubban and Shireen Jejeebhoy (2000), deal with Reproductive Health Issues and Sexual Behaviour. The book, '*Sexuality in the Time of AIDS*' edited by Ravi Verma and others (2004), deals with case studies primarily on Sexual Behaviour in the context of developing strategies to prevent AIDS. The book has been the result of Ford Foundation support for network, to promote social science research on sexuality issues. The current book, '*Sexuality, Sexual Behaviour and Reproductive Health*' also provides ethnographic case studies of similar nature. But, not all chapters in this book deal exclusively with sexual behaviour. Some chapters are dealing with broader issues of gender and reproductive health.

The change in emphasis in India, from family planning to control the risk of HIV has meant a 'paradigm shift' in the research agenda. There are vivid stories about sexual behaviour, highlighting the ignorance of partners about infections due to sex. A Hindi movie '*Mandi*' (1983) about brothel life and trafficking became quite famous. Recently a movie '*Love Sonia*' has discussed brothel life in the context of trafficking of women. There have been other movie, '*Bhumika*' (1977), based on a biopic in Marathi, '*Sangtye Aika*' or recently, '*Natrang*' in Marathi, which present the hardships of female dance actors. These art films are not made in the context of HIV. However, it could provide insights which lead to trafficking of women.

I had a shocking revelation from anthropology trained student couple settled in New York. On inquiry about the source of livelihood, my male student, who apparently received training in Psychology after Anthropology at Pune, he said, he was counselling the 'same sex partners' to resolve their 'partnership discord'.

II

One of the significant fall out of social science research regarding sexuality, sexual behaviour and reproductive health in the context of HIV, is the discussion of private issues in the public domain, in the media, in the judicial courts, giving inputs to the government to take executive and legislative action, when necessary.

As a big step towards women's empowerment, sanitation which was promoted by Mahatma Gandhi as a constructive programme has been reintroduced as a national programme. To address reproductive health of women, government has abolished taxation on the manufacture and sale of sanitary pads. The film media has come out with two Hindi movies '*Toilet*' and '*Padman*' addressing these issues.

Recently the Supreme Court of India struck down century old law about adultery as a criminal offence and dismissing the criminality clause of homo-sexual relationships. The debates have not been in the context of HIV infections but about private behaviour being labelled as criminal behaviour in law, for over a century, subjected to prison punishment by the government.

The issues about Lesbian, Gay, Bisexual and Third Gender (LGBT) require bio-medical and bio-social research about the prevalence and incidence. The cases of sex change are being freely reported and discussed in the media, and the relevant surgeries in public hospitals are being advertised about offering reduced rates, as compared to private sector. On the other hand, media is reporting increased sex violence involving those in power positions or heading the educational institutions. The adolescents and minors are being reported as perpetrators and as victims in sex violence. The latest protest movement initiated in the West by women, is termed as 'Me Too' whereby the women in public position, mainly as film actors, are narrating the sexual harassment, they went through in their lives, in the recent and distant past. Due to female education and economic reasons, age at marriage is increasing for boys and specially for girls. Traditional marriages immediately after puberty are giving way, whereby, the parents are concerned about the risk behaviour leading to risk of infections.

The need for policy research or research providing data for policy framework and implementation is desired from social scientists. There is need of intervention research which may be feasible, if academic institutions develop networks and partnerships with the government and NGOs.

Ideally participatory research would be useful for understanding the behavioural variables, which in the process also empowers the participants, by analyzing the contexts, with objectivity. Such researches addressed to people's behaviour and their concerns, could provide insights for giving solutions, and could lead to conceptualization about the social and economic dynamics about social and cultural change, and about values of morality. The judiciary and media have emerged as the powerful arms of democracy. When would the academic research become significant arm, to contribute to policy framework and implementation, to address the issues of normative and deviant behaviour, as impacting the health and disease, in the scenario of plural medical systems?

Annexure 1

List of Small Grant Awardees

Sl. No.	Name of Small Grant Awardees
1.	Hemant Apte, Medical Anthropology, Pune
2.	B.C. Agrawal, Communication Anthropologist, Ahmedabad
3.	Alka Barua, FRHS, Ahmedabad
4.	Jyotsna Bapat, Anthropologist, Mumbai
5.	Susmita Bhattacharya, BJMC, Pune
6.	S.V. Gandham, BJMC, Pune
7.	R.D. Gambhir, Anthropologist, S.P.P.U.
8.	Anjali Ganpule, Health Science, Pune
9.	Lokesh Gujjarappa, Health Science, Bangaluru
10.	Bhupali Mhaskar, Bajaj Foundation, Pune
11.	Aarti Nagarkar, Anthropologist, S.P.P.U.
12.	R.C. Swarnakar, Anthropologist, Jaipur
Ph.D. Fellows	
13.	P.S. Agashe, Health Sciences, S.P.P.U.
14.	Maushami Joshi, Health Sciences, S.P.P.U.
15.	Abhay Kudale, Health Sciences, S.P.P.U.

Annexure 2

List of Participants who Attended National Meetings

Sl. No.	Name	Sl. No.	Name
1.	Dr. P.S. Agashe	47.	Dr. C.G. Hussain Khan
2.	Dr. B.C. Agrawal	48.	Dr. Vishwanath Koliwad
3.	Dr. Mallika Alexander	49.	Mr. Abhay Kudale
4.	Dr. Hemant Apte	50.	Ms. Sunita Kujur
5.	Dr. A.S. Babu	51.	Dr. Aruna Lakhani
6.	Dr. Kalyan Banerjee	52.	Mr. Daniel Manoharan
7.	Dr. Jyotsna Bapat	53.	Ms. Manjari Maslekar
8.	Dr. Alka Barua	54.	Dr. Nita Mawar
9.	Dr. Peggy Bentley	55.	Dr. Sanjay Mehendale
10.	Dr. Shalini Bharat	56.	Ms. Bhupali Mhaskar
11.	Dr. H.K. Bhat	57.	Dr. Veena Mulgaonkar
12.	Dr. Susmita Bhattacharya	58.	Dr. Nirmala Murthy
13.	Dr. Asha Bhende	59.	Dr. Kalpana Mutatkar
14.	Dr. Sujata Bhobe	60.	Dr. Vimal Nadkarni
15.	Dr. Hemant Chandorkar	61.	Dr. Moni Nag
16.	Dr. N.S. Deodhar	62.	Dr. Ujjawal Nene
17.	Ms. Christina Desa	63.	Mr. Shantanu Ozarkar
18.	Ms. Deepali Deshmukh	64.	Dr. Saroj Pachauri
19.	Mr. Abhijit Deshpande	65.	Dr. Apoorvaa Pandit
20.	Dr. S.R. Deshpande	66.	Dr. R.S. Paranjape
21.	Ms. Sucheta Deshpande	67.	Ms. Geeta Pardeshi
22.	Ms. Anuprita Dikshit	68.	Ms. Varsha Parikh
23.	Mr. Lokesh G.	69.	Ms. Archana Pataskar
24.	Dr. R.D. Gambhir	70.	Dr. Bert Pelto
25.	Dr. Bela Ganatra	71.	Dr. A.D. Pendse
26.	Dr. R.R. Gangakhedkar	72.	Dr. D.S. Phalgune
27.	Ms. Anjali Ganpule	73.	Dr. Mohan Prabhu
28.	Dr. Laila Garda	74.	Ms. Vidula Purohit
29.	Dr. J.S. Gogia	75.	Mr. Sandeep Rasalpurkar
30.	Dr. Kamla Gupta	76.	Dr. Sudhakar Reddy
31.	Dr. R.N. Gupta	77.	Mr. Prakash Rote
32.	Dr. Manisha Gupte	78.	Dr. Rohini Sahani
33.	Ms. Gurbaxani	79.	Ms. Arti Samajpati
34.	Ms. Tillottama Jamadar	80.	Dr. A.G. Sathe
35.	Mr. Mukesh Janbandhu	81.	Dr. B.V. Sharma
36.	Dr. Surinder Jaswal	82.	Ms. Shankari Shinde
37.	Ms. Neelam Joglekar	83.	Ms. Anuprita Shukla
38.	Dr. Renu John	84.	Ms. Sandhya Sundaran
39.	Mr. Saju Joseph	85.	Dr. R.C. Swarnakar
40.	Ms. Maushami Joshi	86.	Dr. Ravi Verma
41.	Dr. Tara Kanitkar	87.	Dr. Sunayana Walia
42.	Dr. Nandita Kapadia-Kundu	88.	Dr. Mahinder C. Watsa
43.	Dr. Anita Kar	89.	Dr. C.A. K. Yesudian
44.	Ms. Anuradha Karkare	90.	Prof. R.K. Mutatkar
45.	Dr. Aarti Kaulagekar	91.	Dr. Bhushan Patwardhan
46.	Dr. S.B. Khadilkar		

References

Acharya, R. *et al.*, (1996). "Inter-spouse communication, contraceptive use and family size: Relationship examined in Bihar and Tamil Nadu", *The Journal of Family Welfare*, 42(4): 5-11.

Andrew, Gracy and Vikram Patel (2002). "Sex, studies or strife? The needs of adolescents in Higher Secondary Schools in Goa," *Report of Research of the Sangath Societ) for Child Development and Family Guidance*. Goa.

Apte, H. (1997). ' Adolescent sexuality and fertility: A study in rural western Maharashtra", Paper presented at the workshop on "Research Related to Male Involvement in Reproductive Health and Contraceptive Use", April, 30-May 7, 1997, Baroda, India.

Apte, Hemant, (1999). "Beginning of a Process: Male Involvement in Reproductive Health", Working Paper. King Edward Memorial Hospital and Research Centre, Pune.

Asif, R. *et al.*, (1994). "Contraceptive behaviour in women carrying an unwanted pregnancy", *The Journal of Family Welfare*, 40(2): 27-30.

Avis, N.E.; Stellato, R.; Crawford, S.; Bromberger, J.; Ganz, P.; Cain, V.; Kagawa-Singer, M. (2001). "Is there a menopausal syndrome? Menopausal status and symptoms across racial/ethnic groups", *Soc. Sci. Med.* 52(3): 345-56.

Balaji, L.N. (1994). "Women and AIDS", *Journal of the Indian Medical Association*. January: 15-16.

BBC News, "Indian Sex Workers Fight for Rights", *BBC News* (01.05.03) Item reported in AIDS-India Forum (Internet Accessed January 2003)

Beine, David K. (2003). *Ensnared by AIDS*, Kathmandu: Mandala Book Point.

Benedict, R. (1934). *Patterns of Culture*, New York: Houghton and Miffin Co.

Bhargava, P. *et al.*, (1987). "Determinants of the status of women and fertility in greater Bombay", *Indian Journal of Social Work*, XLVIII(1).

Bhatia, J. *et al.*, (1980). "Inter-spousal communication and practice of contraception in India", *The Journal of Family Welfare*, 26(4): 18-30.

Bhattacharya, Susmita, (2003). "Brothels and brothel clients in Pune city," In: Verma, R., P.J. Pelto, S.L. Schensul, and A. Joshi (eds.) *Sexuality in the time of AIDS: Contemporary perspectives from communities in India.* New Delhi: Sage Publications.

Bhagat, Rasheeda. (1997). The battered half", *NEXUS*, New Delhi: Population Services International.

Bharat, S., Singhanetra Renard, A. and Aggelton, P. (1992). "Household and community response to HIV-AIDS in Asia: The case of Thailand and India", *AIDS*, 12 (suppl. B): 117-122.

Bhende, A. *et al.*, (1958). "Determinants of contraceptive method: Choices in an industrial city of India", *Asia-Pacific Population Journal*, 6(3).

Bhende, Asha (1994). "A study of sexuality of adolescent girls and boys in underprivileged groups in Bombay." *Indian Journal of Social Work*, 55(4):557-571.

Black, M. (1992). *Aids and Asia: A development crisis*, New Delhi: United Nations Development Programme.

Boulet, M.J.; Oddens, B.J.; Lehert, P.; Vemer, H.M. and Visser, A. (1994). "Climacteric and menopause in the seven South East Asian countries", *Maturitas*, 19, 157-76.

Borgatti, Stephen, ANTHROPAC. Software programme for structured qualitative data. Analytic Technologies, Inc.

Courtenay, W.H. (1999). "Situating Men's Health in the Negotiation of Masculinities", *The Society for the Psychological Study for Men and Masculinity Bulletin (American Psychological Association)*, 4(2): 10-12.

Courtenay, W.H. (2000). "Constructions of masculinity and their influence on men's well-being: A theory of gender and health", *Social Science and. Medicine*, 50: 1385-1401.

CREHPA (2003). "Injection drug users in southeastern terai region." *Report of Research for Family Health International*. Kathmandu, Nepal.

Dandekar, K., (1980). "Vasectomy camps in Maharashtra", *Population Studies*, 17, 63-64.

Dagar, R. (ed.) (1998). *Manual on Women's Development and Gender Justice*, Institute for Development and Communication, Chandigarh.

Deutsche Presse-Agentur (2002). "Chronic Condom Shortage Could Trigger AIDS in Indian Brothels" (Deutsche Presse-Agentur 08.04.02). Item reported in AIDS-India Forum (Internet Accessed August 2002).

Dennerstein, L. (1996). "Well being, symptoms and the menopause transition", *Maturitas* 23: 147-157.

Dennerstein, L., Smith, A.M. and Morse, C. (1994). "Psychological well-being, mid-life and the menopause", *Maturitas*, 20(1): 1-11.

Dixon-Mueller, R. (1993). "The Sexuality connection in reproductive health", In: *"Learning about Sexuality: A Practical Beginning"*, eds. Zeidensteine, S. and K. Moore, The Population Council, Inc., New York.

D'Souza Dominic, IHO (1992). Dominic D'Souza: "The complete story of India first AIDS activist who succumbed to the disease", on May 27th 1992. Bombay, India Health Organization.

Dube, L. (1988). "Socialisation of Hindu girls in patrilineal India", In: K. Channa (Ed.) *"Socialisation, Education and Women: Explorations in Gender Identity"*, New Delhi: Orient Longman.

Dube, L. Leacock, C. Ardener, S. (Ed.) (1986). "Visibility and Power", *"Essays on Women in Society and Development"*, Oxford University Press.

Expert Group on Population Policy, 1994 in Zodgekar A., "Family welfare programme and population stabilisation strategies in India: levels, motivation and differentials", *Asia-Pacific Population Journal*, 11(1).

Foundation for Research in Health Systems, Ahmedabad (2000). "Condom Use Among Married and Unmarried Males: A Report".

Fuhrer, R. and S.A. Stansfeld (2002). "How gender affects patterns of social relations and their impact on health: a comparison of one or multiple sources of support from 'close persons'", *Social Science and Medicine*, Volume 54, Issue 5, March 2002, 811-825.

Ganatra, B., and Hirve, S. (2002). "Induced abortions among adolescent women in rural Maharashtra, India", *Reproductive Health Matters* 10(19): 76-85.

George, Annie (1994). "It happens to us: Menstruation as perceived by poor women in Bombay", In: J. Gittelsohn, M.E. Bentley, P.J. Pelto, M. Nag, S. Pachauri, A.D. Harrison and L.T. Landman (Eds). *Listening to Women Talking About Their Health*, New Delhi: The Ford Foundation and Har-Anand Publications, 168-182.

George, Annie and Surinder Jaswal, (1995). "Understanding sexuality: an ethnographic study of poor women in Bombay, India." *Women and AIDS Research Programme Report,* Washington, D.C.: International Centre for Research on Women. Series, No. 12.

George, A. (1998). "Differential perspectives of men and women in Mumbai, India on sexual relations and negotiations within marriage," *Reproductive Health Matters* 6(12): 87-95.

George, A. (1997). "Sexual Behaviour and Sexual Negotiation among Poor Women and Men in Mumbai: An Exploratory Study", SAHAJ Society for Health Alternatives, Baroda.

Godwin Peter (ed.) (1997). *Socio Economic Implication of the Epidemic. UNDP Regional Project on HIV and Development*, New Delhi.

Goffman, Ervin (1964). *Stigma: Notes in the management of spoiled identity*, New Jersey, Prentice-hall, Inc. Englewood Cliffs.

Gokova, John (1998). "Challenging men to reject gender stereotypes", *Sexual Health Exchange*, 1998/2, www.kit.nl/exchange

Gupta, Hitesh *et al.*, (15-19 March, 1998). *International Conference on Reproductive Health, A study on attitude of female spouse towards male sterilization.*

Guthrie, J.R.; Smith, A.M.; Dennerstein, L. and Morse, C. "Physical activity and the menopause experience: A cross-sectional study", *Maturitas*. 20(2-3): 71-80, 194.

Hilber, A.M. and Colombini, M. (2002). "Promoting sexual health means promoting healthy approaches to sexuality", *Sexual Health Exchange*, 2002/4, www.kit.nl/exchange.

Hunt, Kate (2002). "A generation apart? Gender-related experiences and health in women in early and late mid-life", *Social Science and Medicine*, 54(5): 663-676, March 2002.

IIPS (1994 a). *National Family Health Survey, 1992/93, Mumbai in Supplement to India's Family Welfare Programme*, ed. Measham A. *et al.*, 1996, 27-29.

Jain, A., *et al.*, (1992). "Socio-economic determinants of fertility: What do we know?" *Demography India*, 21(1).

Jamshedji, A. *et al.*, (1990). "Medical Termination of Pregnancy and Concurrent Contraceptive Acceptance", *The Journal of Family Welfare*, 36(3): 39-53.

Jejeebhoy, S. (2000). "Adolescent sexual and reproductive behaviour: A review of the evidence from India", In: R. Ramasubban and S. Jejeebhoy (Eds.), *Women's Reproductive Health in India*, New Delhi: Rawat Publications. 40-101.

Jejeebhoy, S. *et al.*, (1989). "Reproductive motivation: A comparison of wives and husbands in Maharashtra, India", *Studies in Family Planning*, 20(5): 264-272.

Joshi, Archana, Mrinalika Dhapola and Pertti J. Pelto (2004). "Non-marital Sex and Sexual Health Problems in Rural Gujarat." Chapter in R. Verma, P.J. Pelto, S.L. Schensul and A. Joshi (Eds.) *Sexuality in the time of AIDS: Contemporary perspectives from communities in India.*

Jones, J.B. (1997). "Representations of menopause and their health care implications: A qualitative study", *Am J Prev Med.* 13(1): 58-65.

Khan, M.E. and Patel Bella. "How Males Think about Contraception and family Formation. Research Related to the Male Involvement in Reproductive Health and Contraceptive Use", Working Paper. Population Council, Baroda.

Kakar, S. (1989). *Intimate Relations: Exploring Indian Sexuality*, Viking Publications, New Delhi.

Khanna, R. and Price, J. (1994). "Female sexuality, regulation and resistance", *Focus on Gender*, 2(2): 29-34.

Kanitkar, T., (2000). "Changing health scenario in Maharashtra", Prepared for a workshop organised by BAIF, Pune.

Karra, M. *et al.*, (1997). "Husbands' reproductive health knowledge, attitudes, and behaviour in Uttar Pradesh, India", In: *Studies in Family Planning*, 1998; 29(4): 388-399.

Khan, M.E. *et al.* (1990). "Contraceptive use dynamics of couples availing of services from government family planning clinics: A case study of Orissa", *The Journal of Family Welfare*, 36-37, 18-38.

Khan, M.E. *et al.*, (1997). "Involving men in safe motherhood, study of sexual behaviour and reproductive health problems of couples", CORT Baroda and *The Journal of Family Welfare*, 43(2): 18-30.

Kimmel, M. (1995). *Manhood in America: A Cultural History*, Free Press, New York.

Koenig, M. (2000). "Quality of care within the indian family welfare programme: A review of recent evidence", *Studies in Family Planning* 2000, 31(1): 1-18.

Krishnan, P. *et al.*, (1986). in Sujatha, D. *et al.*, (1993). "Religiosity and Fertility among Brahmins", *The Journal of Family Welfare*, 39(1) 13-17.

Kumar, P. *et al.*, (1978). "An Attitudinal and motivational study of early and late adopters of family planning among women", In: *Health and Population, Perspectives and Issues*, 1(1): 79-85.

Kumar, S. (1997). *Demography India*, 26: 63-78.

Lakhani, A. and Ganju, S., "Use of Qualitative Research Methodologies for Situation Assessment of the Sexual Behaviours in the Nandnagar Area in Vadodara District, Gujarat", Unpublished Report to the Department for International Development (DFID).

Linton, R. (1956). *The Cultural Background of Personality*, London: Routledge & Kegan Paul.

Lock, M. (2002). "Symptom reporting at menopause: A review of cross-cultural findings", *J Br Menopause Soc.* 8(4):132-6.

MacCauley (1996). "Meeting the needs of young adults", *Population Reports, Series J.*, 41, July 1996 (Vol. XXIII, No.3) The John Hopkins University, USA.

MAP (Monitoring the AIDS Pandemic). (1997). "Status and Trends of the HIV-AIDS/STD Epidemic in Asia and Pacific", 4th international Conference of AIDS in Asia and the Pacific, October 25-29. Mania: UNAIDS and USAID Funds.

Martin, L. (1987). in Sujatha, D. *et al.*, (1993). "Religiosity and fertility among brahmins", *The Journal of Family Welfare*, 39(1): 13-17.

MAUL, C. *et al.* (1983). "Inter-spouse communication on the domiciliary visit of paramedical staff and family planning acceptance", 4, 52-61.

Merton, Robert. K. (1984). *Stigma: Social Administrative Approach*, Routledge and Kegan Paul, U.K.

Mehta, P., (1975). "Effectiveness of female sterilisation in Greater Bombay: Some vital issues for reconsideration for the national programme", *Demography India*, IV(1).

Mitchell, E.S. and Woods, N.F. (1996). "Symptom experiences of midlife women: observations from the Seattle Midlife Women's Health Study", *Maturitas*. 25(1):1-10.

Mundigo, A. (1996-97). "Reproductive Health research: The new dimensions", *Biennial Report—1996-1997.*

Murthy, R.S. and B.M. Karott "Street boys' perceptions of sexuality and sexual behaviour." Paper presented at Workshop on Reproductive Health in India: New Evidence and Issues, Pune, March.

Nag, Moni (1996). *Sexual Behaviour and AIDS in India*, New Delhi: Vikas Publishing House.

NACO (1998). *Country Scenario 1997-98*, National AIDS Control Organization, Ministry of Health and Family Welfare. New Delhi: Government of India.

Nancy, E. Moss (2002). "Gender equity and socio-economic inequality: a framework for the patterning of women's health", *Social Science and Medicine Volume 54, Issue 5*, March, 649-661.

Narayan, K.A., D.K. Srinivasa, P.J. Pelto and S. Veerammal (2000). "Puberty rituals, reproductive knowledge and health of adolescent schoolgirls in South India." *Asia-Pacific Population Journal* 16(2): 225-238.

Obermeyer, C.M. (2000). "Menopause across cultures: A review of the evidence", *Menopause* 7, 184-192.

Oomman, N. (1998). "Sexuality: Not just a reproductive health matter", *Reproductive Health*, November, 6(12): 10-16.

Pachauri, S. (1995). "Defining a Reproductive Health Package for India: A Proposed Framework", *Regional Working Papers, No. 4*, The Population Council.

Pachauri, S. (ed.) (1999). "Sexuality and sexual behaviour: The current discourse", *Implementing a Reproductive Health Agenda in India: The Beginning*, New Delhi: Population Council, pp. 551-599.

Peedicayil, Abraham (2003). "Male Sexual Health Project in Urban and Rural Areas of Vellore", Report prepared at Christian Medical College for Programme for Appropriate Technology in Health (PATH).

Pelto, P. (2000). "Research on sexuality and sexual behaviour in India", In: R. Ramasubban and S. Jejeebhoy (Eds.), *Women's Reproductive Health in India*, New Delhi: Rawat Publications, 102-133.

Pelto, Pertti J. (1994). "Focused ethnographic studies on sexual behaviour and AIDS/STDs," *The Indian Journal of Social Work* (Special Issue: Sexual Behaviour and AIDS in India) LV (4): 589-602.

Pelto, Pertti. J. (1996). "Qualitative data-gathering for reproductive health research." *Social Change*, September-December, 161-188.

Pelto, Pertti J. (1995). "Challenges of Qualitative Research on High Risk behaviours", Indo U.S. workshop on "Behavioural Research Priorities: Developing effective strategies for the prevention of HIV in India", TISS, Bombay 24-29 April.

Pillai, M., (1974). "Conjugal interaction patterns and fertility behaviour: A multivariate study", *The Journal of Family Welfare*, 33(1): 38–51.

Rajan, S. *et al.*, (1996). "Choosing permanent contraceptive, does son preference matter?", *Economic and Political Weekly*, 31(3): 1980-84.

Ramakrishna, Jayashree, A. Kilaru, S. Mahendra, S. Divakar, and S. Prakash 2000, "Boy-girl relations: cultural influences on sexual perceptions and behaviours among adolescents in South India." Paper presented at 3rd IASSCS Conference. Melbourne.

Rele, J.R. and Kanitkar, T. (1980). In: Sujatha, D. *et al.*, (1993). "Religiosity and Fertility among Brahmins", *The Journal of Family Welfare*, 39(1): 13–17.

Rele, J.R. and Kanitkar, T. (1974). "Residence background and fertility in Greater Bombay", *Population Studies*, 28(2), 299-308.

Redfield, R. (1956). *Peasant Society and Culture: An Anthropological Approach to Culture*, Chicago: University of Chicago Press.

Salunke, S.R., Shaukat, M., Hira, S.K. and Jagtap (1998). "HIV-AIDS in India: a country responds to a challenge", In: Kaldor John (ed.) *AIDS in Asia and the Pacific*, London: Lippincott-Raven Publishers.

Sambamoorthi, Usha, Rakkee Thimothy, Wenhui Wei, S. Irudaya Rajan (2004). "Antenatal Care and AIDS Knowledge among Married Women." *Economic and Political Weekly*, February 14.

Schiller, Nina Glick. Crystal Stephen and Lewellen Denver (1994). "Risky business: The cultural construction of AIDS risk group", *Social Science and Medicine*, 38(10): 1337-1346.

Sethi, G. Carter M. (1996). "HIV-AIDS in India, thinking through the issues and options", *Briefing sheet for policy makers*. New Delhi: The Population Council.

Shyamini, K.A. *et al.* (1995). "A Study of some of the factors in relation to contraceptive use in an urban slum", *Health and Population: Perspectives and Issues*, 18(4): 176-189.

Sidramshettar, S. (1993). "The small family norm: A sociological study of dual earner couples", *The Journal of Family Welfare*, 39(2).

Singh, K. (1998). "Husbands' reproductive health knowledge, attitudes, and behaviour in Uttar Pradesh, India", *Studies in Family Planning*, 29(4): 388-399.

Sodhi, Geeta and Manish Verma (1997). "Report of Research: Exploring adolescent sexual behaviour." SWASTHYA. Report submitted to The Rockfeller Foundation.

Sodhi, G. (2000). "Seeking Gratification: Study of Sexual Behaviour Patterns of Adolescents in an urban slum", Paper presented at Conference on Reproductive Health in India: New Evidence and Issues. Tata Management Training Centre, Pune, Maharashtra, India.

Sodhi, G., Verma, M. and Schensul, S. (2003). "Traditional protection for adolescent girls and sexual risk: Results of research and intervention in an urban community in New Delhi," In: R. Verma, P. Pelto, S. Schensul, and A. Joshi, (Eds.), "*Sexuality in the time of AIDS in India: Contemporary Perspectives from Communities in India*", New Delhi: Sage.

Srivastava, H.C. (1988). "The role of mass media in inter-spouse communication among urban Momin and Kokni Muslims", *The Journal of Family Welfare*, 35(1): 50-60.

Srinivas, M.N. (1956). "A note on Sanskritization and westernization", *The Far Eastern Quarterly*, 15(4): 481-496.

Sujatha, D. *et al.*, (1993). "Religiosity and fertility among brahmins", *The Journal of Family Welfare*, 39(1): 13-17.

The Population Council: District level baseline survey of Family Planning Programme in Agra, Uttar Pradesh, *Monograph*, The Population Council, New Delhi, India, 1995.

Townsend, J. *et al.*, (1993). "Target setting in family planning programme: Problems and potential alternatives", *Demography India*, 22(1).

Tripathy, S. *et al.*, (1994). "Epidemiological study of non-acceptance of female sterilization", *Journal of Obstetrics and Gynaecology of India*, 44(1): 93-97.

United Nations Development Programme (1995). *Human Development Report 1995*, UNDP, New York, USA.

life, 82, 387
managers, 81, 87
owners, 78–79, 81–83, 86–87, 90, 367, 373, 375, 377–79, 381–82
types, 78
Burning urination, 22, 379

Caesarian deliveries, 377–78, 382
Celestial nymph, 65
Celibacy, 12
Centre for AIDS Prevention Studies, 46
Centre for Social Studies (CSS), 150
Child care centre, 193
Child marriage, 97
Child transmission of HIV, 380
Childbearing, 290, 292
Chit funds, 172–73
Christians, 129–30
City lifestyle, 153–54
Cleanliness, 80, 318–19, 323–26, 328
Commercial Sex Workers (CSWs), 13, 18, 48–49, 53, 75–76, 93–94, 96–97, 110–11, 116–21, 127, 130–37, 184–85, 209–11, 226, 385–86
Commercial sex, 13–14, 75, 92, 95, 97–99, 102, 107–9, 384
Common beliefs, 163
Communication
appropriate channels of, 150–51
facilities, 153–54
strategy, 138, 150
Community-based studies, 315–17
Condom
acceptance, 135, 288
access, 136
acquisition, 48
availability, 363
bursting, 134, 136
free, 134
identifying, 134
non-use of, 48, 89, 111, 136
promotion, 47, 77, 90–91, 125–26, 128, 366
role of, 133, 372
wear, 131
Contraception, 48, 89, 116, 126, 128, 133, 135–36, 158, 164, 186, 189–90, 288, 335, 348–49, 371
Contraceptives, 94, 164, 239, 348–50, 367, 371, 382
methods, 283–84, 288, 295–96, 298, 302, 338
Counselling
centre, 110, 112, 114–15, 224, 233–34
sessions, 112–13, 116
Courtesans, 55–56, 58, 61, 64–65, 70, 73
Cross-sexual transmission, 330
Cultural
attitudes, 16, 243
context, 17, 310, 313, 316
determinism, 7–8
ideas, 267
Influence Models, 16, 18, 243
relativism, 8

Damage control measures, 227, 237
Dancing girls, 13–14, 57–58, 61, 70, 97, 385
Data-gathering, 23–25, 36–37, 39, 78, 191–92, 337, 351
Defecation, 267, 318, 325–26
Descriptive information, 25–26
Devdasis, 64–65, 82, 364, 368–70, 375, 377, 381
Diamond workers, 48, 137–40, 143–48, 150–52
Diapers, 250
Divorce, 15–16, 48, 52, 153, 157, 384
Documentation centre, 96
Domestic chores, 273–74, 277

Economic
compulsions, 94, 279
indicators, 275–76
pressures, 137

Enculturation, 267, 353, 360
Eroticism, 191, 239, 242–44, 246–47, 259, 262
Ethnic groups, 48, 94, 235, 268, 306, 367
Ethnic identity, 106
Ethnographic research, 37, 315
Eunuchs, 14, 127, 130, 132, 135, 144
Evil eye, 105, 355–56
Extra-marital sex, 138, 143, 159–60, 162, 164

Fair skinned girls, 13
Familial
  control, 213
  reasons, 359
  responsibilities, 174
Family planning, 11, 128, 242, 284–85, 287–88, 294, 301–2, 313, 350, 387
Family Planning Association of India (FPAI), 129, 134, 209
Family Planning decision, male involvement, 283
Farming activities, 141, 170, 172
Female dancers, 64
Female Sex Workers (FSWs), 43, 45–46, 48, 51, 77, 92–109
  clients of, 100
  peer group of, 95, 103
Female slaves, 61, 68–69
Femininity, 60, 310
Feudal rules, 13–14
Focus Group Discussions (FGDs), 37, 96, 124, 126, 318, 327, 329, 338, 351
Focused ethnographic study (FES), 47
Foothills, 173
Fossils, 23
Foundation for Research in Health Systems (FRHS), 128–29, 211
Friendship circles, 169–70

Ganikaa, 74
Gender
  discrimination, 51, 74, 242
  equality, 239, 242
Genital
  area, 263, 318, 320, 322, 325–26
  functions, 57
  hygiene, 315, 318, 325–27
Geographical mapping, 23
Ghar janwai, 94–95, 97, 101–4, 107–8
Girls
  confining, 266
  courtesan/dancing, 61
  flattering, 196
  Gopi girls, 9
  maid servants/slave, 68
  nauch, 70, 74
  pre-menarche, 335
  school-aged, 342
Gratification, 61
Gupta Period, 9, 56
Gynaecological morbidity, 313, 316, 331
Gynaecologists, 290

Harems, 10, 57, 74, 92
Head bath, 328–29
Health behaviour, 281, 314, 317
Health facilities, 23, 278–79, 331
Health providers, 29, 31, 35
Health-seeking behaviour, 3–4, 345
Heterosexual
  couples, 243
  friendship, 206
  partners, 135
  relations, 52, 54–55, 60, 127, 190, 336
HIV-AIDS, 2–4, 23–24, 27, 43, 110–14, 116–17, 137–38, 144–51, 185, 205–6, 210, 212–13, 218–19, 228, 349–50
  awareness, 77, 144–45, 150
  counselling centres, 113, 233

pandemic, 111, 167, 225
prevention of, 3, 113, 164, 214, 363
risk of, 152–53
transmission of, 103, 186
Home remedies, 30–31, 309, 331
Homosexual
activity, 45
behaviour, 121
experiences, 144
relationship, 214, 221
Homosexuality, 14, 111, 119, 125, 144
Hormone replacement therapy (HRT), 309
Household duties, 250–51, 254, 266
Human Immunodeficiency Virus (HIV), 26, 43–47, 75–77, 93–94, 102, 110–12, 114–16, 118–26, 137–38, 145–46, 186–88, 218, 224–25, 380, 385–87
Husband-wife relationships, 19
Hygiene, 190, 318–19, 326, 328–29, 332, 346, 383
Hygienic practices, 318–19, 324, 332
Hypergamy, 9–10, 13, 384

Ill health, 117, 315
Indian Express, 186, 188
Industrial workers, 138–40
Information
access, 239
authentic, 151
concrete, 25
correct, 47
cultural, 21, 36
holistic, 225
management, 229, 232
networks, 187, 189
official, 28
partial, 26
preparatory, 21
qualitative, 129
reproductive, 302
Injection Drug Users (IDUs), 27, 31–33
International Centre for Research on Women, 46
International Conference on Population and Development (ICPD), 313, 335, 385
International Institute of Population Sciences (IIPS), 93, 166, 283
Inter-spouse communication, 283, 289, 293
Intervention
groups, 38, 168
programmes, 37, 91, 167, 352
research, 2, 388

Jaundice, 367, 381
Jeevan Asha Project (JAP), 103, 105
Joint families, 172–73, 287–89, 291–96, 298–302, 319, 348

Kinship, 7, 15, 95, 106, 231, 353, 386
Kumbhadaasee (water carrier), 58–59

Linguistic
acculturation, 53, 55
groups, 51, 366–67
Love affairs, 176, 202–3
Love marriage, 299
Low-income communities, 190–91, 336, 339, 351

Mahabharata, 10, 15, 55, 58, 72
Marital relations, 306, 308
Marketable commodities, 7, 18
Marriage
alliances, 98, 336, 343
arranged, 133, 203, 291
celebrations, 156, 158
ceremonies, 13, 203
partners, 266
Masculinity, 163–64, 220, 243
Mass media, 147, 154, 164, 192, 213, 224, 226, 336
Masturbation, 11–12, 38, 117, 120–21, 138, 143, 162, 175, 184

Menopause, 303–10
Menstrual
  cycle, 161–62, 306
  hygiene, 318, 323
Migrant
  communities, 185, 222
  hotel workers, 209–13
  populations, 191, 211, 218
  youth, 18, 48–49, 167–74, 177–80, 182–85
Milk party, 14
Monogamous women, 111
Monthly cycles, 305–6
Moral support, 289, 292, 300
Morbidity, 3, 18, 48, 270, 315–16, 319, 323, 328, 367, 382
  reproductive, 3, 286, 315, 317, 332, 335, 384
  self-reported, 315, 317, 319, 327
MTP centre, 380
Mughal Period, 56, 66
Multi-partner, 77, 135–36, 372
Multi-Purpose Health Workers (MPHW), 146, 149
Municipal Health Centre, 150

Nat caste, 97, 109
Nat community, 92, 95–97, 102, 105–8
Nat women, 92–98, 102–3, 105, 108–9
  migration of, 108
Natal homes, 228, 295, 377
National AIDS Control Organization (NACO), 166–67, 211, 216, 222, 225
National AIDS Control Programme (NACPII), 4, 167
Nautch girls, 13, 385
Nomadic life, 92, 94, 98
Non-condom events, 374
Non-Government Organizations (NGOs), 2, 27, 39, 77–79, 90, 95–96, 102–3, 105–6, 108–9, 129, 145–46, 190, 226, 366–67, 380
Non-migrant, 175, 177–80, 182, 184
Non-*rakhel* clients, 87–89
Non-tribals, 154, 165
Normative expectations, 227, 229
Norms
  behavioural, 247, 356
  cultural, 270, 327–28, 332
  sexual, 60–61, 69, 71
  societal, 62, 64
Nuclear families, 97, 231, 287–89, 291–302

Oil massage, 355–56, 359, 361
Oral contraceptive pills, 349, 371
Oral sex, 102, 125, 165

Partnership for Sexual Health (PSH), 150
Patriarchal society, 5, 7, 45, 48, 51, 67, 69, 283, 317
Peer group, 105, 157, 167
Peer pressure, 48, 118, 222
Penetrative sex, 98, 101, 108, 386
Peno-vaginal intercourse, 223, 262–64, 267
People Living with HIV-AIDS (PLHA), 48, 224–28, 230–38
Perineal wash, 324
Personal hygiene, 103, 317–18, 320, 332, 365
Personality traits, 247
Picture cards, 368, 371
Pile sorting, 22, 31, 33–36, 38
Pimps, 94, 100, 109
Plural sex, 13, 164
Police officials, 100, 109
Pregnancy and Child Birth, 374, 377
Premarital sex, 111, 118, 157–59, 164, 179, 214, 255
Premature ejaculations, 38, 146–47
Primary Health Centre, 111, 125, 156, 314
Prostitutes, 10, 45–46, 51–74, 92, 132, 385
  Clandestine, 58–59

Prostitution, 45, 52–58, 60–61, 64, 68, 70, 72, 92–93, 160
  history of, 52, 54
Pubertal changes, 162
Puberty, 18, 45, 94, 107, 119, 162, 187–88, 193, 277, 388
Pubic hair, 162, 325
Pushkar, pilgrimage centre, 93

Qualitative
  data-gathering, 37
  methods, 19–21, 37, 48
  research, 8, 21–22, 24, 28, 37
Quantitative
  research, 26, 39
  surveys, 3, 20–21, 23, 36, 127, 129–30, 205–6, 338–39, 349

Rakhel, 63, 73, 84–91
Red light area, 19, 68, 75, 78, 85, 91, 118, 124, 138, 144, 151, 160, 180–81, 222–23, 363–64
Remarriage, 16, 52, 153, 157
Reproductive health, 1, 6, 37, 154, 187, 189–90, 270, 301–2, 313–14, 316, 335, 337–38, 345–47, 351–53, 387
Reproductive Tract Infections (RTIs), 3–4, 107, 189, 313–14, 316–18, 321, 326–27, 329, 331–32, 336, 338, 382–83
Research
  methodology, 96, 129
  skills, 2–3, 39
Risk behaviour, 17–19, 85, 120, 138, 168, 210, 212, 220, 222, 226, 368, 386, 388

Safe sex, 27, 45–46, 102, 105, 108, 135, 152, 227, 386
  practices, 46, 49, 75–76, 154
Salvation Army Centre, 231
Self-reported morbidity of women, 332
Seminal fluids, 11–12
Sensitization, 174, 185
Sex
  behaviour, 13, 15, 17, 19, 98, 153, 386
  commercialization of, 66, 165
  composition, 234, 284
  diversities, 385
  during pregnancy, 144, 161
  education, 124, 154, 205–6
  extra-marital, 220
  forceful, 119
  gratification, 7, 384
  heterogeneous, 98
  marriage, 14
  multi-partner, 53, 152
  objects, 18, 347
  penetrating, 101
  penetrative vaginal, 126
  ratio, 272
  research, 19
  romanticized, 154
  safer, 128, 134–36
  security, 18
  therapy, 15
  trade, 98, 109
  work, commercial, 52, 62, 93, 99–100, 102–3
  workers and clients, 84
Sex workers, 4, 26, 31, 33, 35–36, 73–75, 77–91, 99–100, 107–9, 143–44, 216, 219–21, 363–73, 375, 377–83
  brothel, 91, 365
  category of, 368, 378
  clients of, 4, 31, 78, 223, 382
  commercial, 314
  ethnic minority, 366
  pregnant, 364, 376, 378–79, 382
  sexual behaviour of, 94–95
  street-based, 81
Sexual
  abstinence, 160–61
  abuse, 5
  activities, 7, 9, 18, 25, 61, 80, 87, 96, 101, 113, 137, 157–59, 164–65, 190, 220

arousal, 142
avenues, 167, 185
career, 223
coercion, 5
commutation, 84
disorders, 142
dynamics, 5
energy, 10
exploitation, 254
exposure, 138, 150
freedom, 167
harassment, 388
health, 184, 313–14, 381
hunger, 220
hygiene, 320, 326
initiation, 49
intercourse, 44, 131, 141, 144, 160–61, 179, 185, 198, 200, 206, 210, 316, 330
involvement, 187, 204
liberty, 67
meaning, 244, 259, 262–63, 267
morality, 53
networks, 5, 75
partners, 75, 87, 101, 166, 168, 179, 184–85, 211, 220–21, 228
partnerships, 126, 244

Sexuality
adolescent, 11
construction of, 4, 240–41
control of, 60
cultural influence models, 16
perceptions of, 189
perspectives of, 186

Sexually Transmitted Diseases (STDs), 76–77, 93–96, 103, 107–8, 111–12, 125–27, 135–36, 146–47, 165–66, 189, 210, 216–17, 220–23, 363, 365–67

Sexually Transmitted Infections (STIs), 3–4, 22, 25, 34, 38, 48, 91, 126–28, 186–90, 205–6, 208, 210, 313, 334–35, 350–51

Surat Diamond Manufacturers Association (SDMA), 138–39

Vyabhichaar (adultry), 61

Water scarcity, 320, 322, 326, 328
Well-to-do families, 157
Wet dreams, 138, 142–43, 147
White-collar workers, 224, 235
Widows, 58, 60–61, 64, 69–70, 74, 110, 114, 124, 228

Women
affluent, 74
asymptomatic, 326
divorced, 159
educated, 302
elder, 295
empowered, 302
honourable, 70
innocent, 45
menopausal, 303, 310
menstruating, 267
midlife, 310
migrated, 108
perceptions of, 316–17
post-menopausal, 310
pregnant, 122–23, 376
rural, 11, 314, 326
symptomatic, 322
unchaste, 61
unmarried, 368

World AIDS Day, 380
World Development Report, 315
World Health Organization, 334
World Women's Day, 380
Worm disease, 105
Wound healing, 360–61
Wrestling, 161

Yellamma, 82
Yoga, 11
Yoga postures, 309

Zagirdars, 97
Zamindari system, 57
Zila Panchayat, 150